THE VEST-POCKET
MARKETER

THE VEST-POCKET MARKETER

Alexander Hiam

PRENTICE HALL
Englewood Cliffs, New Jersey 07632

Prentice-Hall International (UK) Limited, *London*
Prentice-Hall of Australia Pty. Limited, *Sydney*
Prentice-Hall Canada, Inc., *Toronto*
Prentice-Hall Hispanoamericana, S.A., *Mexico*
Prentice-Hall of India Private Limited, *New Delhi*
Prentice-Hall of Japan, Inc., *Tokyo*
Simon & Schuster Asia Pte. Ltd., *Singapore*
Editora Prentice-Hall do Brasil, Ltda., *Rio de Janeiro*

© 1991 by

PRENTICE-HALL, Inc.

Englewood Cliffs, NJ

10 9 8 7 6 5 4 3

Printed in the United States of America

Library of Congress Cataloging-in-Publication Data

Hiam, Alexander.
    The vest-pocket marketer / by Alexander Hiam.
        p.   cm.

    Includes index.
    ISBN 0-13-932302-3
    1. Marketing—Handbooks, manuals, etc. I. Title.
HF5415.H49 1991
658.8—dc20   91-18442
                                                        CIP

ISBN 0-13-932302-3

PRENTICE HALL
Business Information Publishing Division
Englewood Cliffs, NJ 07632

Simon & Schuster, A Paramount Communications Company

Acknowledgments

Thanks to my wife Heather and my sons Eliot and Paul for their patience and support, and also to the many people whose assistance or contributions have helped create this book, including Jay Chiat of Chiat/Day/Mojo, Philip DiPeri of Stonehenge International, Sharon Hollander of Executive Solutions, Chris Hikawa of CBS, John Quincy of the American Marketing Association, Charles Schewe of the School of Business, University of Massachusetts, Amherst, Steven Sinclair of Virginia Polytechnic Institute, Maxwell Sroge of Maxwell Sroge Publishing, and any others whom I may have inadvertently overlooked.

The reader owes thanks to various publishers for their kind permission to include useful material from Jan Carlzon of SAS, Philip Kotler, William Nicholls of the Census Bureau, Tom Peters, Stan Rapp and Tom Collins of Doyle Dane Bernbach, Tom Eisenhart of Business Marketing, and American Express, AT&T, The Conference Board, Dunfey Hotels, DuPont, Motorola, Pfizer, Weyerhaeuser, and probably many other individuals and companies whose names have momentarily slipped my mind. A book like this is not possible without contributions from dozens of practitioners and researchers. Many thanks to them all.

To the Reader

If your work has anything to do with marketing, you need this book.

Why? Because you do not have time to talk with the 100-plus managers and companies who contributed their expertise and insights to this book. Because you don't have time to study the 200-plus journals and books the author reviewed in order to discover what you need to know about marketing in the 1990s. And because you will find immediate uses for many of the checklists, problem solvers, and creative new approaches this book contains.

The Vest-Pocket Marketer is a working document for working managers. It details up-and-coming techniques and strategies, identifying tomorrow's sources of competitive advantage rather than recapitulating yesterday's. It elaborates on the enduring themes in marketing, focusing on the most powerful recent implementations of them. It provides a unique vehicle for cross-fertilization of methods and solutions by uniting the ideas of leading thinkers from many industries and professions.

How to Use This Book

The *Vest-Pocket* format is especially suited to these purposes. Its entries start by listing applications and summarizing procedures so that the practitioner can quickly evaluate alternative methods and select the most applicable. Then the guts of each technique are presented in clear, practical language, copiously seasoned with case histories and advice from expert practitioners. Everything is designed to help the reader find useful ideas and methods and then figure out *how to use them* in context. Nothing is included unless it can be translated directly into actions and benefits by the reader. (The guiding principle is "need to know, not nice to know.")

The first section of the book presents almost a hundred techniques and methods that will guide leading managers and companies in the practice of marketing over the decade to come. Use it to find new ideas and approaches or to serve as an efficient way to bone up on important new directions in marketing, advertising, and sales. (See the introduction to the first section for details.)

The second section gives managers an up-to-date briefing on increasingly critical ethical issues in marketing. In fact, this section provides the *only* action-oriented analysis of these issues we know of that is specifically for practitioners of marketing and related fields as of this publication date.

The third section is a streamlined key to the classic marketing tools and models. Since managers must continue to execute the basics well, even as they seek the new and exciting, it is important to put all the basics in one place and make them easy to find and use. Here they are presented in shortened format, minus the chaff, for quick memory refreshment and easy reference. Accompanying them is a glossary that provides brief, clear definitions of marketing terms—necessary because some of them are sufficiently obscure as to stump even the seasoned marketer.

The Subject/Name Index is also a powerful reference tool. It allows you to search the material by subject, technique name, and company name, often revealing multiple entries of relevance to your query.

The index should be used in conjunction with the unusual tables of contents. A Short Contents summarizes the book to provide orientation. A Detailed Contents lists every method and tool in the book by name. Use it to identify interesting and potentially useful techniques that you might not find your way to through the index or to look for material from your favorite commentators and companies. In addition, each chapter in the first section of the book contains a special Functional Contents that includes cross-references to techniques from other chapters. This makes it easy for the reader with a specific functional interest to identify everything of relevance, including those methods whose multifunctional appeal led them to be slotted elsewhere.

We are very excited about *The Vest-Pocket Marketer*. We expect it will change the way publishers approach the creation of business books, and we know it will give its readers many valuable insights and practices with which to boost performance—both personal and organizational—over the coming years.

The Publisher

From the Author

Peter Drucker wrote in his preface to *The Frontiers of Management* that "the future is being made by totally anonymous people, a CEO here, a marketing manager there, a training director or comptroller yonder doing mundane jobs: building a management team, developing a new pricing strategy, changing a training program. . . . thus tomorrow is being shaped today."

I think Drucker has put his finger on the engine of progress when he describes this process, although I don't believe the jobs managers do are necessarily mundane, and I certainly do not believe their insights and innovations should be totally anonymous. But tomorrow *is* shaped by today's managers and management thinkers, often acting independently and anonymously to find better solutions to common problems. Their breakthroughs spread informally, by word of mouth and with the movement of managers from company to company—an awkward and inefficient path to the future when the pace of opportunity and challenge quickens every year.

With *The Vest-Pocket CEO: Decision-Making Tools for Executives,* I worked with Prentice Hall's editors to straighten this path and to provide recognition for the anonymous pathbreakers. *The Vest-Pocket Marketer* extends the concept to advertising, sales, pricing, research, and all the other elements of marketing-oriented management.

The result is an unique collection of new techniques and new spins on old techniques and methodologies. Here are many of the hot topics we will see heralded in the press and at conferences over the coming years. And here also are the creative and practical presentations of the current state of the art—from checklists and guidelines to strategy selectors and step-by-step instructions. Some of these may be the stuff of future textbooks and encyclopedias, but by the time they are institutionalized in the literature of management, they will have lost much of their value.

This point needs emphasis, because most readers will equate the reference book format of this volume with the typical effort to regurgitate classic techniques and theories. The contrast is best seen by comparing the brief *One-Minute Guides to the Marketing Classics* at the end of this book with the rest of the contents. In the One-Minute Guides you will find the most useful of the material one learns in business school marketing classes. It's good stuff—but nothing earth shattering. However, you will not find the rest of the book's contents on the syllabi of most MBA programs until late in this decade, when certain of them will have become so widely accepted that they too are regarded as classics. In the meantime, I have done my best to make them available for those readers who, out on the front lines of marketing and general management, are charged with the responsibility to shape tomorrow today. They are not alone, and their task is made infinitely easier when they can collaborate and share their experiences more fully.

I hope readers will use *The Vest-Pocket Marketer* in this spirit, dipping into it to find newly broken paths that may lead to solutions for them as well. And I hope readers will take the concept beyond the printed page to increase the rate of idea exchange with their professional colleagues. A good place to start is with a telephone call to the originator of one of the methods described in this book. I have spoken with many managers, consultants, advertising execs, and academic researchers in the course of writing up their techniques, and have been impressed by their openness and ability to share useful insights and information. I believe this spirit of cooperation is stronger than most managers realize, and that both parties benefit whenever common experiences and problems are shared.

Readers are encouraged also to use the publications that are referenced at the end of each technique's write-up. In many cases one can find some written record of recent management experience, although it is admittedly often in an obscure journal, conference proceeding, or small-circulation trade publication. These are treasure troves of information, and I commend those managers who take the time to hunt through them for ideas, and especially those managers who take pen in hand to share their ideas in such forums. Both acts require a certain courage, for it is not easy to seek and act on new visions of the management task in the face of a never-ending stream of daily demands and crises.

These publications, and the professional associations, business schools, and others who publish them, make an important contribution toward the straighter path of cooperative struggle and advancement. While it can be difficult to separate wheat from chaff (a process I found quite painful as I compiled this book!), there is definitely much wheat to be found. In fact, I see this as the principal author's task and believe *The Vest-Pocket Marketer* gains much of its value because of this careful selection process.

I have drawn on my varied consulting and management experience to try to pick the most interesting and valuable of new approaches in marketing. For example, as I examined current practices and problems in consumer research, I became convinced that we will see a rebirth of interest in qualitative techniques that probe deeper into the motivations and needs of our customers. This guided the selection of material for the "Market Research and Analysis" chapter, which includes interesting approaches to focus groups and a variety of projective techniques that many researchers may not be familiar with at present. In another example, I have integrated several important lines of thought into an entry on service recovery because I am convinced that solving customer problems is the key to service success.

I have attempted to create a book that combines the best guides to today's top techniques with blueprints to tomorrow's hot techniques, because I believe the manager's principal responsibility is to be a change agent within his or her company—and this requires every manager to be on the forefront of marketing thought. As Harlan Cleveland put it years ago in *The Knowledge Executive*, "The executive function is to bring people together in organizations to make something *different* happen" [my emphasis]. His prediction that this "executive function" would be required of more and more managers has proven true. As managers wrestle with increasingly competitive and fast-changing markets, they need more and better access to those sources of new ideas that can be used to make the right "something different" happen. *The Vest-Pocket Marketer*, it is hoped, will make it easier for managers to perform as change agents by creating competitive advantage from new approaches to the diverse tasks of marketing and by using the tools of marketing to better serve their many customers.

The Author

Alexander Hiam's management experience ranges from the marketing department of a *Fortune* 100 to the management teams of several Silicon-Valley start-ups. He is currently president of a management consulting firm based in Amherst, Massachusetts, which specializes in marketing and strategy for a wide range of clients. Educated at Harvard and U.C. Berkeley, he has an MBA in marketing and strategic planning and is currently an adjunct professor in the Marketing Department at Western New England College in Springfield. His articles on marketing and management have been published widely, and he is the author of *The Vest-Pocket CEO: Decision-Making Tools for Executives*. He is currently researching a book on quality in U.S. companies in collaboration with the Conference Board and is also at work on the up-coming *Prentice Hall Encyclopedia of Marketing and Advertising*.

Short Contents

Detailed Contents

PART I

TOOLS AND TECHNIQUES FROM INDUSTRY INNOVATORS

INTRODUCTION

Most books on marketing emphasize the body of knowledge as we learned it in business school. But managers are more interested in the latest innovations and issues—the practice of marketing is ever changing, and a good reference must bring its readers to the cutting edge in each of the fields of marketing. The following chapters collect the best and most innovative ideas from leading practitioners and theorists.

This is a radically different picture of the field of marketing than the one we normally see. Here marketing is visualized as an evolving, exciting, multifaceted practice, offering creative managers of all titles a rich source of good ideas and winning strategies. This picture of marketing emerges from the search for rich veins, the ideas and techniques that can yield competitive advantage to firms today and tomorrow, not yesterday. Sometimes these are rich because of their novelty, and sometimes they are rich because they have not yet been fully mined, even though they may have first been mapped some years ago.

Managers need techniques that offer the potential of advantage, not just parity.

If you need to look up the 4Ps, you can find it in the back of the book under One-Minute Guides to the Marketing Classics. But not here. Because most of your competitors already know about the 4Ps, there is generally little advantage to be gained by applying the concept. However, you are very likely to find and apply something completely new to your company and maybe even your industry in the following chapters. In the competitive environment of business, managers need techniques that offer the potential of advantage, not just parity. The following collection is intended to include the techniques that tomorrow's successes will be built upon.

*Competitive advantage comes both from innovating and from using existing techniques **better.***

Read these chapters for inspiration, treating each like a short essay on a topical subject from the cutting edge of management practice. Or use them as a reference tool, looking up specific methods and approaches in response to specific problems or questions raised by your work. For example, you will find practical guides to selecting the right pricing strategies, advertising media, marketing plan outlines, planning processes, and primary market research techniques in this section, along with many creative new theories and methods in these and other areas. This mixture reflects the fact that competitive advantage can come either from innovating or from using existing techniques better than competitors.

Managers need to know what to do—and how to do it!

Most books for managers are long on what is happening in the world of business and why. But what managers really need to know is *what to do* and *how to do it*. The following chapters provide the whats and hows in sufficient detail to guide the practitioner through difficult decisions, problems, and opportunities.

Benchmark your methods against others.

Xerox has pioneered the use of benchmarking as part of its total quality program. Each business process is compared with an exemplar, often from another industry, to help make the process better. For example, Xerox used L.L. Bean's shipping operation as a model for its parts distribution operation. This concept can be applied in marketing and planning as well. In fact, Xerox's strategic planners used the manuscript of this book as a source of model planning methods for their benchmarking efforts and report that it's useful for this purpose.

Chapter 1

Marketing Strategy and Planning

A-1 Tool's Planning Worksheets

Bonoma's Implementation Model

Booz, Allen Customer Return-on-Assets Method

Coattails Marketing: The IBM-Barrister Principles

Communicating the Plan

DiMingo's Defensive Marketing

Marketing Plan Outlines

Performance Standards Checklist

Planning Processes and Procedures

Shanklin's Marketing Blunders

Also see:
   Dovel's Positioning Process
   Recompetitive Strategy
   Market Research Department Structure
   Capsugel Crisis Management Checklist
   Vielhaber's Crisis Communication
      Strategies

A-1 TOOL'S PLANNING WORKSHEETS

*We call it planning, but it's really just
running a business.*

—Walter R. Lovejoy

Applications

- Forcing planners to think hard about where they are and what they should be doing.
- Making sure plans address concerns you think are important.
- Bringing creativity and open-mindedness into planning processes that have become too rigid and routine.

Procedures

1. Develop a list of the types of questions you want managers to address as they prepare their plans.
2. Prepare a workbook based on these questions and have managers complete it as the first step of the planning process.

A-1 Tool Co. was founded as a tool-and-die shop by Walter Lovejoy and, when its revenues reached $4 million, was acquired by Beatrice Foods. Lovejoy went on to manage Beatrice's Metal Products Division, then its Industrial Division, and finally took back control of A-1 in a leveraged buyout of several of the industrial companies owned by Beatrice. Lovejoy developed a low opinion of the planning process while at Beatrice, finding that many managers there "thought planning was an exercise on their calculators." Planning by rote often produces meaningless numbers because the planning process does not force anyone to think hard about where they are and what they should be doing.

The insight Lovejoy brought to the planning process was that it should be "built around *questions*, not numbers," as *Inc.* magazine puts it. Lovejoy developed a list of the types of questions he hoped managers would be addressing. The list is broken down by functional area. Questions for marketing include:

What is the age of existing products?

What is the future product mix?

What are the competitors' strengths?

What are competitors' costs?

What would you do if you lost your biggest account?

The questions are prepared in workbook format, and managers discuss them, complete the workbooks, then send the responses back as the first stage of an annual planning process.

The merit of this simple device is that it forces an examination of assumptions before any sales quotas or budgets are prepared, presumably making them a little more intelligent as a result. Warning: Managers are sometimes resistant to the idea of filling out a workbook. It may take several tries before everyone accepts the approach.

Reference

"Planning Without Calculators," *Inc.*, November 1985, p. 130.

BONOMA'S IMPLEMENTATION MODEL

*The results are usually as instructive
as they are shocking.*

—Thomas Bonoma,
Harvard Business School

Applications

- Diagnosing problems in implementation of marketing strategy.
- Problem-proofing marketing plans by considering all the likely implementation problems and developing plans that avoid them.

Procedures

Review the four-level model of implementation and use it to identify the forces at work within your organization at each level. The model helps you see where and how implementation problems arise, making it possible to develop responses to the most critical problems.

When the "best-laid plans" do not produce expected sales, Thomas Bonoma of Harvard Business School argues that bad implementation is usually the problem. In a study of the marketing function at 35 companies, he observed the implementation process and identified four common families of problems corresponding to four levels at which he found implementation issues typically arise. Use the resulting model to analyze your own company's ability to implement. Or use it to make the implementation phase of a marketing plan more robust and trouble-free by identifying likely sources of trouble in advance.

The model splits marketing implementation into four levels and identifies the common pitfalls on each level. The model is hierarchical, with top-level *policies* filtering through the organization's many *systems*, resulting in marketing *programs* that are ultimately implemented by the multiple marketing *functions*. Thus the four levels of marketing implementation are policies, systems, programs, and functions:

Level 4—Policy. Typically the responsibility of the CEO and marketing and sales managers. Definition: Formal and informal directives by which management guides the execution of marketing strategy.

Level 3—Systems. Typically the responsibility of managers in marketing, sales, accounting, and data processing. Definition: Budgeting; the organization chart; cost and revenue accounting; sales force reporting and control; and other systems that inform and constrain marketing managers, staff, and the sales force.

Level 2—Programs. Typically the responsibility of the marketing manager, product managers, and advertising and sales managers. Definition: Coordinated efforts to sell a particular product or implement a strategy using a variety of marketing and nonmarketing functions.

Level 1—Functions. Typically the responsibility of sales, advertising, and distribution managers; ad agencies; customer service managers; training managers; and distributors. Definition: The basic tasks of marketing, such as sales, advertising, distribution, customer service, and trade promotion.

The study identified specific implementation problems to watch out for at each level. (Idea: A marketing plan could benefit from a short section addressing how proper implementation will be assured at each of these levels, with plans for avoiding the common problems of each level.)

Policy Problems. If a company lacks a clear vision of where its marketing should be going—it does not have a strong "marketing theme," in Bonoma's words—then identity problems are likely to plague implementation. A strong, agreed-upon theme gives everyone in marketing the common vision needed for smooth, coordinated implementation. For example, in one of the cases he studied Bonoma was impressed by the fact that everyone in management and in the 10,000-person sales force could recite with conviction, "We are the premier vendor of snack foods in this country. Our products are great. But we have only two seconds to reach the supermarket shopper, so we live or die on service." While this may seem simplistic, it gave everyone a clear sense of mission and produced superior sales performance. Bonoma advises testing to see whether there is a clear marketing theme in your company by having the CEO and key managers write a single sentence describing your company's "marketing essence." He warns that "The results are usually as instructive as they are shocking."

The "marketing culture" can also be a source of problems when conventional ways of thinking about or doing things become obstacles to implementation. Bonoma warns managers to look out for comfortable ruts. A third source of problems at the policy level is poor-quality marketing leadership. It is up to the top marketing managers to establish marketing themes and shape the culture to the needs of the day. Charismatic leadership can make this happen effectively, and so can good coordination, delegation, and planning.

System Problems. Errors of ritual are, in my mind, the most prevalent source of implementation problems in most companies. The term refers to situations where established systems drive the company "down habitual pathways, even when good judgement dictates a different course," as Bonoma puts it. The conventions of measurement used in the accounting system can shape the way an entire organization views its market, including its customers and competitors. Example: I recall a company that used a complex formula to measure market share, a formula that showed it way ahead of competitors. But when a more conventional and realistic measure of share was calculated, it actually was in a close tie for leadership. Marketing programs were designed to help break this tie, but managers who refused to adopt the new measure of market share did not see any urgency in the programs and failed to support them. The company moved into second place as a result.

Political processes can also cause problems at the system level. For example, the raw data going into a reporting system is sometimes modified or falsified by those who have learned to use the system for political purposes. Much of the data used to support management decision making is biased in one way or another by political processes, and some biases can have an unexpected negative impact on program implementation.

Bonoma finds that unavailability is the most pervasive system problem. In many cases systems simply do not provide the information, materials, or people when and where needed in order to implement a program. He reports that in almost all of the 35 companies studied, "the financial accounting and sales accounting systems can only be called perverse in failing to meet marketing's requests."

Program Problems. Some programs are so out of step with the reality of the organization that they simply will never deliver what they are supposed to. Bonoma calls this problem "empty promises" marketing, and gives the example of a computer vendor that sold primarily to small businesses through a national sales force. A national account program was initiated in order to sell more hardware to big companies, and a national account manager was hired to implement it. But the program failed because the rest of the company, including the entire sales force, was focused on selling to small companies, not large, and did not have the motivation, resources and skills needed to make the program work. "Bunny marketing" is another common program problem, arising when too many programs are created and marketing finds itself going in every direction at once. The result, a "diffusion of effort and random results."

Function Problems. In larger companies, management relies on specialists for sales, trade promotion, and all the other basic functions of marketing. It is easy for managers to lose touch with the specifics of how each function works and to make false assumptions when defining policies or programs. Faulty assumptions by managers are an important source of problems at the function level. Structural contradiction is also a major source of problems, and it arises from conflict between the basic structure at the functional level and the implied structure of policies. If a policy is inconsistent with the existing distribution channel, this is a structural contradiction, and the policy is likely to run into implementation problems.

The final source of problems at the function level is what Bonoma terms "global mediocrity," the lack of a functional specialization. No company can be superior at all the many marketing functions, yet many managers and policies place equal reliance on all functions. A better strategy is to take advantage of the organization's strengths in certain functions. For example, if your company is strong in advertising because it has a consumer products division, then industrial programs would do well to emphasize advertising.

Program Design Note: The 4Ps approach to the marketing mix that is taught at business schools rests on the assumption that there is an optimal mix of marketing functions for any program. This optimal mix, it is assumed, will produce optimal results regardless of the company, and the role of marketing is to uphold the general principles of marketing and find the optimal mix. However, this belief is likely to lead to global mediocrity. Bonoma's observations suggest that the marketing mix for any program must reflect not only general marketing principles but also a company's strengths and weaknesses. There are almost always many means to a desired end in marketing, and you avoid implementation problems and take advantage of competitive strengths if you select a mix that gets you where you are going using the functions at which your company excels.

Reference

Thomas V. Bonoma, "Making Your Marketing Strategy Work," *Harvard Business Review*, March/April 1984: 69–76.

BOOZ, ALLEN CUSTOMER RETURN-ON-ASSETS METHOD

Applications

- Managing customers to maximize profits.
- Countering the growing power of large retailers.

Procedures

1. Measure customer return on profit (CRA) according to the formula that follows in order to measure profits per customer.
2. Segment customers and establish groups to manage each group of customers so as to maximize CRA.
3. Measure team performance.
4. Establish benchmarks.

In most consumer goods markets the emergence of large, powerful retailers has shifted the balance of power away from suppliers. Retailers are increasingly able to call the shots, demanding JIT (just-in-time) deliveries to stores instead of less frequent deliveries to central warehouses, for example. The large retailers use their buying power to shift costs off their income statements and to their suppliers. For example, the food industry has seen a 25% increase in supplier costs in recent years. Randy Myer of Booz, Allen & Hamilton argues that dozens of costs, from shelf stocking to inventory carrying to late delivery fees, require suppliers to take a new approach to managing their customers. If you supply a Wal-Mart, J. C. Penney, Toys "R" Us, or Stop and Shop, you need to take stock of the services you provide, what the customer costs you, and, through this analysis, decide whether the customer is worth the effort.

Randy Myer of Booz, Allen observes that, "Suppliers tend to focus on product performance, but they should pay equal attention to customer performance." He suggests the following steps to achieve sufficient customer focus.

1. Measure CRA. Customer return on assets is a variant of return on assets (ROA) that gives management a clear measure of the contribution of each customer and a way to identify the most profitable. The formula for CRA is·

> Revenue from the customer −
>   cost of goods sold
>   reserves for damaged/returned merchandise
>   discounts and allowances
> = gross margin for the customer
> gross margin −
>   sales cost
>   promotion costs (excluding media advertising)
>   direct product development cost
>   direct warehousing cost
>   customer freight cost
>   postsale service cost
> = customer contribution to overhead
> customer contribution ÷ by direct asset costs
> (which are accounts receivable and finished goods inventories)
> = customer return on assets

Surprisingly, CRA is generally not a function of customer size. In one study reported by Myer, it was inversely related to customer growth rate. Fast-growing companies, both large and small, tended to "cherry-pick" products in order to take continual advantage of discounts and other special promotions. Their suppliers only sold to them at discounted prices or with other associated promotional expenses. The cherry-picking strategy may have been one of the reasons for the fast growth of these customers, giving them the option of low prices or high margins. Or it may simply reflect more aggressive management and controls, a trait that might carry over into other aspects of the business and lead to success and above-average growth. Whatever the reason, the message is to be suspicious of fast-growing companies and not to expect profitability to vary directly with customer size.

CRA can vary significantly—at one consumer goods producer the average was 30% but the range was 5% to 55%. Promotion expenses are usually a major source of variation. Sales cost varies quite a bit as well, since call frequency and the number of buying locations may differ for customers of similar size. Accounts receivable can vary by a month or more, and some customers will take discounts even when they pay late. A comparison of these and other figures that go into the CRA formula can be quite eye opening, especially since accounting systems usually do not reveal these variations. As Myer puts it, "Imagine headquarters' reaction if product performance had ranged from 5% to 50% ROA."

2. Set up customer teams. A new orientation on individual customers and their profitability will create new requirements and responsibilities. Assigning these to product managers and salespeople is burdensome and ineffective. It is preferable to create teams of experts from sales, product management, distribution, finance, product development, or any other relevant functions to manage groups of customers (see "P&G's Brand Teams," in Chapter Ten, "Marketing Management," for an analagous approach to product management). This requires grouping the customers, and it is important to identify an effective strategy for customer segmentation. Options include segmenting by region, type of customer, or size. The best approach will be whichever one creates groups of customers with common service requirements and market strategies. It is important to give teams full responsibility for the performance of customers (tracked by CRA) and the authority to allocate resources and make and implement all customer management decisions.

Customer teams might decide to drop unprofitable customers. But in most cases they will redefine certain elements of sales, promotion, distribution, and other policies in order to improve CRA.

Application Note: What can you do about low-profit customers? In many cases, playing tough will result in a mad customer and a lost account. A punitive approach to customer management does not work. A better approach is to improve communications with the customer and make your needs better understood so the customer will be able to select the services that are most important and will be more willing to pay for services you provide. Here are Myer's four steps for improving customer relations, as they appeared in the referenced article:

- Define certain deviations as acceptable, but know where and when to draw the line.
- Create a menu of options for the customer.
- Emphasize that every service has its price.

- Establish prices that create appropriate incentives without alienating the customer. (This means a menu of price/service options, and buyers may need to be eased into this format if pricing is usually simple in your industry.)

3. Measure team performance. Performance reviews and rewards ought to reflect team performance, for example, by reflecting changes in CRA. Mechanisms are needed to ensure accountability. This is the simplest step, but note that it can be complicated too. For example, management may want to set CRA targets for each team. But teams may work with customers that have inherently different profit potentials, so the same CRA target will not be appropriate for each group.

4. Establish benchmarks. Track the progress of the program by establishing benchmarks such as market share of key accounts, CRA goals, cooperativeness of customers, and perceptions of customers and the entire supply chain.

Reference

Randy Myer, "Suppliers—Manage Your Customers," *Harvard Business Review*, November/December 1989: 160–168.

COATTAILS MARKETING:
THE IBM-BARRISTER PRINCIPLES

Applications

- An alternative to "guerilla marketing" or retreat when faced with an overwhelmingly strong competitor.
- Taking advantage of an emerging industry standard that is not your own.
- Gaining access to the sales force and image of a major competitor.

Procedures

1. Sign a nonexclusive partnership agreement with the industry leader that gives each company the right to sell the other's products. Do not press for a formal joint venture.
2. Maintain good communication with contacts at the other company.
3. Build the business relationship slowly. Apply the principles described below to create and maintain a workable and successful relationship.

I came across an article on Barrister Information Systems Corp. as I was thinking about a small computer company I had taken on as a client. And just in time, as a matter of fact. They needed to raise substantial capital and put together a nationwide dealer network to introduce an innovation in memory systems for a specific vertical market—a market that did not buy most of its hardware from computer retailers. None of their past experience was really of any use, and the plan did not look very appealing to investors, until we joined forces with the leading producer of software for the vertical market. Their name recognition with customers and network of specialized dealers, their sales leads, their endorsements, in fact, everything and anything available from the marketing department, was just what was needed. But how to structure a deal and gain access to these critical resources? The strategy changed after learning about Barrister's experiences.

Fortunately, Barrister and a number of other companies have already given a lot of thought to the question of how to structure deals like this. Barrister, which produced its own hardware and software for lawyers' offices since 1972, faced a severe challenge for the first time when IBM introduced its PC in 1982. Law offices liked Barrister's products, but wanted to be IBM compatible. Barrister fought IBM for a while, but now is an "authorized IBM business partner." IBM salespeople handle Barrister's software, and Barrister sells IBM systems as well as their own. The relationship is nonexclusive and somewhat informal. One of the best pieces of advice in the article is *not* to pursue a joint venture in cases like this.

Why not? A formal business partnership with a much larger company will inevitably put you on an uneven playing field. The little guy will be jerked around, taken over completely, or replaced. You simply do not have the resources and strengths to survive that close of an encounter, even if you could convince the big company to sign a joint venture agreement with you. This seems counterintuitive at first; why not make the relationship as formal as possible in order to reduce the chances of it falling apart? But when you come right down to it, the deal will only stay together as long as there is mutual benefit, and your only weapon, your slingshot when dealing with an industry giant, is the access you can provide to a vertical market. If you have a reputation, specialized products, and other assets that give you a good position in a small market, the giant may well see you as the easy way to move into your market. But enough of what I think. Here are the four principles to follow when negotiating a partnership with a much larger firm.

1. *Deal only with Goliath.* By this they mean you should avoid cutting deals with anyone except a clear industry leader. The runner-up will not do because the leader may come into your niche market and your deal offers you no firm protection in this case.

2. *Go slowly.* This advice is important because it can be difficult to deal with a much larger company. A track record of experience, and success, needs to precede any entity invest-

ment or other close and formal relationship in most cases.

3. *Make sure you're not forgotten.* Your partner has a lot of other things to worry about, and you will have to take responsibility for keeping their sales force up to date and excited about your products. Key managers should also be on your list for regular calls and letters.

4. *Be separate but equal.* The advice, literally, is to repeat over and over to yourself, "This is not a joint venture, this is not a joint venture," for the reasons discussed. The alternative is to sign a nonexclusive partnership agreement that simply gives each company the right to sell the other's products. (Compatibility will in some cases have to be engineered into the little guy's product to make this feasible.) Once a marketing partnership agreement is signed, it provides a foundation for developing a working relationship with the sales and marketing operations of the big company. The key to the success of the partnership is really what the little company does with it; see rule 2.

Reference

Paul B. Brown, "David and Goliath Do a Deal," *Inc.*, February 1990, pp. 87–88.

COMMUNICATING THE PLAN

. . . improving the quality of how the plan is communicated may be more beneficial than improving the quality of the plan itself.

—Journal of Business Strategy.

Applications

- Communicating the mission and contents of a plan to improve implementation.
- Adding communication processes and goals to the planning process.
- Building support for a new plan.

Procedures

Follow Calhoun and Lederer's eight guidelines to improve communication of marketing plans. Assess the effectiveness of current communications by evaluating your firm's performance on each of the eight points. Integrate communication strategies based on these guidelines into scheduled company events using the rhythm method of Tregoe and Tobia.

Nobody will follow a plan unless they know about it and support it. Obvious, perhaps, but a recent study by two business school professors found that communication problems were often at the heart of implementation problems. Kenneth J. Calhoun of Slippery Rock University and Albert L. Lederer of Oakland University developed the following guidelines after studying the planning process at manufacturing firms:

GUIDELINES FOR COMMUNICATING PLANS

1. *Document the contents in writing.* Written communication of the plan works much better than oral communication.
2. *Summarize the plan.* Prepare short, clear summaries for reference by the managers who need to implement your plan. (Idea: Customize the summaries to the interests and responsibilities of each manager. Why waste their time with irrelevant details?)
3. *Increase management/employee communications.* Senior managers are especially effec-

tive for communicating a plan to the organization. Schedule meetings for this purpose.

4. *Maintain a senior management presence.* If upper-level managers cannot make a meeting, the planner should stand in for them and present the plan anyway.

5. *Weave communication into ongoing activities.* Routine meetings and training sessions are good vehicles for communicating a plan. (See the Tregoe/Tobia Rhythm Method, following.)

6. *Keep the plan alive.* This means actually using it. If it is used as a performance measure, for example, it will receive a lot of attention and interest.

7. *Publicize the mission statement.* The vision driving a plan should be shared with the entire organization. Display it, talk about it, and make sure everyone knows about it. (Note: If the mission statement does not seem worthy of such special treatment, perhaps you should go back to the drawing board. I find that plans are only as strong as their missions.)

8. *Hand out the plan.* Give it to as many people as you can without compromising any confidential material it may contain. Try to write a best-seller!

The Tregoe/Tobia Rhythm Method

Benjamin Tregoe and Peter Tobia of Kepner-Tregoe, Inc., advocate something they call the *rhythm method* for communicating strategy. As suggested in guideline 5, the "rhythm method" takes advantage of the "certain pulse and momentum" that is unique to an organization. Annual planning processes, directors' meetings, sales meetings, and many other events occur on a predictable schedule and create a series of rhythms that can be used by the planner to speed implementation and strengthen communication. A good understanding of these rhythms gives the planner useful insights, both concerning how and where the plan can be communicated and concerning the pace and timing of implementation.

References

"Idea Forum: Strategic Concepts at a Glance," *The Journal of Business Strategy*, January/February 1990: 63. You might also want to look at "Peters's Leadership Tools," in Alexander Hiam, *The Vest-Pocket CEO: Decision-Making Tools for Executives* (Englewood Cliffs, NJ: Prentice Hall, 1990), for Tom Peters's creative approach to communicating the mission to employees.

Benjamin B. Tregoe and Peter M. Tobia, "An Action-Oriented Approach to Strategy," *The Journal of Business Strategy*, January/February 1990: 16–21.

DIMINGO'S DEFENSIVE MARKETING

*Good old-fashioned dollar volume
share is all that counts in marketing.
There is no other type of meaningful
leadership.*

—Edward DiMingo,
Infotron Systems Corp.

Applications

- Maintaining market share leadership.
- Formulating responses to challengers.
- Selecting the appropriate defensive strategy.
- If you are not the leader, use this strategy selector to anticipate the leader's defensive moves. See ideas for Market Followers, following, for ways to take advantage of a challenger's entry.

Procedures

This chapter lists alternative defensive strategies and provides examples and advice on how to use them. Start by verifying your leadership position—do you really have a firm lead as measured in market share? And is your method of measuring market share reasonable? (Some firms proclaim leadership based on an overly narrow definition of the market, which is fine for public relations but awful for strategy selection!) If you have a clear leadership position, your key strategy issue should be how to hold onto it. Review DiMingo's collection of defensive strategies for leaders in order to consider all the options that other firms and theorists have invented to date. Just remember that, "While a given firm might really be number one in research, product design, or even profitability, or "first," "best," "latest and greatest" in some other area," it must be number one in market share for these strategies to be effective. For this reason, DiMingo's strategies for leaders have been supplemented with some strategies for nonleaders, who are generally eager to respond to the latest challenger as well, and who will be frustrated by the general wisdom that keeps them on the sidelines.

Market Share Leadership Strategies

1. Raise structural barriers to entry (shark repellent). The goal is to make it prohibitively expensive for challengers. Sometimes the existing barriers are already substantial enough to offer protection, but if history has not created a wall and moat around your position, you can.

- Fill gaps in the product line, as Seiko did with its acquisition of Pulsar in order to block attacks at the low end from Citizen and Timex.

- Block access to the requisite distribution channels, as IBM does by packaging "all feasible sizes and permutations of its hardware, software, and service support, thus crowding competitors out of many market channels."

- Increase the economies of scale, for example, by increasing the emphasis on new product development (much of the development expense consists of fixed costs that are more economical when spread over a larger product line).

- Increase the amount of capital needed to compete, for example, by offering customized service, equipment, or even facilities.

- Foreclose alternative technologies, as Xerox did in the early days of photocopying through its acquisitive practices in patents and licensing, its aggressive research and development, and its joint ventures with technology innovators.

- Protect technological leadership as Michelin does through "aggressive patenting and litigation of all infringers."

- Limit access to sources, as Coca-Cola does through its long-term purchase contracts for sweeteners.

- Raise production costs, for example, through bidding up the cost of labor when your plants are more automated than competitors'.

- Form coalitions with likely challengers.

2. Signal retaliation (the warning shot). The goal is to make your commitment to the market clear so that the challenger fears a long, costly battle and decides avoidance is a better strategy.

> Establish an effective plan (using approaches from strategy 1) and publicize it, as Dow Chemical did whenever it would publicize a large addition to its capacity for magnesium production.

- Leak information about a future barrier, for example, a new technology under development.

- Make a commitment to having the lowest price ("we will not be undersold"). This is effective against a low-priced challenger when your costs are lower. (But be sure a low-price response is appropriate—see step 6 of "The Pricing Advisor's Pricing Policy Audit" in Chapter Nine.)

3. Lower the inducement for attack (prepare for a siege).

- "Raise the penalty for exit or lost share" by "increasing capacity well ahead of demand, entering into long-term supply contracts, increasing vertical integration, and investing in specialized facilities."

- Stockpile weapons and make them visible. The obvious existence of "retaliatory resources" like excess cash reserves and new models in the pipeline will make you a less appealing target.

- Encourage competition among existing players and use them as a first line of defense.

Ideas for Market Followers

What do you do if you are not the market leader, and your market is under attack from a new entrant? DiMingo is very clear on the point that these strategies are designed for leaders only. In most cases, a follower does not have the resources and strength of position to implement them effectively. In some cases, trying to implement one of these strategies could be disastrous. A low-share player's efforts to raise barriers might push it out of the market and benefit its larger competitors, for example. Unfortunately, managers often find themselves in second place or follower companies (there are more of these than there are leaders, after all). And despite the advice of experts, it usually does not feel right to sit on the sidelines and await the outcome of the battle. Here are some ideas I have developed for clients for how the market follower might be able to gain by taking sides in the battle. If you choose to participate, or if circumstances force your hand, just remember that it would be a very grave mistake to think you can use the leader's strategies described earlier.

Make sure the leader defends.

The first step is generally to look to the leader. Is the leader using publicity and investments to signal its commitment? Has the leader fired a warning shot? If not, perhaps you should send the leader's chief executive a copy of this chapter—anonymously, of course, since you do not want to be accused of collusion by the challenger!

Take advantage of the confusion.

The second step is also to look to the leader, but this time with an eye to how you can gain share from the leader during the ensuing melee. Any confusion in the market can provide opportunity for the followers. Can you act more quickly than the leader? Can you flank the leader without immediate retaliation because of the distraction of a new challenge from another direction?

Become indispensable to the leader.

As market followers know only too well, the third step is to look to the leader again! This time, look for ways of mending fences in the face of a common enemy. Will the leader consider forming a coalition with you that is to your mutual advantage? A joint venture, shared resources, and so forth—there are many legitimate ways to cooperate that will strengthen the leader's ability to defend against the intruder—and as a by-product also strengthen your position. Look closely at the leader's options, as given previously, and think of creative ways to assist the leader that are to your mutual benefit.

Become indispensable to the challenger.

The fourth step probably ought to be to look to the challenger. If there is no way to gain significant advantage by helping the leader, try to gain advantage by helping the new challenger instead. You may be able to provide access to distribution channels, technology, and other resources that will greatly lower the challenger's barriers to entry. And the challenger may have new technology, capital, or other resources that will allow you to gain on the leader, and possibly even displace the leader.

Reference

Edward P. DiMingo, "Marketing Strategies for Small-Share Players," *The Journal of Business Strategy*, January/February 1990: 26–30.

MARKETING PLAN OUTLINES

Applications

- Designing a formal, written marketing plan.
- Reviewing plans used by Du Pont, Fidelity Bank, Philip Kotler, and others for inspiration in developing a plan format best suited to your organization
- Also includes an issue-based plan for responding to specific problems or opportunities.

Procedures

1. Evaluate the unique information and objectives of your plan.
2. Identify the kinds of issues that the plan must address in order to accomplish the five principal functions of a marketing plan.
3. Use the sample outlines as a source of ideas as you develop a customized format that is especially well suited to your plan's focus and audience. Just be sure to include an executive summary—the rest of the plan is variable.

Cross-reference

See also "Planning Processes and Procedures" in this chapter.

There are as many formats as there are marketing plans—at least there ought to be. Most references on marketing present a single format as the standard, but this is misleading. The subject matter, emphasis, and order will vary depending upon the situation, plan, and audience. After all, every plan is designed to achieve unique objectives in a unique situation and to inform and persuade a unique audience. The key issue is how well the plan fulfills these two basic roles. David Luck, O. C. Ferrell, and George Lucas take a functional approach in their classic book on marketing strategy and plans, identifying five principal functions for the marketing plan.

Luck/Ferrell/Lucas Marketing Plan Functions

1. *Explain the situation.* A thorough situation analysis, ranging from historical data

through future projections, must be coupled with a description of the "planning gap" or change in position that the plan must achieve.

2. *Specify the results.* A description of expected results and anticipated position at the end of the planning period is always necessary.

3. *Identify necessary resources.* People, materials, funding, and other resources needed to implement the plan must be identified, both to allow evaluation of the plan and to facilitate implementation. Some form of budget is generally necessary for this purpose.

4. *Describe required actions.* Who will have to do what in order for the plan to be implemented?

5. *Permit monitoring of results.* Benchmarks or other measures of success, combined with an assignment of responsibility for monitoring, are essential in order to ensure control over the plan during implementation and to allow changes in tactics if results are disappointing.

Any plan that performs these functions effectively and efficiently for your organization is a good one. The details of structure are less important than the details of function. In fact, when form is subservient to function, a better plan is often produced. The slavish adherence to a textbook outline or one of the currently popular planning workbooks produces a fine table of contents, but not necessarily a good plan! The only element of the outline that you should insist on is a one-page executive summary at the very beginning. For some reason, it does not appear in all the outlines presented here, but it is essential for any plan. Why? Because most readers, and certainly the most important readers, will not read your plan carefully if at all. And because it forces you to condense and clarify the key points of your plan into a single page of text, which is a wonderful mental exercise and a good test of the strength of your plan. If you simply cannot focus on a handful of key elements, expressed in short, punchy sentences, then you do not have an original, insightful, and powerful plan. And I am sure you need one—everybody does!

Having said all this, the fact remains that you must decide upon a specific format in order to write your plan. The right format will help ensure that the plan performs the five requisite functions well and will make the plan a better communicator and persuader. The best way to select a good format is to start by thinking about the specific information needs and the general focus of your plan. Then look at a bunch of plans to see the range of options and decide upon a format that will work best for you. Looking at a pile of your company's plans is probably not very helpful, as most companies evolve a standard format and style that limits variation and (in my opinion) quality as well. For this reason I am including several outlines that cover a wide range of styles and approaches.

A Du Pont Divisional Marketing Plan

SITUATION ANALYSIS

Sales history
Market profile
Sales versus objective
Factors affecting sales
Profitability
Factors affecting profitability

MARKET ENVIRONMENT

Growth rate
Trends, changes in customer attitude
Recent or anticipated competitor actions
Government and activity

PROBLEMS AND OPPORTUNITIES

Problem areas
Opportunities

MARKETING AND PROFITABILITY OBJECTIVES

Sales
Market profile
Gross margin

MARKETING STRATEGY

MARKETING

Marketing programs

PRODUCT ASSUMPTIONS

A Fidelity Bank (of Philadelphia) Marketing Plan

(A plan in this format is written for each major service.)

MANAGEMENT SUMMARY

ECONOMIC PROJECTIONS

Economic factors affecting the service next year

THE MARKET—QUALITATIVE

Prospects
Profiles of potential customers

THE MARKET—QUANTITATIVE

Size of the potential market
Market shares
Current competitive position

TREND ANALYSIS

Historical data by quarter for last five years
Projections

COMPETITION

Competitors, direct and indirect
Current competitive position
Anticipated competitor actions

PROBLEMS AND OPPORTUNITIES

Internal problems
External problems
Opportunities

OBJECTIVES AND GOALS

Next year's objectives

Long-range objectives (five years)

Includes both qualitative (rationale) and quantitative (targets) analysis

ACTION PROGRAMS

Short-term actions to achieve goals, including

Advertising
Direct mail
Brochures

also

Completion schedules
Methods of evaluation
Assignment of responsibilities for execution and evaluation

Kotler's Marketing Plan

Philip Kotler proposed a general format for marketing plans that defines the contents clearly and provides a good boilerplate for most businesses. I used to use it as a starting point for all client plans.

EXECUTIVE SUMMARY

This presents an abbreviated overview of the proposed plan for quick management skimming.

CURRENT MARKETING SITUATION

This presents relevant background data on the market, product, competition, distribution, and macroenvironment.

OPPORTUNITY AND ISSUE ANALYSIS

This summarizes the main opportunities/threats, strengths/weaknesses, and issues facing the product that the plan must deal with.

OBJECTIVES

This defines the goals the plan wants to reach in the areas of sales volume, market share, and profit.

MARKETING STRATEGIES

This presents the broad marketing approach that will be used to meet the plan's objectives.

ACTION PROGRAMS

This answers *What* will be done? *Who* will do it? *When* will it be done? and *How much* will it cost?

PROJECTED PROFIT-AND-LOSS STATEMENT

This summarizes the expected financial payoff from the plan.

CONTROLS

This tells how the plan will be monitored.

The Issue/Problem Plan

This is a format I have used in cases where a company is planning because of specific performance problems or situational challenges it faces. Unfortunately, the unexpected often happens and plans must sometimes be rewritten in order to respond to unplanned problems or opportunities. I find that standard outlines are not as useful in this situation, and they generally take too long to prepare since they include a full-blown situation analysis.

This format supports a problem-solving approach through its emphasis on issue analysis rather than the standard recitation of market statistics. Specific situation analyses are undertaken and presented in order to resolve any questions that are difficult to answer and important to the resolution of the problem—a conventional analysis is replaced by an issue-based situation analysis. The analysis therefore need not be exhaustive—only relevant to the issues. This format also encourages managers to think about how to modify planning and information systems in order to avoid similar problems in the future.

EXECUTIVE SUMMARY

The problem

Key issues (asks penetrating questions)

Proposed resolution of issues (answers questions)

Proposed solution

Major challenges faced by the planners (a constructive gripe list)

Summary of resources needed

Deviations from previous plans

Anticipated results

THE PROBLEM

Complaints prompting analysis (the problem as given)

Restatement of problem (based on issue analysis)

KEY ISSUES

Definition of issues (see King's strategic issue analysis in *The Vest-Pocket CEO*)

Issue analysis and resolution (include a separate section for each issue)

ALTERNATIVES

Review of "on-the-table" solutions

Other viable alternatives

Conclusions from issue analysis

Favored alternative

PROPOSED SOLUTION (A DETAILED DESCRIPTION OF THE FAVORED ALTERNATIVE)

Summary of solution

Action time line

Responsibilities and resources

Budget and financial projections

Anticipated results (qualitative and quantitative, several scenarios)

Certainty of results

Benchmarks and controls

Fallback strategies if benchmarks are not achieved

MAJOR CHALLENGES FACING THE PLANNERS

Unmet information needs

Organizational constraints

Political constraints

Time constraints

Applicability of existing mission and strategy
statements

Implications for certainty of analysis and projections

Implications for future planning process

SUMMARY OF EXPECTED RESULTS

WHEN SHOULD THE NEXT PLAN BE PREPARED?

APPENDIX: HOW ARE COMPETITORS REACTING?

Review of competitor strategies (for those competitors facing a similar challenge or opportunity)

References

David J. Luck, O. C. Ferrell, and George H. Lucas, Jr., *Marketing Strategy and Plans* (Englewood Cliffs, NJ: Prentice
Hall, 1989). Marketing plan functions are from page 297.

The Conference Board, *The Marketing Plan*, Report No. 801
(New York: The Board, 1981). The Du Pont plan is from
page 62. The Fidelity Bank plan is from pages 63–64,
Copyright 1981.

Philip Kotler, *Marketing Management: Analysis, Planning,
Implementation, and Control*, 6th ed., 1984: 77. Re-
printed by permission of Prentice Hall, Englewood Cliffs,
NJ.

Alexander Hiam, *The Vest-Pocket CEO: Decision-Making
Tools for Executives* (Englewood Cliffs, NJ: Prentice Hall,
1990).

PERFORMANCE STANDARDS CHECKLIST

Applications

- Setting control standards and criteria for monitoring marketing plan implementation.
- Developing criteria for evaluating personnel performance and linking performance measures to marketing objectives.

Procedures

Use the checklist as a resource for identifying possible standards whenever reviewing performance against objectives, developing controls for marketing plans, or designing management information reports.

How do you measure success in marketing? There are a surprising number of ways, and it is important to choose measures that are appropriate to specific objectives and that provide the most useful information for management decision making. The selection of performance measures ought to be a central part of the planning process, but it often is not. Instead, many companies allow performance measurement to be based on the existing set of reports generated by accounting or management information systems. These reflect, at best, historical marketing objectives rather than current objectives, and are of little use in monitoring performance, diagnosing problems, or identifying opportunities. Further, when applied to personnel evaluations, the old performance measures often create conflicting and suboptimal measures that motivate employees to pull in the wrong direction or frustrate them so much that motivation is actually reduced.

Planners can set specific performance standards, selecting the best criteria for measurement. This is best done at the time the marketing plan is prepared and assignments are handed out. If the standards differ significantly from last year's, the marketing plan will need to include a brief section on how new measures will be developed, who will do the work, and when it should be done. Conflict with other departments is possible, since other departments may control information flows within the company, so try to bring the appropriate managers into the planning process early on. Use the following list as a resource when trying to identify the most effective performance standards. Raise the issue of performance standards for each objective or component of the plan, as different standards may be optimal for different objectives.

Commonly Used Performance Standards

EFFECTIVENESS STANDARDS

A. SALES CRITERIA

1. Total sales
2. Sales by product or product line
3. Sales by geographic region
4. Sales by salesperson
5. Sales by customer type
6. Sales by market segment
7. Sales by size of order
8. Sales by sales territory
9. Sales by intermediary
10. Market share
11. Percentage change in sales

B. CUSTOMER SATISFACTION

1. Quantity purchased
2. Degree of brand loyalty
3. Repeat purchase rates
4. Perceived product quality
5. Brand image
6. Number of letters of complaint

EFFICIENCY STANDARDS

C. COST

1. Total costs
2. Costs by product or product line
3. Costs by geographic region
4. Costs by salesperson

5. Costs by customer type
6. Costs by market segment
7. Costs by size of order
8. Costs by sales territory
9. Costs by intermediary
10. Percentage change in costs

EFFECTIVENESS-EFFICIENCY STANDARDS

D. PROFITS

1. Total profits
2. Profits by product or product line
3. Profits by geographic region
4. Profits by salesperson
5. Profits by customer type
6. Profits by market segment
7. Profits by size of order
8. Profits by sales territory
9. Profits by intermediary

Reference

Charles D. Schewe, *Marketing Principles and Strategies* (New York: Random House, 1987), p. 593; accompanying list is from Table 18–1.

PLANNING PROCESSES
AND PROCEDURES

Plans are nothing; planning is everything.

—Dwight D. Eisenhower

Applications

- Designing a planning process to produce marketing plans.
- Reviewing processes used by Dunfey Hotels, Celanese Company, and Celestial Seasonings for inspiration in developing a planning process best suited to your organization.
- Evaluating and improving your planning process. Producing better plans.

Procedures

1. Identify objectives and problems that apply to your planning process.
2. Use the sample planning processes as a source of ideas as you develop a customized process that is especially well suited to your company.

Cross-reference

See also "Marketing Plan Outlines" in this chapter.

How a plan is generated is often more important than what the plan says, as Eisenhower learned through his experience in military planning. The planning process drives both the quality and quantity of marketing objectives and strategies. How and when people participate drives their involvement, motivation, and performance to a large measure. The planning process can bog a company down, slowing its product development cycle and its reaction to opportunities and challenges in the market. The planning process can also provide a competitive advantage, allowing one company to edge ahead of another through better ideas implemented more efficiently and effectively.

Much attention is usually focused on the plan's format, but the planning process deserves at least as much attention. Companies need to evaluate their planning process every time they plan, and to modify it whenever they can think of ways to do their planning better. Unless the process evolves with changes in the company and its markets, the company itself will stop evolving and begin to stagnate. One way to keep improving the planning process, or to create a good one if your firm currently has no formal process, is to look for ideas from other companies. The following process descriptions are intended to support this window-shopping approach, and they ought to provide useful ideas for further development as well as specific instructions.

Dunfey Hotels' Planning Process

Dunfey's mission statement includes the following: "To create and/or maintain the structure that provides for the appropriate satisfaction of specifically defined needs of targeted customers, owners, and employees." It is a little unusual in its use of the concept of creating structure. What is this all about?

Jon Canas developed a sophisticated planning process for Dunfey when he came on board as CEO in 1975, and it has been further refined since. It translates the corporate-level goals into missions and strategies for individual hotels and the employees who run them. It creates a vehicle for forecasting and for planning all the major activities of each hotel. It dictates a rhythm and style of management at all the hotels, despite the fact that each is in a unique environment and faces unique challenges. The planning process is the structure referred to in Dunfey's mission statement, and it is a structure that may suit other organizations as well. As Canas says, "The structure is our management philosophy and our planning process, which, when implemented properly, will provide for the needs of owners, employees, and customers." Without further ado, here is Dunfey's planning process.

Annual Corporate Planning. Performed by an executive committee that includes the heads of all major functions/departments. Based on a marketing assessment, financial assessment, and where relevant, an assessment of the objectives of outside owners (since some hotels are managed by Dunfey for outside owners).

Corporate planning results in a mission statement for the business and a traffic-light assessment of their current situation. A "green" is given to units that are on track, a "yellow" is given to units that are on track except for specific items that should be addressed, and a "red" is given to units that are off track. "Red" also means that corporate staff are assigned to the unit to turn it around.

Annual Unit Planning. Performed by an on-site executive operating committee (EOC) at each unit. The EOC, in cooperation with a corporate manager, develops a mission statement whose cornerstone is the "ideal business mix" or IBM. It is a clear definition of target customer segments and how they ought to be represented in the unit's sales effort and revenues over the course of the year. It sometimes results in a major repositioning strategy and associated capital investments. It always drives sales and marketing.

Once the mission statement is approved, the task of the EOC is to translate it into specific actions to be taken, which are called key result areas or KRAs at Dunfey. To help with this process, and to standardize it across units, three planning forms are used:

FORM	FUNCTION
V-1s	Define unit objectives and strategies
V-2s	Define departmental objectives and strategies
V-3s	Set specific goals for each objective from the V-1s and V-2s

Performance Evaluation. The specific goals generated by unit-level KRA planning are translated into an incentive plan for employees.

Short-Term Plans. At Dunfey these are called "Quadimester" plans, and they are prepared, three times a year, for the next four months. They follow a similar format, even to the extent of having Q-1, Q-2, and Q-3 forms, but are less likely to involve a new mission statement.

Reference

Robert J. Kopp and Christopher Lovelock, "The Planning Process," Volume II in *Marketing Management: Strategy, Planning and Implementation*, eds. Benson P. Shapiro, Robert J. Dolan, and John A. Quelch (Homewood, IL: Richard D. Irwin, 1985), pp. 403–420.

Celanese Company's Planning Process

Although this methodology is from an older source, and has probably changed since, it is worthy of note because it represents the classic approach to market and business planning in a product management-oriented organization.

August. Senior management receives market research reports, develops specific volume and profit goals, sends a guidance letter to all product managers stating these goals in late August.

September. Product managers collaborate with the field sales manager and marketing vice president to develop an overall marketing plan, including specific plans for each product.

Field sales manager collaborates with regional sales managers to develop field sales plans.

Mid-October. Marketing vice president reviews plans. Possible give and take required with authors for revision. Upon approval, marketing VP submits them to the president for approval.

Late October. Comptroller prepares operating budget on the basis of the plan.

Early November. Submitted to top management for final approval.

Reference

The Conference Board, *The Development of Marketing Objectives and Plans: A Symposium* (New York: The Conference Board, 1963), p. 38.

Celestial Seasonings' Gap Planning

1. The management team performs a situation analysis, identifying key issues. Strengths/weaknesses analysis and opportunity analysis can be helpful as well.

2. Targets are established for the coming year (for example, in 1984 Celestial Seasonings' goal was to sell 2,600,000 units versus 2,257,000 in 1983).

3. Assumptions are generated concerning the expected *decline* in sales that would result from doing nothing new. Attrition and competitive actions are assumed to make inroads

in sales—this is the first gap that needs to be closed.

4. The total gap between last year's sales minus expected decline and next year's target is identified. Celestial Seasonings' 1984 plan assumed a 100,000 unit decline from 1983 sales as a baseline, and the total gap the planners had to address was therefore 443,000 units.

5. Next, management identifies sources of new revenue that, in combination, appear able to "overfill the gap." It is important to incorporate extra revenues into the marketing plan because an ambitious plan is likely to identify objectives that are hard to reach. (Celestial Seasonings expects to achieve about 85% of objectives.)

The sources of new revenues are derived from the initial analysis of the situation and identification of opportunities (step 1). A clearly articulated mission statement is applied during gap analysis to keep the plan focused on objectives that are consistent with the company's vision. For example, in Celestial Seasonings' 1984 gap analysis the company's philosophy was summarized as "Celestial Seasonings' success = quality products + filling customer/consumer needs," and this formula appeared on key planning documents.

The expected impact of each opportunity is estimated and a chart is prepared to summarize all contributions to next year's unit sales, both negative and positive. Its horizontal axis has only two points—this year on the left and next year on the right. Its vertical axis is unit sales. This year's sales are drawn as a straight, horizontal line. So are next year's units—they appear as another line near the top of the chart. The expected decline due to attrition/competition is drawn below this line. Then each objective for next year's marketing program is entered above this line as a new line based on how much it is expected to contribute to unit sales. Celestial Seasonings' 1984 plan had the following items in its gap analysis chart:

- −100,000 units lost in declining health food business
- +150,000 units for the effect of a conversion to direct sales (includes increasing share, improved distribution, feature support, parity pricing with Lipton, 40% share of shelf)
- +65,000 units from Sunburst C (a new product)
- +50,000 from West Coast Market Development
- +50,000 from Kroger-Peyton distribution
- +50,000 from increased distribution in nondirect markets
- +70,000 from Health Food Tea of the Month Club
- +100,000 from food service, nonfood accounts
- +25,000 from advertising, including TV
- +50,000 from international increases

This list brought the plan about 167,000 units over target to provide about 6.5% in padding. It provided a very specific breakdown of where sales were expected to come from and how much each program had to contribute.

6. Next, Celestial Seasonings develops a *marketing action plan*, in which each item from the gap analysis is addressed by one or more objectives. Every objective is stated in specific, qualitative form, and a strategy is developed for each objective. (Note: You can either develop this plan as a group or delegate the strategy development to individual product managers.) The strategies really get into the tactical level in Celestial Seasonings' marketing action plans. Specific actions and a time frame are defined. Here is a short example from their 1984 plan (other strategies are more lengthy and detailed, but not very intelligible to a company outsider):

   Objective: Improve relative product quality index by 15%.

Strategies:

    a. Improve at least four of the top seven brands plus Lemon Mist through flavor improvement.

    b. Identify greatest areas for RPQ (relative product quality) improvement in packaging modifications.

7. Finally, incentives and a review process are defined in order to encourage achievement of the objectives in the marketing action plan. Celestial Seasonings' founder, Mo Siegel, explains that, "We reviewed the plan quarterly. And I had every officer bonused on the sales and profit objectives. At the end of the year, we did a performance review. How people did versus what they said they'd do. And we had a score."

Reference

David E. Gumpert, "How to REALLY Create a Successful Business Plan, Inc.," 1990, pp. 41, 113–118, 166.

Schewe's Planning Process

This process description comes from Charles Schewe, a marketing professor at the University of Massachusetts, Amherst. Its chief value is that it identifies all the key elements any planning process ought to contain. It divides the process into four key stages: planning→organization→implementation→control. Any customized planning process needs to address each of these areas in order to succeed, so this process description is perhaps best viewed as the basic template from which companies develop their own processes—much as Philip Kotler's outline has become the template for many marketing plans.

PLANNING

1. *Review the organization's mission and objectives.* Mission will generally stay the same from year to year, but objectives will usually change.

2. *Analyze the current marketing situation.* Start by defining the company's current target markets and its position in those markets. This should include "a description of the market and its main segments, the major product in the company's line, the chief competitors and their products and strategies, and recent trends in all areas of marketing," according to Dr. Schewe.

3. *Review the threats and opportunities facing the company in light of its objectives, and use this information to develop marketing strategies.* Opportunities "arise when an environmental change results in an unsatisfied want or need." A principal focus of this step is the identification of unmet needs. Another important focus is on predicting the major threats or challenges the company will face over the next few years.

The analysis of threats and opportunities supports the development of specific objectives (and it is therefore important to have the same people involved in both the analysis and the setting of objectives). Objectives may be expressed "in terms of market share, profits before taxes, return on investment, or some similar marketing or financial goal."

ORGANIZATION

4. *Develop an organization structure to carry out the strategy.* (You cannot assume that the existing structure is suited to the new strategy.) Options are (a) functional organization, that is, research, development, advertising and promotion, sales, and other functions; (b) product organization, using product managers or product family managers; and (c) regional organization (preferable "when the needs of customers vary greatly from one region to another, when customers are located far from one another, and when relationships with customers are important to the marketing effort"). Customer-type organization (by customer groups) and matrix organization are also possibilities.

5. *Develop action programs and establish budgets for those programs.* This is where the specific tactics are defined—the who, what, when, and how questions are answered at this stage of the planning process. Income and expenditures also need to be projected at this point in order to develop detailed budgets. (See "Promotion Budgeting Strategy Selector" in Chapter Two for specific budgeting methods.)

IMPLEMENTATION

6. *Implement the programs.* The key issues in implementation are delegation, coordination, communication, and motivation, and all should be considered when thinking about how to implement the plan. It may also be useful to look at implementation from the perspective of McKinsey's 7 S framework (each of the seven components is linked to the others in the McKinsey diagram, with shared values providing a hub and the other six forming spokes). The 7 Ss of the framework are

- Shared values
- Structure
- Systems
- Style
- Staff
- Skills
- Strategy

7. *Monitor the programs.* This involves setting performance standards (based on sales criteria, customer satisfaction criteria, cost criteria, or profit criteria; see this chapter's "Performance Standards Checklist"), evaluating actual performance, and designing the information systems necessary to do so.

8. *Analyze the results.* It is especially important to obtain information that permits analysis of results by specific products and market segments. Sales reports broken down according to the percentage of sales contributed by each region or each product and

product group are helpful. Sales variance analysis, showing the percent variance of actual from forecasted sales, can also be helpful. Other analytical tools include marketing control charts (actual sales plotted by week against the forecast level, with an upper and lower action line added for control purposes) and marketing cost analysis (based on the income statement).

9. *If necessary, take corrective action.* But note that "corrective action should not be undertaken without a thorough understanding of the cause (or causes) of the problem." Corrective actions can take three general forms (quoted from Schewe, p. 602):

   a. *Eliminating the cause* of the difference between actual and planned performance.
   b. *Adapting* to situations beyond the marketer's control by making changes in tactical plans.
   c. *Taking no action in the short run* while modifying long-term strategy.

Reference

Charles D. Schewe, *Marketing Principles and Strategies* (New York: Random House, 1987), pp. 576–603.

SHANKLIN'S MARKETING BLUNDERS

Applications

- Avoiding classic errors in formulating marketing strategy.
- Training managers to improve their planning and forecasting skills.

Procedures

Use as a checklist when preparing or reviewing marketing plans and strategies.

No, these blunders were not *made* by Shanklin. They are the most common errors underlying failed marketing strategies *according to* consultant and Kent State University professor William L. Shanklin. He finds that a large number of problems arise from a small number of common misconceptions. These misconceptions produce what Shanklin calls "timeless marketing blunders," timeless because they are repeated so often over the years and because they are always mistakes. The list is a valuable defense against conventional wisdom, a defense that is clearly needed when you consider that the majority of new businesses and new products fail. As Shanklin puts it, "If people learn from their mistakes, many are getting a fantastic education."

1. Building better mousetraps. Emerson's advice that the world will beat a path to your door if you build a better mousetrap is perhaps true for dramatic technical breakthroughs. Unfortunately most inventions and product improvements do not create new markets. But it is easy to fall in love with your product and fail to look at it from the consumer's perspective. Many new products are of little interest to the consumer. And those that are may require a long-term marketing program to educate and penetrate the potential market.

It is also important to remember that customers evaluate "better mousetraps" on the basis of value, which means that the added performance features of the new mousetrap had better be worth the added price or consumers will stick with the old version.

2. Practicing Chinese marketing. The term comes from Carl Crow's classic *Four Hundred Million Cus-*

tomers, in which he argued that the Depression could be cured by exporting to a market as large as China. China has one and a quarter billion people now, and it still does not account for a significant share of U.S. exports. The size of the market has little to do with its sales potential. But many marketers select target markets on the basis of size, and advertisers frequently rationalize media selections on the basis of number of exposures. The problem can be acute in direct mail, where it is tempting to assume the typical return of 1–3% and maximize the size of the mailing to maximize sales. It usually works a lot better to focus more narrowly, to improve the quality of exposures or lists rather than the quantity, and to target the most receptive, least contested customer segments rather than the largest.

3. Having too much faith in forecasting. Most forecasts are wrong. And studies suggest that the difference between the quality of inexpert and expert forecasters is negligible. So why do companies rely so heavily on forecasts? J. Scott Armstrong of Wharton says this is the "seer-sucker theory" at work. It states that "No matter how much evidence exists that seers do not exist, suckers will pay for seers." Because forecasting change is an inexact science, planning needs to be robust enough to accommodate unexpected events. Plans built on several forecasts, for example, through the use of multiple scenarios or low-, mid-, and high-range projections, are more likely to succeed.

4. Oversubscribing to conventional wisdom. There are two issues here. First, the conventional wisdom is often wrong. This is especially true of facts reported about economic and social issues. If the newspapers all say fewer young people can afford houses today than in the past, it is probably not true (in fact, you see this frequently, but long-term statistics say the opposite is true). Basing a marketing plan or a positioning strategy on false conventional wisdom is likely to cause trouble. The second issue is more subtle, but equally important. Even where conventional wisdom is based on fact, following it can be poor strategy since everyone else follows it too. In fact, if conventional wisdom is pointing everyone in the same direction, other directions may provide better opportunity for the independent-minded marketer.

5. Selling the sizzle instead of the steak. According to Shanklin, "Marketers add value and a little sizzle, of course, to what the factory provides. But quality and everything it denotes and connotes is basically determined at the development and manufacturing levels." It is a mistake to ask marketing to "bail out" a bad product with flash and hype. Marketing is far more successful when there is some real benefit to communicate. Note that this wisdom runs counter to the trend toward psychographic marketing, in which the unique selling proposition is a novel positioning strategy rather than better performance. As long as the product is not perceived as *worse*, this approach can work. But when competitors focus on quality and value, the fancy positioning strategy may fall flat—witness the share gains of Japanese versus U.S. autos during the 1980s.

6. Confusing financial/marketing cause and effect. Marketing plans often derive revenue projections from the financial requirements of the firm. A start-up projects rapid growth to show investors a good return. A lower-risk, larger company projects lower growth as this is all investors will require. But if a liquidity squeeze is anticipated, sales and revenue projections will be jacked up to justify further debt. Why? Because it is easy to forget that marketing drives finance, and not the opposite. As Shanklin puts it, "Revenues and profits depend squarely on how well company executives discern and meet customer problems and needs." He argues that the rise of Japanese companies in consumer electronics and other industries reflects their willingness to focus on building market position in the short term and to let financial performance flow from market performance in the long term. The shortsighted focus on quarterly financials is a symptom of blunder 6.

References

J. Scott Armstrong, "How Expert Are the Experts?" *Inc.*, December 1981, pp. 15–16. See, also, William L. Shanklin, "Six Timeless Marketing Blunders," *The Journal of Business & Industrial Marketing*, Vol. 2, Spring 1987: 17–25.

Chapter 2

Advertising and Promotion

Berger's Attitude Model

Bovee/Arens Advertising Checklists

Chiat/Day Advertising Rules

"Copy Chaser" Criteria for Business-to-Business Ads

Leo Burnett Drama Scale

Promotion Budgeting Strategy Selector

Retention Marketing

Robinson's Promotion Guidelines

Schultz's Four Challenges

TV Ad Censorship Rules

Also see:
  Maxwell Sroge's Catalogue Planning Guide
  Business Marketing Media Selector
  Zap-Proofing Advertising
  Word-of-Mouth Marketing Objectives
  McElnea's Promotion Agency Selection Guide
  Rapp & Collins' Double-Duty Advertising

BERGER'S ATTITUDE MODEL

An academic perspective on how advertising influences purchase behavior, and how its influence might be increased.

Applications

- Developing stategies to convert awareness into trial.
- Understanding contradictions between survey results concerning consumer attitude and actual purchase behavior.
- Evaluating and refining advertisements to make them more action oriented.
- Developing communication objectives and strategies for use in the creative process.

Procedures

Analyze the marketing task, and evaluate specific campaigns, from the perspective offered by the model. Specifically, consider how effectively ads encourage viewers to evaluate the information they present, how viewers' confidence in the information can be strengthened, and how the attitude conveyed by the ad can be made more accessible and memorable for the viewer. Review the experimental results to see if they offer any clues to improved advertising strategy.

Advertising is usually assumed to influence the consumer's purchase decision by creating a favorable attitude toward a particular brand. Advertising can create awareness of the brand, and information in ads can shape this awareness into a positive perception. Then, hopefully, consumers holding this positive perception of a brand will go out and buy it over competing brands. But exactly how does this process work? If we knew, we might be able to develop better advertising. Here is one model of the relationship among advertising, attitude, and behavior that sheds light on the mystery and has some useful implications for advertising strategy.

Building on a model of attitude developed by social psychologist Russell Fazio, Ida Berger and Andrew Mitchell of the University of Toronto have proposed and tested the following proposition:

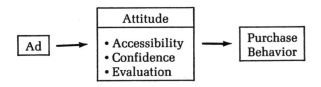

Attitude accessibility and attitude confidence moderate the attitude-behavior relationship.

"So what?" the practitioner is likely to say. To understand the significance of this, you need to look briefly at what Fazio discovered. He found that attitude is not a simple thing, that in fact it has several dimensions. There is an evaluative dimension—how good or bad you think something is—and this is what we normally refer to when we speak of and measure consumer attitudes. But there are also nonevaluative dimensions influencing how accessible and strong the evaluative dimension is. Berger's model portrays two nonevaluative dimensions, *accessibility* and *attitude confidence*, each having the ability to increase or decrease the relationship between attitude and behavior. For example, if accessibility is low, the consumer may not recall and apply an attitude at the moment a purchase decision is made.

One of the tougher problems marketers face is that attitudes do not necessarily predict behavior. Consumers might say in a survey that they prefer brand X, but then they go out and buy brands Y and Z in greater numbers. Advertising research might indicate that a TV campaign has built awareness significantly, but sales results may show that awareness was not converted to trial and use at a high rate. This model offers some clues for strengthening the relationship between attitude and behavior. Specifically, it suggests that advertising needs to strengthen attitude confidence and increase accessibility of the attitude in the consumer's memory. How?

Berger and Mitchell demonstrated in an experiment that repetition of ads can, under certain circumstances, accomplish both of these goals and result in a closer link between attitude toward a brand

and purchase of the brand. But it is important to make sure that you achieve the same circumstances they did. They focused on the evaluative dimension of attitude in their experimental ads. Here is what they have to say about it:

> *To the extent that an individual is motivated to evaluate brand information and either form evaluations or activate and reconsider previously formed evaluations, any ad exposure should result in either the formation or strengthening of the association between representation of the brand in memory and its evaluation.*

The problem is that after repeated exposure to an ad, "individuals may cease to process the information in evaluative terms." How do you overcome this problem? One strategy is to do "direct experience" pretests, in which subjects use, evaluate, and describe their responses to the product as vividly as possible. Then include these direct experiences in the advertisement in order to simulate a direct experience through the indirect experience of advertising. Another strategy is to focus on building high involvement in the advertising audience. Under experimental conditions this can be done by giving special instructions. In a real advertisement, the ad itself must demand and hold attention, for example, through encouraging vicarious participation. There is no pat formula to accomplish this goal, and arguably good advertising already does. The most useful point is simply that **the model suggests a new set of goals that copywriters can aim for and market researchers can use for pre- and posttesting.**

In an elaborate set of experiments involving the comparison of direct experience (which produces high-confidence, accessible attitudes) with advertising (which often does not), Berger and Mitchell found that "advertising can influence more than just the evaluative dimension of attitudes. When individuals are highly motivated to process brand information, advertising via repeated exposures can influence how easily an evaluation is accessed, how confidently it is held, and ultimately how likely it is to influence subsequent behavior." Their study found that several repetitions of an ad could result in attitudes that were as accessible and strongly held as attitudes formed through direct experience.

I suspect that most advertising falls far short of this level of influence over buying behavior, but it should be encouraging to advertisers that it is possible to create such high-impact ads. A strong focus on building motivation to process brand information is important, especially when repetition of the ad is planned. And copywriters may find it interesting to think about making attitudes more accessible and creating greater confidence in attitudes, along with their current focus on creating favorable attitudes toward brands. For example, an advertising strategy could include a description of the purchase context and a goal of making consumers recall their evaluative attitudes *in this specific context* through some point-of-purchase reminder or mnemonic device aimed at nonevaluative dimensions of attitude.

References

Ida E. Berger and Andrew A. Mitchell, "The Effect of Advertising on Attitude Accessibility, Attitude Confidence, and the Attitude-Behavior Relationship," *Journal of Consumer Research*, Vol. 16, December 1989: 269–279. See also, Russell H. Fazio, "How Do Attitudes Guide Behavior?" in *Handbook of Motivation and Cognition: Foundations of Social Behavior*, eds. Richard M. Sorrentino and E. Tory Higgins (New York: Guilford), pp. 204–243.

BOVEE/ARENS ADVERTISING CHECKLISTS

Applications

- Developing and evaluating advertising.
- Identifying the critical issues for advertising in a specific medium (there are checklists for print, television, radio, direct mail, and outdoor).

Procedures

Review the appropriate checklist to identify winning strategies in a chosen medium. Use the checklist to guide review of proposed or existing advertisements and identify problems and improvements. Checklists of what works best are provided for print, TV, radio, direct mail, and outdoor.

Cross-reference

A PR checklist can be found in Chapter Six, "Public Relations and Corporate Marketing."

Checklist of What Works Best in Print

☐ Use simple layouts. One big picture works better than several small pictures. Avoid cluttered pages. (Layouts that resemble the magazine's editorial format are well read.)

☐ Always put a caption under a photograph. Readership of picture captions is generally twice as great as that of body copy. The picture caption can be an advertisement by itself.

☐ Don't be afraid of long copy. The people who read beyond the headline are *prospects for your product or your service.* If your product is expensive—like a car, a vacation, or an industrial product—prospects are hungry for the information long copy gives them. Consider long copy if you have a complex story to tell, many different product points to make, or an expensive product or service to sell.

☐ Avoid negative headlines. People are literal minded and may remember only the negatives. Sell the positive benefits in your product—not that it won't harm or that some defect has been solved. Look for emotional words that attract and motivate, like *free* and *new* and *love*.

☐ Don't be afraid of long headlines. Research shows that, on the average, long headlines sell more merchandise than short ones.

☐ Look for story appeal. After the headline, a striking visual is the most effective way to get a reader's attention. Try for story appeal—the kind of visual that makes the reader ask: "What's going on here?"

☐ Photographs are better than drawings. Research says that photography increases recall an average of 26% over artwork.

☐ Look at your advertisement in its editorial environment. Ask to see your advertisement pasted into the magazine in which it will appear—or for newspapers, photostated in the same tone as the newspaper page. Beautifully mounted layouts are deceptive. The reader will never see your advertisement printed on high-gloss paper, with a big white border, mounted on a board. It is misleading for you to look at it this way.

☐ Develop a single advertising format. An overall format for all print advertising can double recognition. This rule holds special meaning for industrial advertisers. One format will help readers see your advertisements as coming from one large corporation, rather than several small companies.

☐ Before-and-after photographs make a point better than words. If you can, show a visual contrast—a change in the consumer or a demonstration of product superiority.

☐ Do not print copy in reverse type. It may look attractive, but it reduces readability. For the same reason, don't surprint copy on the illustration of your advertisement.

☐ Make each advertisement a complete sale. Your message must be contained in the headline. React to the overall impression as the reader will. Only the advertiser reads all his advertisements. Any advertisement in a series must make a complete sale. Assume it will be the only advertisement for your product a reader will ever see.

Checklist of What Works Best in Television

☐ The picture must tell the story. Forget every other rule in this chapter, and you will still be ahead of the game. Television is a *visual* medium. That's why the people in front of a set are called *viewers*. Try this trick for looking at a storyboard. *Cover the words.* What is the message of the commercial with the sound turned off? Is there a message at all?

☐ Look for a "key visual." Here's another test to apply to the storyboard. Can you pick out one frame that visually sums up the whole message? Most good commercials can be reduced to this single "key visual." A commercial with many different scenes may look interesting in storyboard form but can turn out to be an overly complicated piece of film.

☐ Grab the viewer's attention. The *first 5 seconds* of a commercial are crucial. Analyses of audience reaction show either a sharp drop or a sharp rise in interest during this time. *Commercial attention does not build.* Your audience can only become less interested, never more. The level you reach in the first 5 seconds is the highest you will get, so don't save your punches. Offer the viewer something right off the bat: *news,* a *problem* to which you have the solution, a *conflict* that is involving.

☐ Be single minded. A good commercial is uncomplicated, direct. It never makes the viewer do a lot of mental work. The basic commercial length in U.S. television is 30 seconds. The content possible in that time is outlined in the phrase "name-claim-demonstration": the name of your product, your consumer benefit, and the reason the consumer should believe it. Longer commercials *should not add copy points.* A 60-second commercial tells the same story as the 30-second one, with more leisure and detail. Or—best of all—*repetition.* The 60-second commercial allows time for a mood to be created; the 30-second one generally does not. The 10-second and 15-second commercials are one-point messages. The 10-second registers the brand name and promise. The 15-second makes the promise more explicit.

☐ Register the name of your product. Too often, a viewer will remember the commercial but not the name of your brand. This is a problem particularly troublesome with new products. Showing the package on screen and mouthing the name is not enough. Take extra pains to implant your product name in the viewer's mind.

☐ The tone of your advertising must reflect your product personality. If you are fortunate enough to have a product with an established brand image, your advertising *must* reflect that image. It takes dedication on the part of advertiser and agency to build a brand personality. Discipline yourself to reject advertising that conflicts with it. (It helps to have a written "personality statement" of your product; if it were a person, what sort of person would it be?) When you launch a new product, the very *tone* of your announcement commercial tells viewers what to expect. From that moment on, it is hard to change their minds. Once you have decided on a personality for your product, sustain it in every commercial. Change campaigns when you must, but retain the same tone of voice.

☐ Avoid "talky" commercials. Look for the simplest, and most memorable, set of words to get across your consumer benefit. Every word must work hard. A 30-second commercial usually allows you *no more* than 65 words, a 60-second commercial twice that amount. Be specific. Pounce on cliches, flabbiness, and superlatives. Try this discipline. When you ask for 10 words to be added to a commercial, decide which 10 you would *delete* to make room for them.

Checklist of What Works Best in Radio

☐ Stretch the listener's imagination. Voices and sounds can evoke pictures.

☐ Listen for a memorable sound. What will make your commercial stand out from the clutter? Offer a distinctive voice, a memorable jingle, a solution to the listener's problem.

☐ Present one idea. It is difficult to communicate more than one idea in a television commercial. In radio, which is subject to more distractions, it is nearly impossible. Be direct and clear.

☐ Select your audience quickly. It pays to flag your segment of the audience at the beginning of the commercial—before they can switch to another station.

☐ Mention your brand name and your promise early. Commercials that do so get higher awareness. It heightens awareness if you mention the brand name and promise *more than once.*

☐ Capitalize on events. Exploit the flexibility of radio to tie in with fads, fashions, news events, or the weather.

☐ Use radio to reach teenagers. Teenagers don't watch much television. They do listen to a lot of radio. Media experts say it's the best way to reach teens. Some say it's the *only* way.

☐ Music can help. It is particularly effective in reaching teenagers who prefer the "now sounds" offered by music stations. You can give your campaign infinite variety with the same lyrics arranged in different ways and sung by different people.

☐ Ask listeners to take action. People respond to radio requests for action. They call the station to exchange views with the disc jockey or ask for certain music. Don't be afraid to ask listeners to call now, or write in, or send money.

☐ Make use of radio's merchandising services. Associate your business with a popular on-air personality; sponsor promotions such as contests and giveaways.

Checklist of What Works Best in Direct Mail

☐ Make sure your offer is right. More than any other element, what you offer the consumer—in terms of product, price, or premium—will make the difference. Consider combinations instead of single units, optional extras, different opening offers, and commitment periods. Free is the most powerful offer you can make, but beware of its attracting lookers instead of buyers.

☐ Demonstrate your product. Offer a free sample, or enclose a sample if you can. Sampling is the most expensive promotion in absolute cost but is often so effective that the investment is quickly paid back with a larger business base. If you measure response on a profit per piece mailed, it sometimes pays to spend a few more cents.

☐ Use the envelope to telegraph your message. Direct mail must work fast. Your envelope has only seconds to interest the prospect or go unopened into the wastebasket.

☐ Have a copy strategy. Like any other advertising medium, direct mail will be more productive if you decide *in advance* the important issues of target audience; consumer benefit; and support, tone, and personality. While your promise should relate specifically to your product, experts say the most potent appeals in direct mail are how to make money, save money, save time, or avoid effort.

☐ Grab the reader's attention. Every beginning copywriter in direct mail learns the AIDA formula. The letters stand for the ideal structure of a sales letter: attention, interest, desire, action. Look for a dramatic opening, one that speaks to the reader in a very *personal* way.

☐ Don't be afraid of long copy. The more you tell, the more you sell—particularly if you're asking the reader to spend a great deal of money or invest time. A Mercedes-Benz diesel car letter was five pages long. A Cunard Line letter for ocean cruises was eight pages long. The key to long copy is *facts*. Be specific, not general. Make the letter visually appealing. Break up the copy into smaller paragraphs and emphasize important points with underlines or handwritten notes. Including several pieces in a direct-mail package often improves response.

☐ Don't let the reader off the hook. Leave your readers with something to do, so that they won't procrastinate. It's too easy to put off a decision. Use action devices like a yes/no token to be stuck on a reply card. *Involvement* is important. Prod them to act *now*. Set a fixed period of time, like ten days. Or make only a limited supply available. Make it extremely easy for the reader to respond to your offer. But always ask for the order.

☐ Pretest your promises and headlines. Don't guess at what will appeal to the reader. There are many ways to sell your product benefits and as many inexpensive testing methods. Avoid humor, tricks, or gimmicks. It pays to be serious and helpful.

Checklist of What Works Best in Outdoor

☐ Look for a big idea. This is no place for subtleties. Outdoor is a bold medium. You need a poster that registers the idea quickly and memorably—"visual scandal" that shocks the viewer into awareness.

☐ Keep it simple. Cut out all extraneous words and pictures, and concentrate on the essentials. Outdoor is the art of brevity. Use only one picture and no more than seven words of copy—preferably fewer.

☐ Personalize when you can. Personalized posters are practical, even for short runs. Mention a specific geographic area ("New Chicago") or the name of a local dealer.

☐ Look for human, emotional content for memorability. It can be an entertainment medium for travelers who are hungry or bored.

☐ Use color for readability. The most readable combination is black on yellow. Other combinations may gain more attention, but stay with primary colors—and *stay away from reverse.*

☐ Use the location to your advantage. Many new housing developments capitalize on their convenient locations with a poster saying, "If you lived here, you'd be home now." Use outdoor to tell drivers that your restaurant is down the road, your department store is across the street. Don't ignore the ability of outdoor to reach ethnic neighborhoods. Tailor the language and the models to your consumer.

Reference

Courtland L. Bovee and William F. Arens, *Contemporary Advertising*, 3rd ed. (Homewood, IL: Richard D. Irwin, 1989). All checklists reproduced with permission of the publisher.

CHIAT/DAY ADVERTISING RULES

Applications

- Controlling the quality of work done by advertising agencies.
- Introducing standards to maintain high-quality, creative work as an ad agency or advertising department grows.
- Coming up with tough questions to keep your ad agency on its toes.

Procedures

Jay Chiat of Chiat/Day, Inc., developed these simple rules to ensure continuing high-quality work as his advertising agency grew. It is easy for an agency to allow some bad work to slip by, but obviously it is important to their reputation that they avoid bad work under any circumstances. Agencies, both independent and in-house, will find it constructive to compare Chiat-Day's rules with their own policies and past performance. And agency clients have an obvious interest in seeing the quality of work maintained, so they might find the guidelines useful in evaluating their agency or selecting a new agency. Without further ado, here are Jay Chiat's rules for avoiding bad advertising.

HOW TO AVOID DOING BAD ADVERTISING

1. Realize that your agency cannot work for everyone.
2. Recognize that there are no shortcuts. It's hard work to do great advertising.
3. Hire only those you believe can do the job better than you can. It makes the work brighter, and it makes your work brighter.
4. Fire quickly those who do not measure up. They contaminate the agency by making good people question their judgment.
5. Recognize that all your people have creative capabilities, and demand creativity from all departments.
6. Make sure your account management people are smart marketers. It takes brilliant marketing support to quiet client nervousness.

7. Never stop at the first creative solution. Explore alternatives.

8. Dig for facts. Interview relentlessly. Your research must be unquestioned.

9. Know your target better than you know yourself.

10. Make sure a clear, concise, creative brief is written for every ad. Yes, *every* ad.

11. Treat all advertising as equal. The trade is as important as the TV commercial. Perhaps more so.

12. Do not permit "closet" accounts. If the work is not good enough to show to new business prospects, the account is not good enough to keep.

13. Spend time training. Do not assume that people automatically understand what is expected of them.

14. Promote from within when possible. But do not hesitate to seek expertise elsewhere if it is lacking at the agency.

15. Treat everyone with the same level of dignity you expect yourself.

16. Have no expectations. You have the privilege of working on an account for as long as the client allows you to.

17. Perhaps most important, try to relax and have some fun.

    (Thanks to Jay Chiat for permission to print this material.)

Incidentally, it is interesting to note that David Ogilvy of Ogilvy & Mather finds rule 3 very important too. He wrote that "When someone is made the head of an office in the Ogilvy & Mather chain, I send him a Matrioshka doll from Gorky. If he has the curiosity to open it, and keep opening it until he comes to the inside of the smallest doll, he finds this message:

> *If each of us hires people who are*
> *smaller than we are, we shall become*
> *a company of dwarfs. But if each of us*

> hires people who are bigger than we
> are, we shall become a company of
> giants.

References

Jay Chiat, of Chiat/Day, Inc., unpublished document. See also, David Ogilvy, *Ogilvy on Advertising* (New York: Vintage Books, 1983), p. 47.

"COPY CHASER" CRITERIA FOR BUSINESS-TO-BUSINESS ADS

Applications

- Evaluating advertising copy.
- Improving the effectiveness of advertising, especially business-to-business and industrial advertising, by making the copy more effective and memorable.
- Training copywriters.

Procedures

Review and score copy (for print, TV, and other media) against each of the ten criteria. Or use the criteria as a set of principles and guidelines when training copywriters or establishing policies for practice.

The Copy Chasers are an anonymous panel of experts in business-to-business advertising who evaluate ads for *Business Marketing* magazine each month. Their evaluation criteria are also used to select winners of the annual Sawyer Award for top business advertising. The Copy Chasers are anonymous for good reason—they stick their necks out once a year to choose the single best business or industrial ad, and also deal rather severely with a lot of bad advertising during the rest of the year.

The ten criteria were developed by Howard G. Sawyer. His identity as founder and long-time panelist for the "Copy Chaser" column was only revealed posthumously. But he was a well-known executive of Marsteller, Inc., now HDM. No further introduction to the criteria is needed. Their obvious application is for evaluating ads, and they also are useful in training. Although designed for business-to-business and industrial ads, you will find them helpful with consumer print advertising as well.

*Copy Chaser Criteria**

1. The successful ad has a high degree of visual magnetism. On average, only a small number of ads in an issue of a magazine will capture the attention of any one reader. Some ads will be passed by because the subject matter is of no concern. But others,

*Reprinted from *Business Marketing*, January 1990, pp. 77–78. Copyright Crain Communications, Inc.

even though they may have something to offer, fail the very first test of stopping the reader in his or her scanning of the pages.

Ads perish right at the start because, at one extreme, they just lie there on the page, flat and gray, and at the other extreme, they are cluttered, noisy, and hard to read.

An ad should be constructed so that a single component dominates the area—a picture, the headline, or the text—but not the company name or the logo.

Obviously, the more pertinent the picture, the more arresting the headline; the more informative the copy appears to be, the better.

2. The successful ad selects the right audience. Often, an ad is the first meeting place of two parties looking for each other.

So there should be something in the ad that at first glance will enable readers to identify it as a source of information relating to *their* job interests—a problem they have or an opportunity they will welcome.

This is done with either a picture or a headline—preferably both—the ad should say immediately to the reader, "Hey, this is for you."

3. The successful ad invites the reader into the scene. Within the framework of the layout, the art director's job is to visualize, illuminate, and dramatize the selling proposition.

And the art director must take into consideration the fact that the type of job a reader has dictates the selection of the illustrative material. Design engineers work with drawings. Construction engineers like to see products at work. Chemical engineers are comfortable with flowcharts. Managers relate to pictures of people. And so on.

4. The successful ad promises a reward. An ad will survive the qualifying round only if readers are given reason to expect that if they continue on, they will learn something of value. A brag-and-boast headline, a generalization, an advertising platitude will turn readers off before they get into the message.

The reward that the ad offers can be explicit or implicit, and can even be stated negatively, in the form of a warning or possible loss.

The promise should be specific. The headline "Less maintenance cost" is not as effective as "You can cut maintenance costs 25%."

5. The successful ad backs up the promise. To make the promise believable, the ad must provide hard evidence that the claim is valid.

Sometimes, a description of the product's design or operating characteristics will be enough to support the claim.

Comparisons with competition can be convincing. Case histories make the reward appear attainable. Best of all are testimonials: "they-say" advertising carries more weight than does "we-say" advertising.

6. The successful ad presents the selling proposition in logical sequence. The job of the art director is to organize the parts of an ad so that there is an unmistakable entry point (the single dominant component referred to earlier) and the reader is guided through the material in a sequence consistent with the logical development of the selling proposition.

A layout should not call attention to itself. It should be a frame within which the various components are arranged.

7. The successful ad talks "person to person." Much industrial advertising, unlike consumer goods advertising, consists of one company talking to another company—or even to an entire industry.

But copy is more persuasive when it speaks to the reader as an individual—as if it were one friend telling another friend about a good thing.

First, the terms should be the terms of the reader's business, not the advertiser's business. But more than that, the writing style should be simple: short words, short sentences, short paragraphs, active rather than passive voice, no advertising cliches, frequent use of the personal pronoun *you*. A more friendly tone results when the copy refers to the advertiser in the first person: "we" rather than "the company name."

8. Successful advertising is easy to read. This is a principle that shouldn't need to be stated, but the fact is that typography is the least understood part of our business.

The business press is loaded with ads in which the most essential part of the advertiser's message— the copy—appears in type too small for easy reading or is squeezed into a corner or is printed over part of the illustration.

Text type should be no smaller than 9 point. It should appear black on white. It should stand clear of interference from any other part of the ad. Column width should not be more than half the width of the ad.

9. Successful advertising emphasizes the service, not the source. Many industrial advertisers insist that the company name or logo be the biggest thing in the ad, that the company name appear in the headline, that it be set in boldface wherever it appears in the copy. That's too much.

An ad should make readers want to buy—or at least consider buying—before telling them *where* to buy.

10. Successful advertising reflects the company's character. A company's advertising represents the best opportunity it has—better than the sales force—to portray the company's personality—the things that will make the company liked, respected, admired.

A messy ad tends to indicate a messy company. A brag-and-boast ad suggests the company is *maker* oriented, not *user* oriented. A dull-looking ad raises the possibility that the company has nothing to get excited about, and is behind the times, is slowing down.

What we are talking about is a matter of subtleties, but the fact remains: like sex appeal (which is not easy to define), some companies have it, some don't. And whatever it is, it should be consistent over time and across the spectrum of corporate structure and product lines.

Reference

"Copy Chasers," *Business Marketing*, January 1990: 72–78.

LEO BURNETT DRAMA SCALE
(for TV Ads)

Applications

- Thinking about the form a TV ad should take.
- Evaluating alternative storyboards.
- Using form-based criteria for designing and pretesting ads.

Procedures

1. Evaluate an ad by placing it on the drama scale. (Or review the discussion of theory to decide where on the scale a new ad should be.)

2. Rate the ad, using qualitative judgment, on four dimensions: whether it inspires counterarguments, how believable it is, how much feeling it arouses, and how realistic or authentic it is.

3. The drama scale can provide a basis for testing ad concepts. Develop ad concepts representing all four categories on the drama scale, with more than one ad concept for each category. Present the concepts to a panel of consumers and look for any relationship between ratings and placement on the scale—the panel results may indicate that one of the categories is most effective.

4. A formal survey can be used to evaluate ad concepts on the four dimensions listed in "procedure" and evaluate its effectiveness on these dimensions. Use a consumer panel and develop questions based on the samples provided.

Much of the research literature on advertising is completely unintelligible to practitioners. My source for this tool is, unfortunately, a good example. Strange diagrams, statistical tables, and talk of "binary judgments," "Cronbach's alpha," and "linear transformations" brought back dark memories of grad school days, and I would have passed the article by happily except for the fact that two-thirds of the author team hails from Leo Burnett. I figured there must be something useful here, and, after five or six readings, I think I have found it.

The authors start by defining a spectrum for the form of commercials. It ranges from pure argument to pure drama, with most commercials falling somewhere in between. They divide the scale into four basic ad types:

The Drama Scale

AD FORM	CHARACTERISTICS
Argument	Narrated, no character, no plot
Demonstration	Narrated, no character, plot
Story	Narrated, character, plot
Drama	Unnarrated, character, plot

They hypothesize—and then prove through methods that are best not described in a practitioners' book—that viewers evaluate an argument rationally, expecting it to be supported and often developing counterarguments to it. Arguments elicit expressions of belief or disbelief, depending upon how persuasive they are.

On the other hand, dramas are evaluated on the basis of whether they ring true to life—their verisimilitude—and when persuasive, they communicate value. Value may be thought of in terms of how useful a product is, how enjoyable it is, or other dimensions. If the viewer does develop counterarguments (which is less common with dramas than arguments), the verisimilitude of the drama becomes especially important in determining whether the viewer is persuaded.

The study classifies commercials on the argument/drama scale and also evaluates the effectiveness of the ads. It does *not* find that argument is a better form than drama, or vice versa. It's not that simple, of course! Some arguments work, others don't, and the same may be said for dramas. But *which* will work? The study does find that viewers differentiate good from bad ads on the basis of:

- Whether they inspire counterarguments

- How believable they are
- How much feeling they arouse
- How realistic or authentic they were

Further, it finds a relation between believability and counterarguments, and a relation between feelings and realism. The former is of use in evaluating argument-based ads, the latter for dramas.

Application Ideas: You have developed a basic strategy for an ad campaign, and have sketched out a variety of concepts in storyboard form. You plan to show them to a panel of consumers and explore their reactions before committing to a specific concept. You wonder whether to take a "proof" approach or to dramatize the product's use and benefits. One simple application is to review the drama scale, and be sure to include a number of concepts in each category. After the session, review consumer reactions and comments to see whether there is any relationship between them and the drama scale. Was one category favored? Was one a disaster? This will give some form-oriented feedback you might not otherwise have obtained from the concept test.

Another idea is to supplement the qualitative feedback you receive from your concept-testing panel or focus group with a survey in which viewers report how they responded to each commercial according to dimensions from the Leo Burnett study. Specifically, ask viewers to describe how they felt on four dimensions, using a 1-to-6 scale for not true–true. You will need to develop a minimum of several questions for each dimension. The dimensions are:

1. Counterargument. How inclined the viewers were to argue back.

SAMPLE QUESTIONS:

I thought of reasons not to use the product while watching this commercial.

I felt like arguing with the narrator.

2. Expression of belief. How believable the ad and its claims were.

SAMPLE QUESTIONS:

This ad made good sense to me as I viewed it.

This ad seemed important to me.

I felt that the ad illustrated the qualities of the product realistically.

3. Expression of feeling. How good the viewer feels about the ad as they watch it.

SAMPLE QUESTIONS:

I felt that this commercial was clever and entertaining.

It was exciting.

It was enjoyable.

4. Verisimilitude. How well the commercial draws in the viewers and how authentic and realistic it is.

SAMPLE QUESTIONS:

If I could, I would have stepped into the commercial and joined in.

This commercial was true to life.

I could relate to the feelings of the people in this commercial.

On the simplest level, this survey will give you some interesting feedback you might not have otherwise collected. It is nonevaluative—it does not ask the viewers whether they think the commercial is a good one. Instead, it asks them how they reacted to it on four dimensions that you expect will be related to the power of the commercial. On a more complex level, you could also try to relate the "drama score" or position of the commercial on the argument-drama scale to the reactions in your viewer survey. If the ad's form leans toward drama, you ought to look closely at the answers to questions concerning attributes 3 and 4, as the Leo Burnett study showed these to be especially relevant. For an argument-oriented form, on the other hand, your primary concern is to receive high marks on items 1 and 2.

Some day, researchers will get to the bottom of how advertising works. Until then, we will have to settle for whatever little inspirations may trickle down from their work. I think there is considerable food for thought in this study, and hope my application ideas will help practitioners develop novel concept-testing tools and better ads. Oh, and there is one other conclusion that comes through loud and clear in this study. I know your job is difficult, but it can't be half as hard to design a good ad as it seems to be to analyze what makes ads work. For example, the study's authors concede that, "We do not rule out the possibility that argument might be more effective in establishing usefulness and drama in establishing enjoyment value, but the question could not be resolved by our data . . ." This after interviewing well over a thousand people in ten different malls. Now I know why I am not in academia!

Reference

John Deighton, Daniel Romer, and Josh McQueen, "Using Drama to Persuade," *Journal of Consumer Research*, Vol. 16, December 1989: 335–343.

PROMOTION BUDGETING STRATEGY SELECTOR

Applications

- Deciding how much to spend on promotion (advertising, sales, etc.).
- Comparing different methods of budgeting and their impact on the total promotion budget.
- Selecting the most appropriate strategy (or combination of strategies) for establishing the promotion budget.

Procedures

Review the descriptions of budgeting strategies. Evaluate the strategy(ies) used in the past in your company and industry. Choose the method considered most appropriate in your situation based on the listings of applications.

Note: Promotion is used as an umbrella term encompassing all marketing-related communications between seller and buyer, including advertising, retail and trade promotions, coupons, direct mail, sales collateral materials, and direct sales. However, some firms do not include the cost of a sales force or sales representatives in their promotion budget.

How much should a company spend on advertising, sales, and sales promotions—the three components of the promotion budget? Setting the promotion budget is a complicated and sometimes controversial task. It is therefore difficult to change the budget substantially from year to year, and difficult to know whether the traditional approach to budgeting is appropriate.

It is very helpful to take a strategic approach, identifying the preferred budgeting method in any given situation before worrying about specific numbers. This way, the budget more accurately reflects the situation, and is able to change as the situation does. Descriptions of known promotion budgeting strategies follow.

Percentage-of-Sales Strategy

Applications. Setting total promotion budgets for a company's annual plan. Allocating advertising and sales promotion dollars to individual products. Setting promotion level higher or lower than competitors to achieve specific share gain or margin goals and other strategic objectives.

Tactics. Provides a convenient method for comparing promotion expenditures among competitors. Convert data on competitor expenditures to a percentage-of-sales basis to compare level of funding or set funding high or low relative to a competitor. Establish a standard percentage allocation for your company's promotion budget; then use last period's sales or a projection of next period's sales as the basis for calculating the budget.

Here is a selection of industry average percentage-of-sales figures, as compiled by Schonfeld & Associates and published in *Advertising Age*.

Airlines	1.8%
Apparel and Accessory Stores	2.4%
Beverages	9.5%
Book Publishing	3.3%
Candy	10.6%
Cigarettes	5.7%
Computer/Software Stores	0.9%
Department Stores	2.9%
Electromedical Apparatus	1.3%
Financial Services	0.6%
Food Products	7.8%
Guided Missiles	5.3%
Hardware and Gardening Stores	4.0%
Hospitals	5.0%
Industrial Chemicals, Inorganic	16.5%
Movie/Video Production	9.8%
Paper Mills	3.6%
Pharmaceuticals	6.8%
Photofinishing Laboratories	4.0%
Poultry Slaughter/Processing	3.1%
Radio Stations	8.6%
Restaurants	3.3%
Television Stations	2.5%
Variety Stores	1.9%

Pro/Con. Subhash C. Jain explains the pros and cons of this strategy in detail: "This approach is followed by many companies because it is simple, it is easy to understand, and it gives managers the flexibility to cut corners during periods of economic slowdown. Among its flaws is the fact that basing promotion appreciation on sales puts the cart before the horse. Further, the logic of this approach fails to consider the cumulative effect of promotion" or "the relationship of promotion to competitors' activities or its influence on sales revenues."

Competitive Parity Strategy

Applications. Setting budgets in maturity and decline stages of the product life cycle, in a brand war, and in other situations in which competitor advertising and sales promotion is especially important. Maintaining relative parity in promotion effort (as measured by percentage of sales) to maintain relative position and market share. Increasing promotion relative to competitors to gain share, or decreasing it to harvest a product or company (sometimes called *self-defense method*).

Tactics. Make reference to trade publications, public reports from competitors, and other references to discover how much competitors spend on promotion as a percentage of sales. Set your budget at parity, or above or below it, depending upon whether you want to maintain, grow, or reduce your share relative to competitors. Also possible is to set the promotion budget so as to achieve absolute parity (i.e., dollar expenditures not to fall below those of competitor X) rather than percentage-of-sales parity.

Pro/Con. Makes it easy to develop competitive promotion strategies and to take the competitors' strategies into consideration in setting promotion level. Acknowledges the importance of competitor activities in determining the effectiveness of promotional spending. Makes it possible to invest in promotion for a new product or company in advance of substantial sales (by budgeting for absolute parity rather than relative parity—see Tactics). However, if followed religiously, this strategy leads to a me-too approach with little room for novel or creative marketing strategies. Also, the assumptions companies use to justify the method are sometimes flawed. As Philip Kotler explains, "Two arguments are advanced for this method. One is that competitors' expenditures represent the collective wisdom of the industry. The other is that maintaining a competitive parity helps prevent promotion wars. Neither argument is valid."

Objective/Task Strategy

Applications. Achieving specific marketing goals, such as a target gain in market share. Building a budget on the basis of reasonable assumptions about the reach and impact of sales, advertising and sales promotion, and the likely response of the market. An especially good way to force consideration of optimal promotion mix and spending levels prior to setting a ceiling on spending; the result may avoid waste or provide greater efficiencies (sometimes called *task method*).

Tactics. Follow Maxwell Ule's six-step methodology, quoted here as illustrated by a fictitious brand of cigarette.

1. Establish the market share goal. The advertiser wants 8% of the market. Since there are 50 million cigarette smokers, the company wants to switch 4 million smokers to Sputnik.

2. Determine the percentage of the market that should be reached by Sputnik advertising. The advertiser hopes to reach 80% (40 million smokers) with the advertising.

3. Determine the percentage of aware smokers that should be persuaded to try the brand. The advertiser would be pleased if 25% of aware smokers, or 10 million smokers, tried Sputnik. This is because he estimates that 40% of all triers, or 4 million persons, would become loyal users. This is the market goal.

4. Determine the number of advertising impressions per 1% trial rate. The advertiser estimates that 40 advertising impressions (exposures) for every 1% of the population would bring about a 25% trial rate.

5. Determine the number of gross rating points that would have to be purchased. A gross rating point is one exposure to 1% of the

target population. Since the company wants to achieve 40 exposures to 80% of the population, it will want to buy 3,200 gross rating points.

6. Determine the necessary advertising budget on the basis of the average cost of buying a gross rating point. To expose 1% of the target population to one impression costs an average of $3,277. Therefore, 3,200 gross rating points would cost $10,486,400 (= $3,277 × 3,200) in the introductory year. (Warning: Cost figures are not current.)

The example illustrates the setting of a specific market share objective and the description of the specific advertising needed to achieve this objective. It can as easily be adapted to any other promotion methods, including personal selling, sales promotions, telemarketing, and direct-mail solicitations. In each case, or when the marketing plan calls for a mix, the specific tasks needed to accomplish the objective are first planned and costed carefully; then the budget is set based on the total cost of achieving the objective.

Note: This is the most popular method among large companies. Lancaster and Stern find that *80% of major national advertisers use the method,* and many have developed computerized aids based on it. The most common form the method takes is a three-step process in which objectives are defined, strategies are determined to accomplish the objectives, and costs of implementing the strategies are estimated.

Pro/Con. Forces attention on specifics of the marketing plan in the early stages of budgeting, therefore making the budget more realistic and suited to the objectives. Brings the marketing and advertising departments into the budgeting process. However, it can be difficult to work out all the details of the marketing program by the time promotion expenses have to be budgeted, so the tendency may be to submit slight modifications of last year's numbers. This method can give the impression of a well-conceived promotion budget when in fact it is based on last year's numbers. Also, it fails to anticipate competitor actions and their impact on trial and usage rates.

Buildup Strategy

Applications. Basing the promotion budget on estimates of need by managers of each functional area (i.e., advertising, sales, marketing communications, and merchandising managers). Building the budget on the basis of specific objectives and tasks as defined by each manager reporting to the director of marketing.

Tactics. Form a committee consisting of all those managers who have responsibility for any promotion expenditures. Make the committee responsible for setting promotion objectives and resolving promotion mix issues to translate overall objectives into specific department objectives. Each manager then prepares a budget for his or her department and negotiates it with the marketing manager (or, more rarely, the committee).

Pro/Con. According to Jain, "The buildup method forces managers to analyze scientifically the role they expect promotion to play and the contribution it can make toward achieving marketing objectives. It also helps maintain control over promotion expenditure and avoid the frustrations often faced by promotion managers as a result of cuts in promotion appropriations due to economic slowdown. On the other hand, this approach can become overly scientific." The complexity of the budgeting process makes it difficult to revise plans quickly in response to new opportunities.

Also, the buildup process can degenerate into an effort to produce numbers the company wants to see, as in the classic example quoted in a *Fortune* article (December 1956: 123): "Why it's simple. First, I go upstairs to the controller and ask how much they can afford to give us this year. He says a million and a half. Later, the boss comes to me and asks how much we should spend and I say, 'Oh, about a million and a half.' "

Share-of-Market Strategy

Applications. Setting promotion budgets for individual products that compete closely with very similar products. Budgeting for promotions when a gain in market share is the primary objective. Budgeting promotions for a new product launch.

Tactics. Confirm that products and marketing strategies are similar among competing companies. There should be a close correlation between companies' share of market and share of industry advertising. J. O. Peckham of A. C. Nielsen Company developed share-of-market budgeting for markets where this correlation is high and argued that a company should keep share of advertising slightly ahead of market share in order to hold share. To grow market share, share of advertising should be significantly higher.

For a *new product,* base share of advertising on target share of market, not current share (i.e., expected market share in two years). It is common to set share of advertising at 1.5 × target market share.

Pro/Con. In competitive markets, especially for consumer products, this method ensures a promotional effort that is in proportion to competitors' efforts. It bases promotion budget on the appealing logic that the size of the budget is related to the "share of mind" it captures, which in turn drives market share. However, because it is necessary to base calculations on historical industry advertising/ promotion figures, the method may fail to anticipate changes in competitors' budgets. Also, companies sometimes fall into the trap of believing that market share is gained simply by increasing share of promotional expenditures, and they fail to consider product positioning, media selection, and the many other strategic issues that determine whether a target market share will be achieved.

References

"Advertising-to-Sales Ratios, 1989," *Advertising Age,* November 12, 1989, p. 32.

Courtland L. Bovee and William F. Arens, *Contemporary Advertising,* 3rd ed. (Homewood, IL: Richard D. Irwin, 1989), p. 245.

Subhash C. Jain, *Marketing Planning & Strategy,* 3rd edition (Cincinnati: South-Western Publishing, 1990), pp. 550–555.

Philip Kotler, *Marketing Management: Analysis, Planning and Control,* 5th ed. (Englewood Cliffs, NJ: Prentice Hall, 1984), pp. 621–623.

Kent M. Lancaster and Judith A. Stern, "Computer-Based Advertising Budgeting Practices of Leading U.S. Consumer Advertisers," *Journal of Advertising*, Vol. 12, 1983: 4–9.

G. Maxwell Ule, "A Media Plan for 'Sputnik' Cigarettes," in *How to Plan Media Strategy* (New York: American Association of Advertising Agencies, 1957), pp. 41–52.

RETENTION MARKETING

Applications

- Building consumer awareness of brand and company names.
- Reaching consumers in a nonadvertising setting and when they are relaxed and more likely to retain brand or company information.

Procedures

Retention marketing reaches consumers at home or in other relaxed situations, especially situations in which consumers have high involvement (although the advertising slots on TV do reach people at home, they are characterized by low involvement). When a product is featured as a prop or as part of a set in a movie, viewers may infer and retain detailed information about the product and its benefits. This low-key approach to awareness and image building can be quite effective, and some companies pay fees or contribute free goods in order to appear in movies, TV shows, and even novels.

ESM Marketing Group has a new vehicle for retention marketing. The company developed a board game with a large cash prize that is given away to one of the game players in a drawing. ESM sells slots on the board to companies as a form of advertising, and also packages coupon books with the game. The game, in which players go on a shopping spree, was launched "with a $2 million ad and promotion package that included TV, distribution of 50 million circulars nationwide, in-store video presentation, special events, and radio spots." Someone obviously takes retention marketing seriously! The vehicle seems to have the greatest appeal to large retail chains, including Ames/Zayre.

The challenge for marketers is to think of new ways of showcasing their names and products in the context of entertainment and relaxation, either in passive form, such as by having them appear in a movie, or in some participatory promotion like a game. The impact of any specific retention marketing strategy is likely to fade as consumers become familiar with it. After all, the wall calendar at one time would have qualified as retention marketing, but it is so commonplace now that consumers have little use for it.

Reference

Helene Diamond, "It's Only a Game, But Players Have a Chance to Win $400,000," *Marketing News,* October 23, 1989, p. 10.

ROBINSON'S PROMOTION GUIDELINES

If a product is unacceptable to consumers, promotion won't change that. If an established product is experiencing declining sales, promotion won't turn it around. Promotion can't create an "image" for a brand. And a single promotion won't motivate consumers to buy over a long period of time.

—William A. Robinson

Applications

- Picking the right sales promotion for the job.
- Evaluating or reviewing a promotion plan.

Procedures

Knowing which promotions do what is half the battle, and many companies launch unsuccessful programs simply because they pick an inappropriate promotional technique. If you do not promote frequently, are trying a new technique, or have to review a marketing plan, these simple guidelines from William Robinson will be a big help. (His agency has developed sales promotions for Apple Computer, Federal Express, McDonald's, and many other companies.)

TECHNIQUE	APPROPRIATE USES
Samplings	Generating trial
Coupons	Generating trial
Value packs	Loading present users Converting triers to users
Refund offers	Building brand loyalty
Trade allowances	Gaining distribution Building trade inventories
Contests, sweepstakes	Extend brand image Increase ad readership
Premium offers	Loading present users Reinforcing brand loyalty
Premium packs	Attracting new triers
Mail-in premiums	Obtaining store displays
Continuity programs	Differentiating "parity" products Building brand loyalty
Special events	Enhancing brand image

Of course, the success of a trade promotion depends not only on picking the right technique, but also on implementing it creatively and effectively. If you want to see copious examples of good trade promotions in each of these categories, look up Robinson's annual review book, *Best Sales Promotion*. It is based on the Robbie Awards for best promotions of the year, an annual feature of *Advertising Age*.

Reference

William A. Robinson, as quoted in Courtland L. Bovee and William F. Arens, *Contemporary Advertising*, 3rd ed. (Homewood, IL: Richard D. Irwin, 1989), pp. 528–529.

SCHULTZ'S FOUR CHALLENGES

What's wrong in the world of sales promotion?

Applications

- Managing the sales promotion function.
- Improving the effectiveness of consumer product promotions to the trade and to the consumer.

Procedures

Don Schultz of Northwestern University believes that all is not well in the world of sales promotion, and argues in his regular *Marketing News* column on sales promotion that the leading promoters need to change their strategy to keep promotions effective in the future. Here are the four challenges they face:

---

1. Controlling the price promotion spiral. Promotions too often focus on price reduction. Widespread discounting makes consumers more price-sensitive and "deal-prone" and makes retailers very price-sensitive as well. According to Schultz, "the more you price promote, the more you must price promote." He suggests developing sales promotions that add value to the brand instead of simply reducing its price.

Part of the problem is the growth of trade promotions. Forward buying by retailers (stocking up when the product is on discount) and diverting (purchasing for other locations to take advantage of regional discounts) are two ways retailers abuse trade deals. Even when they do not take unfair advantage of trade deals, the retailers may simply be shifting the time of purchase in response to these deals and not buying more in the long run. An *Advertising Age* article argues that this is still an open question:

> The main bone of contention for marketers is whether trade promotions bring about incremental profits through increased use of products, or whether the products eventually would have been sold anyway, regardless of promotions.

The challenge of ending the price promotion spiral addresses this problem directly. Discounts alone will not bring about incremental profits through increased use of products, but category-building promotions can.

2. Moving from brand switching to category building. Schultz predicts that retailers will be increasingly unwilling to support promotions that are directed at market share alone. Why does the retailer care to invest in brand switching if it does not produce more sales of the category as a whole? (Only, I suppose, if there are fatter margins or other benefits—the net result being a promotion-cost spiral at the wholesale level that mirrors the price promotion spiral at the retail level.) Instead, he suggests that promotions always have a category-building goal along with whatever brand-switching goal the manufacturer is pursuing. This may require some collaboration between manufacturer and retailer or between manufacturers within an industry.

3. Integrating sales promotion into the marketing communications mix. The typical organization chart divides marketing functions and separates sales promotion from advertising, public relations, and other functions. It is surprisingly difficult to integrate all the functions into a single marketing program, as this requires close collaboration among the different functions from the idea stage onward. Better integration can be a source of efficiencies and improved effectiveness. According to Schultz, "Only with a broader view can the sales promotion manager advise brand and marketing managers on the best way to achieve their goals."

4. Education and development. Succession is likely to be a problem in the coming years. There are not enough good people "in the pipeline" to replace senior sales promotion professionals. A general lack of interest in recruiting people to this profession, little emphasis on sales promotion in the business schools, and a lack of concern with this issue at companies are the major causes. Schultz suggests that the activities of the Direct Marketing Educational Foundation provide a good model for sales promoters.

Examples

These are good goals. How can they be achieved? A great variety of promotions are used, and some of them clearly address these challenges. S. C. Johnson & Son's introduction of Agree creme rinse and conditioner is a successful example of integrating sales promotion into the overall marketing strategy. The introduction called for expenditures of $6 million in advertising and $6 million more in sampling to generate considerable demand for the new product among targeted 14- to 30-year-old women. The details of the mix, such as an unusually heavy emphasis on radio, were optimized through experiments in test markets. The program gained 20% of the market nationwide in five months and generated heavy demand for the product, convincing the trade that the product is worth the shelf space.

QuillMark, the leading producer of blank, cloth-covered diary books in the United States, emphasizes displays in its trade promotion. Freestanding, rotating book racks of lucite or metal have been placed in hundreds of drug, stationery, and bookstores. These displays allow stores to carry a broader line of blank books than they would otherwise, bring the books to the attention of customers, and have convinced many stores to try blank books for the first time. For these reasons the display program has been highly effective at building sales for the category. The company has not found it necessary to rely on price-based promotions.

Some trade deals are designed to encourage better selling by the stores and their employees. For example, *push money* ("spiffs") is commonly used to provide shoe store salespeople a commission if they sell ancillary products (such as polish or insoles) along with the shoes. If this becomes routine, its value is probably minimal, but as a short-term strategy to build awareness and trial for a new product, it can work quite well to build category sales. Where there is an educational component to a sale, as is the case in the introductory stage of a product's life cycle, push money can provide a vehicle for educating retailers and encouraging them to educate their customers. (Issue: Should customers be informed that the salesperson receives a commission for selling certain products?)

Note: Combination offers can also be used to introduce a new product, especially in retail settings such as supermarkets where no personal selling takes place.

Collateral materials from the automaker BMW have two purposes—informing customers and educating dealers. The material aimed at dealers provides detailed information about the market and BMW's marketing program. Demographics, ad campaigns, and other specifics are communicated to the dealers through collateral material. This addresses Schultz's concern for integration and better communication—it brings the dealers into the loop concerning the activities of the marketing department.

Fifth Challenge?

It is tempting to add a fifth challenge to Schultz's list, based on a recent column (see the April 2, 1990, *Marketing News*), in which he argues that much consumer products promotion is wasted because it takes a mass market approach even though the product is not consumed by the majority of the mass market. The challenge: *Focusing promotions on prospects.*

For example, he points to a recent *Chicago Tribune* Sunday edition that carried cents-off coupons and discount offers in freestanding inserts (FSIs). While this is a well-accepted approach to advertising a promotion, the fact is that the majority of products in the FSI are *not used* by the majority of *Tribune* readers. Here are some of his examples:

- Carpet deodorizers. Average household penetration according to a spring 1989 report from Mediamark Research is 14.5%. The average redemption rate for FSIs is 3.2%. Given a circulation of 1.5 million, this means a total of only 6,960 potential coupons redeemed. The problem is that the advertisers are paying for exposure to only 217,500 households that use carpet deodorizers, and wasting their money on another *1,282,500 households* that do not!

- Cat litter. Household penetration averages 15.3%, for a total of only 7,344 potential coupons redeemed. According to Schultz, "there's very little likelihood that the 76% of households that don't own a cat will get one just to take advantage of the cat litter coupon."

- Other product categories that should not have been advertised in FSIs, according to Schultz, include children's vitamins (12.9% penetration), cigarettes (33.2%), dishwasher detergent (43.0%), disposable diapers (10.7%), dog treats (18.5%), and floor polish (32.0%). I don't know about you, but it would take substantial discounts on vitamins and diapers to convince me I need more children.

At issue here is whether to use a "tonnage approach" in which promotional dollars are spent on a high volume aimed at the general consumer, or whether to take advantage of the excellent data on usage to pinpoint prospects and focus more efficiently and effectively on them. Direct mail, specialized publications, and other targeted vehicles exist for reaching them intelligently. Schultz's conclusion: "It just doesn't make sense, in a time when marketing budgets are going down instead of up, to buy into the concept of mass distribution."

Reference

Richard Edel, "Trade Wars Threaten Future Peace of Marketers," *Advertising Age*, August 15, 1985, p. 18. See also, Don F. Schultz, "It's Not Time for Laurel-Resting Yet," *Marketing News*, January 22, 1990, p. 14, and Don E. Schultz, "Promotion 'Waste' Defies Definition," *Marketing News*, April 2, 1990, p. 13.

TV AD CENSORSHIP RULES

*No open-mouthed or lengthy kissing,
please!*

Applications

- Reviewing ad concepts to identify possible problems early in an ad's development.
- Deciding whether a print or radio ad campaign can be translated directly into TV ads (often they cannot).

Procedures

Review the set of guidelines following and use them when developing or evaluating TV ads. If an ad is borderline, contact networks for an up-to-date judgment on the concept *before* you spend a lot of money shooting it!

"Open-mouth kissing I would think would have gone too far" is how *The Wall Street Journal* quotes Alan Wurtzel, ex-vice president of broadcast standards at ABC. He goes on to explain that "Perfume companies . . . have tried to do some pretty hot things, but we've prevented that." Yes, indeed, and he and his counterparts at NBC and CBS have also prevented women from eating too much ice cream, toilet bowls from flushing, and many other objectionable events from appearing in TV advertising. Although programming is quite liberated these days, TV ads are still rigorously censored. If you want to run an ad on the networks, you will need to have it reviewed by their censors first. Agencies with experience in TV advertising usually show storyboards to the networks before developing the commercial, as it can be difficult to predict what they will object to. For example, they may reject a fanciful ad in which people are depicted inside a refrigerator for fear that some child will climb in and try it, but they do not object to auto advertising in which people drive dangerously and illegally.

Here is a list of basic criteria applied by the networks. There may be exceptions, in either direction, but it gives the marketer a good general idea of the standards applied by the networks and will help avoid unrealistic advertising plans and wasted production time and money. Be forewarned, however, that censorship rules are a moving target. (Major ad agencies usually maintain their own guidelines.)

THE NOS OF TV ADVERTISING

No breasts.

No open-mouthed or lengthy kissing.

No pill taking or medicine consumption (the concern: imitative behavior by children or addicts).

No toilet paper in context (it can only be shown *away from* the toilet and bathroom).

No douches in context (see previous item).

No tampons. They may be named and shown in an abstract manner, but not photographed directly.

Minimal use of words relating to feminine hygiene (e.g., do not repeat the word "period" more than once or twice in a 30-second spot).

No direct representation or description of bodily fluids, even sweat!

No humor. Well, almost no humor. The censors usually don't get the joke.

Minimal representation of toilets. While bowls have been shown on occasion, they never flush, and the word "toilet" itself is generally a no-no.

No one in a potentially dangerous situation. (The concern: Children might imitate and be hurt. An ad featuring a pizza chef handing a woman a pizza from inside her refrigerator was rejected for this reason. Bungee-jumping was also nixed recently.) Exception: Dangerous automobile driving.

No unmarried couples. (This rule may be relaxing, but in general if a close intimate or sexual relationship is implied, the couple must be shown as married. Show those wedding bands!)

No nudity. Even commercials like one for Calgon bathbeads showing a woman in a bath can be rejected if the networks view it as showing too much "flesh" or looking too "sexy."

Not even a *hint* of homosexuality.

No excessive consumption of food. (Do not portray someone as "out of control.")

No violence.

No consumption or depiction of alcoholic beverages or anything that might be mistaken for one. Period. Even the *sound* of drinking has been censored.

Okay, you get the idea! Now go forth and make insipid commercials.

Update

Competition from cable alternatives (such as MTV) and general competition from other media seems to be loosening the standards at the networks. According to Chris Hikawa, who recently succeeded Alan Wurtzel as V.P., Broadcast Standards and Practices at CBS, "It's no longer possible to say, 'You can't do this on TV.' " While nudity and sex are still out, "What has changed is the aggressiveness of the claims being made. The substantiation levels are a little different." What once might have been evaluated as a hard claim is more likely to be classified as "puffery" now, which means that it may not be held to as high a standard of proof. Also, she notes that "The three networks used to be very very similar. But we've really gone our own ways in the last three years." This means that, while in general the standards are similar, each network will differ in particulars. (Quotes are from a telephone conversation with the author on December 6, 1990.)

The networks continue to review ads, and each has its own published book of advertising guidelines. But the guidelines are not available to the general public, or even to most marketing managers. Their distribution is usually restricted to major advertising agencies. At CBS the guidelines are currently being revised under the direction of Harvey Dzodin, and new guidelines should be available from his office for the use of ad agencies by the time this book is in print.

The current guidelines are extensive, covering everything from abortion clinics and the American flag to vitamins and weight reduction. My review of them suggests several restrictions that ought to be added to the Nos of TV advertising:

No scaring the viewer. For example, "References which tended to play upon the fears and anxieties of the general public regarding coronary heart disease are prohibited."

No new-age silliness. "The advertising of astrology, character reading, fortune telling, mind reading, numerology, occultism, palm reading, phrenology, or similar subjects is unacceptable."

No training of criminals. "Advertising may not contain the portrayal of specific, detailed techniques involved in the commission of crimes, the use of weapons, or the avoidance of detection."

There is, believe it or not, a serious side to such restrictions. TV ads have a significant social impact, and the networks must try to balance ethical and commercial issues as a result. The easiest way to develop acceptable advertising is to think through issues of social importance *before* submitting an ad for review. The hook, of course, is that your morals may be a few decades more up-to-date than theirs!

Reference

Joanne Lipman, "Censored Scenes: Why You Rarely See Some Things in Television Ads," *The Wall Street Journal*, August 17, 1987, p. 21. Also, contact the networks for their latest written guidelines.

Capital Cities/ABC, Inc. Department of Broadcast Standards and Practices, *Advertising Standards and Guidelines*.

Chapter 3

Product Development and Introduction

Campbell's New Product Rules
Center for Concept Development's Evaluation
   Form
General Foods' Principles of Disciplined
   Creativity
Johnson Controls' False Product Launch
The "Misfortune 500" Product Failure List
"New Products Power" Test
Peters's Product Team Success Factors
Rosenau's Phased Product Development
Thamhain's Team Innovation Model

Also see:
   Bozell, Jacobs' Two-Way Focus Groups
   Projective Techniques
   Weyerhaeuser Determinant Attribute Analysis

CAMPBELL'S NEW PRODUCT RULES

Here are the five rules that have worked best for us at Campbell Soup Company.

Herbert M. Baum

Applications

- Managing new product development and introduction.
- Analyzing new product proposals.
- Preparing marketing plans for new product introductions.

Note: This discussion includes descriptions of the Grass Roots and Campbell's in the Kitchen research programs and the MBP Model for forecasting new product returns.

Procedures

Use the five rules presented here as a basis for evaluating new product proposals or developing new product policy and strategy. Also see specific procedures described under rule 2 ("Research Ideas") for instructions on grass-roots research and procedures described under rule 4 ("Forecasting Note") for instruction on minimum business proposition analysis using a computer spreadsheet program.

Herbert Baum of the Campbell Soup Company has been involved in many successful product introductions, and he believes product development is the province of senior managers. Companies that put their junior product managers on new products are ignoring the fact that it takes a lot more expertise and effort to market a new product than an old one. Managers should learn on the existing products, and only work with new products when properly seasoned. In addition to this advice, he offers a five-point recipe to improve the quality of new product development that I think readers will find applicable at other consumer products companies and also applicable to industrial products and services.

Rule 1. Go for the home run. Baum sites statistics showing that the number of new products is rising every year, but that the number grossing more than

$1 million in their first year is *declining*. Oops. This means many more new products fall on their faces or limp through life, never breaking the $1 million barrier let alone becoming hundred-million-dollar best-sellers. This is due, at least in part, to the popularity of line and brand extensions. While these are an important part of most marketing strategies, it is also essential to create new brands that will stand on their own and spin off their own extensions.

Rule 2. Be sure of the consumer: The consumer is the most important member of your product team. Baum advocates developing an intimate, long-term relationship with the consumer: ". . . I'm not talking about a one-night stand like a focus group, I'm talking about a relationship." By this he means that you must look behind the statistics and recognize that the consumer is actually a diverse group of real and distinct individuals whom you may be able to target as a group on the basis of some common concern or behavior. Use consumers to test your new product ideas, not only in focus groups, but also by studying usage (in the home if it is a consumer product) and by studying the purchase process (in the store if it is a consumer product). And plan to check back with consumers frequently as you incorporate their reactions and modify your ideas.

This intimacy gives an edge to marketing as well as product development. Campbell is a leader in regional advertising, increasing its use of spot TV to customize its message in light of regional differences in eating habits. (See the Paskowski article in the footnote for more on regional advertising.)

Research Ideas. Campbell has developed a "grass-roots" research program in which researchers periodically visit supermarkets in major cities, intercept consumers in the aisles, and talk to them about products. Questions focus on why someone chose a particular brand, whether they have tried others, what their eating and cooking habits are, what they think of the competition. The answers are transcribed verbatim and distributed widely at Campbell. Baum says "Consumer talk is idea food, and we like to chew on it." Another Campbell technique, called "Campbell's in the Kitchen," uses a panel of 300 consumers who are periodically queried by phone or questionnaire on an issue and also are given new products to review. Both these methods are qualitative and designed to help decision makers get to know consumers better; Campbell's goal is "breaking bread with consumers, crawling into their heads, and finding out what turns them on." (See the *Marketing News* article for more on Campbell's research techniques.)

Rule 3. Before you go for the home run, make sure you have money and staying power. Baum observes that most markets are mature, characterized by flat sales. Any new product must gain share primarily at the expense of another product. You can therefore assume that competitors will "stop at nothing to discourage you from starting, continuing, or finishing the job." This means every test market may be messed up by a competitor's promotions and coupons, so it is a good idea to plan a simulated test market as well. Also, even in the test market it is important to support the new product—many good new products fail because they lack sufficient marketing support to push them to the number one or number two position in their categories. Baum describes underspending as "the unspeakable crime!"

Rule 4. Know your economics. A careful financial analysis of a new product's projected market is helpful in planning its introduction, and sometimes reveals hidden problems that allow you to avoid disasters. Campbell uses an analytical model called MBP, the minimum business proposition. It incorporates

- The influence of volume (based on trial, repeat and package rates), growth rate, marketing costs, effectiveness of marketing, price, price sensitivity, attrition to other product lines, capital flows, and various costs on ROI. All are treated as variables, and the model allows you to explore many scenarios before committing to the new product.

- The returns over a long time period. First-year break-evens are not necessarily required. A model that allows you to look at the present value of projected cash flows over many years may encourage long-term investment in those "home runs" referred to in rule 1.

- The probability of various scenarios occurring. A judgmental approach is used to assess the likelihood of scenarios developed in the sensitivity analysis (see the first bullet). Presumably this approach supports the use of payoff tables in which the expected value of the business proposition can be calculated by summing the return from each scenario, weighted by its probability of occurrence.

Forecasting Note. The details of the MBP model have not been released by Campbell, but it would not be difficult to create a similar model for your company using any spreadsheet program; instructions for creating a simple model follow. Try starting with a detailed income statement or cost breakdown for a related product. Identify all the relevant variables, as previously outlined. Create a template spreadsheet that calculates yearly profit or loss for at least five years, or over the length of the expected life cycle. Add to its bottom line a discounting formula to determine the present value of annual cash flows using your firm's borrowing rate or hurdle rate. Then use this to support noodling around with the variables until you have created three to five plausible scenarios. Assign each a probability of occurring such that the sum is 1; then weight the present value figure from each by the scenario's probability. This gives you an expected value for the project. Also look at individual scenarios to see if there is an unacceptable risk of disaster or insufficient likelihood of a home run.

Rule 5. The product is hero. This means you cannot succeed without a good product—actually, Campbell insists on a *better* product. Baum says that "we insist on a preference rating of at least 1.6 to 1 versus the competition" before they will introduce a new product. And Campbell's CEO, Gordon McGovern, says that "The consumer is ready for improved quality and service. Delivering it is the true secret of new product success." Note that this amounts to a strong argument against cost-based product innovations. While Campbell is open to new products that cost less, they also must have higher quality to be introduced. Product quality must be maintained throughout the product's life—customer surveys providing satisfaction or performance ratings should be used to keep track of product quality on a regular basis.

Reference

Herbert M. Baum, "Realities of New Products Management: What to Do—What to Avoid," in *The New Products Handbook*, ed. Larry Wizenberg (Homewood, IL: Dow Jones-Irwin, 1986), pp. 34—43. See also Herbert M. Baum, "You Need to 'Press the Flesh' to Get Close to Consumers," *Marketing News*, April 2, 1990, p. 14, and Marianne Paskowski, "See Spot Jump," *Marketing and Media Decisions*, April 1986, p. 66.

CENTER FOR CONCEPT DEVELOPMENT'S EVALUATION FORM

> *. . . the more concepts you look at the more likely you are to wind up with one or two good business propositions.*
>
> Eugene J. Cafarelli
> Center for Concept Development

Applications

- Screening new product or service concepts
- Speeding the initial evaluation of concepts to increase the rate of concept development.

Procedures

To take advantage of this "law of large numbers," product developers must be prepared to generate and evaluate a large number of ideas. And the more ideas you produce, the more you must dispose of! Screening of concepts can actually become a bottleneck, and for this reason it is often standardized as much as possible at companies that do a lot of product development. Screening needs to address consistency with strategy, suitability to the business, and consumer interest. While consumer interest is best judged by the consumers themselves, a quick assessment of at least the first two issues can be made. Here is a broadly applicable screening instrument from the Center for Concept Development that you can adapt slightly if necessary in order to make it applicable to your organization.

Instructions

Rate the strength of each new product concept on each factor, using a 1–3 scale (which this form is designed for) or a 1–5 or 1–10 scale. Find the mean factor scores for each factor group and major aspect. Fill in a new form for each concept; then summarize major aspect scores for all concepts in a comparative table. If you want to refine the analysis, weight each factor based on your organization's strength in the factor (i.e., on a 1 = weak to 3 = strong scale), and create a computerized spreadsheet to compute weighted factor, factor group, and major aspect scores.

NEW PRODUCT EVALUATION FORM

Factor				Factor Group	Major Aspect
Effectiveness	___	___	___		
Reliability	___	___	___		
Simplicity	___	___	___	Performance	
Convenience	___	___	___		
Appearance	___	___	___		
Uniqueness	___	___	___		
Economy	___	___	___		
Timeliness	___	___	___		Item
Understandability	___	___	___	Salability	
Tradability	___	___	___		
Buyability	___	___	___		
Legal	___	___	___		
Newness	___	___	___	Defensibility	
Proprietary	___	___	___		
Experience	___	___	___		
Support Services	___	___	___		
Technical Services	___	___	___		
Market Coverage	___	___	___		
Entrenchment	___	___	___	Marketing	
Dependency	___	___	___		
Volume	___	___	___		
Penetration	___	___	___		
Management					
Design	___	___	___		
Engineering	___	___	___		
Materials	___	___	___		Company
Techniques	___	___	___	Technology	
Labor	___	___	___		
Facilities	___	___	___		
Purchasing	___	___	___		
Dependency	___	___	___		
Capacity	___	___	___	Production	
Location	___	___	___		
Management	___	___	___		
Potential Volume	___	___	___		
Proportion	___	___	___		
Fertility	___	___	___		
Growth	___	___	___	Market	
Stability	___	___	___		
Outlook	___	___	___		
Size	___	___	___		
Specialization	___	___	___		
Entrenchment	___	___	___		
Pricing	___	___	___	Competition	
Entry Reaction	___	___	___		Environment
Materials	___	___	___		
Equipment	___	___	___		
Services	___	___	___	Suppliers	
Dependency	___	___	___		
Regulations	___	___	___		
Taxes	___	___	___		
Programs	___	___	___	Government	
Politics	___	___	___		
Chief Executive	___	___	___		
Management Group	___	___	___		
Trade	___	___	___	Support	
Customers	___	___	___		
Size	___	___	___		
Commitment	___	___	___		
Maturity Rate	___	___	___		
Risk	___	___	___	Investment	Venture
Return	___	___	___		
Salvability	___	___	___		
Consistency	___	___	___		
Appropriateness	___	___	___		
Improvement	___	___	___		
Preemption	___	___	___		
Necessity	___	___	___	Strategy	
Intuition	___	___	___		

Source: From Eugene J. Catarelli, "Screening New Products," pp. 130–131

Reference

Eugene J. Cafarelli, "Screening New Products," in *The New Products Handbook*, ed. Larry Wizenberg (Homewood, IL: Dow Jones-Irwin, 1986), pp. 111–135. See also Eugene J. Cafarelli, *Developing New Products and Repositioning Mature Brands*, (New York: John Wiley & Sons, 1980), and W. R. Park and J. B. Maillie, *Strategic Analysis for Venture Evaluation: The Save Approach to Business Decisions* (New York: Van Nostrand Reinhold, 1982).

GENERAL FOODS' PRINCIPLES
OF DISCIPLINED CREATIVITY

Applications

- Developing new products.
- Strengthening the links between research, strategy, and marketing to improve the product development process.

Procedures

Use the principles as a foundation for product development strategy and policy. Also can be used to implement specific practices that have been successful at General Foods. For example, the principles provide guidance in implementing the following policies and procedures:

1. Define the link between mission and strategy and the product development function, clarifying the mission and strategy if necessary.

2. Form *Technical Strategy Boards* made up of divisional managers, research managers, and senior managers at three levels within the company: division, operating company, and senior management levels.

3. Research and development proposals are reviewed at each level by the appropriate strategy board.

4. Bring managers from different functional areas together periodically to discuss product development.

5. Allocate R&D funds where they have the greatest leverage (often correlates with poor historical performance).

6. Audit or review all research projects periodically to make sure they continue to be focused on the mission and strategies of senior management.

> *You want the business and research sides to*
> *agree on a set of needs and opportunities so*
> *that luck can flow out to create better products*
> *and produce shareholder wealth.*

> Philip L. Smith, chairman,
> General Foods, 1987

These principles are designed to coordinate the diverse efforts of senior management, division managers, and product managers and to focus research by incorporating the organization's strategic vision and the insights of marketing into the product development process. The principles were developed after General Foods decentralized control of technical research to its product groups. While the decentralized approach has the advantage of incorporating the insights of line managers into product development decisions, it can lead to a lack of focus and poor coordination. These principles help General Foods' research produce products that advance its strategies and target the needs of its customers—this is the discipline product research needs in a decentralized environment.

The Principles of Disciplined Creativity

1. The linkage between research, business strategy, and marketing must begin with an overall corporate vision. A clear mission defining the company in the future, translated into specific goals and growth requirements, provides the unifying framework for all research efforts. When research efforts, strategies, and marketing are each guided by the "sense of destiny" that a clear mission and strategy provide, the role each plays in achieving this destiny is clarified.

2. Direction for research is both a top-down and a bottom-up process. According to Philip Smith, bottom-up control over research programs leads to overemphasis on the short term and on mature products and technologies. By looking for rapid impact on the performance of individual products in the market, such research may miss opportunities for major advances in the long term. Top-down direction for research is more likely to emphasize long-term strategic goals, but on the other hand it often lacks the market and product knowledge that bottom-up direction brings to research. Both perspectives are required. This is accomplished at General Foods by having two-way communications at the division, operating company, and senior management levels—all the levels where resources are allocated to research. A Technical Strategy Board made up of divisional managers, research managers, and senior managers reviews proposals at each level, and all research proposals must compete for resources. This competition is considered essential. According to Smith, "If the process doesn't create tension at these points, then it probably isn't working."

3. Interaction between research, business planning, and marketing must be forced. It will come as no surprise to most managers that researchers, operating managers, and marketers at General Foods tend not to communicate fully on their own. Operating managers, lacking technical knowledge, hesitate when it comes to the details of program content. Researchers, fearful that their projects will not be understood by other departments, sometimes hold back information. General Foods' Technical Strategy Board helps dialogue develop, and the company also holds an annual President's Conference on Technology. One hundred top managers with different backgrounds and responsibilities spend a day studying and discussing a technical topic of importance to the company.

4. Different businesses inherently have different levels of technical intensity. The importance of technology to a business can vary greatly. It even varies for different divisions of a business or the same business at different times. Assessing the importance of technology, the technical intensity, helps in allocating resources. This principle is important because without it the tendency is to allocate technical resources (including expertise and funding) based on profit performance. However, past profit performance does not have anything to do with the potential contribution of research to future profits, so resources should be allocated where technology offers the greatest possible *leverage* instead. This may mean cutting research funds for a division after it has just introduced a novel and profitable new technology in order to fund another division that has not but has the potential to.

Warning: To division managers this may seem like rewarding poor performance and penalizing good performance, so senior management must make the logic of this principle clear and be prepared to deal with conflicts.

5. Look beyond your own walls for new ideas. Small research firms, universities, customers, and other industries are all important sources of new ideas for General Foods. But there is a tendency to focus on the ideas and problems voiced under your own roof. Smith argues that "your research is never as basic or imaginative as you think."

6. There has to be enough flexibility to permit some amount of scientific dabbling. This is an often-debated point. Some of the most successful R&D companies take special care to allow and encourage "noodling" or "dabbling," while other companies try to keep staff and resources strictly focused on projects. Even though General Foods' approach is designed to add discipline to the creative process, the company allows enough freedom to permit creative investigation and dumb luck to play a role.

7. Make periodic checks on your research spending. The goal is to keep research focused on the company's mission and strategies. Goals change and a project can evolve and shift emphasis as it develops its own life, so it is necessary to make a formal top-down review every few years. This review also offers senior management another chance to maintain the balance between short-term and long-term research goals.

Reference

Philip L. Smith, "The Seven Principles of Disciplined Creativity," address at "R&D Technology/1987: Key Issues for Management," a Conference Board conference. Published in *Across the Board*, October 1987, pp. 43–46.

JOHNSON CONTROLS' FALSE PRODUCT LAUNCH

Applications

- Taking countermeasures to keep a new product or development project secret when you suspect competitors have discovered its existence.

Procedures

1. Monitor competitors' intelligence gathering and decide whether they suspect you are developing a new product.

2. If they do, confuse them and misdirect their response by feeding them false information about the new product.

3. Identify the new product by a code name, leak the code name, then attach the code name to a minor product upgrade. When the upgrade is introduced, the competitor may mistake it for the major product still under development.

What do you do to keep a competitor from anticipating and reacting to a major new product launch? In many cases, companies rely on secrecy to give them the advantage of surprise when they are developing and introducing an important new product. But secrecy is difficult to maintain. As the product moves from the lab to the market, it often goes through several steps, from beta testing by customers to presentations and training for the sales force, and leaks and rumors often result in these intermediate stages. A long-term R&D project can even be discovered by competitors while still in the lab, conceivably allowing them to bring a competing product out first. One response to leaks is to speed up the product launch, but in many cases this compromises the launch. There may be bugs in the product, the sales force might not be ready, and so forth. Johnson Controls has developed another alternative: throw the competitor off the scent with a dummy product launch that does not have all the fancy new features of your planned product launch. Hopefully, the decoy product will be mistaken for the product that they have heard rumors about, and the competitors will lose interest and give you time to complete a proper launch for your major new product.

Is this ethical? I am not sure. It is clearly deceptive, though if done with finesse it only deceives the competitor suspected of "spying" on you and developing countermoves. If done poorly, which seems likely if it is adopted widely, it will deceive and confuse customers as well. When you are head to head with a competitor and you know they have been gathering information about your new product, you could make the argument that they have an unfair information advantage and you should be permitted to use any legal tactics that will make the playing field level again. If you buy this argument, this is just the method for you!

Here is how it worked at Johnson Controls. The company makes computerized building controls, used to manage heating, security, and other building systems. A new system code named Loba, developed at a cost of $20 million over three years, was in beta testing when management found out that Honeywell, the largest competitor, had learned of the project. Customers reported that Honeywell salespeople "had approached Johnson customers and asked them to pump Johnson on the project," which they mistakenly referred to as "Lobo." Honeywell denies this, but it is a credible story since salespeople are used to gather competitor intelligence from customers in many companies.

Rather than rush the product introduction, Johnson took a scheduled update of an existing building controls system and renamed it Logical Option for Building Operation system, giving it the acronym Lobo. A splashy publicity campaign was used to introduce what *The Wall Street Journal* characterized as a "relatively minor upgrade." Heavy coverage in the trade press helped confuse Honeywell's competitor intelligence efforts, and John Bernaden of Johnson Controls reported that, "After we came out with the Lobo smokescreen, there wasn't that pressure through Honeywell's various means to attempt to learn what we were doing." The Lobo smokescreen took the heat off the Loba project, giving Johnson time to introduce a more major advance to their product line. The new system, called Metasys, was introduced in early 1990.

Military Rules Applied to Competitor Disinformation

I called an acquaintance who is an expert on military intelligence to find out what he thought about the Johnson Controls case. He said it was a classic example of disinformation. It uses misdirection in much the same way a magician does to focus the attention of the competitor away from what you do not want them to see. It was a success in his opinion because Honeywell thought they had something figured out on their own. This is an important element, and it gives the recipient a higher level of confidence in the information than in any information that was not discovered through competitor intelligence. There are several rules that can be borrowed from the military textbooks on disinformation and applied to cases like this:

- Disinformation should refocus attention.
- Disinformation will be more effective if the targets believe they have discovered the information on their own.
- Targets should be unaware that they have been detected.

The Johnson technique could be used for other purposes, for example, to pretend you have a major breakthrough on the way as a disincentive to a company that you fear may be planning to enter your market. But, in general, it is likely to send misleading signals to customers, suppliers, and other innocent parties in the process of misleading the competitor.

Other techniques from military intelligence might be useful in competitor counterintelligence. The double-cross, in which the agents (or sources of information) are found and turned against the competitor, gives you the ability to feed false intelligence to the competitor through their own network. This sounds like a complicated thing to do in business, but it has the advantage of leaving the customers entirely out of the equation since it only uses channels that are received by companies that are collecting competitor intelligence.

Another classic military tactic (according to my friend) is "the man who never was," a body that is allowed to wash up or be captured by the other side, with a false ID and misleading plans or other intelligence in its pockets. I hope competitor intelligence never degenerates to this point, but business variants of the technique could be envisioned. For example, a manager's notepad or briefcase could be carefully lost in a strategic location, ready to be discovered by an unscrupulous member of the competitor's management.

A general rule to keep in mind with any disinformation effort is that you can do anything once. But only once. As soon as the competitor discovers the deceit, a new and more disingenuous trick will be needed. One can imagine that an intelligence war between two fierce competitors could escalate into an involved, costly, and undesirable exchange unless care was taken to limit it and maintain a certain amount of trust.

Another concept from the military that may be especially useful in evaluating disinformation tactics is the idea of passive versus active disinformation. Passive disinformation is designed to mislead no one who is not actively engaged in intelligence gathering already. It is designed to "sting" only the company that engages in what you consider to be unfair or unethical behavior. The Johnson Controls technique is a fairly good example, as Honeywell would only have been deceived by the decoy product introduction if the report that they were snooping for information on "Lobo" was true. The sting operations used by the FBI and DEA to catch prominent people red handed fall into the category of passive disinformation—for example, no one will be hurt by an undercover agent portraying a drug dealer unless they try to buy drugs. While passive disinformation is definitely hardball and may be unethical in some cases, it is far less likely to violate rules of ethics and law than any active disinformation technique.

Reference

Eben Shapiro, "How Johnson Controls Guarded Its Big Secret," *The New York Times*, February 19, 1990, p. D2.

THE "MISFORTUNE 500" PRODUCT FAILURE LIST

Blunders don't get the attention they deserve. . . . Companies just don't want to talk about them.

Bruce Nash and Allan Zullo, in
The Misfortune 500

Applications

- Reminding yourself that bad ideas can slip through the evaluative net and lose big in the marketplace.
- Putting the product development process in perspective.
- Laughing at others' misfortunes.

Procedures

None really necessary. Just read the list and try to stay off it in the future! Also, consider creating a similar list for your company. If a certain amount of humor can be maintained about failures, this list could be a good source of learning.

Bruce Nash and Allan Zullo have been collecting stories of blunders and bloopers for years and have published many in their series of Hall of Shame books. *The Misfortune 500* applied their concept to business with a vengeance.

A lot of bad decisions are made in business, but Nash and Zullo are probably right when they state that "execs prefer to stay mum and bury their heads in books on motivation and excellence." While no one likes to talk about mistakes, it is pretty important to learn from them. I hope Decca Recording looked hard at its forecasting methods after earning Nash and Zullo's award for Worst Business Decision by a Record Company: "In 1962, Decca Recording refused to sign a group named The Beatles, saying, 'Groups with guitars are on their way out.' "

The "false negatives" of missed opportunities hurt, but not nearly as much as the costly "false positives" of failed product introductions. However, failures are more often examined from the anonymity of sweeping statistics than on a case-by-case basis. Examination of individual failures provides more insight, revealing both what made an idea deceptively appealing and what doomed it to failure. Much can be learned from qualitative analysis of individual failures, and all companies ought to keep a well-documented Hall of Shame file of their own on the flops of their industry. Application Note: I have modified Nash and Zullo's presentation to include a description of the principal errors in each case. Companies developing their own lists will probably want to do the analysis necessary to also include principal errors.

Use the following collection of classic product failures from Nash and Zullo as a reminder that many ideas that seem good at first will seem really dumb in retrospect. Their book is intended to be humorous, but it may be difficult for anyone in product development to laugh at these stories—it is too easy to fall into the same trap and too easy to add up the millions in wasted development and marketing costs these failures represent!

Hall of Shame Product Failures

The following vignettes are adapted from "Ideas That Should Have Been Killed But Weren't," pages 22–28.

Wine and Dine Dinner from Heublein, Inc. (1970s). This packaged meal included an upscale entree and small bottle of wine. But the wine "was more like swill," a cooking wine with salt and spices that many consumers drank instead of mixing it with the food as the producer intended.

- Principal Errors: Misunderstanding of consumer behavior and wants. Poor communication of instructions. Misleading name.

Singles from Gerber Products, Inc. (1970s and 1980s). Large jars of foods like creamed beef and Mediterranean vegetables were positioned to appeal to busy young adults. But the packaging was distinctly reminiscent of Gerber's baby foods, and adults did not want to eat baby food.

- Principal Error: Inappropriate line extension due to lack of knowledge of customer perception.

Gourmet Foods from General Foods (1950s) were premium specialties like "lingonberry preserves," distributed through upscale department stores rather than supermarkets. Nash and Zullo explain,

> *Before it died . . . Gourmet Foods cost the giant company $30 million. General Foods chairman Edward Mortimer said he knew instantly why it flopped: "The wife of some fancy businessman sat next to me at a party and said, 'Oh, Mr. Mortimer, your Gourmet Foods are wonderful. We stock the yacht with them.' I thought to myself, 'Yeah, that's what's wrong—not enough yachts.' "*

- Principal Error: Pursued a market that was too small and specialized for the volume requirements of its business.

I Hate Peas, I Hate Spinach, and *I Hate Beets* from American Kitchen Foods (1970s) were french fry–style vegetables for the freezer case of grocery stores. They proved that children really do hate vegetables, even if they look like french fries.

- Principal Errors: Tried to sell customers products they don't like. Used a negative communication strategy that reminded them they did not like the products.

Napa Natural from Adams Natural Beverage Co. (1980s) was positioned by Nevins and Stevens of Perrier fame as the "world's first natural soft drink." The cans of fruit juice–based soda sold very well during the first six months of the rollout, but the high juice content (67%) meant that the soda fermented, and eventually exploding cans forced a recall. By the time a reformulated product was introduced, momentum was lost and the soda never made it in the marketplace.

- Principal Error: Failed to test product sufficiently before rollout.

SelectaVision VideoDisc from RCA Corp. (1980s) bombed to the tune of $80 million and 15 years of development time. Consumers did not want to buy a new video machine that could only play prerecorded discs and could not record TV programs.

- Principal Errors: Too technology oriented. Failed to understand consumer usage of product.

The *880* and *990* from Convair (1960s) were developed for the intermediate-range jet transport market. But lack of advance orders and little consumer interest, combined with excessively high costs, turned these models into a $425 million loss.

- Principal Errors: Too product oriented. Unwilling to reexamine assumptions once committed to the project.

TV-Cable Week from Time, Inc. (1980s), was positioned to compete against *TV Guide* with editions customized to individual cable systems. The costs of producing customized magazines soared and it folded in five months. *Picture Week* met a similar fate several years later.

- Principal Errors: Overdependence on technological gimmick. Underestimation of entrenched competitor's strength. Failed to learn from experience.

PCjr from IBM (1980s) was aimed at the home computer market, but the product failed to excite consumers. Complaints focused on the small keyboard, lack of memory, and high price relative to more serious machines from competitors. Introduction in 1983 missed the Christmas season, taking much of the wind out of the rollout.

- Principal Errors: Failed to provide sufficient value relative to competing products. Underestimated the sophistication of the target market and overestimated its size.

Viewtron from Knight-Ridder (1980s) was a sophisticated, expensive videotext machine for the home. Knight-Ridder positioned this product to provide a substitute for newspapers on the then popular theory that electronic media would replace the printed word. It didn't, and the product produced a $50 million loss.

- Principal Error: Jumping the gun on an anticipated technological development due to excessive product orientation and insufficient understanding of customer behavior and preference.

Unfortunately, the list goes on. There are many products that seem doomed to failure from the very start, even based on a simple reading of their name and concept. Quaker Bonnet's *Buffalo Chip* chocolate cookies. Revlon's *Private*, a deodorant for male genitalia, and on the same subject, MLO Products' *Gorilla Balls* protein supplement snack. *Sea Lion* seafood bologna from Jac Creative Foods and *A Touch of Yogurt* shampoo from Clairol seem to have started with the wrong ingredient lists, as did International Yogurt Co.'s *Yogurt Face & Body Powder*, which was advertised as containing "a large amount of living yogurt culture." How do these failures slip by management and test markets and find their way onto the income statement? A good answer to that question would take all the risk out of product development, but also a little of the fun!

Reference

Bruce Nash and Allan Zullo, *The Misfortune 500: Featuring the Business Hall of Shame* (New York: Pocket Books, 1988).

"NEW PRODUCTS POWER" TEST

I never cease to be amazed at the shabby job most companies do when it comes to systematically generating new products and setting up a disciplined process for turning ideas into commercial successes.

Thomas Kuczmarski

Applications

- Rating your company's product development effort.
- Forecasting the likelihood of generating significant revenues from new products over the time span covered by a long-range plan.
- Comparing the strength of the product function at different companies or business units (including competitors, acquisition candidates, joint venture candidates, suppliers).

Procedures

1. Review strategic plans, management style, organization, compensation, proposal screening, and product-based accounting, as each of these functions relates to product development and introduction. Note: Review available documentation and interview managers and employees (anonymously) in order to evaluate competitors, acquisition candidates, and other companies where you may lack intimate knowledge of policies and culture.

2. Rate the company(ies) on each of the six questions to evaluate (or compare) new products' power.

3. Take action on items receiving a low rating. Modify your company's policies and management style if necessary. Avoid acquisition candidates that have no new products power. Use product innovation to take share from competitors who lack new products power. Favor suppliers who are more likely to provide you with innovative products and services.

You would not do business with a company whose balance sheet signaled serious financial trouble in the future. You would not acquire it or purchase components from it. If your balance sheet looked bad, your company would turn itself inside out to improve the picture.

But other components of long-term strength are less closely monitored and less likely to receive close attention. New products power, as Thomas Kuczmarski terms the company's ability to generate revenues from innovations in the future, is given a lot less attention than the balance sheet. But in many markets it is equally important to future market strength and financial performance. The company that is able to produce new products more frequently and more quickly has a long-term advantage in most industries.

The strength of the product development function is traditionally measured by historical performance and by the amount of money budgeted for R&D. But organizational culture plays an important role in the process of innovation, and these measures are frequently misleading. Many large companies spend millions on development, but fail to support innovation in other ways. In the referenced article on Ingersoll-Rand's Strykeforce, it was necessary to form a commando-style group (the leader wore army fatigues) and go to war in order to cut through internal obstacles and bring out a new product in a timely manner.

Thomas Kuczmarski (of Northwestern's Kellogg Graduate School and Kuczmarski & Associates) has proposed six questions that measure the organizational aspects of new product development. Together, they provide an indication of an organization's new products' power. I have added a rating scale to his instrument to support the various analytical approaches described in "Applications" and "Procedures." This simple instrument ought to be used whenever new product performance needs to be evaluated or forecasted, whether for a marketing plan, long-term strategic plan, competitor study, or other purposes. The rating created by summing the scores on each question ought to be considered alongside historical performance and the R&D budget. And, it is hoped, these three factors will capture new products power with sufficient clarity that management will treat it with the reverence currently reserved for balance sheets and other standard financial statements.

The optimal score is 30. Anything below 15 is sufficient reason to pull the nearest fire alarm (1 = not at all, 5 = definitely).

1 2 3 4 5   Does the strategic plan define the financial growth gap and roles that new products should satisfy during the next five years?

1 2 3 4 5   Does top management foster an environment of "disciplined freedom," providing consistent commitment to new product funding and allocating the best managers with high-powered skills and know-how to the new products effort?

1 2 3 4 5   Is there a clear understanding of who is responsible for new product development and accountable for performance? Is the decision-making process understood, and are go/no-go approval points understood and adhered to?

1 2 3 4 5   Are there performance-based compensation programs that encourage entrepreneurship, reward risk takers, and reinforce innovative thinking and actions?

1 2 3 4 5   Are there screening criteria, based on varying levels of risk, to evaluate new product concepts?

1 2 3 4 5   Is there a formal tracking system to measure costs/returns from new products?

(All questions are quoted and adapted from the *Marketing News* article.)

Reference

Thomas Kuczmarski, "Shame on America for Bogging Down Innovation," *Marketing News,* July 9, 1990, p. 16, and "How Strykeforce Beat the Clock," *The New York Times,* March 21, 1990.

PETERS'S PRODUCT TEAM SUCCESS FACTORS

Use multifunction teams for all development activities.

Tom Peters

Applications

- Setting up and managing product development teams.
- Reducing the cost and development time for new products.
- Diagnosing problems with product development teams.

Procedures

Before using the team approach to product development, prepare a clear, written statement of how teams should operate and how the organization will treat both teams and their individual members. The items addressed in this statement can be drawn from Peters's principles, Honeywell's tactics, and possibly sources not described in this chapter. Senior management needs to sign off on all elements of the statement, and changes in compensation, reporting, funding, design and allocation of office space, and many other fundamentals are often required.

If your organization currently uses product development teams, evaluate them based on the principles presented here. A formal ranking (for example, using a 1 = not at all through 5 = definitely scale) can be performed for each of the principles by each member of the group (anonymity is important). Or an individual manager can use the principles and tactics as a guide to informal, judgmental analysis.

A growing number of managers believe products are best designed "all at once" through a team-based collaboration of engineering, marketing, production, and any other functions of relevance to the design, testing, production, and introduction of the new product (or service). As the introductory quote indicates, Tom Peters is firmly in this camp. He sites the development of the Ford Taurus and successes at Chaparral Steel, 3M, Hewlett-Packard, and Frito-Lay as evidence that product development teams shorten the development cycle and produce better products quicker and faster.

The development of the Taurus at Ford illustrates the power of this approach. Here are some of the participants in the design process and the contributions they made:

Dealers	Helped make the car more user friendly and easier to sell.
Insurance companies	Showed how to minimize the cost of repairing the car after a collision.
Lawyers	Incorporated anticipated laws into current design.
Hourly production workers	Provided thousands of suggestions on how to make it easier to build.
Suppliers	Assisted in design and drafting of the components they supply. Innovated to provide special features and options for customers.
Consumers	Tested prototypes and identified problems.

The design process was radically different as a result of the incorporation of multiple perspectives and inputs. An open process was needed to ensure serious and useful involvement from many parties, and Ford's relationships with these parties changed as a result. After the designers put their blueprints on the walls of stamping and assembly plants and solicited suggestions from hourly workers, the director of the Team Taurus project, Lew Veraldi, found the participation increased employee motivation. "It's amazing the dedication and commitment you can get from people. . . . We will never go back to the old ways because we know so much [about] what they can bring to the party." In another example, Ford's relationship with suppliers became more long term when it brought car frame manufacturer A. O. Smith into the design process in its earliest stages. Smith was awarded a five-year contract three years before production, as opposed to the more common one-year contract awarded shortly before production and in exchange played a major role in refining the car's design.

Peters identifies five factors that he finds in each successful case of product development teams. These factors address both the mechanics of who should be involved and what role they should play and are designed to help avoid pitfalls that can confound the team's development efforts.

Team Development Success Factors

This discussion is taken from Tom Peters, *Thriving on Chaos: Handbook for a Management Revolution*, pp. 262–264.

1. Multifunctional involvement. Multiple-function representation means, at best, the Ford approach: customers, dealers, suppliers, marketers, lawyers, manufacturing personnel, engineers, designers—and non-managers as well as managers; and all of these from the start.

Short of that, the lead of Hewlett-Packard and 3M . . . suggests that development teams at a minimum consist of (a) a designer/engineer, (b) a representative of manufacturing, (c) a purchaser, (d) an accountant, (e) a marketer, and (f) a field sales or service representative.

2. Simultaneous full-time involvement. Key team members—at least design, manufacturing, and marketing—must be represented full-time from the start. The involvement of others, even of lawyers, should be full-time for the duration of the most intense activity. The idea here is simple co-optation. There is no such thing as a part-time passion. The part-time team member is not really a team member. The part-timer knows where his or her bread is buttered, and is first and foremost a "functional representative," more interested in discovering reasons why things won't work than driven by champion/ entrepreneur's passion to smash down barriers and make things work. The part-timer is evaluated and paid by the "home" function; a win is seeing to it that no "surprises" occur when she or he goes back home.

Rewards should go to teams as a whole. Evaluation, even for members who are only full-time for a while, should be based principally upon team performance. This is simple to state, but tough to execute. It's a piece of a larger issue—the actual shifting of the entire focus of evaluation, including pay and promotion, from functional performance . . . to team performance, where a team leader, regardless of which function she or he comes from, dominates the evaluation process.

But what about the member of the purchasing department who may be full-time for only a few months in a multi-year process? The ideal answer is an approach like Chaparral's, where functional barriers essentially don't exist [Chaparral Steel is a successful mini-mill]. Short of that, it is vital that the purchasing team member be rewarded, in the short or the long run, by his contribution to the team's success, rather than the purchasing department's success. If a purchasing person was on two teams, for two months each during the year, most of his or her annual evaluation should be based on the team leader's appraisals, not that of the nominal boss in purchasing.

A related element is rewards for cooperation. A few pioneering firms give large and numerous awards to honor acts of cooperation. For instance, if you, the manager, give out ten dinners or $100 checks or send fifty thank-you notes this month— why not make a rule, formal or informal, that at least half of these acts of recognition must go to people in other functions who have helped you and your teams?

3. Co-location. Walls of concrete and plaster are very important—and inimical to team work. Numerous studies chronicle the exponential decrease in communication when even thin walls or a few dozen feet of segregation are introduced. Hence all team members must "live" together. It's as simple as that. Want factory people and engineers to talk? Put them in the same room, with no dividers. Space management is yet another tough nut to crack, but I can state unequivocally that regardless of expense, you can't overdo it when it comes to putting people together.

4. Communication. In *A Passion for Excellence*, the original Skunk Works at Lockheed was described. This renegade band regularly completed complex projects in a tenth or less of average development time, at a tiny fraction of expected cost. Tom West's Data General skunkwork (the subject of *Soul of a New Machine*) and Gerhard Neumann's exceptional General Electric aircraft engine development operation were also analyzed. Many things were special about these three leaders, but nothing more than their insistence on constant communication across typically troublesome functional boundaries. Daily meetings and brief, written status reports, circulated to everyone, were the norm in all three cases. There is no substitute.

It is essential that regular decision-making sessions be held, with all functions represented. More important is instituting what I call the "no substitutes" rule. That is, whoever attends the meeting representing purchasing must be authorized to sign off for purchasing as a whole. Decisions subsequently undone because a junior rep attended a meeting for his or her boss are a leading source of project delays—and then sore feelings about wasted time, which cause further delays.

5. The "shared resource" trap. Recent research reported in the *Journal of Business Venturing* concludes that the sharing of resources between new-product/service teams and main-line activities—including manufacturing, marketing, and sales—is a leading cause of sandbagged product development and introduction efforts. My best advice is to urge that you at least try to wholly dedicate bits of labs or factories, or parts of marketing or field service operations, to the new-product efforts when you feel you can't afford full duplication. That is, approximate duplication as best you can, even if the costs seem high. They usually aren't when measured in retrospect.

6. Outside involvement. Suppliers, dealers (or other distribution channel members), and ultimate customers must become partners in the development process from the start. Much, if not most, innovation will come from these constituents, if you trust them (i.e., show them all information from the start) and they trust you. This is one of the most important instances of the urgent need for a shift from adversarial to cooperative relationships.

Another Approach: Honeywell's Product Development Tactics

Peters's principles will produce a product development team and environment that is similar to the one Honeywell finds most effective—but they approach the problem from different directions. There is virtually no overlap in the specifications provided. At the risk of confusing the issue, the Honeywell approach is presented here. The reader will, it is hoped, find it useful to compare this list with Peters's and will presumably be able to patch together a good approach for his or her organization from parts of both.

Honeywell's seven product development tactics are a useful addition to Peters's comments, and the combination of the two provides a strong framework for creating and managing product development teams. Here are the tactics from Honeywell, as presented in *The Vest-Pocket CEO* (original source was The Conference Board):

The procedures are

1. Gather a team from all the departments responsible for product development and introduction.
2. Cross-train the members so they understand the role each department plays.
3. Use the seven tactics to define how the group works together, how it interacts with the rest of the company, and how it will be evaluated.

The tactics are

1. *Parity.* Each individual and department involved has equal input.
2. *Frozen specification.* The team settles on firm specifications in advance. This means market research must precede design.
3. *Consulting gurus.* Technical gurus should be kept off the team, contributing in a consulting role only.
4. *Simple rules.* The team must be evaluated simply (e.g., according to how well it achieves scheduled milestones).
5. *Championship.* Necessary support and recognition can be provided through championship by a high-level manager.

6. *Risk.* By eliminating punishments and other organizational deterrents, risk taking can be encouraged.

7. *Communication.* The team must communicate freely with the rest of the organization (e.g., don't send them to a remote location without a mechanism to stay in touch daily with their peers).

Reference

Tom Peters, *Thriving on Chaos: Handbook for a Management Revolution* (New York: Harper & Row, 1987), Chapters 1–2. Also see Alexander Hiam, *The Vest-Pocket CEO: Decision-Making Tools for Executives* (Englewood Cliffs, NJ: Prentice Hall, 1990), pp. 258–260, and Clint Larson, "Team Tactics Can Cut Product Development Costs," *Journal of Business Strategy,* September/October 1988: 22–26.

ROSENAU'S PHASED PRODUCT DEVELOPMENT

A short phase can be focused more sharply and planned better than can a long phase or an unphased program.

Milton Rosenau, Jr.

Applications

- Shortening the product development cycle.
- Reallocating development funds based on intermediate assessments of competing projects.
- Improving feasibility studies and screening

Procedures

Start with a feasibility assessment of the proposed product, as in an unphased program. But if the initial study indicates feasibility, divide the program into four phases: optimization, design, preproduction, and production (or more if needed). Assess the project at the beginning of each phase—each phase requires a separate authorization. Termination is possible at any of these points. Plan each phase carefully as it begins, but do not plan beyond that phase in any detail.

Milton Rosenau of Rosenau Consulting recommends a four-phase model which can be adapted to the needs of many product development efforts. Why divide development into formal phases? He finds that a "greater urgency" applies when a short, well-defined phase is the goal than when everyone is looking at the entire project. It makes the development effort more manageable by focusing attention on well-defined, tangible objectives. It also reduces risk by formalizing the periodic review of each development effort. As the end of each phase is reached, evaluation and planning begin anew, and an objective evaluation of the project is easier. Because of this feature, the phased approach tends to optimize allocation of development funds over the short term. Whenever one project begins to look worse than others, funding is shifted away from it.

The four-phase model consists of the following:

1. Optimization. The purpose of this phase is to develop product specifications. Specifically, the goal is to focus the design phase on "the best combination of product features (e.g., performance, cost)." Rosenau recommends developing lists of the "must" and the "want" attributes of the proposed product, which will help in making trade-offs during the design phase. Marketing input is of considerable importance to the optimization phase, and Rosenau recommends secondary research as needed to provide a foundation for later test marketing efforts. Any primary consumer research that can be performed to support the selection of product attributes would clearly be helpful in this phase as well. Trade-off analysis of attributes and an exploration of the current positioning of both direct and indirect competitors will help optimize the new product's specifications.

2. Design. Optimization produced a firm specification for the product, and the purpose of the design phase is to figure out how—and if—the specification can be met. The design phase is primarily a technical exercise for most products, but a marketing orientation is assured by the preceding phase.

3. Preproduction. The goal of this phase is to prepare the new product for production. All necessary documentation is assembled, and its accuracy and completeness are established. Also, likely sources of delayed production are identified, and critical material or equipment may be ordered now so as to shorten the production phase. However, even when funds are used for this purpose the new product is reassessed before moving to the production phase.

4. Production. If it still makes sense, the new product moves on to production. This phase can be defined to cover enough units or time to demonstrate that the product can be produced to specifications, and it may also include testing or refining any novel production methods and equipment required. It may coincide with the initiation of test marketing or rollout.

In planning each phase, make sure that the requisite marketing, manufacturing, and engineering people are available and have them commit to schedules and goals. Rosenau also argues that "promoting teamwork . . . is crucial. Disharmony is a frequent correlate of new product failure." A multidisciplinary team can be formed for each phase to encourage cooperation. Also, the teams can be charged with finding ways to reduce the duration of each phase. Critical path methods can be utilized by the team for planning and managing a phase, and the team can also propose acquisition of new equipment intended to increase productivity and reduce the length of the phase. Rosenau recommends freeing team members from feasibility and maintenance work on other products—or on the new product itself—to permit them to focus completely on development for the duration of the phase.

The time between phases is also critical to the speed of development. Review of the results of each phase needs to be scheduled so as to follow immediately upon the completion of the phase, and the preparation of necessary documents should be streamlined. If the teams take a few weeks to write up their reports, and another week or two is wasted trying to obtain a go/no-go decision from management, the time between phases might add several months to the development effort!

Note on Feasibility Studies: Rosenau assumes that a feasibility study is performed prior to Phase 1, and if this first step is considered, there are really five phases. A recent Booz, Allen & Hamilton study concluded, not surprisingly, that the most successful firms generally put more effort into the "predevelopment stages," which would include the feasibility and optimization phases as defined by Rosenau. Feasibility needs to address at minimum these three broad areas: fit with the company's strategy, the nature and extent of the customer need the product is intended to satisfy, and the technical feasibility of the product. A recent study by Brentani and Droge favored the following five-factor screening model:

The Brentani-Droge Five-Factor Screening Model

- Overall corporate synergy
- Production/technical synergy
- Marketing synergy

- Competitive advantage
- Expected performance

They report that managers generally weigh expected performance highest, and that this factor is generally the hardest to predict. They used a rating scale for new product proposals that ranged from 1 = failure almost certain to 7 = success extremely likely for each of these five factors.

The major problem with feasibility studies and screening models is that they do not necessarily pick all the winners and screen out all the losers—and that is a major problem indeed! To improve the accuracy of feasibility studies, some managers are beginning to look at the potential *durability* of the new product—that is, the expected life cycle and the strength of competitive advantage provided by any innovations in the new product. This is a difficult thing to assess, but it is obviously helpful in anticipating returns and thus in evaluating the required investment.

Lawless's New Product Durability Test

Michael Lawless, director of the High Technology Management Research Center at the University of Colorado, Boulder, observes that durability, including likelihood of being imitated, depends upon innovations in one or more of the following areas:

- Product form
- Product function
- Product intangibles (including service, warrantees)
- Pricing
- Promotion
- Distribution
- Firm characteristics (resources of the company)

Assessment of the uniqueness and likelihood of being imitated should be divided into individual assessments of each of these areas. Innovations in multiple areas, or a hard-to-imitate innovation in any single area, should contribute to a favorable assessment during the feasibility phase. The optimization phase could also use this checklist in an effort to develop specifications that make the new product less likely to be imitated and more likely to be perceived as a real innovation.

Rogers's Customer Acceptance Test

A related issue, both in feasibility and optimization, is how easily the new product will be accepted by customers. Feasibility studies need to pass judgment on this, and indicate whether a problem may exist. The optimization phase can target specific problems identified during feasibility in an effort to improve acceptance. The simplest way to look at the acceptance issue is to evaluate novelty—a more novel product may be accepted more slowly. However, it usually is not that simple. A more sophisticated approach is to look at specific attributes that are linked with the speed of acceptance (see Rogers's book):

- Relative advantage over existing products (higher = faster acceptance)
- Compatibility (higher = faster acceptance)
- Triability, which is often related to divisibility (higher = faster acceptance)
- Communicability, which is often related to observability (higher = faster acceptance)
- Perceived risk of trying (lower = faster acceptance)

Each of these attributes will provide some insight into the acceptance question, and will be of use as marketing plans are developed. The optimization phase can be used to improve ratings on any problem attributes to develop specifications for a product that is more likely to be accepted quickly by consumers.

References

Milton Rosenau, Jr., "Phased Approach Speeds Up New Product Development," *Research & Development*, November 1988: 52–55.

Ulrike de Brentani and Cornelia Droge, "Determinants of the New Product Screening Decision: A Structural Model Analysis," *International Journal of Research in Marketing*, No. 2, 1988: 91–106.

Michael W. Lawless and Robert J. Fisher, "Sources of Durable Competitive Advantage in New Products," *Journal of Product Innovation Management*, Vol. 7, March 1990: 35–44.

E. M. Rogers, *Diffusion of Innovations* (New York: The Free Press, 1983).

THAMHAIN'S TEAM INNOVATION MODEL

Applications

- Enhancing drivers and removing barriers to innovative performance of new product teams.
- Improving the work environment for new product teams.
- Diagnosing problems with team management and structure when product teams do not perform up to expectations.

Procedures

To improve team performance or overcome problems with a team, rate the team and its environment on each of the variables that drive or block team performance (see the table that follows). Make modifications to remove the major blocks and enhance drivers as needed. Also refer to the listing of early warning signs when evaluating groups or diagnosing problems.

To improve the organizational climate for new product groups, refer to the model and list of drivers when planning the project and establishing the group.

To evaluate the innovativeness of a team or an entire department or business unit over time, rate it using the performance measurement (output) variables, in the second table.

. . . of the fifty influence factors mentioned by managers as drivers or barriers toward innovative team performance during the pilot study, only fifteen of these were found to be statistically significant.

Hans J. Thamhain

As this quote suggests, managers have a wealth of opinions concerning what makes teams work. However, many of the widely held beliefs do not hold up to scientific scrutiny. If only 15 of the factors studied actually correlated with new product success and failure, then 35 were red herrings, diverting resources and attention from the relevant factors.

Perhaps this explains another of Thamhain's findings, that "on average, first line managers rate their group's innovative characteristics as 'good' ... while their superior's perception is considerably less favorable, ranging from 'marginal' to 'satisfactory'. . . ." The team members think they are doing well, but their senior managers do not. (The results come from a study of 360 new product managers from 52 high-tech companies.)

Clearly the efforts of product development teams need to be focused on the factors that count, and managers need effective ways of evaluating and improving the performance of groups. Thamhain's model helps on both counts.

The model identifies three groups of variables that drive team performance and determine how successful their efforts at innovation will be. It also identifies four characteristics of successful innovation and creativity—these provide effective measures of group performance. The model is simple and process oriented: it has input variables, a process, and output variables. Its focus is on manipulating the input variables to improve the output. Process is left as a black box. For this reason, the model is especially useful for senior managers who are trying to assess or improve the product development function from above, rather than for individual members of a team, who have control over the process but not necessarily the input variables. (See Peters's Product Team Success Factors for methods that address the process more directly.)

Input-Output Model of Innovative Team Performance

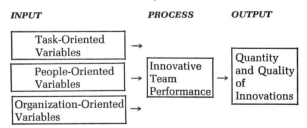

Inputs. The great virtue of this model is that both the input and output variables have been enumerated through analysis of actual product development teams at many companies. The user can say with considerable certainty that certain variables have proved good at predicting and evaluating group performance in the product development context and that others represent the desired output of the group process accurately. First, here are the input variables.

Variables Driving (or Blocking) Team Performance

VARIABLES	MANAGEMENT IMPLICATIONS
TASK RELATED	NEED TO DEFINE THE TASK CLEARLY.
Plans	Need comprehensive planning early in the project, including requirements analysis, project definition, feasibility assessment. Should involve the entire team.
Leadership	Teams need effective "people" leadership and proper technical direction.
Autonomy	Members must have a sense of autonomy and feel that they are performing professionally challenging work.
Experience	The team must consist of experienced and qualified personnel.
Visibility and involvement	All members of the team need to feel that they are fully involved in the team's work, from planning onward. And they need to feel that their team is working on an important project that is highly visible to senior management.
PEOPLE RELATED	NEED TO COORDINATE AND MOTIVATE THE TEAM MEMBERS.
Satisfaction	Individual members need to find their work with the team satisfying. Select people for work they find interesting, and build an image of importance for the project within the organization.

Trust	A sense of mutual trust and team spirit is needed. Participatory management, equitable allocation of workspace, and a minimum of supervisory reporting requirements help.
Communications	Clear, ample flow of communications (both vertical and horizontal) should be encouraged through meetings, workspace design, reviews, and information sessions.
Conflict	Power struggles and other structural tensions resulting in unresolved conflict must be avoided.
Threats	There should be no increase in personal risk associated with team participation. Job security needs to be emphasized.
ORGANIZATION RELATED	*NEED TO PROVIDE SUPPORT FOR TEAM PARTICIPANTS.*
Stability	Performance depends on the sense of security of the team. The team needs to perceive a stable environment within the organization—see Threats.
Resources	Materials, equipment, facilities, and other resources need to be adequate. Relevant to stability, threats, as well as having a practical impact on performance.
Management involvement	Senior management's support of the project must be adequate to maintain team leader's credibility. Team leader should update management routinely and aggressively cultivate their involvement.
Rewards and recognition	Proper, timely recognition of the team's accomplishments is essential. Applies to interim benchmarks as well as final results.

Goals and priorities	They must be stable. The team should try to define its plan clearly and stick with it, and senior management must not shift the ground on which the team stands.

While all these variables have a significant impact on innovative performance of teams, it is interesting to note that the task-related variables were of the greatest importance. If you have to narrow your focus, it ought to be on these variables rather than the organization-related or people-related variables. Without a sense that the task is well defined and compelling, no group will perform well. And with high task clarity, groups can, it is hoped, overcome whatever other problems might remain.

Using These Variables. The most obvious and powerful way to use this model is to evaluate a team and its environment on each of the variables described in the preceding table. If the team is new, the model will help to identify potential barriers to high performance in advance, and efforts can be made to minimize the barriers. On the other hand, it may also be useful to identify those drivers in which the organization and team are already strong and accentuate those. If the team is an existing one, working on an ongoing project, it probably does not make sense to reexamine and manipulate all the variables described. However, it will be helpful to identify specific problems or complaints and use the model to relate these to problem variables. The model will help narrow down the search to specific factors that are likely to be at the root of problems.

Outputs. Thamhain also identifies four important output variables, and these provide useful measures of team performance. They reflect the desired result of the team development process from the senior manager's view. If teams do not rate high on each, then they are not performing well—regardless of whether the optimal mix of input variables seems to present. For this reason they provide a good scaffolding for performance evaluation of groups and their members. Here are the output variables.

Characteristics of Successful Innovation

- Number of new ideas adopted
- Ability to meet preestablished goals
- Adaptability
- Commitment

All four of these characteristics were correlated with the performance ratings given groups by senior management in Thamhain's study, and presumably with the success of the projects they worked on. Managers can make the working assumption that groups who are rated low on one or more of these characteristics are off track and not likely to produce up to expectations in the future.

Early Warning Signs. Thamhain provides one additional tool for managers of new product development programs that is likely to be of value as a "checkup" or routine screen for trouble. It gives the team leader and/or the senior manager an excuse to step back and evaluate the overall health of the development effort on a routine basis, and it will help identify problems in their early stages if used this way. Use it as a checklist, running through the list either on your own or with the entire group at least once a quarter. If used as a group exercise, it may provide a good starting point for an open discussion of problems and how to address them.

Checklist of Early Warning Signs

(From *J. Product Innovation Management* article, Table 4. Copyright 1990 by Elsevier Science Publishing Co., Inc.)

- Project perceived as unimportant
- Unclear task/project goals and objectives
- Excessive conflict among team members
- Unclear mission and business objectives
- Unclear requirements
- Perceived technical uncertainty and risks
- Low motivation, apathy, low team spirit

- Little team involvement during project planning
- Disinterested, uninvolved management
- Poor communications among team members
- Poor communications with support groups
- Problems in attracting and holding team members
- Unclear role definition, role conflict, power struggle
- No agreement on project plans
- Lack of performance feedback
- Professional skill obsolescence
- Perception of inadequate rewards and incentives
- Poor recognition and visibility of accomplishments
- Little work challenge (not stimulating professionally)
- Fear of failure, potential penalty
- Fear of evaluation
- Mistrust, collusion, protectionism
- Excessive request for directions
- Complaints about insufficient resources
- Strong resistance to change

Using the Checklist. While this can be used informally by a manager to aid in reviewing a group or project, it can also provide a vehicle for formal self-assessment by the group. The group leader needs to assess the openness of the group's members, and in some cases will decide that honest answers to these questions will not be given in an open meeting. If this is the case, have each group member complete a checklist anonymously by checking any problem statements that apply. Collect and summarize the results, and disclose them fully to members in summarized form (e.g., how many checks each early warning sign received). Then use the summary as a basis for an open discussion of how to resolve problems and improve the climate for innovation.

Reference

Hans J. Thamhain, "Managing Technologically Innovative Team Efforts Toward New Product Success," *Journal of Product Innovation Management*, Vol. 7 March 1990: 5–18. Also see Hans J. Thamhain and David L. Wilemon, "Building High Performing Engineering Project Teams," *IEEE Transactions on Engineering Management*, Vol. 34, August 1987: 130–137, and Wilemon and Thamhain, "Team Building in Project Management," *Project Management Quarterly*, July 1983.

Chapter 4

Direct Marketing

ALPERT'S YIELD-BASED LEAD ANALYSIS

Applications

- Developing direct-mail lead-generation strategies for lead-driven businesses, especially those with a limited universe of prospect lists.
- Evaluating test results to select the most effective premium promotion strategy.

Procedures

Some readers may recall Shell Alpert of Alpert, O'Neil, Tigre & Co. as the opinionated author of the "Direct Marketing Clinic" column in *Business Marketing*. Here is a simple concept Alpert proposes as an alternative to conventional methods for evaluating direct-mail promotions designed to generate sales leads. This concept may be controversial, as it is liable to lead you to spend more money and time on converting leads to sales, but he makes a convincing case for doing so under certain circumstances.

Many companies use direct mailings to generate sales leads, then have salespeople or commission-based sales reps follow up on the leads. A common analytical approach is to look at the mailing costs per lead. Costs go up if premiums or other expensive promotional tools are used, of course, but if the promotion is expensive the cost per lead will usually go down. So far, so good, but the next issue is whether the increased yield of sales leads results in lower-quality leads. In many cases it does, and reps complain about the extra sales calls they must make.

Example: An insurance agency selling medical plans to small businesses found that the use of a special premium (worth $6.50 versus the usual $1.90 premium) boosted the response and cut the cost per lead by nearly 50%. However, the reps' closure rate fell from the normal 40% of leads to only 30%. This meant that the cost per sale was only 25% less using the special premium (versus 50% reduction in cost per lead), and reps had to make one extra sales call on average for every sale made. The company figured the extra sales call cost more than the 25% reduction in mailing costs per sale, and decided to stick with their usual premium and avoid the grumbling from the reps.

Alpert's approach is to calculate *sales yield per M*, defined as "the total number of consummated sales yielded by each thousand-name increment of your list universe." If a promotion gives you a higher yield, and costs a little more, then you should use it anyway based on this measure. Why? Because, for many sales lead–driven companies, high margins make it profitable to use expensive promotions, and the real limitation is the availability of good lists. With a finite number of prospects to whom the company can send mail, repeat mailings become an issue. Response rates may fall if you pester people with your mailings. Also, each list is "highly perishable," becoming less accurate over time. For these reasons Alpert argues that it is of overriding importance to harvest the maximum number of sales in the minimum amount of time from the lists that are currently available. The strategy can be expressed as maximizing yield from mailing lists within the bounds of profitability (which could be defined by management as a target margin). According to Alpert, sales lead–driven businesses characteristically have "the kind of wide profit margins that tend to minimize the relative significance of costs in favor of yields. Yet it never ceases to amaze me how many otherwise bright managers never seem to grasp that major truth."

Reference

Shell R. Alpert, "How Much Those Leads Really Cost," *Business Marketing*, January 1990, p. 8.

MAXWELL SROGE'S CATALOG PLANNING GUIDE

Applications

- Planning and producing a catalog.
- Managing catalog production in the context of a marketing plan or schedule.
- Understanding the roles and terminology of the printer and designer of a catalog.
- Identifying and using "hotspots" to maximize catalog sales of targeted items.

Procedures

Review the seven-step process. Use as a structure for planning and scheduling the design and production of a catalog. Refer to the Application Note for information relevant to catalog design and product management.

An outgrowth of a workshop by catalog publishers Maxwell Sroge Publishing, these guidelines identify the key steps in planning and producing a catalog—and who is supposed to do them. They find that creating a catalog requires *seven major tasks*, as described here (reproduced by permission from *How to Create Successful Catalogs*):

1. Dummying the catalog [the placement and grouping of products to maximize sales] is primarily the job of the merchandiser. Why? Isn't the visual effect of the catalog important in attracting the customer and selling the products? Doesn't it matter what products are put side by side? Yes, to all questions, except that the merchandiser is aware of product sales and seasonality, and it is the merchandiser who must be concerned with placement, creating additional sales with specific products, and taking advantage of catalogue "Hotspots" to boost selected product sales. [I have included a list of these in the "Application Note" following.]

The format you choose for your catalog (the way you group products, such as by product category or theme-function category mixed product) and the technique you choose (the physical design of the grouping, such as symmetrical or asymmetrical) dictate how soon and how deeply the graphic designer and product artist become involved with the dummying process. If you have chosen to have a symmetrical layout with a product or theme/function format, it is fairly easy for the merchandiser to proceed with the dummying. Art and copy sizes are balanced proportionately and may be predetermined by the merchandiser because of a limited number of common sizes. Keeping the products in categories such as stationery, kitchen, office forms, desks, and twine is pretty cut and dried. But when an asymmetrical layout is chosen requiring different sizes per individual product, the knowledge, talent, and guidance of a graphic designer and artist become critical to outcome. All of these factors must be considered when you're making up a schedule: a symmetrical layout will take less time and most likely involve fewer people; the asymmetrical layout will take longer to dummy and will involve a number of people and perhaps several meetings.

2. Product review by the copywriters and artists, along with the merchandiser and other product buyers, is how the selling message to the customer begins. In product work sessions, new products are introduced to the creative staff and the catalogue art and copy are planned. These sessions are vitally important and productive. A minimum of 15 minutes should be devoted to each new product, to bring out why it was selected, why the customer will purchase it, which competitors have run it, how the art might be approached, and what needs to be included in the copy. If you have only a few new products (9 or 10) you might be able to get by with one long review session. But if you have 100 new products, you may have to schedule many sessions. *Do not expect the artist to work on layout or design or the copywriter to produce copy without the benefit of these meetings—your bottom line will suffer if they are skipped.*

3. Design layout will take considerable time. Even though the products have been assigned to their pages and the basic idea as to how they should be presented has been formed, ample time should be allowed for the artists to wave the creative wand . . . the visual presentation must catch the customer's eye.

4. Copy. The copywriters must assemble the facts, emphasize the benefits, and sell the customer. If legal releases from the manufacturer are needed for copy claim protection—this takes extra time. Rewrite time must be considered, too. And the duty of revising copy on the products or for seasonal changes usually falls on the shoulders of the copywriter. Don't shortchange this time.

5. Photography can be either extremely involved (if done on location in Greece) or less complicated (if done in the studio). But do not think that photographing catalogue products is easy just because the photographer is provided with detailed, to-size layout sketches of how the shot should look. The right props have to be found, the models arranged for, the background readied, and lighting planned. The layout provided for the photographer may not work well once the real products are positioned and viewed through the photographic lens. Time for reshooting needs to be allowed.

6. Press preparation. Much is included in this task. Typesetting, mechanical pasteups, transparency assembly, and color separation all take a good share of time. The better prepared the work is, the fewer problems will occur at press. If the camera-ready art is expertly done—no smudges; photography/art edges smooth; no headlines, type, inserts, or photos missing; everything in line—the printer won't have to piece things together and there will be minimal error. So the time spent at this stage will save time and trouble at press.

7. Printing/lettershop. The time it takes at this stage is pretty standard. Four-color printing generally takes six weeks from the time the job is received by the printer to the time the first catalogue drops in the mail. (If your camera-ready art is as slick as a whistle and the color separations have been provided—maybe five weeks, but don't count on it.)

Reference

How to Create Successful Catalogs (Colorado Springs, CO: Maxwell Sroge Publishing, 1985).

Application Note: Catalog hotspots that sell especially are

- Inside front cover
- Page three, opposite the inside front cover

- Center spread (or middle)
- Inside back cover
- Page opposite the inside back cover
- any pages referenced on the front or back cover
- special bind-in sections

NOVICH'S TELEMARKETING DO'S AND DON'TS

Applications

- Training and managing telemarketers.
- Improving telephone sales skills (for salespeople and managers as well as telemarketers).
- Overcoming psychological obstacles and bad habits to improve telephone skills.
- Developing or improving sales strategy when it involves telephone contact.

Procedures

Review these checklists quickly; then refer to them before or after making a call to improve your technique. Also use them as a training tool when training telemarketers or when teaching telemarketing skills to salespeople and sales support people. These tips are just as helpful in scheduling direct sales calls as they are in selling over the telephone. (Also review these checklists for ideas and advice on sales strategy when developing strategy and plans.)

Do's and Don'ts of Speaking to a Prospect

DO

Maintain a moderate tone and use inflections in your voice; never speak too loudly or softly.

DON'T

Feel too at ease when talking to a prospect. Examine the reason why. You are possibly being manipulated into a comfortable feeling, taking away your effectiveness.

DO

Take the time to train your voice: tone, enunciation, and proper use of inflection. These are basic to good telephone selling.

DON'T

Be careless in your dialogue. Clearly state everything you think about the product or service for sale.

DO

Seek out a professional voice therapist. Their help could be the difference in whether or not you have a successful telemarketing career.

Do's and Don'ts of Listening

DO

Always be well rested and physically up to par.

DON'T

Allow yourself to be distracted by side conversation with others while you are on the phone with a prospect.

DO

Anticipate the prospect's conclusion in order to concentrate on the concept of what is being said.

DON'T

Interrupt the prospect—you want participation. Encourage it.

DO

Listen to the person's tone of voice. Determine the temperament. Is this person introverted or extroverted?

Do's and Don'ts of Cold Calling

DO

Remember that cold calling is a search for new business; it is nothing to be afraid of. Without new customers and the business they bring, you cannot achieve personal growth, nor can your company grow.

DON'T

Confront the prospect with the service or product's cost on the cold call. The prospect is concerned with value; therefore, price is not the only consideration. There are other factors that contribute to value which you will explain in future calls to the prospect.

DO

Offer the prospect something, such as "saving money" or "better service." At the very least, offer an interesting personality to talk to.

DON'T

Prospect if you are not enthusiastic.

DO

Speak to the prospect's eye—not ear. You must visualize your product's or service's usage and project it so that your prospect, in turn will visualize what you describe. This gives the telephone sale a tangible overtone and makes it viable.

DON'T

Think for a moment that you will make a prospect out of everyone you cold call. Turning one name in ten that are called would be an above average figure.

DO

Always identify with the party you are calling. In that way you will discover how to make your cold call interesting. DO ask yourself if you would listen to your voice; is it interesting enough?

DON'T

Make claims about the product that are not true and that you cannot back up.

DO

Describe the highlights and *some* of the benefits of the product, not all or even most of them. In describing some benefits and usage, you lay the foundation for the closing call. You will get to know the prospect better on that future call which will give you the advantage of putting your empathy to work. Your purpose on the cold call is to bring the product into sharper focus.

DON'T

Be passive if the prospect says no to your cold call. Use an assertive technique, but don't be rude. You are entitled to know why your prospect has said no. Ask!

DO

Keep a written record of all your calls. They are invaluable in determining the validity of your prospecting list and the effectiveness of your cold calling effort.

DON'T

Just send literature to a person to make yourself feel good or prove that you are working hard. It is expensive to send information, so why waste money or time in mailing to someone with little or no interest?

Do's and Don'ts of Using the Prospect List

DO

Make sure all prospecting lists are current and have correct phone numbers.

DON'T

Make any assumptions on a prospect list because you have bad memories of an area or certain group of people. Do not trust your bias or prejudice, only your own ability with people.

DO

Pay careful attention to how your calls are received by at least two dozen people on the prospect list. Spot check the list choosing any names or phone numbers at random. In this way you can tell whether the list has accurate phone numbers and whether the people on it possess the right market profile to purchase your wares.

DON'T

Expect a list to get you sales. It will help, but you must close the sale. A good list only guarantees you someone to call.

Do's and Don'ts of the Trial Close

DO

Prepare yourself to requalify your prospect and close the sale if you can, but only if you can develop enough interest within the prospect for what you are selling.

DON'T

Talk about topics that are controversial without testing the prospect's views. Keep the conversation strictly business for the first few minutes of the second call. If the prospect offers personal information, accept it in a positive light. Never be critical.

DO

Move to the next prospect if your feelings tell you the prospect is definitely not interested. Your own feelings are never wrong for you. If you are not sure about the prospect, do not directly confront his evaluation of your product or service. You must test his assertiveness by asking for suggestions on the performance of the product he would like to see or have included.

DON'T

Knock the product or service the prospect is using in lieu of yours. It makes you seem like a sore loser. Instead, point out the benefits or services your product offers.

DO

Continue to talk if in your judgment a possibility of a sale exists.

DON'T

Get involved with a "stroker." Here again, you must pay attention to your feelings for signs of your frustration to determine if you are wasting your time.

DO

Lecture the prospect after you have established your credibility. Ask her to take written notes and take on a parental authority with her by personalizing the conversation. Show her she is special by your consideration of her needs or wants.

DON'T

Ever present an illogical presentation. Skipping details can make a sales presentation confusing.

DO

Give a testimonial of your product, but make sure it is in good taste.

DON'T

Be discouraged if, after the first closing attempt, the prospect says, "I want to think it over."

DO

Ask for the order if you feel the lecture and testimonial have been effective.

DON'T

Get caught up in the rhythm of your prospect's questions. Answer the questions slowly and with thought on your part. A question and answer rhythm is manipulation by the prospect in order for you to make an error. An analogy would be a trial attorney cross-examining a hostile witness.

DO

Discover the prospect's hidden agenda, or the expectations from the product or service. If they are too much, modify the expectations into the reality of the product or service.

Do's and Don'ts of Closing the Sale

DO

Begin the closing call with a summation of the previous calls by going over the information previously given.

DON'T

Add more information without reviewing the old.

DO

Give more information than what you set out to give. Remember, every product or service has a link with what surrounds its use of benefits.

DON'T

Limit your thinking. Expand your thoughts about the product, the industry, and other factors.

DO

Direct your prospect to give you an order by asking for it.

DON'T

Ever break your prospect's mood if he is silent at this point in the sale. You are disturbing his privacy.

DO

Hold back your anxiety if it is prevalent. Turn the mouthpiece of the telephone away. Heavy breathing is a sign of nervousness, and your prospect may hear it and react negatively because of it.

DON'T

Let the silence go on too long. Use your knowledge of the prospect and your empathy to determine when he has had enough time to think things through.

DO

Gently bring the prospect out of his silence with reassuring words, not manipulative ones.

DON'T

Think you can force silence on any prospect. Your prospect must determine this for himself.

Reference

Reprinted by permission of publisher, from Martin M. Novich, *Success on the Line: The ABC's of Telephone Selling* (New York: AMACOM/American Management Association, 1989). All rights reserved.

OGILVY & MATHER DIRECT'S TEN COMMANDMENTS

Applications

- Managing direct marketing.
- Avoiding common mistakes in direct marketing.
- Looking at the "big picture" issues to make sure the program is on track.

Procedures

Use as guidelines for developing a direct marketing strategy and making decisions about how to allocate funds. Also provides a scaffolding for reviewing the effectiveness of an ongoing direct marketing program.

Program Managers: These commandments may be useful in persuading senior management to cough up the extra funding you need for continued testing, additional mailings, or whatever needs you think they won't understand!

These "ten commandments" for direct marketing come from Drayton Bird, president of Ogilvy & Mather Direct in London. They provide a general philosophy of direct marketing that can be used to guide strategy and management choices and also to critique an ongoing program. They are included here because they concentrate on the "big picture" issues of importance to management, in contrast to the technical focus most experts bring to the subject of direct marketing. The manager overseeing direct marketing does not need to know how to compile a list or what a Johnson box is, but he or she definitely needs to know where the program is going and how it can best get there!

*Ten Commandments for Direct Marketing**

1. Do not take the name of direct marketing in vain. It's hard to use direct marketing effectively if you don't understand its full scope. Many still think of it as a medium, often confusing it with direct mail or thinking of it as below the line. Direct marketing is a

*Reproduced by permission of the Conference Board.

method of marketing. It includes any activity whereby you reach your prospect or customer directly, or they respond to you directly. The objective is to build a direct relationship between you and your customers as individuals so that they stay with you longer—and you make more money.

2. Build your database and exploit it. A database is simply a list of names with relevant facts placed on computer software. These facts enable you to communicate with individuals or companies more effectively, and thus more profitably. Every piece of data combines to make your targeting more accurate, and thus your message more credible and persuasive.

3. Remember your positioning. Positioning is the most important factor in successful, creative work and in accurate targeting. The promotion for the American Express Card, for example, is determined by its positioning as the world's most prestigious financial instrument for business or pleasure. This applies right down to the solicitation letter with an opening sentence: "Frankly, the American Express Card is not for everyone . . ." which has run unchanged all over the world for 13 years.

4. Discover the value of a customer and invest accordingly. Only if you discover how much a customer is worth to you over time can you set proper recruitment objectives. You are working in the dark if you don't know.

5. Honor your existing customers before seeking new ones. Your best customer is your existing customer. You can pay ten times as much to recruit a new customer as to sell to an existing one. Surveys show that the vast majority of customers who stop buying do so because they feel a lack of concern. One way to show you do care is to mail more often.

6. Never forget to test and keep on testing. One company showed that in a series of tests, the best combination of creative, list, price, timing, and response vehicle was 58 times as effective as the worst combination.

7. Seek out and understand new technology. Technology is making remarkable things possible. For instance, the magazine *Farm Journal* is now segmented. A farmer on one side of the road raising cattle for milk gets a different magazine from the farmer on the other side who raises cattle for beef. It's all done through the database.

8. Make your budgets flexible, or you will miss opportunities. Many think in terms of fixed budgets—which is outmoded. If you know the value of a customer over time, your budget should be determined by how many additional customers you can get at an acceptable cost. If you can afford to recruit customers at break-even, spend as much as you can doing so.

9. Most direct mail richly merits the description "junk mail." That's because marketers don't know enough about the people they are writing to, what interests them, or how they think. The answer, of course, is to do research. Research should also be conducted after mailing. The most important people to us in future mailings will not be the 12% who respond but the 88% who don't.

10. Use direct marketing throughout your business. Even when not going for an immediate sale, direct marketing has great persuasive power. Its objective is to build loyalty over time, and it can be used in any area of your business—not merely with your customers, but with your suppliers and even your staff.

Reference

"Ten Commandments for Direct Marketing," *Management Briefing: Marketing* (The Conference Board), April/May 1988: 5–6.

RAPP & COLLINS'S DIRECT STRATEGIES FOR INDIRECT MARKETERS

Applications

- Supplementing a marketing channel with database-driven direct marketing without alienating intermediaries in the channel.
- Using direct marketing in a nondirect market in order to improve marketing productivity.

Procedures

Review the four basic strategies and select the one that fits both your product (or service) and the constraints imposed by your channel of distribution.

How can you build a customer database and use it to expand your distribution without alienating retailers or agents?

- Stan Rapp and Thomas Collins

The founders of Rapp and Collins (the large direct-response agency now part of Omnicom) have some useful advice for companies that want to mix direct marketing with indirect forms of marketing. This is fundamentally difficult to do because retailers, distributors, or reps handling a company's products do not want to compete with the company for customers and sales. Direct marketing is, after all, a competing channel of distribution.

Many companies that market through indirect channels have, or can build, customer databases. Warranty cards and other vehicles for direct communication give the company a core database that can often be supplemented with the lists of intermediaries or through list acquisitions. Note: Intermediaries may be protective of their lists, in which case the strategy can be shifted to helping them market to their lists better. In fact, any company with an appropriate database may be interested in mailing your promotions and handling the orders for you, even if they are not currently an intermediary. According to Rapp and Collins, "Unless you have a huge customer base, like Sears or Avon or American Express, you may find it not only desirable but necessary to graze on outside databases to feed your own."

When an indirect marketer moves into direct marketing, whether with its own list or others, the potential for competition with existing intermediaries requires a certain delicacy. Benefits can be obtained from direct marketing without corresponding detriments to established channels as long as one of the following strategies is pursued.

1. Closing the gaps. Many producers find that retailers, distributors, and even reps do not carry their entire line of products. The broader the line, the larger the gaps in coverage by intermediaries, and the greater the opportunity cost. Another kind of gap is that caused by incomplete geographic representation. Many companies are weak in certain geographic areas, often because their intermediaries are not strong in those areas.

Direct marketing focused specifically on obvious gaps in intermediaries' coverage is fairly easy to explain to the intermediaries, and by definition not likely to offer competition for them. It can take the form of a second, independent marketing channel, as it does at Pfaltzgraff. This company produces dinnerware patterns with dozens and dozens of different pieces to a set. Most retailers do not carry the full sets. Customers collect sets, and were frustrated that they could not obtain rarer pieces from retailers. The company now puts out a catalogue of its products, from which customers can order any of the pieces produced. Retailers continue to offer the basic collections of Pfaltzgraff's dinnerware. According to Pfaltzgraff's director of marketing, Jerry King, "From a marketing standpoint, there's nothing worse than having a product that you want to sell and a consumer on the other end who is quite eager to buy with no way to get it to them. So we began to pursue mail order as a way, not to compete with our retailers that were out there, but as a way to supplement that channel of distribution."

In this case, direct marketing not only fills a gap by selling the items that retailers do not keep in stock, it also fills a gap by meeting the needs of collectors. New and casual customers are served well by the retailers, but the serious repeat buyer is not. Direct mail gives the company better access to this segment of the customer base, and a good example of Rapp & Collins' advice that direct marketing should be used to "round out your line and plug the geographical gaps in your distribution."

2. Using intermediaries' databases. This strategy is prescribed when your data base is inadequate, and also when relationships with intermediaries are threatened by your use of direct marketing. In fact, the strategy can also be used to strengthen relationships with intermediaries, and is most likely to produce a win-win situation when direct and indirect marketing are combined.

The strategy can take two forms. *Syndication* involves developing a specific product offering and promotional piece and syndicating it by turning it over to anyone with an appropriate mailing list to market under their name. Rapp and Collins explain that "a winery might prepare a syndicated mailing on a wine-of-the-week club and offer to provide it to their retailers at cost, imprinted with the retailer's name throughout." *Third-party promotion* is similar in form, but the producer's name and identity are marketed through the promotion by the third parties that send out the mailing. For example, *Reader's Digest* sells Metropolitan Life Insurance policies to its subscribers through a direct-mail program.

3. Either-or selling. The concept behind either-or strategies is simple: give the customer a choice of buying it direct or through a retailer. By offering this choice, you provide marketing support to the retailers as well as reaching prospects who would not purchase through retail.

There are three forms of either-or selling, and they differ according to the emphasis placed on direct versus retail. The 90-10 mix emphasizes retail sales. Copy urges recipients to purchase the product at retail, and the mailing probably includes the names of local retailers or dealers. Retail promotions such as a discount certificate can also be included. The option of ordering direct is presented as a fallback in case a retailer is not convenient to the recipient.

The 50-50 mix presents both options and gives them equal weight. The recipient is told something like, "You can order the electronic tongue depressor from you local dealer, or mail this coupon directly to Tongue Equipment Manufacturers Ltd."

The 10-90 mix is basically a direct-mail piece, but it adds a brief reference to the fact that the product is also available at retail stores. However, the main focus of the mailing is stimulating the recipient to fill in an enclosed order form or call an "800" number to place an order direct.

Note: Either-or selling reduces the response rate, since some recipients will respond by buying at retail rather than direct. The response rate obviously will go down as the emphasis is shifted toward retail, with a resulting increase in the net cost of the mailing. The increased costs are properly considered as advertising costs, not direct-mail costs, and should be justified on the basis of their impact on retail sales. It might even be appropriate to treat some either-or mailings as a form of cooperative advertising.

Retailers often react negatively when a company starts using direct mail. But once the direct channel is established, it often complements the indirect channel. Book and record clubs are able to coexist with retailers, but they were quite controversial when first introduced by the publishers. To overcome the initial objections and phase in the direct channel slowly it is often advisable to start with a 90-10 mix, working slowly to 10-90 over time.

4. Forced retail distribution. Sometimes a company lacks retail distribution for a product—especially if the product is a new one. Direct marketing can be used to create the pull needed to convince retailers to make room for the new item on their shelves. Giorgio Parfum used both direct mail and magazine advertising to introduce its new, expensive fragrance in 1982. By 1984, retailers were demanding the product (they had been uninterested in it in 1982), and by 1985 the product was grossing over $100 million through 250 retail outlets. According to Rapp and Collins, a similar strategy was employed by Calvin Klein to introduce Obsession. They comment, "Did any stores decide to boycott Calvin Klein fragrances because of direct competition with their own selling effort? Of course not. Not while customers are asking for and buying Obsession in record numbers. The Calvin Klein experience could be a turning point— proof that a respected brand name can do double-duty advertising: reaping direct sales from consumers beyond the reach of department store retailers while stimulating retail sales for those same stores."

References

Stan Rapp and Thomas L. Collins, *MaxiMarketing: The New Direction in Advertising, Promotion and Marketing Strategy* (New York: McGraw-Hill, 1987), Chapter 11. See also "Manufacturer Complements Retail with Mail Order Catalogue," *Direct Marketing*, September 1983, pp. 72–77.

THROCKMORTON'S COLLECTED RULES AND GUIDELINES

Applications

- Improving the quality of direct-marketing pieces and practices.
- Learning the collected wisdom on direct marketing in a hurry.
- Evaluating a specific direct-marketing piece to improve it, that is, through identifying a better offer for it.

Procedures

Each method provides specific instructions on how to do successful direct marketing. Use the methods as checklists against which a specific piece is reviewed. Or use them as the fastest way to bring yourself up to speed on aspects of direct marketing with which you lack familiarity.

Direct marketing is a rapidly growing field. Many companies are finding a role for it in their marketing, and a growing number rely on it completely. The fallout of this trend is that more and more managers find it necessary to develop, review, or authorize direct-response mailings, and most of them find it necessary to scramble around for the expertise needed to play these new roles. After all, the principles and practice of direct-response advertising are not taught in most business school curricula to this date!

Joan Throckmorton has performed a valuable service by collecting the wisdom of this field in her recent book, *Winning Direct Response Advertising*. Of course, the book does a great deal else as well, but for our purposes the following rules and guidelines are of greatest value. (And this collection is bound to contain something new, even for the hoariest old direct-response writers!)

The 4 Ps of Direct Marketing

Picture. Get attention early in the copy to create desire.

Promise. Tell what the product or service will do; describe its benefits to the reader.

Prove. Show value, backed up with personal testimonials or endorsements.

Push. Ask for the order.

(From Henry Hoke, Sr., as quoted on p. 306 of Martin Baier, *Elements of Direct Marketing*, McGraw-Hill, New York (1983.)

The Star, Chain, and Hook

The star. A bright, brisk opening paragraph to get the reader's attention.

The chain. The facts and benefits that convince the reader that this is something he or she needs.

The hook. The final step is to ask the reader to act and make it as easy as possible to do so.

(From Frank Dignan, also in *Elements of Direct Marketing*.)

Throckmorton's Letter Framework

The successful letter needs to contain

Your big benefits

Your offer

Your qualifications

Other benefits

Involvement devises

Motivation to respond

Throckmorton explains: "Offer for you—with benefits to you—equals involvement from you. That's how you start to gain attention. But before you can say "free" or "50 percent off" credibility comes in. . . . When your prospect goes inside [the envelope], the letter should immediately take over the same theme, embellish it with secondary benefits and features, then add motivation to act. . . ." (from Throckmorton, p. 75).

The A-B-C Checklist

Attain attention.

Bang out benefits.

Create verbal pictures.

Describe success incidents.

Endorse with testimonials.

Feature special details.

Gild with values.

Honor claims with guarantees.

Inject action in reader.

Jell with postscript.

Does your direct piece accomplish all these goals? Usually they fall short on at least one. (From William Steinhardt, also quoted in *Elements of Direct Marketing*.)

The Seven Possible Offers

Each direct piece has to make some kind of credible offer to the reader. Here are the options:

1. **The offer with premium.** Premium needs to be closely related to the product or service for sale, and should not overshadow it.

2. **Introductory offers.** A charter offer and trial and sample are examples. Free sampling generates 30% to 50% more response in general.

3. **Club and continuity plans.** An offer in which the customer joins requires significant commitment. Often combined with a premium or trial offer.

4. **Sale or discount offers.** "It's common practice to have sales for mail order customers when there's a reason—time of year, specific holiday, anniversary, back-to-school sale, or warehouse clearance." Need an established retail price against which the sale price can be compared.

5. **Sweepstakes offers.** Throckmorton advises, "Although you cannot legally combine the sweeps offer and your main offer, see if you can get your prospect to combine the two mentally."

6. **The inquiry offer.** A two-step promotion designed to qualify the prospect for a more

expensive mail or personal selling effort. Make sure the steps are clear and will make sense to the prospect.

7. **Fund-raising.** Requires a "clear and imminent need to give." Should encourage small as well as large gifts, and make clear *how* to give.

Note: Combinations of these offers are possible as well, and Throckmorton advises that "You should try to combine two or *even three* if you can."

The Four Basic Sales Guidelines

1. Establish and maintain credibility.
2. Create and sustain involvement.
3. Overcome inertia (which she calls "the dread disease of direct").
4. Structure a compelling offer.

Sounds simple, but the acid test is to read a direct piece from the prospect's point of view. Most fail on one or more of these objectives. Before you throw away the next batch of direct mail that hits your in-box, look at each piece as you reject it to see where it failed. In my experience, most pieces never get past step 1! (from Throckmorton, pp. 47–54).

Bob Stone's Seven-Step Formula for Good Letters

1. Promise a benefit in your headline or first paragraph, your most important benefit.
2. Immediately enlarge upon your most important benefit.
3. Tell the reader specifically what he or she is going to get.
4. Back up your statements with proofs and endorsements.
5. Tell the reader what will be lost by not acting.
6. Rephrase your prominent benefits in the closing offer.
7. Incite action now.

(From Bob Stone, *Successful Direct Marketing Methods*, Crain Books, National Textbook Company, 1984, p. 192.)

Tom Collins's Creative Checklist for Direct-Mail Packages

1. Do you have a good proposition?
2. Do you have a good offer?
3. Does your outside envelope select the prospect?
4. Does your outside envelope put your best foot forward?
5. Does your outside envelope provide reading motivation?
6. Does your copy provide instant orientation?
7. Does your mailing visually reinforce the message?
8. Does it employ readable typography?
9. Is it written in readable, concrete language?
10. Is it personal?
11. Does it strike a responsive cord?
12. Is it dramatic?
13. Does it talk in the language of life, not "advertise at"?
14. Is it credible?
15. Is it structured?
16. Does it leave no stone unturned?
17. Does it present an ultimate benefit?
18. Are details presented as advantages?
19. Does it use, if possible, the power of disinterestedness?
20. Does it use, if possible, the power of negative selling?
21. Does it touch on the reader's deepest relevant daydreams?
22. Does it use subtle flattery?
23. Does it prove and dramatize the value?
24. Does it provide strong assurances of satisfaction?

25. Does it repeat the key points?

26. Is it backed by authority?

27. Does it give a reason for immediate response?

28. Do you make it easy to order?

(From Throckmorton, pp. 90–91)

Obviously someone has written a formula for almost everything! And these formulaic approaches can be very helpful in diagnosing a problem or spurring the writer or agency on to better work. But they can also give a false sense of confidence, as Joan Throckmorton demonstrates by writing a four-page direct-response letter for a fictitious product, the jim-jam, that is technically perfect in every way—but totally ridiculous (see pages 92–95 of her book). The point is that a stiff, mechanical execution according to a standard formula will not produce desirable results. Whether evaluating a package or developing one, you must always make sure that the product or service makes sense and is presented in a creative and exciting manner. The formulas and guidelines are best used as a foundation for innovative marketing, not a substitute.

References

Joan Throckmorton, *Winning Direct Response Advertising: How to Recognize it, Evaluate it, Inspire it, Create it* (Englewood Cliffs, NJ: Prentice Hall, 1986). See also Bob Stone, *Successful Direct Marketing Method*, Crain Books National Textbook Company, 1984, and Martin Baier, *Elements of Direct Marketing* (New York: McGraw-Hill, 1983).

Chapter 5

Sales and Sales Management

American Express Target List
Dr Pepper and Drackett Co. Closes
Gellerman's Sales Management Guidelines
Graham's Sales Killers
Nashua's "Blind Spot" Customer
  Research
Sauers's Sales Presentation Training
Smith's Negotiating Tactics
Szymanski's Declarative Knowledge Sales
  Model

Also see:
  Alpert's Yield-Based Lead Analysis
  Novich's Telemarketing Do's and Don'ts
  Caterpillar's Distributor Training Program

AMERICAN EXPRESS TARGET LIST

Applications

- Identifying prospects, especially for industrial and business-to-business sales.
- Helping individual salespeople keep track of prospects and making sure they contact all prospects in their territory.
- Also included is a discussion of AmEx's selling strategy for initial presentations.

Procedures

This method is used by the salespeople who sell American Express Travel Management Services to large companies. The method is a two-step process.

---

1. Management establishes guidelines for identifying prospects. The guidelines set target size ranges for each SIC (Standard Industrial Classification) category. For example, an electronics manufacturer with more than 100 employees might be defined as a prospect. Guidelines can of course be modified and reissued when knowledge about prospect identification improves or when strategies change.

Guidelines can also be probabilistic, giving salespeople an estimate of the potential of making a sale to a prospect based on its size or other characteristics. This gives salespeople the freedom to place their own bets.

2. Salespeople research companies in their territories, identifying all companies that meet the guidelines. Salespeople at American Express use the following sources for this task:

> Dun's Million Dollar Directory
>
> Dun's state sales guides
>
> National Register Publishing's Directory of Corporate Affiliations
>
> Local chamber of commerce lists
>
> State directories and registers of manufacturers

The list then forms an agenda for sales calls. According to Greg Deming of American Express, "The objective of the salesperson is to turn the names on these target lists into clients by moving them, one by one, from the target list to a first presentation." American Express uses telemarketing, mail marketing, industry networking, and trade affiliations to help get a foot in the door with prospects.

Initial Presentation. What do you do once that first meeting is scheduled? Because American Express's travel service for companies is a complex product with a lengthy sales cycle, the objective is not to close the sale right away. The initial call strategy, which will be useful for others selling complex services and products to business or industry as well, is as follows (quoted from Porter Henry's write-up of an interview with Greg Deming):

- Earn the right to ask questions.
- Agree on objectives of the call. (Take note of this—an underused technique for business-to-business selling!)
- Ask enough open-ended questions to determine
  - Organizational needs.
  - Personal needs of your contact.
  - Potential obstacles.
- Summarize needs from organization's perspective, always testing that the needs are mutually understood.
- Ask and make statements regarding how the needs can be fulfilled.
- Reinforce the benefits of fulfilling the needs.
- Test for client reaction in terms of personal needs.
- State the benefits of moving to the next step in the cycle: the needs analysis. Outline what each of you needs to do to prepare for that next step, and set a date for the next contact.

In many complex business-to-business sales, it is fairly easy to identify problems (what business doesn't have problems?), but it can be very difficult to state these problems as organizational goals that the contact will agree with. They may not see your solution as compelling, or may simply not be prepared to focus on and solve a problem at present. The first presentation strategy is designed to explore and map the journey from problems to solutions. It gets at the heart of the problem faced by many salespeople, especially those who are directed to sell solutions or told to take a consultative approach. The key to making this type of sale work is to make sure the contact sees the problems the same way you do. According to Deming, "When your contact's level of awareness is equal to yours, you can begin to apply features and benefits to that need, but not before!"

Reference

Porter Henry, *Secrets of the Master Sellers* (New York: AMACOM/American Management Association, 1987), pp. 24–26, 102–103.

DR PEPPER AND DRACKETT CO. CLOSES

Applications

- Improving one's skill at closing sales.
- Training salespeople in sales closing techniques.

Procedures

Use the lists of closing techniques from Dr Pepper and Drackett to identify a specific method that is suited to a particular sales call. (Refer to the lists when developing a call strategy.) Also use the lists in training by memorizing the closes and role-playing them until they feel comfortable and natural.

In my business, management consulting, it's a very bad idea to use strong-arm close techniques, and just writing about some of the techniques used at Dr Pepper and Drackett is enough to make me cringe! The last thing a consultant wants is to talk someone into a project before they are truly committed to it and ready to support and implement it. But in many selling situations an aggressive close *is* appropriate, as the salesperson needs to overcome inertia and encourage the prospect to take immediate action. This is especially true with retail products that are supported by "pull" advertising and will definitely sell, as long as the salesperson can talk the retail buyer into giving them shelf space.

Many techniques exist for making a close, but the basic principle behind most of them is that the prospect should have to say *no*, not yes. Aggressive closes presume that the prospect will buy, and throw the ball into their court. If they do not want to, they can raise a specific objection, give a negative response that permits you to probe for an objection, or throw you out the door. As long as you can elicit objections, you can address them and, by removing them, set the stage for another attempt at closing. The rationale for this is that natural resistance to change is best overcome by creating an equal resistance to not changing. Making it slightly uncomfortable for the prospect to say "no" creates a countervailing force.

That is the principle behind a good close, but in practice most of us find it difficult to make it work.

When I am on the road as an observer for a client, and am able to watch a good salesperson handle the close, it seems more like an art than a science. Fortunately, some companies have developed detailed descriptions of successful closing techniques, and have success in training people in this art by giving them a portfolio of techniques to draw from. Dr Pepper trains salespeople how to use the following seven techniques.

Dr Pepper Closing Techniques

1. *Trial close.* A hypothetical question to test their willingness to purchase. Example: "If you pick up Dr Pepper, which brand will you drop?" If they respond by giving a brand name, they are obviously ready to switch to Dr Pepper. Otherwise, they will probably raise an objection that can be addressed.

2. *Assume assent.* Act like the prospect will buy, and ask only questions about the specifics, like when and how. If the prospect objects that they never committed to buying, continue with the presentations and try another close.

3. *Offer a choice.* Ask a question that does not by its structure permit a "no" answer. Example: "How many do you think you'll need? Six or seven?"

4. *Action close.* Start going through the motions of a close, filling order forms or other paperwork. At Dr Pepper the action close is executed by filling in a form that establishes the prospect as a national account.

5. *Inducement close.* A special promotional offer, often a discount, is used to convince the difficult prospect to close. This technique is used only if others fail, and never to make a sale when the salesperson judges that the product is not appealing otherwise (since the customer will probably not make another purchase in this case).

6. *Summary close.* Summarize the product positioning, benefits, and other material covered in the sales presentation. This signals to the

prospect that the time has come to make a purchase. It is a good lead-in to the action close. At Dr Pepper it is used in slide presentations to large target accounts. The presentation ends with a "Summary" slide followed by a "Next Steps" side.

7. *The balancing act close.* A pro/con analysis is used to show that the balance is in favor of the pros, for example, by writing down a list of risks and benefits.

This bag of tricks gives the salesperson a lot of options for closing, depending on how the presentation is going. It also means they can make several attempts to close, getting a good read on the prospect's attitude each time, and not run out of closing techniques. The more closing techniques you know, the better, so it is useful to supplement the Dr Pepper list with one from The Drackett Company (which wholesales household products). Some of these techniques overlap with the Dr Pepper list, but some are unique.

Drackett Co. Closes

1. *Direct close.* Ask for the order you want, for example, by saying, "May I write up an order for . . ." or "Will X amount be enough?"

2. *The order-form close.* Like Dr Pepper's "action close." Fill in the order form, asking for the necessary information as you go. Do not say "sign this"; a variant like "just okay this" is preferable.

3. *The either-or close.* Like Dr Pepper's "offer a choice" close.

4. *The "half-nelson" close.* When an objection is raised, ask the prospect to agree to make the purchase if you can convince them that the objection is unfounded. This commits them in advance. Of course you should only use it when you are confident you can overcome the objection convincingly.

5. *The cautionary tale close.* Mention another buyer who adopted your recommendations, who shared your prospect's objection but

found after purchasing that it was not a problem or who otherwise illustrates the wisdom of purchasing.

6. *The lost-sale close.* When you are ready to give up, ask the prospect why you were unsuccessful. For example, say "Why didn't I convince you?" This close may reveal a hidden objection.

7. *The process-of-elimination close.* When the prospect refuses to purchase, use this close to identify a hidden objection. Ask the prospect if they did not purchase because of objection x, and if not, objection y, and so forth, until you have covered all the common objections. Like the lost-sale close, this one does not seem advisable except when the sale seems lost anyway.

8. *The "I'll think it over" close.* Prospects often respond to closes by saying "I'll think it over," which means the salesperson will go away empty handed. In this close, respond by saying something like "That's good—I am sure you wouldn't need to think about it if you weren't interested. To make sure you have all the information you'll need, tell me, what are you still uncertain about?" This strategy can turn the "I'll think about it" response into specific objections, allowing you to address them and try another close.

9. *The final-objection close.* Get the prospect to agree that she is not purchasing because, and only because, of a specific objection. Then overcome this objection. Rich Ziegler of The Drackett Company suggests the wording, "If I understand you correctly, the only reason you're not buying is . . .".

Reference

Porter Henry, *Secrets of the Master Sellers* (New York: AMACOM/American Management Association, 1987), pp. 214–219.

GELLERMAN'S SALES MANAGEMENT GUIDELINES

Applications

- Improving the productivity of a sales force by maximizing customer predisposition to purchase.
- Increasing the effectiveness of recruiting and support by sales managers.

Procedures

Review the arguments to adapt the model to your company's situation. Consider using or adapting the suggestions to ensure that salespeople call on the customers who are most predisposed to purchase. Suggestions include training salespeople in call management (wait time, focus of conversation, making polite retreats). The approach also emphasizes on-the-job training and coaching to increase salespeople's utilization of sales techniques.

Saul Gellerman of the University of Dallas's School of Management spent 25 days in the field observing an industrial sales force in action, and his observations led to a shift in focus from seller to customer. His study of automotive parts sales found three critical behavioral descriptors of the salesperson-customer interaction that were strongly related to sales performance. They are:

- Appropriateness of the discussion focus.
- Time management, especially while at prospect companies.
- Staying power, or whether a salesperson will "neglect the fundamentals of the craft" after encountering several rejections.

They are important because they each influence the customer's predisposition to buy during a sales call. Gellerman's research led to the insight that

It was clearly customers' predisposition to buy, or resist a long sales pitch, or ignore pleas, or use the seller much as a talkative drinker uses a bartender that largely determined the outcome of the call.

Most salespeople will find this argument obvious—of course the mood of the buyer is critical to the success of a sales call. If the customer needs to place an order, if you call at a convenient time, and if you are considered a reliable source for the needed item—you are guaranteed a good order. But sales trainers, sales managers, and academic researchers generally overlook the predisposition of the customer and focus on the behavior of the salesperson. Because if you assume customer behavior is more important than salesperson behavior, you run smack into the problem that you cannot train and manage customers the way you can train and manage salespeople. So the general assumption is that one should ignore the customer's attitude and behavior (beyond qualifying a prospect) and focus on what *can* be controlled—salesperson attitude and behavior. But what if it is possible to manipulate the customer's attitude toward buying?

Gellerman found that each of the three factors listed holds a key to the customer's predisposition to buy during the individual sales call—that is, at the specific time a salesperson tries to ask the customer for an order. Each is described here.

Discussion Focus

There was an inverse relationship between small talk and size of order. Why? He found "the focus of discussion seemed to depend on how seriously the customer took the seller. It was a matter of whether the seller had demonstrated both competence and usefulness to the customer." The customer's opinion of the salesperson was usually formed in the first few sales calls. If the customer took the seller seriously, the customer would readily participate in a discussion focused on purchasing. If not, the customer would slip into a pattern of making small talk, exchanging views on sports, and so on—the kind of personal relationship salespeople are traditionally supposed to build. Unfortunately, this relationship turned out to be counterproductive.

While the opening calls shape the customer's perception of the salesperson, and thus the discussion focus the customer establishes, the salesperson can also exert some control over the focus of discussion.

Higher-producing salespeople are generally more adept at steering the conversation back to the sales task.

Time Management

Much attention is given to optimal routing of salespeople as they travel from call to call, and many companies also attempt to improve time management by setting quotas for number of calls and by streamlining paperwork and providing prospecting and clerical support. However, Gellerman observed that time management *while on a call* was very different for top producers than for the less successful salespeople. Time management on the call is a potent technique for controlling the predisposition of customers to purchase in the short run. Customers who are eager to purchase do not keep salespeople waiting for long, they do not want to talk about baseball for a half hour, and they do not interrupt to take phone calls or talk to associates. The most successful salespeople in Gellerman's study heeded these clues and "courteously withdrew," usually setting up another appointment at a better time for the customer. Less successful salespeople were more persistent, waiting for 20 minutes to be seen, and tolerating interruptions and divided attention if they were seen. This proved to be poor time management. For example, waiting for more than a few minutes to be seen generally did not result in significant orders.

Note that this finding contradicts the well-worn advice to persist. Patience is not an effective sales tool when it leads to a small number of calls on customers who are not predisposed to buy. Better to keep moving in search of customers who are eager to purchase, and try the disinterested customer later.

Does this strategy sacrifice account development for maximum orders today? It could, if the salesperson's withdrawal burns any bridges. Perhaps sales managers need to provide training in withdrawal etiquette appropriate to their industry. However, it is likely that a salesperson's willingness to be kept waiting signals low self-value and encourages the customer not to take the seller seriously. This could initiate the pattern of unfocused discussion that works against order taking, as discussed. When Gellerman's findings are considered, it seems likely that the time management strategy is preferable for long-term account development as well as short-term order taking.

Another way to look at this finding is that prospects should be defined both in traditional terms—which tend to have a long-term, macro focus, and also in behavioral terms—which ought to have a short-term focus. Salespeople need to be taught how to qualify buyers on this behavioral dimension every time they make a sales call.

Staying Power

"The basic problem is the extreme difficulty of the seller's job," concluded Gellerman. It is a tough job, and "a typical seller runs into more rejection in the course of a day than most of us have to absorb in weeks, if not months." The top salespeople are better at coping with rejection than are others. Most do not bounce back from several failures at the beginning of the day, and they limp through the rest of their day with the certain knowledge that it will not go well. They take long lunches and otherwise try to avoid further rejection, and, most significant, "Like a badly shaken athlete, the seller will neglect the fundamentals of the craft."

The staying power of the salesperson is evidenced by the ability to keep selling properly and wait out a run of bad luck. The best salespeople persevere, continuing to have faith in sales technique. The others fall to pieces and stop applying the sales knowledge they have. Gellerman found that most salespeople do not apply their knowledge of how to sell consistently, even though most of them share this knowledge.

The implication is that more training in sales technique is a poor investment. What is needed instead is "good coaching" to increase the staying power of salespeople. The objectivity, maturity, and faith in technique that are the requisites of staying power are probably best taught in the field and through reinforcement and encouragement. Gellerman argues that

> Good sales managers should be in the field with their low producers, and their new sellers, as much as possible. Like good athletic

> *coaches, they should constantly remind the sellers of the fundamentals, constantly encourage, and constantly praise effective performance. The objective is to break bad habits and to build good ones.*

This advice bucks a trend as well. Sales managers have turned increasingly to centralized sales training programs to bring salespeople up to speed on sales technique, and large sales forces make it hard to work one on one with salespeople. But the coaching role is very different from the training role, and training is a poor substitute for coaching. Coaching is needed for all but the exceptional salesperson in order to help them implement the lessons of training effectively and consistently.

While training cannot substitute for coaching, it is possible that sales training can help build staying power. The staying power issue needs to be addressed explicitly during sales training, both descriptively and through role-playing. And the salesperson's attribution of causality should also be addressed in sales training. Many salespeople will attribute several tough calls in a row to fate. Gellerman reports that almost all the salespeople he studied "were convinced that there are good days and bad days, and that the outcome is almost preordained." A bad first few calls was a clear signal of a bad day. This form of attribution is obviously damaging to staying power. If training can help salespeople to see a few bad calls in the morning as a coincidental series of unrelated events, staying power is more likely to survive intact.

Reference

Saul W. Gellerman, "The Test of a Good Salesperson," *Harvard Business Review*, May/June 1990: 64–69.

GRAHAM'S SALES KILLERS

*Even the best salespeople develop
attitudes that destroy sales.*

- John R. Graham, president,
Graham Communications

Applications

- Improving your sales effectiveness by identifying and eliminating bad habits of thought.
- Training a sales force to avoid common errors.
- Scoring salespeople in the field or in role-playing to identify problem areas that need improvement (used by supervisors/sales managers).

Procedures

Use this chapter as a checklist of common errors and false assumptions that plague salespeople. *Trainers* should present these "sales killers" and give examples of them from their industry and context in the course of basic sales training or during follow-up training events. (They will take about an hour to present and discuss, and another hour or two could be used for role-playing based on them.) *Sales managers* will find this checklist useful when spot-checking their sales force. Whenever the sales manager goes on a call with a salesperson, the manager can fill in a copy of this checklist and keep it in the salesperson's file. Over time, the checklists will provide an accurate record of any bad habits that have been observed and can be used for customized training. *Salespeople* will also find it useful to keep track of personal performance using this checklist and to change their thought and behavior if they find they are guilty of uttering any of the sales killers.

The Sales Killers' Checklist

(Adapted from the *Marketing News* article already cited. The headers are quoted directly.)

☐ I know more than my customer.

It is easy to translate product expertise into an unintended sense of superiority—a sense that customers will pick up on even if the salesperson does not intend to "talk down" to them. There is a fine line between confidence and condescension, and the latter always turns off customers.

☐ My customer knows more than I do.

Sometimes customers feel they should know more than they do, and hide their insecurity with a false assuredness. The salesperson needs to see through this bravado and provide full information and instruction (without disputing the customer's expertise, however). Holding back information is a mistake.

☐ There's no doubt about it. My customers think of me when a need arises.

A long and friendly relationship is no guarantee that the customer will seek out the salesperson. Variety seeking by the customer or the aggressive selling of a rival may steal the business that is taken for granted. Continued effort is always required.

☐ When there's a problem to be solved, my customers turn to me.

Salespeople often think they are viewed as problem solvers, but customers are more likely to see them as providers. To make sure the customer does not go elsewhere when there is a problem, the salesperson must demonstrate an ability to solve problems and reinforce the fact that he or she has the ability, resources, and desire to do so.

☐ Forget it. That customer will never place a big order.

When salespeople decide how much business they expect a customer to give them, their assessment carries over into behaviors that are noticed by that customer. The customers who are pegged as small accounts will feel they are being treated that way. It is easy to underestimate the potential of an account. And even if the account is not huge, the customer needs to feel valuable or the business will go elsewhere.

☐ I've worked hard to make sure I'm "in solid" with my customers.

Customers do not like to feel they are taken for granted, and this is just the way they often feel when the salesperson thinks the relationship is solid. The key is to make sure the salesperson is still working for the business, regardless of how strong the relationship is historically.

☐ A big sale is the best sale.

John Graham observes that "big sales alone do not make great salespeople—except in their own minds. Anyone who has spent too much time sitting on a stool with one leg knows how precarious a perch it really is. As the moments go by, all the effort goes into maintaining your balance." Other accounts suffer when the Holy Grail of "the big account" dominates a salesperson's attention.

☐ I know my customers trust me.

All the salesperson really knows is what customers have done in the past. Inferring their attitudes is a risky occupation, and it can lead to dashed expectations. That a customer has given the salesperson small orders in the past is no guarantee that "he trusts me" and will therefore give the salesperson big orders as well. In general, customers do not trust salespeople to perform until the salesperson has asked for and earned that trust.

Reference

John R. Graham, "Eight Sales 'Killers' Are on the Loose," *Marketing News*, Dec. 18, 1989, p. 6.

NASHUA'S "BLIND SPOT" CUSTOMER RESEARCH

Applications

- Filling in blind spots in customer knowledge that arise when there are too many customers for managers to keep track of individually.
- Making sales and customer service more customized and responsive at business-to-business and industrial companies.

Procedures

A blind spot, according to Eric Birch of Nashua Corporation, is the lack of insight into a customer that arises "when managers stop asking specific questions about customers." It is likely to occur at business-to-business or industrial companies with between 10 and 1,000 customers—companies in this size range often start to rely on statistical reports about customer activity to such an extent that they lose sight of the specifics of each customer's situation. But individual customers are still important enough that these companies cannot afford to treat them like statistics.

Birch suggests asking the following questions as a way of diagnosing, and shedding light on, a blind spot (as quoted from the referenced publication):

1. How many customers bought from you last month?

2. How many of those were first-time customers? Of the others, how many bought in their normal or regular pattern and how many were out of the pattern, on either the high or low side?

3. How many customers stopped buying from you or sharply reduced their volume this year? Do you know why?

4. What reports do you get routinely that give you customer-specific information? Do any of them give you pattern information that might provide you with either defensive or offensive clues about what you should be working on?

In addition, he recommends that managers reinforce the customer orientation by asking customer-specific questions and by insisting that statistical reports provide as much information on a customer-specific basis as possible.

Reference

"Overcoming the Blind Spot," *The Conference Board's Management Briefing: Marketing*, Vol. 3, August/September 1988.

SAUERS'S SALES PRESENTATION TRAINING

Applications

- Preparing for an important sales presentation.
- Overcoming nervousness and bad presentation habits that occur during tense "cold call" presentations.

Procedures

"Practice makes perfect," says Professor Daniel Sauers of Louisiana Tech about difficult sales presentations. Of course, but salespeople rarely practice for individual presentations. Sales training usually focuses on generalized skills, and even when role-playing is included, it does not provide practice specific to any single presentation. When a salesperson has a major sales presentation to make, for example, with the purchasing manager of a competitor's largest account, the abstractions of last year's training session are of little help. What is needed, according to Sauers, is mental training specific to this sales call that will "channel the nervous energy into productive energy—you're not going to do away with the nervousness, so use it to your advantage."

Here is a set of "mental exercises" that can be used to prepare for the major sales presentation. They are analogous to the training an athelete does in preparation for a major contest.

Imagine the Meeting. Use your imagination to generate an image of the building and the person you will call on, and then work through the entire presentation in your imagination, from greeting to close. This exercise helps develop a full strategy for the presentation, including the tone you will use and the way your nonverbal and verbal presentation will be coordinated. By seeing yourself in the situation, you can prepare yourself on many levels for it.

Create "What Ifs." Develop a list of scenarios for what might happen—and go wrong—in the meeting. Think about your response to each scenario. Use your imagination to visualize and rehearse responses to the objections you think may be raised.

Role-play with a Co-worker. (*Sales managers*— Consider asking salespeople to role-play with you before going into a major presentation.) Write down a list of possible objections, prepare your answers, then rehearse the presentation with a coworker who has the list of objections in hand and raises them at will. This is pretty good practice, and it forces you to verbalize your responses and see how they sound. Also, it overcomes the problem that "we tend to let ourselves off too easily, or we formulate incomplete answers and move on" when trying to prepare for objections on our own, according to Sauers. Note: Give and take is important here. The coworker needs to be familiar with the sales task and able to give constructive feedback as well as to play the role realistically.

Practice the Nonverbal Presentation too. Practice, according to Sauers, is the only effective way to control bad habits like pulling on your tie, drumming your fingers, or using too expansive gestures. Again, use role-playing to identify and improve on any bad habits in nonverbal presentation. (A related idea is to work on your nonverbal skills during less stressful meetings, like those with old and friendly clients.)

Time Constraints. The typical salesperson is on the road constantly and has a challenging quota of calls to make. Back at the office, there is a mound of paperwork to be completed and tomorrow's calls to be scheduled by phone. Preparation for important presentations does not fit into this typical schedule. Probably the most important benefit of using these preparation techniques is that it forces the salesperson to find time for formal preparation. Sales managers need to help and encourage this effort, even if it means allowing flexibility in quotas and other requirements in order to ensure that salespeople take the time to prepare.

Reference

Daniel A. Sauers, "Limber Up Mentally Before Big Sales Presentation," *Marketing News*, March 19, 1990, p. 10.

SMITH'S NEGOTIATING TACTICS

Applications

- Improving business-to-business selling skills.
- Diganosing and responding to buyer negotiating tactics.

Procedures

Review and role-play each tactic in sales training. Also use the list of tactics as a guide when developing sales strategy, planning sales calls, analyzing what went wrong during a sales negotiation, or responding to a buyer's negotiating position. (Idea: Keep a copy in your brief case or car for reference on the road.)

———————————————

Homer B. Smith of Marketing Education Associates believes that "negotiation enters the selling scene at any point where persuasion has stalled, where the salesperson and buyer have not agreed on a common goal and some give and take are needed." Buyers and sellers often disagree—in fact, in most sales calls they disagree right at the outset! And even when the buyer indicates interest in the product, the seller usually finds some give-and-take negotiation is required to make the sale. Negotiation is therefore a central part of selling, and Marketing Education Associates emphasizes negotiating skills in their sales training.

Note: In general negotiation is most important during the final stages of the sales call. Smith divides the sales cycle into prospecting, planning the sales negotiation (in which negotiation power and strategies are added to the normal list of items for call planning), the approach, the presentation, and then two stages in which negotiation is central. The first, called "negotiating resistance," involves probing for objections and then responding to them and negotiating solutions. The second (and the final) stage in the sales cycle, called "closing the negotiation," involves applying closing skills to reach agreement on the negotiated terms.

One of the most useful tools to come out of Marketing Education's training in sales negotiation is a compilation of negotiating tactics that buyers use on

salespeople. Smith discusses these tactics and the
most effective responses to them in detail in the book
cited. Here they are presented in a summary checklist form for quick reference when planning a sales
call or responding to a buyer demand. Note that they
are derived from a study of business-to-business
sales, and not all are directly applicable to personal
sales (but most are).

Twenty-four Buyer Tactics

TACTIC	RESPONSE
Extreme initial price demand	Act on the assumption that buyer is unaware of market prices.
Budget limitations	Probe to see if it is real. If so, find out how flexible it is; then work within its limitations. If not real, try making concessions on other fronts, like time and quantity, in return for movement on price.
"You gotta do better than that, Charlie."	May not mean a better price is necessary. If anticipated, seller can start high to leave room for movement. Be prepared to defend the price.
Time pressure	Test deadlines to see if they can change. If not, try to meet them. Sometimes they can be used to pressure your own company to respond more rapidly than normal.
"Take it or leave it."	A "final offer" from buyer can be ignored—act like you didn't hear it. Go over terms, identifying areas of agreement, to point out the small distance between positions. Concede on one factor, but continue to negotiate on others. Try nonprice concessions before conceding to a final price offer. If you accept the final offer, make sure you get a commitment from buyer to place an order immediately.

"I have to get it approved."	Initial homework on buyer authority and the buying process is the best defense against this closing tactic, because it allows you to call on the real decision maker. If you are told approval is needed, make it clear that you intend to treat the agreement as a draft so that you can change your mind also. Or set a time limit on how long you will be committed to what you offered.
Good guy/bad guy	Don't fall for the good guy's "saving offer" to you, because it is all part of the act. Thank him for his consideration, but return to your initial position if you feel it is reasonable.
Threats ("I'll take my business elsewhere")	Other variants include threatening to tell other companies about the salesperson or complaining to the salesperson's boss. If it is a bluff, call it in a professional manner. (I think the principles applied to dealing with terrorists should apply here, but others may feel concession is all right under some circumstances.)
The competitive "super contract"	Competitors are called together to bid on a major contract. Forces low-margin bidding; buyer usually wins this one! Do a careful proposal, emphasizing any nonprice benefits.
"I'm short on time. What is your rock-bottom price?"	Don't give it. Suggest a reasonable price, and ask them what they think. Try asking what quantities they want, or other trial-close questions, before suggesting a price.
"What if"	Often a useful approach for both seller and buyer. Use hypothetical questions to explore solutions without commitment. But do not let

buyers treat past answers as absolute concessions—keep track of the contingencies and remind the seller of them. Avoid excessive "what if" questions from the buyer, as you may give a hasty answer you will later regret.

Misleading facts

Some buyers will give misleading information about quantity, credit, and so forth. If suspicious, say that your company routinely checks relevant facts before making a final commitment. Then do the necessary investigation before finalizing the deal.

Escalation tactics and low balling

When the buyer tries to add one more concession after you thought you had an agreement, try calling the bluff, or counterescalating with your own add-on. Another approach is to ask for time to reconsider, which will cause some buyers to back down. Avoid escalation by asking for verbal commitment to an agreement as it is developed and by getting a contract signed fast.

The nibble ("I thought it would be included.")

Often used after a contract is signed to win a small additional concession. Response: "I'm sorry, but I don't have authority to make additional concessions." Or try responding as though you view the effort as humorous—"Good try!" A small concession is sometimes advisable, and when nibbling is expected you can withhold a concession for this purpose. A great approach is to include items usually found in nibble requests in the basic package; then the buyer can negotiate to trade them for the appropriate price concession instead of trying to get them free.

Pick-and-choose scam or cherry-picking	When the buyer asks for a discounted price on a long list of items, and then tries to order only a few of the items, do you stick to the original discount? A variant—asking you to match the lowest-price supplier of each item. Avoid mistakenly underpricing a single product on the list, as you may be held to just this price later. Argue the advantages of single-sourcing. Try countering with a small drop in the total bid rather than switching to a product-by-product sale.
Switching/adding negotiators	When a new buyer is brought into the negotiation, he or she can often break a deadlock but may go back on previous concessions. Be prepared to go back on your concessions in response. If the new person has greater purchasing authority, try to close with him or her. Otherwise, consider breaking off negotiations until you can work with the original buyer.
"Meet me halfway."	Splitting the difference often favors the buyer over the seller, especially if the buyer has not made important concessions yet. If half the difference is too much, take advantage of the willingness to negotiate by proposing an alternative split.
Withholding information	Some buyers conceal their real interests and needs. They may ask for a proposal on something they have no interest in, turn down the proposal, then say, "By the way . . ." in the hope of getting a better deal on what they really want. Knowledge is power, and the best defense is for the salesperson to gain as much knowledge of the buyer as possible in the early stages— background research and

	probing questions during prospecting and approach.
Intimidation by experts	If the buyer is (or has access to) an expert, be careful not to be swayed by one's natural deference to expertise. Be open to the information provided, but emphasize your expertise as well. Avoid being defensive. Make sure the expert is actually expert on your product and not on something unrelated. Use the expert to support your presentation by asking them for information you would normally have provided yourself.
Browbeating	Teasing and put-downs from the buyer are best met with objectivity—remember you are there to get a sale, not have fun. If the abuse is bothering you, there is nothing wrong with letting your preference be known, politely and professionally, of course. Remember, however, that the best way to "get even" is to prove to yourself that your selling and negotiating abilities are unaffected by the abuse.
Rudeness	Some buyers take it even further, acting rude and angry toward salespeople. Avoid escalation—do not raise your voice or respond in kind. Use questions to change their attitudes and give them a chance to cool down. If you are losing your temper, or the sale isn't worth the abuse, leave (but do not burn any bridges!).
"What's your cost breakdown?"	If you sell services, buyers may try this tactic on you. A cost breakdown reveals how much profit there is and where it comes from. Do not give out this information since it will no doubt be used against you. Blame the estimators, your boss—come up with some excuse and politely refuse.

| The silent treatment | Some buyers do not respond and participate. Use probing questions to bring them out. And don't let their silence rattle you into saying anything you would not have otherwise. |
| The power play | Veiled threats or reminders like "Last year we had to switch suppliers because . . ." are designed to communicate the buyer's power. Let them know that you recognize this power. If they appear to be abusing it, appeal to their sense of fairness. |

Other Strategies

Even with effective responses to buyer negotiating tactics, you will inevitably have to make concessions. That is what negotiating is all about. Be sure to think through your options in advance, identifying your fallback position and alternatives. Also, decide how much negotiating you are willing to do. Some sales are not worth the trouble of a lengthy negotiation, either because they are too small or because your chances of negotiating successfully are too low. And some buyers drag negotiations out while others make it easy.

If you know you will have to negotiate the sale, start with a position that leaves you plenty of room to move. Try not to make the first big concession. Be sure you always get something in return for your concessions. Move slowly—a big concession may be read as a sign that there is still plenty of room for movement. Do not accept the buyer's first concession—people usually expect to go through several rounds. Do be sure to explain the value of each of your concessions—their importance may not be recognized by the buyer. And do not feel that you have to stick to everything you have said—if you made an honest mistake, most buyers will allow you to correct it.

Reference

Adapted by permission of the publisher, from Homer B. Smith, *Selling Through Negotiation: The Handbook of Sales Negotiation* (New York: AMACOM American Management Association, 1988. All rights reserved. Smith's book is the classic application of conventional negotiating principles to sales. But for a completely different approach to negotiation in which a cooperative, open relationship is developed, see Roger Fisher and William Ury, *Getting to Yes: Negotiating Without Giving In* (Boston: Houghton Mifflin, 1981). Or see Harvard Negotiation Project Rules in Alexander Hiam, *The Vest-Pocket CEO* (Englewood Cliffs, NJ: Prentice Hall, 1990). Also in *The Vest-Pocket CEO*, see Hendon's Negotiating Tactics.

SZYMANSKI'S DECLARATIVE KNOWLEDGE SALES MODEL

Applications

- Evaluating individual or company performance in prospecting, sales calls, sales presentations, and closing.
- Investigating sales force performance from a customer perspective to improve effectiveness of sales functions.
- Guiding sales training methods and goals.
- Providing a framework for sales managers and salespeople for making the transition to a consultative selling strategy.

Procedures

Familiarize yourself with the model of how salespeople categorize prospects, as described below. Apply it to training to improve the categorization skills of salespeople by presenting categories of buyers and their attributes and teaching appropriate sales strategies for each category. Teach salespeople the types of buyer categories to look for at each stage of the sales cycle. Develop customer categories specific to your company through observation of and discussions with successful salespeople.

Use a category-based training system to implement new strategies. Train salespeople in any new categories of prospects that they can be expected to encounter in implementing a strategy (expansion into new segments is likely to require new categories).

Integrate category-based sales training into existing training and sales management by implementing the four practices of the behavior modeling technique, as described here.

The salesperson gathers information about clients and, on the basis of the information obtained, places customers into one selling category at each stage of the sales process. . . . An effective salesperson therefore can be defined as someone who makes fewer errors when categorizing sales leads.

- David M. Szymanski

David Szymanski of Texas A&M University based this tool on the premise that knowledge of customer needs is critical at all stages of the sales cycle. Customer knowledge permits the salesperson to adapt selling style to the needs and preferences of each customer. Of course the importance of customer knowledge is recognized at many companies, and quite a few make customer and industry knowledge a specific focus of advanced sales training. What is really novel about Szymanski's approach is the notion that *how* you store or organize that knowledge is more important to performance than how *much* knowledge you have. In fact, he argues that most members of a sales force have roughly the same amount of customer knowledge, and it is how they apply that knowledge that sets the top performers apart.

Szymanski's model views the sales task as forecasting the prospect's preferences by assigning the prospect to one of a number of stereotypical customer types. These customer types—there may be a few or dozens—are specific to the industry and are typically learned on the job. The categories of customers in the salesperson's memory are defined by "declarative knowledge"—a term that is not in my dictionary, and probably not in yours either, but which basically means the list of attributes that describe each category. For example, an industrial salesperson might recognize a category of "red-tape buyers," characterized by attributes such as computer printouts on desk, vague and lengthy titles on their business cards, employment by large companies, and a lack of hands-on experience with the product.

Salespeople may also associate "procedural knowledge" with a category. For example, the red-tape buyer has little independent authority, so the salesperson will plan a lengthy sales cycle, provide a lot of quantitative information, and try to involve the buyer's boss before closing. This procedural knowledge is obviously worse than useless if the salesperson uses it on the wrong type of buyer. A buyer who prefers to make quick decisions will be turned off by the painfully slow sales procedures designed for the red-tape buyer.

Categorizing Prospects

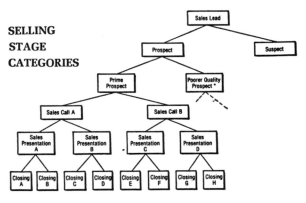

Reprinted by permission of the American Marketing Association

The model says that salespeople must decide what category the prospect fits in, and must make this decision (or at least make sure it is right) at each stage of the sales process. The first categorization determines whether to treat a sales lead as a prospect or not. Next, the prospects may be divided into two groups based on how likely they are to make large purchases if there is not time to pursue all of them at once. Obviously the quality of the categorization decisions at these two stages determines how good the list of primary prospects will be, and many marketing departments have formalized the decision-making process to improve its accuracy.

The third decision is typically made by the salesperson alone. Each primary prospect is assigned to a customer category in order to decide how to approach the initial sales call. Should it be a cold call, or should a letter or telephone call precede it? Will a special strategy be required to get past a receptionist? If the lead is a company, what person or position is the right point of entry? These are difficult decisions, and the model says they are made based on the salesperson's assessment of the type of prospect so that procedures can be applied that worked with other prospects of the same type.

The fourth important decision is the type of sales presentation to make. Different presentations may, in the opinion of the salesperson, be preferable with different types of prospects. And it may be necessary to put the prospect into a more narrow, specific category than that used to select a sales call strategy. There will certainly be more information once the salesperson calls on the prospect, so a more careful categorization of the prospect is possible.

The model includes a fifth categorization of the prospect to decide what type of closing to use. A different set of categories may be used at this stage, and all the information gathered during the sales call can be applied to make this decision. Some people like fast, direct closes, for example—deciding that the prospect is one of these people during the sales presentation will help make the close successful.

Do salespeople really think this way? It is certainly a simplification, but it rings true for me when I think about the times I have been on the road to observe salespeople at a variety of companies, and Szymanski cites evidence from academic studies to support the model. The model goes on to describe *how* the salesperson makes the decision at each stage, and here it rests on less solid ground. It hypothesizes that salespeople store a list of attributes in their memory for each category of prospect. Further, the attributes are ordered, as though in a list, with the most *unique* attributes at the top. Attributes are ranked according to their "discriminating power." When the salesperson wants to see if someone fits in a category, he or she looks at the attributes at the top of the list first, and tries to avoid going through the entire list. This simplifies the task of categorizing people by making it unnecessary in most cases to review everything you know before deciding. And it is efficient to focus on the attributes that are most unique to each category. In fact, quite a bit of evidence has been collected to support the idea that salespeople (and people in general) are "cognitive misers" and rely on a limited number of attributes in classifying prospects. If brains do not literally work in this manner, the model still provides a useful simplification that leads to some interesting conclusions.

Szymanski argues that if salespeople are collecting and ranking attributes for each category, then matching people to categories by using the top-ranked attributes, three types of errors are likely:

Error 1. Incorrect Ranking. According to Dr. Szymanski, "good salespeople . . . have discerned the attributes truly descriptive of category members." Others may have the attributes in the wrong order. When they try to classify a prospect, they may rely on an attribute that is not unique to a category and mistakenly assign the prospect to the wrong category.

Error 2. Poorly Defined Attributes. Even if a salesperson looks for the right attributes, mistakes can occur if he or she does not define the attributes quite right. For example, age and income could be the most important attributes to look at, but if the salesperson thinks the category includes everyone over 30 and with an income greater than $40,000, whereas it really includes only those over 40 with an income of $45,000, many mistakes will be made. This type of error is likely unless salespeople are exposed to good, representative examples of the categories when they are first learning them.

Error 3. Incorrect Understanding of Attribute Importance. In addition to ranking attributes by their discriminating power, salespeople also rely on some attributes more heavily than others. How they assign importance will affect their decision, especially in ambiguous cases where some attributes point to one category and some to another. Ideally, salespeople will consider the attributes at the top of the list—the most unique to each category—to be most important. However, if the list is incorrectly ordered (error 1), the salesperson will have trouble categorizing prospects, and may start relying on more of the attributes in an effort to get better results. The importance of top-of-the-list attributes will be reduced and weight will be spread more evenly over the entire list in an effort to reduce the risk of incorrect classification. This error might be easily discerned through testing (i.e., just by asking salespeople to assign importance weights to attributes on a list) and could help identify those salespeople who would benefit from training based on Szymanski's model.

Practical Applications

The model focuses attention on the decision making and behavior of salespeople, and gives trainers and managers clues to how it can be improved. The most basic, and most useful, idea to come out of it is that you can improve the categorization skills of salespeople by presenting categories of buyers and their attributes and teaching appropriate sales strategies for each category. When salespeople are trained in the stages of the sales cycle, from prospecting through closing, they can also be taught the types of buyer categories to look for at each stage. If categorizing the buyer or prospect helps salespeople select the right approach, then sales technique ought to be taught in the context of customer categories. The model articulates the cognitive processes of the salesperson in a way that makes it easier to begin to formalize and teach the cognitive skills required.

Trainers can develop customer categories specific to their company through observation of and discussions with successful salespeople. (The categories are probably different for every company, and perhaps differ even from region to region and market to market within a single company.) Managers can use a category-based training system to implement strategy once it is in place—if management wishes the sales force to focus on a new segment of the market, for example, new categories and associated sales strategies could be introduced to the sales force. Market research could be used to help support the development of new categories if no one has enough sales experience with the new segment to develop an optimal category model from their own knowledge.

Behavior Modeling Technique. Szymanski argues that since "the organization of sales category information in long-term memory depends greatly on the salesperson's selling-related experiences," lecture-oriented training will not help salespeople as much as training techniques that provide relevant experience. He recommends the behavior modeling technique, in which the following four activities are used to teach salespeople:

1. *Modeling.* Films or videotapes portray proper salesperson behavior, especially in problem situations.

2. *Role-playing exercises.* Used to reinforce behavior learned in lectures or films.
3. *Social reinforcement.* Provided through recognition of good work. Praise is important.
4. *Transfer of training.* Sales management needs
   to reinforce the training by encouraging the
   learned behavior. Note: This obviously requires closer coordination between trainers
   and managers than exists in most companies.

I have tried to use these techniques at a number of
companies and have found that salespeople often
resist a change to more participatory training styles.
Where training is voluntary (as advanced training
programs are at quite a few companies), some salespeople will not attend if they hear that role-playing
is required. However, once they gain some experience with it, the technique is less intimidating and
no longer controversial. It may be a good idea to
introduce all four of the training methods cited during mandatory introductory training so that eventually the entire sales force will be familiar with the
methods when advanced training in categorization
skills is undertaken.

Problem: How do you know what categories and
attributes apply in your markets? Interviews with
and observations of top salespeople have been suggested already. But Szymanski suggests a more formal technique that could be used to refine the attribute lists once the categories are defined. Ask
salespeople to categorize a number of "mystery prospects." Draw up a profile of each, but do not make it
available. Instead, salespeople must guess the correct category by asking a series of specific
questions—perhaps a prize could be given to the
salesperson who guesses the category after the few-
est questions? However you structure this, the series
of questions salespeople ask will help you develop a
clearer idea of which attributes are used and how
they are typically prioritized. It may also point to
common mistakes that can be addressed in training.

Reference

David M. Szymanski. "Determinants of Selling Effective-
ness: The Importance of Declarative Knowledge to the
Personal Selling Concept," *Journal of Marketing*, Vol. 52,
January 1988: 64–77.

Chapter 6

Industrial and Business-to-Business Marketing

Business Marketing Media Selector
Caterpillar's Distributor Training Program
Dovel's Positioning Process
Planning Perspectives' Guidelines for
    Competing with In-House Suppliers
Recompetitive Strategy

Also see:
Booz, Allen Customer Return-on-Assets
    Method
"Copy Chaser" Criteria for Business-to-
    Business Ads
American Express Target List
FireKing's Channel Management Strategy

BUSINESS MARKETING MEDIA SELECTOR

Applications

- Selecting media for business-to-business marketing of services or products.
- Allocating the communications budget.
- Developing marketing communications strategy or auditing current strategy.

Procedures

Use this as a guide for finding the right medium or combination of media in any specific business-to-business marketing situation by reviewing pros and cons of each option. Also use it to analyze the current media plan by looking up each medium in current use to see whether it is indicated or not.

———————————

Which medium or combination of media is right for a particular marketing campaign? Conventional wisdom is based on consumer marketing, and is not always applicable to business-to-business or industrial marketing. What's the difference between card decks and regular direct mail? Is a display ad in the Yellow Pages a good investment? When do unselective media, like television and outdoor, make sense for business or industrial marketing? There are many media options, and the choices are not always easy.

Tom Eisenhart of *Business Marketing* magazine recently analyzed each option and developed a list of pros and cons for each (based on a survey of media buyers and marketers—see note on sources at end of chapter). His simple analytical device is especially helpful when designing a marketing program or when trying to refine the balance of media. I have redesigned it here to make it shorter and easier to use for quick reference. See the footnoted article for a lengthy discussion that includes a number of comments and suggestions from managers at the various companies Eisenhart polled in developing his analysis.

Note: Data from ABP are used to indicate the percentage of total business-to-business media spending that went to each medium in 1989. Media are listed from most popular to least based on these statistics.

Business Publications

Share of total medial spending: 31.5%

Trade Publications

Pros: A cost-effective way to reach customers if the
        publication is properly targeted. Offer spe-
        cialized vertical markets. Readers may be
        more involved and loyal to a trade magazine
        than to a general business publication. Usu-
        ally offer many reader service options.
        Single-topic special issues and special edi-
        torial sections provide opportunities to reach
        segments of a trade publication's readership.

Cons: Trade publications usually do not support
        regional or job title targeting. In some mar-
        kets there are too many trade magazines and
        no publication delivers sufficient reach as a
        result. (Although *Business Marketing* does
        not mention it, some buyers complain that
        trade magazines suffer from unsophisticated
        writing and are not read by the more experi-
        enced and senior people in the market as a
        result.)

General Business Publications

Pros: Offer broad access to middle and upper man-
        agers. Frequency of publication permits flex-
        ibility in advertising. Good for corporate
        awareness advertising and for services pur-
        chased by a wide range of managers.

Cons: Lack of focus makes them a costly alternative
        in many cases. Higher cost than trade pub-
        lications. Advertising needs to have high vis-
        ibility to stand out from the many ads placed
        in this medium.

Regional Business Publications

Pros: More focused on managers and professionals
        than metropolitan newspapers. Special-topic
        sections can provide narrow industry target-
        ing. Good for cooperative advertising with
        dealers or distributors.

Cons: Lower frequency than newspapers. Reach of-
        ten limited by low circulation. Not targeted
        for industry- or title-specific advertising.

Direct Mail

Share of total media spending: 31.4%

One-Company Direct Mailings

Pros: Best for focusing on narrowly defined audiences. Very flexible. Can be personalized. Good for reinforcing and elaborating on a message placed in print or broadcast media. Good for generating leads or sales.

Cons: Costly. Requires considerable planning and lead time. Many prospects are unlikely to read a direct-mail piece. May be screened and discarded in mailroom or by a secretary.

Card Decks

Pros: Inexpensive, quick way to generate leads and sometimes sales. Permit easy tracking of cost per response, as with other direct-response media. Split runs are offered by many decks; use for an inexpensive test of different creative messages.

Cons: Small format reduces flexibility and impact of message. Readers tend to flip through decks quickly. Not usually effective with complex or expensive products and services. Most decks are not as specific as direct mail can be. Many users complain about clutter in decks.

Yellow Pages Directories

Share of total media spending: 15.2%

Pros: Provides access to prospects when they are ready to buy. Sometimes used by prospects to narrow their choice of vendors. Popular for cooperative advertising with dealers and distributors. Good for building awareness of your presence in a metropolitan area. Can be paid for on a monthly basis during the year.

Cons: Inflexible—message is fixed for a year. Increasing competition among Yellow Pages publishers is cluttering the market with competing directories. Circulation is not necessarily audited. Your message usually competes with many similar messages.

Consumer Publications

Share of total media spending: 11.0%

Newspapers

Pros: Allow large, detailed ads and frequent repetition. Good for cooperative ads with dealers and distributors. Zoned editions can be used to target geographically defined segments. Financial/business newspapers are read by senior managers/executives, and are good for corporate advertising and investor relation campaigns.

Cons: Advertising costs are increasing, and circulation decreasing, at most newspapers. Lack of specificity in circulation means business marketers pay for a lot of wasted exposures. The cost of achieving ad dominance, or even prominence, in newspapers is usually prohibitive for business marketers. Attention of readers is harder to capture since the time spent reading newspapers is declining.

Consumer Magazines

Pros: Favored for awareness building for office equipment, computer equipment, and business services. Also used for corporate advertising because of their ability to provide broad reach among upscale consumers (who presumably are in management positions) and to "catch them in a different frame of mind." Generally less cluttered with business-to-business ads than business and trade publications. Sometimes regional and business editions are available.

Cons: Consumer magazines are very expensive when circulation waste is considered. Clutter from consumer product and service ads can dilute the message.

Radio

Share of total media spending: 3.5%

Pros: Good for reaching the business community

in a local area, both during morning/evening business news and daytime programming. Programming permits targeting by age and social group.

Cons: Reach limited except during drive time. Listeners do not pay close attention to most ads. This, plus short duration of ads, limits complexity of message.

Directories

Share of total media spending: 3.1%

Pros: A majority of purchasing agents rely on directories. They have long shelf life. Like Yellow Pages, they reach prospects when they are ready to buy.

Cons: Many directories are ineffective (focus on the well-known ones to be safe). Not useful for building awareness. Can be costly, especially when multiple ads (for different sections/ headings) are required.

Television

Share of total media spending: 3.1%

Pros: Useful for building awareness quickly. Can convey message more powerfully than other media. Useful for corporate image building and for generating awareness of office equipment, microcomputers, and business service. Cable TV (especially financial, news, and sports programs) provides a more efficient alternative to network schedules. Can use spot advertising on network TV (or through local affiliates) to complement less expensive advertising in print media or on cable TV.

Cons: Expensive. Wasted exposures are costly for business-to-business marketers. Both time costs and production costs are escalating at between 10% and 15% per year. TV is generally inadequate for making business-to-business sales—limited to awareness-building function.

Outdoor

Share of total media spending: 0.17%

Pros: Permits targeting to local areas. Gives messages considerable impact for relatively little cost. Good for building awareness and name recognition. "Out-of-home advertising" is expanding the options for outdoor from the traditional billboard to buses, trains, airports, phone booths, even the ski lifts! Outdoor advertising can be effective for attracting attention to a booth during a trade show.

Cons: Use limited primarily to generating awareness. Message must be kept short and simple—cannot be used to explain a complex product or service. Lacks focus for most business-to-business marketers.

Reference

Tom Eisenhart, "What's Right, What's Wrong with Each Medium," in "Orchestrating Your Media Options" by Tom Eisenhart and Sue Kapp, *Business Marketing*, April 1990: 38–47.

The conclusions in this chapter are based on *Business Marketing's* survey of the following experts: Donald Purtill, group communications director, Truck Components Division, Eaton Corp., Toronto; Steven Ulett, advertising director, Penstock, Inc., Sunnyvale, CA; Christopher W. Umble, director of marketing communications, glass group, PPG, Pittsburgh, PA; William Loos, sales manager, Loos and Co., Pomfret, CT; Jean Coppenbardger, manager of corporate communications, MobilComm, Ridgeland, MS; Earl Medintz, VP-associate media director, Campbell-Mithum-Esty, Minneapolis, MN; Lynda Rudge, sales manager, Midco, Inc., Chicago, IL; Gordon Savoie, chairman, Skyline Displays, Inc., St. Paul, MN; Robert Bembenek, director of sales and marketing, Active Homes Corp., Marlette, MI; Maury Eikner, media director, Good Advertising, Inc., Memphis, TN; Barbara Thompson, media supervisor, DDB Needham Worldwide, Inc., Los Angeles, CA; Edward C. MacEwen, vice president of corporate communications, GTE Corp., Stamford, CT; and

Scott Silk, director of marketing-alternative channels, Unisys Corp., Blue Bell, PA. They are the real
authors of this chapter, bringing far more experience
and wisdom to it than any single author could, and
their contributions are appreciated.

CATERPILLAR'S DISTRIBUTOR TRAINING PROGRAM

Applications:

- Building a closer working relationship with distributors.

- Creating a training program that makes distributors into better managers of their own businesses, better at selling, and better representatives of the manufacturer.

- Organizing and managing informal, team-oriented approaches to distributor training.

Procedures

1. Organize sales training teams that include expertise in training, marketing and other manufacturer functions, distributors, and sales.

2. Use the seven questions to design a training and support program.

Caterpillar relies on superior distribution to compete against Komatsu and other competitors worldwide. It has more dealers than any other manufacturer of earth-moving equipment, and it maintains a close relationship with dealers through support and training. Caterpillar's dealer support system focuses on dealer motivation, morale, and control in order to boost sales and maintain a high standard of service and a good reputation among customers.

The Sales Training Development System (STDS) is one of the cornerstones of dealer training. It is reported to have boosted net revenues for dealers and to have led to improvements in organization skills, planning skills, product knowledge, and sales skills. A 12-month pilot study produced a 102% increase in net revenues of participating dealers (the comparable figure for nonparticipants was not reported). While the specifics of this program may not be applicable to other companies and their distributors, the success of dealer training at Caterpillar can probably be replicated elsewhere, and the process by which a successful program was designed is certainly applicable to other companies.

Professor Cavusgil of Michigan State describes the STDS as "a system that provides professional assistance in utilizing all the resources that are available through Caterpillar and the dealer." This emphasis on the dealer-manufacturer relationship is one of its strengths. It combines standard training with specific training and awareness building about resources available to the manufacturer. It not only educates dealers, it also helps bring dealers and the manufacturer closer together by teaching dealers and participating employees of the manufacturer how to work together. Also important is its long-term nature—it must be "a series of interconnected training programs and follow-up efforts to help dealers become fully autonomous professionals."

Consulting teams are formed to conduct some of the training and to act as coordinator of the training process. Team members should include both dealer specialists and experts from the manufacturer (Caterpillar draws heavily on its marketing staff). The consulting team works with the sales manager and salespeople at the dealership, providing both structured training on specific topics and informal, ongoing support and involvement. The team becomes an additional source of advice and resources for the dealer.

The specifics of training and team-dealer interaction are supposed to remain flexible, but they are guided by a question-driven process for program design. The consulting teams and presumably the program manager need to address the following seven questions:

1. Who should receive training? The purpose of the question is to focus the inevitably limited training resources on those distributors who will produce the highest return on the training investment. Every company may define return differently, but Caterpillar screens dealers according to the following criteria:

- The probability of full commitment from the dealer.
- The ability of the dealer to invest time/people in the program.
- The stability of the dealer's organizational structure/staffing.
- The attractiveness of the market (country) in which the dealer is located.

- Potential for growth in the dealer's revenues, market share, and margins.

2. What topics should be covered? Caterpillar found that training needs included

- General sales skills
- Overcoming client objections
- Using team selling
- Product knowledge
- Increasing involvement in marketing
- Time management skills

In general, content needs fall into four categories, and an evaluation of needs should look at each. The categories are product knowledge, selling techniques, forecasting future demand, and customer orientation (which includes market analysis skills). According to Cavusgil, content included "why and how to examine industry trends, develop customer profiles, and identify competitive strengths and sales opportunities. After a territory is analyzed and opportunities are identified, specific goals would be established."

3. Where should the training take place? Centralized training offers the advantages of senior management participation, specialized audiovisual equipment and facilities, and consistency of method and content. Its disadvantages include high travel costs, lack of customization to local needs, and commonly, a lack of realism that makes application more difficult for participants. Local training overcomes the negatives of centralized training, but quality can vary and the commitment of managers at the local level often varies. Caterpillar looks at individual components of the training program separately, weighing the strengths and weaknesses of local and centralized training for each. The result is a program that combines centralized training with on-site training.

4. Who should do the training? Caterpillar uses staff specialists who are professional trainers to prepare centralized training programs. Outside specialists are used to conduct some of the training sessions—they are recruited from nontraining functions for specific training programs. In addition, Caterpillar uses line trainers as well—they are trainers whose background includes successful sales experience. Finally, Caterpillar's consulting teams work directly with the dealers to teach them market analysis and other hands-on, complex skills. The variety of options is striking, allowing Caterpillar to use a situational approach to the decision of who to use for training. The emphasis is on choosing the type of trainer who is best suited to the specific content of a training session.

5. What methods should be used? Again, Caterpillar does not favor any specific method, but prefers a situational approach in which trainers can select from direct observation, role-playing, videotaping, and teleconferencing. However, in most cases one of these methods has proven more effective than traditional lecturing or self-learning methods.

6. When should retraining take place? The answer will depend upon the rate of change in the subject (product knowledge retraining needs generally cycle with product development, for example). It may also depend upon changes in territories and markets and reported need at the dealerships. Caterpillar combines retraining with other events like dealer meetings whenever possible in order to reduce the cost and make retraining more regular. The most important reason for asking when retraining should take place is to ensure that it does take place—it is often neglected and the impact of training is often short-lived as a result.

7. How should the training be evaluated? Evaluating training is a perennial problem. There are many possible approaches, each with unique flaws. Rather than focusing on traditional debates such as how to test recipients of training most fairly or whether it is possible to measure return on training investments accurately, Caterpillar decentralizes evaluation and insists only that it be conducted according to the following principles:

- Evaluation is done by the sales team (at the dealership).
- The evaluation must be constructive.
- Any changes suggested in evaluation should be implemented.

This makes evaluation a useful tool for the dealers rather than a budget management device for the manufacturer.

Any informal or team-oriented approach to training that addresses these seven questions will be certain to address the core issues that a more structured, formal program would. Use these questions to create an agenda and avoid the largest negative of flexible training efforts—the lack of professionalism that can lead to incomplete execution, suboptimal programs, and poor follow-through and evaluation.

Reference

S. Tamer Cavusgil, "The Importance of Distributor Training at Caterpillar," *Industrial Marketing Management*, Vol. 19, February 1990: 1–5. See also J. Taylor Sims, "Japanese Market Entry Strategy at Work: Komatsu vs. Caterpillar," *International Marketing Review*, Vol. 3, Autumn 1986, which describes the competitive situation that led to Caterpillar's current emphasis on distributor training and development.

DOVEL'S POSITIONING PROCESS

*. . . if you've actually tried to achieve
a position in the marketplace, you
know that the gulf between theory and
practice can be distressingly wide.*

—George P. Dovel

Applications

- Creating a positioning statement for a business-to-business product.
- Identifying or refining the positioning strategy for a product.

Procedures

This practical approach to positioning comes from George Dovel, who recently left Hewlett-Packard Co. to found the Dovel Group. His experience is that product positioning must be based on a careful effort to segment the market, and it must be implemented through effective communications, not only in promotional materials but also in personal communications through the sales force, support personnel, and other customer contacts, as well as other communications (such as Christmas cards) that are not necessarily considered part of the marketing mix.

His approach creates a *positioning statement,* a brief written description of the customer benefits offered and the value position to be occupied that makes this position clear and promotable. It forms the basis for all marketing decisions concerning the product, ranging from what the brochure says to who the sales force calls on. It is created in an eight-step process.

1. *List the environmental influences of importance to this positioning effort,* especially noting established product positions and how these affect your product. Also look at technological factors, your company's position and constraints, and other relevant issues. Situation analysis tools can be applied here, and qualitative research may also be appropriate. Analysis should include clear identification of historical position (or in-

tended, if this is a new product) and how the environmental influences shape your ability to amplify this position.

2. *Compare product strategy and business strategy.* A quick reality check to see that what you have in mind for the product is consistent with, and will be supported by, business strategy. Check also that your emerging positioning plan does not put your product into direct competition with any of the company's other products.

3. *Identify the attributes customers use to differentiate products.* List the attributes customers are known (or thought) to use—a separate list is needed for each segment targeted. Focus on the key dimensions—not more than three since you will need to map them. Perceptual maps can be generated by "hunch" or through formal market research and analysis. Dovel observes that, while theory says you should always prepare a formal perceptual map based on quantitative research, "perceptual maps are not practical or possible in many situations because they require a fairly mature market, with a representative sample that readily understands existing products." New products, complex products, and markets with highly varied product offerings are generally disqualified for these reasons. He advocates "some combination of qualitative research, judgement and guesswork." In other words, it's all right to wing it.

4. *Understand the positions of existing products.* This should flow out of your perceptual mapping efforts in "3" and your analysis for "1" as well. But the purpose of this step is to take the time to write down or map out "where customers in target segments place the products your competitors offer."

5. *Pick the best position.* This builds on the positioning information about your product from "1" and about competing products from "2." Also it should reflect the product strategy and your analysis of how business strategy

impacts your choices. This "should be a strategic planning effort, with all the research and consideration that implies." Note that in some cases a competitor will have the only really desirable position. If so, your choices are to back off (abandon the product in those segments and try others), try to dislodge the competitor, or try to reposition competing products. The latter is viable when you have something new and interesting that gives you the leverage to modify the perceptual map.

6. Create a concise statement of the targeted position. Keep it short and from the customer's perspective. It helps to think about segment dimensions, the problem your product solves, the people who need your solution.

   Examples

   Scientech, Inc., positioned its laser measurement equipment as providing the greatest confidence to the segment of its market for whom accuracy is the most important differentiating attribute. Communications stress this position with phrases like "The measure of confidence" and "Nothing less than absolute precision."

   The Skinner Valve Division of **Honeywell, Inc.**, is positioned as "a partner to customers solving tough production problems." Advertising messages communicate this position, for example, "Tokheim needed a special solenoid valve to help maintain its position of leadership in gasoline-pump metering. Skinner helped find the answer." Also, "Together, we can find the answers."

7. *Attack the proposed position.* Look for ways the competitors might respond and identify any weaknesses. The purpose is either to figure out how to shield the product and company from these attacks in advance or, if this in not feasible, to modify the positioning strategy so as to minimize vulnerability.

8. *Test the positioning to "make sure you can effectively communicate the positioning statement."* The simplest way is to try out

the statement on peers and the sales force. More accurate, but more expensive, is the use of customer focus groups. More formal techniques like customer choice modeling and test marketing can also be used for this purpose. The end result should be an assessment of whether the positioning statement flies with customers—does it make sense to them and are they moved by it?

There is quite a bit of work hiding between the lines in these eight steps, and the practitioner can expand the project by doing supporting market research until it becomes quite expensive as well. (The source article discusses research strategies in greater detail.) How long you should linger over each step is really a judgment call, and should be based on an evaluation of the increased certainty of business results to be gained from further research and analysis—balanced, of course, by the cost of the further work in time, money, and lost opportunities in the marketplace. But whether your positioning statement takes a week or a year, you may well agree with Dovel when he says,

> It might seem a lot of work to develop one little sentence. But everything you do—from developing the product to writing ad copy—will be much easier if you've nailed the positioning statement up front.

Reference

Based on George P. Dovel, "Stake It Out: Positioning Success, Step by Step," *Business Marketing*, July 1990, pp. 43–51.

PLANNING PERSPECTIVES' GUIDELINES FOR COMPETING WITH IN-HOUSE SUPPLIERS

Applications

- Deciding whether it is worthwhile to try to compete against an in-house supplier.
- Analyzing the prospect and developing a sales strategy when competing against an in-house supplier.

Procedures

1. Find out what the in-house supplier's status is in the mind of the buyer.
2. Assess the buyer's attitude toward change.
3. Assess the strength of the in-house supplier's power base.
4. Evaluate the in-house supplier's support role.
5. Find out how much of your information the buyer will share with the in-house supplier.
6. Analyze the basis of cost comparison used by the buyer.
7. If the in-house supplier is unionized, explore the implications of a switch.

Many large companies have captive, or in-house, suppliers. For example, at Anheuser-Busch, Ford, G.E., McDonald's, Textron, and Unisys one or more in-house or affiliated suppliers provide competition for any outside supplier wanting to make a sale. How do you develop a relationship with a business when the competition has an unfair advantage? Is it worth the trouble even to try? If you do try, should you treat the sale like any other?

Three consultants from Planning Perspectives, Inc., argue that it is often worthwhile to compete against an in-house supplier, but that a special approach is required. Their methodology is probably going to be of increased importance as many industries are seeing consolidation through acquisitions and failures, forcing suppliers to focus on a smaller number of larger prospects—many of which have in-house suppliers.

Note: In-house suppliers can take many forms.

They may be subsidiaries, independent but affiliated companies, and even fully integrated in-house plants or departments. Companies face make-or-buy decisions in almost every area, from sourcing product components to hiring a temp versus using existing clerical personnel. For this reason, it may be beneficial for service providers, as well as traditional suppliers, to apply the Planning Perspectives method.

The method involves asking a series of questions about the in-house supplier and the buyer. If the answer to the first question is favorable, then it is not an obstacle to competing with the in-house supplier and you should go on to the second question. If, however, the analysis reveals a barrier at any point, it is probably best not to compete with the in-house supplier. However, it may be possible in this case to sell to the in-house supplier instead.

1. Assess the opportunity. Before deciding whether to proceed, it is essential to find out what the in-house supplier's status is in the mind of the buyer. Buyers do not like suppliers just because they are in-house. The buyer will evaluate the in-house supplier in terms of their ability to meet standards, either through an informal, qualitative approach or through a formal, quantitative ranking. According to Henke, Krachenberg, and Lyons of Planning Perspectives,

> One Fortune 50 company with whom we are acquainted assesses the parts, components, and subassemblies supplied by its in-house suppliers on a three-rank scale. A green status ranking indicates that the in-house supplier is at least equal to the best available outside supplier and is anticipated to maintain that position in the near term. In this case, buyers within the firm are told not to go to outside suppliers.

If, however, the in-house supplier receives a yellow ranking (slightly below marketplace standards) or a red ranking (unacceptable), the buyer is permitted to go to outside suppliers. Whether the evaluation of in-house suppliers is formal or informal, however, it is generally inadvisable to try to compete against the in-house supplier who is perceived as providing a high level of service.

2. Assess the buyer's attitude toward change. The openness of individual buyers and buyer groups can differ, and not all buyers are open to change even when the in-house supplier is doing a bad job. This assessment can be done directly, by asking them how open they are. But it should also be checked by a review of past performance. If there is no evidence that the buyer or the company has been willing to work with outside suppliers in the past, in spite of a history of problems with the in-house supplier, there may be an underlying policy problem or obstacle that the buyer has not mentioned. In some cases, the openness of the buyer to change is unclear, and it may be worthwhile for the president of the supplier to contact the president of the buyer and discreetly inquire as to whether the supplier will be given a fair opportunity.

3. Assess the strength of the in-house supplier's power base. One of the risks of competing against an in-house supplier is that they will have sufficient power within the organization to override your contacts and retain the business despite the buyer's efforts to replace them. Power may be related to the nature of the relationship with the buying organization—if it is bottom line, power will be greater. Also, the relative size of the supplier will be important. If the supplier contributes a large percentage of revenues and profits, power will probably be greater. Finally, the individuals involved will be important. Any insights into the stature of the supplier's management, the nature of political dynamics, and the like will help in assessing the in-house supplier's power.

4. Evaluate the in-house supplier's support role. The in-house supplier may provide a wide range of services in addition to the central service or product—sometimes more than an outside vendor is accustomed to supplying. Look at customer support, technical assistance, inventorying, and so forth, and compare the level of service with what you offer. It may be necessary to modify your package in order to be truly competitive. If it is not possible to provide all the services the in-house supplier does, it is probably unrealistic to pursue the business. (In some cases, the outside supplier cannot provide the support provided by an in-house supplier at a reasonable cost.)

5. Find out how much of your information the buyer will share with the in-house supplier. This is an important issue, because if the details of your proposal are shared with the in-house supplier, it will give them a dramatic advantage in preparing a counterbid. Some buyers feel that information from outside suppliers should be shared with an in-house supplier, and others treat the information as confidential. You need to know what your contact's approach is, and the best way to find out is to ask. What if the buyer is determined to share your information with the in-house supplier? You need to assess the strength of the advantage this gives the competition. If the in-house supplier's performance is so far below yours that the shared information will not make a significant difference, proceed. Otherwise, treat the sharing of your information as a serious impediment to competing for the business.

6. Analyze the basis of cost comparison used by the buyer. This is important because, again according to Henke, Krachenberg, and Lyons,

> In some companies studied, the goods provided by the in-house supplier are considered on a variable cost basis rather than on a full cost basis, i.e., the fixed costs of production capital equipment are regarded as sunk costs. As a result, if an outside supplier attempts to displace this in-house supplier, the buyer does not consider the fixed costs associated with the in-house supplier's equipment for comparative purposes.

Cost accounting practices can hide an in-house supplier's cost disadvantage. It is very important to explore this issue with the buyer, and if the buying company's cost accounting creates a bias toward the in-house supplier that cannot be removed, it will probably not be worthwhile to pursue the business.

7. If the in-house supplier is unionized, explore the implications of a switch. In some cases, the union contract includes provisions concerning loss of work to outside suppliers—sometime the union has a right of first refusal to produce the goods at the supplier's price, for example. Union pressures can be strong, even if such a provision does not exist. For example, if most of the buyer company's employees work for the same union, that union may have considerable bargaining power. A strong union or a strong union contract can put the outside supplier at a critical disadvantage.

If the qualifying effort made it through all seven stages without revealing a major obstacle, the indications are good for the outside supplier. However, it is important to remember that the outsider is always going to be at some disadvantage. The sales cycle will be long, and the outsider needs to go into it with sufficient advantages in cost and quality to offset the inherent bias toward the in-house supplier.

Reference

John W. Henke, Jr., A Richard Krachenberg, and Thomas F. Lyons. "Competing Against an In-House Supplier," *Industrial Marketing Management*, Vol. 18, August 1989: 147–154.

RECOMPETITIVE STRATEGY

In most mature businesses, the most mature component is the manager.

—Mack Hanan

Applications

- Revitalizing mature brands to increase profitability and growth, especially those with strong relative market shares.
- Developing market plans for products and services in the maturity and decline stages of the product life cycle.
- Changing preconceptions about mature products that limit their performance.

Note: The methodology is designed to be applied to supplier industries, but the philosophy may be adaptable to consumer goods and services as well.

Procedures

1. Select a service or product that is currently suffering from a mature, commodity-type market.
2. Form a growth team consisting of five or more people from multiple functions within your company.
3. Adopt the "branding strategy"—an application of the philosophy of customer growth through consultative, value-added team selling.
4. Select target customers, focusing on a small number with the greatest promise (not necessarily the largest).
5. Combine customers to form growth teams and collaborate with your company's growth team.
6. Meet regularly with the customer growth team to analyze their business, find problems, develop solutions that involve the application of your company's product/service, and analyze the contribution to profits made by your solution.

This method was developed through a decade of Hanan's work on mature products and represents not only a practical methodology for turning them around but a philosophical break with the life-cycle model. If you accept the product life cycle, then you implicitly accept the idea that products will reach the end of their lives. In many cases this belief hastens the death of products—the product life cycle can be a self-fulfilling prophecy.

The product life-cycle model says that maturity and decline are characterized by reduction in demand, increasingly competitive pricing, squeezed margins, and in response, a reduction in marketing costs and other investments (see Product Life Cycle in Part 3). Hanan argues that maturity and decline are hastened by marketing strategies that were developed for the many mature products in most company's portfolios and are totally inappropriate for new products. But he sees these strategies applied to new products as well as old. Marketing skills have been honed by the challenges of keeping me-too products alive and kicking, and many companies are skilled in this dubious art. When confronted with an introduction or growth-stage product, they treat it as though it were mature by featuring the product, its performance, and its price in ways that make it vulnerable to price-oriented competition. "New products are born old: they are mature from the inception, selling on price-performance and inviting margin erosion at the hands of both rival producers and customers."

A new philosophy. The technique of making old brands recompetitive rests on the belief that what a company really sells is customer growth and profitability. Whether the product is an industrial solvent, a fastener, a raw material, a telecommunications service, or anything else with specific performance and benefits, the real benefit to the customer is the product's financial impact. Does it allow the purchasing company to do its work better and more profitably? Does it help the purchaser excel and grow? This means that a supplier should evaluate its products in terms of their impact on customers' margins and prices. To make your product get back on a growth curve, all you need to do is change the product in a manner that allows your customers to reduce costs or increase prices. These are the most tangible of benefits to the customer, as they go straight to the bottom line. Product performance, service and support, and even price are less tangible than the product's impact on customer growth—from the customer's perspective.

Note on Application to Consumer Goods

This argument was developed in supplier industries, but I see no reason why it cannot be extended to consumer goods. In some cases, customer growth will still be best measured as financial growth. (For example, Cadillac buyers traditionally benefited from a higher trade-in value than Lincoln buyers.) In most cases, however, it is more appropriate to think of it as personal growth in a broader sense. Personal growth could be measured in terms of life-style, social status, emotional security, financial security, and perhaps other measures as well.

The human being's "bottom line" is multifaceted and harder to measure than a company's, of course, but I believe the argument still holds. A product that contributes more to personal growth will be more successful. This is the most tangible benefit of the product, more important than the operationally oriented product performance features that we in marketing normally consider the core benefits. In the recompetitiveness philosophy, the most important and tangible benefit of a Mercedes automobile is its contribution to personal growth in social status and self-image, not its performance as a form of transportation.

The philosophy may in fact be easier to grasp when applied to consumer products, as we are accustomed to the idea that a psychological dimension to product performance should exist (although we generally think of this as the less tangible dimension). After all, only a small fraction of the Mercedes' price is required to provide physical transportation—a used Ford will do just as well. So customers are paying far more for personal growth than transportation, suggesting they agree that this is the most important and tangible of the product's benefits.

Customer Growth

The philosophy of customer growth is an essential foundation for recompetitive strategy because the basic thrust of it is adding value to the product that is well in excess of the cost of adding that value. This means taking an innovative and aggressive approach and introducing significant changes when the product is in maturity. The changes made are all focused on customer growth in order to avoid the trap of product-oriented, cosmetic changes so common in mature markets. In most cases, they are *not* changes to the product itself, but rather marketing-oriented changes in the relationship of the product's manufacturer with its customers. And this can be a difficult, costly process, so it is usually focused on the most profitable, "top-tier" customers. The method described here will change the way you relate to your customer—communication channels are built that allow you to help your customer grow using your product or service.

If the philosophy is adopted and the product is modified successfully (through "branding," as explained here), customers will see it as worth considerably more than the commodity price that it may have been selling for previously. The strategy, when successful, allows the company to regain control over its margins. "*Maturity*," according to Hanan, "*occurs when we lose margin control*. When customers set our margins, it is they who are marketing to us. It is we who pay the price." Loss of margin control is a good working definition of maturity, and it is inevitable when competitors replicate your product's performance benefits and customers no longer see your product as unique and essential. Perceived value falls *relative to price*. Price will inevitably come down, unless value goes up.

Conventional product management accepts the fall in price and cuts investment in order to keep return on investment from going ballistic. This is what the Boston Consulting Group's famous growth/share matrix prescribes, and it labels these products "dogs" or "cash cows," depending on their competitive position, neither of which is considered worthy of much additional investment. The key to the phi-

losophy of recompetitive strategy is that it focuses on
the opposite; it asks how perceived value can be
increased in order to halt and even reverse the fall in
margins. A focus on customer growth guides management in the development of strategies that build
customer value and therefore regain control over
margins. I believe that this philosophy is the most
important element in the recompetitive strategy
methodology because it gives management a vital
alternative vision of the product life cycle and leads
to an aggressive, customer-oriented effort to innovate
back into a growth market. If you keep this philosophy in mind as you review the following instructions, you are bound to think of variations on them
that will work especially well in your business.

Instructions

The following step-by-step instructions are based
loosely on Hanan's book, *Re-Competitive Strategies,*
(see footnote), but as the book does not set out a
formal process it was necessary to restructure the
presentation of material and in some cases make
modifications and between-the-lines suggestions to
create these instructions.

   1. Select a product. Start by analyzing the current
portfolio of products or services to select those with
the greatest potential for breaking free of their commodity status and commanding a high price again. In
general, these are the products that have the greatest
potential impact on customer operations, offering
you leverage over customer costs or revenues. The
products need not be the best on the market in terms
of performance, but they ought to at least be in the
running. The goal is to take these products and reposition them so as to earn higher profits on lower
volume (a reversal of the trend that normally drives
mature products). So pick those products that seem
to have this potential.

   Unfortunately, the referenced source gives little
concrete advice about selection criteria, but a review
of the rest of the steps will give you a clear idea of
what must be done and perhaps will give you some
ideas about which of your products this technique
could apply to. Hanan suggests that all products (or
businesses) without the potential for branding be

dropped or harvested, but given the lack of selection criteria my preference would be to start with a single product line and see if the method works before adjusting the entire portfolio.

2. Form a growth team. The team consists of a minimum of five people drawn from marketing and other functions within your firm. It is probably more important to find people with an entrepreneurial streak than to worry about representing different functions fairly. Members should also come from middle or upper management, as they will have to sell to and work with middle managers at a client company.

The team should consist of a sales manager and a technical manager whose expertise should allow them to identify ways to apply your product to a customer's operations so as to grow the customer's profits. Knowledge of customer industries is an obvious requirement. Hanan describes these members of the team as the "how-men," as their job is to figure out how to make your customers grow.

The team needs a data manager, someone who can do the research needed to pick customers and find the opportunities within them. This person is described as the "where-man."

A financial manager is needed to chart the progress of the team by quantifying "the amount and rate of new profit contribution," both at the customer and at your firm. This person is called the "how-much-man."

Finally, a "driver" is needed to act as growth team manager, coordinating the activities of members and providing leadership and dispute resolution—the "who-man."

The driver sets customer profit objectives and profit objectives for the growth team. The driver acts as a "guardian" of the product, keeping anyone from fooling around with it. The focus of the growth team is toward marketing and the customer, not toward technical product development. The driver is responsible for the group's development of growth strategies for each customer, and must take care that these strategies are simple, few, and achievable. The driver is responsible for guiding the team through the implementation of the strategy in step 3.

Growth teams should be given financial incentives in the form of bonuses tied to the accomplishment of specific growth objectives for target customers and for the product they are working with.

3. Adopt the branding strategy. The team has a free hand in developing specific strategies for increasing the profitability of customers. But its basic strategic mission is fixed—it must use marketing and customer consultation to find and develop customer growth opportunities, ultimately positioning the team and its company as the "dominant source of profit supply" for the industry and making possible a branded image and premium price for the company's product.

Team members will need to adopt the recompetitive strategy and make it their own. A good start might be to review the description of the underlying philosophy, first individually, then in a group discussion. The group discussion could be guided toward a written mission statement or other activities that will help members buy into a common vision of what the group's mission should be. Group members should probably read Hanan's *Re-Competitive Strategies* as well to make sure they have reviewed all the information available on the subject.

A special warning is in order as the group prepares to begin work. The group will be required to change the focus to customer growth, which is really a fundamentally different perspective for most managers. You and your customer must be able to place a customer-growth objective first and to act on this objective. Hanan warns that "Suppliers who have never partnered find it difficult to maintain their commitment, lapsing back into merchandising their products, wrapping them in purchase orders, and pricing them on performance benefits." Even if your group avoids this pitfall, it will probably have to run interference from people in sales and marketing who raise objections to the way customer accounts are being handled.

4. Select target customers. Pick a small number of customers with the greatest potential for growth. These may not be the high-volume customers that currently get all the attention. They may be companies that are already growing fast, or they may be companies that are in a good position to participate in growth opportunities. An analysis of customer profitability will probably reveal a small number of customers that already pay a premium price for the product. These are companies where the product probably is making a significant contribution already, and these companies should be targeted and the way they perceive the product explored. The 80–20 rule may apply, with 80% of profits coming from 20% of customers. It may make sense to focus on that 20% of the customer base and ignore the remaining 80% as you begin to implement a branding strategy.

Although Hanan does not discuss it, I suspect that it also makes sense to pick customers with whom you already have a good working relationship. Connections to management are going to be very helpful when it comes to step 5.

5. Convince customers to form growth teams. The first task of the growth team is to convince target customers to form corresponding growth teams and accept the idea of collaborating to create growth. This is a sales task, requiring the team to sell customers on the idea of "partnering" with a supplier for growth (make sure you convince them you're talking about *their* growth!). You only have to sell the idea, and ideas are free. No financial commitments or formal contracts are required.

You will not be able to make this sale at the level of purchasing manager. It is important to find mid-level operating managers with the power to implement changes and to get them excited about this idea. Then teach them how to form a growth team, structured like yours, and convey the basic philosophy and objectives to this new team. The customer growth team is actually the one that acts to reduce costs or increase revenues, and the supplier growth team plays a consultative role, acting as catalyst and educator.

Can the supplier growth team really teach the customer team anything new and useful about its business? Customers may at first be skeptical, but if they are dependent upon products or services that the supplier produces, they will accept the fact that the supplier's growth team may know something useful in this area. And the supplier growth team can expand from this "foot in the door" for the simple reason that any group of managers, if they focus their research and thinking on a particular goal, are bound to accomplish something. It is simply a matter of focusing the supplier's people on the search for sources of customer growth, and you can always sell the idea as providing more "warm bodies" where they are needed most.

Another objection I expect customers will raise is the motivation of the growth team. They are quite accustomed to sales calls, and will tend to see this as a disguised effort to sell more of the supplier's product. The growth team will need to convince them that they are sincerely committed to creating customer growth and see it as the only long-term source of their own growth. If customers see that the growth team's motivation is entirely consistent with their own they should be willing to collaborate.

6. Plan with the customer. Develop a working relationship between the growth teams at the customer and the supplier through regularly scheduled meetings and exchange of ideas and information. (I imagine a strict nondisclosure may be required by some customers.) The key goal is to develop a working relationship with the customer's growth team that is based on identifying and pursuing customer growth opportunities. Hanan explains in *Re-Competitive Strategies* that, "Recompetitiveness can be said to begin when a customer perceives a supplier growth team as a source of growth. This means that the team is no longer positioned as a source of products, services, or systems. It is no longer an alternate vendor. It's business is to supply improved products on a price-performance basis" (p. 62).

Working with a customer team made up of key function and profit center managers to find new revenues and profits for the customer is an extreme example of consultative selling. To do it well, you will have to act more like consultants than vendors, even if this means working on problems that do not result in more sales; otherwise, your sincerity will be questioned! Will you be able to help them grow? Most likely. The managers you will be working with are accustomed to working alone when it comes to planning, and they probably have never sat down in an interdisciplinary group within their own company to do growth planning. When they start to share information and ideas within their company and with your team, and when their participation gets them to focus more time on the search for growth, something is bound to happen.

Customer Research Techniques

Hanan suggests that the supplier and customer teams develop a joint database. Records should be kept of information gathered and ideas developed, and the database should also chronicle the efforts of the growth teams and include financial analysis of impacts. The primary purpose of analysis performed by the teams is to identify problems and opportunities at the customer that the supplier can assist with. One technique advocated by Hanan in another book, *Key Account Selling* (pp. 103–105), is to analyze monthly profit contribution by function for the customer (perhaps by region or other specific descriptor). For example, a convenience store's profits could be broken down into outlets versus home office, and each broken down farther as follows:

OUTLET

Credit control

Inventory control

Cash control

Staff productivity

Maintenance

Throughput productivity

Site layout/size

HOME OFFICE

Data control and report

Cash management

Supervisor productivity

Communications

These estimates will indicate certain problem areas. In Hanan's example, inventory control shows a negative contribution to profit, and is therefore subjected to the second step, a problem analysis screen. This will take various forms depending upon the problem. An inventory control problem might be analyzed by identifying average time out of stock, number of times out of stock per year, and other relevant statistics. The third and final step in the analysis is a benefit analysis screen, in which the supplier's team identifies ways in which their products could address the problem and the teams calculate the impact of each solution on profit contribution. If the product or service really improves profit contribution, it can be analyzed in terms of the return on investment it offers to the customer and, if this is high, will be seen as high in value.

You Need a Growth Plan

It is a good idea to formalize the growth planning effort by writing a joint growth plan describing "mutual growth objectives and the strategy mix to achieve them that is prepared, implemented, and controlled in concert by the planners." This may mean significant changes at the customer company, and it may also require customization of your products and the services associated with them.

References

Mack Hanan, Re-Competitive Strategies: How to Regain Growth Profits for Mature Businesses (New York: AMACOM American Management Association), 1986, and Key Account Selling: New Strategies for Maximizing Profit and Penetration (New York: AMACOM American Management Association, 1982).

Chapter 7

Market Research and Analysis

Backward Market Research
Bozell, Jacobs' Two-Way Focus Groups
Computer-Assisted Telephone Interviewing
Conference Board Competitor Intelligence
   Survey
Ethnographic Research Method
G.M. Research Information System
The Primary Research Technique Selector
Projective Techniques
Sinkula/Hampton Study of Market Research
   Department Structure
Thoughts on Applying Competitor
   Intelligence
Weyerhaeuser Determinant Attribute Analysis
Zap-Proofing Advertising

Also see:
   Dowling's Corporate Image Measurement
   Principles of Service Recovery

BACKWARD MARKET RESEARCH

What I propose here is a technique that requires marketing executives to give up their valuable time so that market research can be made more valuable.

—Alan R. Andreasen

Applications

- Designing market research projects so that they will be more useful and more directly focused on specific decisions and actions of management.
- Addressing management's frustration that research results are too general, not action oriented, or tell them what they already know.

Procedures

Start by identifying the intended effect of the research, rather than by leaving details of how to react to the information until after the study has been completed as is usually done. Follow the eight steps described here. Note: Requires advance participation by managers whose work may be affected by a research study.

Alan R. Andreasen's call for marketing executives' time strikes right to the heart of the problem facing market research at many companies. When people in marketing complain, it is likely to be about research. Common complaints are: "The results tell me what I already knew." "The results are interesting, but we don't see what to do with them right now." "They didn't ask the right questions." "The study was too general and does not give us the specifics we need for implementation." And so on. According to Andreasen this is the natural result of a research process that leaves until the end the translation of research results into actions by marketing executives.

Instructions

The first step in a research project is always to define the research problem. But in most cases the problem is defined in a broad or general manner. An "area of ignorance" is recognized, and research is performed to fill in the information gap in the expectation that new information will give management a clearer idea of what to do. But it may not if the study was not specifically designed to lead to a management decision. In Andreasen's model, that final stage of management decision making and analysis is put at the beginning to identify a *specific marketing decision* that will be driven by the research results. Here are the procedures of *backward market research* in Andreasen's own words (as originally printed in the *Harvard Business Review*):

1. Determine how the research results will be implemented (which helps define the problem).

2. To ensure the implementation of the results, determine what the final report should contain and how it should look.

3. Specify the analyses necessary to "fill in the blanks" in the research report.

4. Determine the kind of data that must be assembled to carry out these analyses.

5. Scan the available secondary sources and/or syndicated services to see whether the specified data already exist or can be obtained quickly and cheaply from others. (While you are at it, observe how others have tried to meet data needs like your own.)

6. If no such easy way out presents itself, design instruments and a sampling plan that will yield that data to fit the analyses you have to undertake.

7. Carry out the field work, continually checking to see whether the data will meet your needs.

8. Do the analysis, write the report, and watch it have its intended effect.

Step 1 is clearly critical to the success of the procedure. Its purpose is to give the researcher a crystal-clear picture of the decision alternatives and the information needed to select the best one. If the decision is viewed in the abstract, the picture will not be sufficiently clear. For example, starting with the statement that "we need to identify different types of users to see if we can target specific segments in our marketing program" sounds like a good place to begin. But it is not. It really is just another way of saying that you would like more information about customer segments. And that is all you will get. Even if you identify an interesting segment, you will probably still be uncertain as to:

- Whether the segment will respond favorably to a disproportionately high share of marketing resources (how much brand loyalty is there?).
- How to appeal to and motivate the segment.
- Whether discrete channels exist to target the segment; or if not,
- Whether the appeal to this segment might turn off customers in other segments.

These implementation issues will come into sharp focus at the end of the study when the results are presented. Even if an opportunity is identified, management will be frustrated by the lack of specifics to help decide whether and how to pursue it.

If, however, a careful effort is made to develop a decision scenario in advance, the researchers will be able to design a study that leaves fewer loose ends and actually supports an action by management. Management should start with a list of all the decision alternatives. A helpful second step is to develop hypothesis tables in which an effort is made to define the alternative research results. Use these to lay out the decision alternatives that will be chosen with each specific result and to make sure that you have thought through the implications of all likely results. Only collect information that does support a decision, and be sure to collect all the information needed for a quality decision.

As results are hypothesized and their implications for decision making explored, the original view of the decision may be called into question. Andreasen recommends a "recycling" in which you take advantage of this to reformulate the decision and develop a second generation of results hypotheses. Collaboration between researcher and manager is helpful in this "what if" process, and the researcher can refine the study design considerably at the same time management refines the decision model. It probably will work best to have the researcher prepare the hypothetical results and for management and researcher to review the decision model in light of the results table together. Note: One likely finding at this stage is that management will tend to make some decisions the same way regardless of the results of the study. If you know this in advance, you can avoid the cost of gathering the information.

The implementation of backward market research requires management to participate in a lengthy and careful analysis of decision alternatives. It requires researchers to prepare dummy tables, drafts of all questions, and so forth to support the analysis of how results will affect decisions. It takes a lot more work than usually goes into ordering a study. But the likelihood of firms doing fewer and better studies as a result seems well worth the trouble. And while the method was first proposed in 1985, I assure you that your firm can still be the first in its industry to implement it. Research continues to be done forward — and it continues in its failure to support direct management action.

Reference

Alan R. Andreasen, "Backward Market Research," *Harvard Business Review*, May/June 1985: 176–182.

BOZELL, JACOBS' TWO-WAY FOCUS GROUPS

Applications

- Supporting creative development of advertising when ads are directed to two or more constituencies.
- Exploring attitudes and possible misconceptions in the relationship between two related markets, such as doctors and patients.

Procedures

1. Run conventional focus groups for each of the constituencies of interest. Use the results to identify issues in the relationship among the groups.
2. Run a second round of focus groups in which members of one constituency observe a focus group from the other constituency; then participate in a focus group that addresses the issues from step 1.
3. Use the results to illuminate attitudes of each constituency or group toward the other, to find out how one group reacts to new information about the other group's perceptions and behavior, and to develop creative themes that build on this information.

Cross Reference

See "Fireking's Channel Management Strategy" in Chapter 10 for a method that might benefit from this type of research.

The New York firm of Bozell, Jacobs, Kenyon & Eckhardt developed this research technique to help them explore attitudes of doctors and patients for a study of drugs designed to treat arthritis. Conventional focus groups revealed that patients did not feel doctors talked to them enough. Follow-up focus groups with doctors suggested they were not aware of this problem and in general did not understand what patients were thinking. While these findings were interesting, the firm felt that more insight was needed, which led them to try a focus group of patients in which doctors were observers. Immediately following, a focus group was held with the doctors who had observed the patient focus group. According to Michael Silverstein, marketing director of

Bozell, Jacobs, "The effect of the patient group on the physicians was startling. They emerged from behind the viewing room's one-way glass flushed and glassy-eyed. ... We knew we had a wining technique when . . . we saw the transforming effect the patient group had on the physicians."

A number of insights emerged from the two-way focus group. For example, it turns out doctors assume patients "put control of their pain" into the doctor's hands. Not so; the patients want to feel that they can control their own pain, which means that more information from doctors and a sense of sharing in decisions is important to them. And it means that they try many over-the-counter medications even when they are in a doctor's care. The method revealed that doctors were shocked to hear patients talk about their use of many over-the-counter medications that may interact negatively with prescribed medications.

Other Applications. Bozell, Jacobs has subsequently found the method useful with other pharmaceuticals (example: to understand parent/child influences in choice of analgesic) and telephone systems (example: sophisticated versus casual users' perceptions of services). They also see applications in "closing the gap between financial consultants and investors, retail store mangers and shoppers, and franchisees and customers." Whenever you market to, or through, multiple groups whose interests and perceptions may differ, a two-way focus group is likely to reveal misunderstandings, conflicts, and other surprises that can form a basis for novel product positioning and creative advertising.

Another possible application is managing distribution channels and developing promotions and advertising targeted at multiple parties in a channel. Conflict, misunderstanding, and unexpected purchase influences may all be found in distribution channels, and knowledge of them may provide insight into the creation of promotions and advertising.

Reference

Michael Silverstein, "Two-Way Focus Groups Can Provide Startling Information," *Marketing News*, January 4, 1988, p. 31.

COMPUTER-ASSISTED TELEPHONE INTERVIEWING

Applications

- Reviewing CATI system capabilities to decide whether to acquire/use one.
- Designing questionnaires and market studies for a CATI system.

Procedures

Review the types of CATI systems and their characteristics. Use the Census Bureau Checklist of CATI Capabilities to identify options when designing research projects or instruments.

CATI Systems

Computer-assisted data collection has much to recommend it. The dreadful interim step of coding responses into a computer program for analysis is eliminated. Checking and feedback can be built into systems for interviewers. Research instruments can be considerably more flexible and complex, since the computer is immune to confusion. Computers also make it possible to reduce bias and cost by eliminating the interviewer entirely—a mixed blessing, I suppose, like any automation is. In any event, a number of academicians and research firms are developing surveys in which respondents simply input their opinions directly into a computer, either through a keyboard or through various simplified interfaces such as joy sticks or levers. No doubt some of these methods will be of importance in the future, but right now computers are of greatest importance in telephone interviewing.

There are several different schools of thought when it comes to computer-assisted telephone interviewing, or CATI. They are reflected in three different formats for questionnaire design, and it is important to decide which format your project requires, and sometimes you also need to know which your research firm's facility is set up for, before designing a questionnaire.

Item Based. These are linear or sequential systems in which the screen displays a single question at a time, waiting for the answer to be input before the next item is displayed. Branching is controlled by the computer, so the interviewer has no opportunity to mess it up. This style is very clear and simple, as it only displays a single question on screen at any one time and the cursor is automatically positioned for answering. The interviewer has an opportunity to edit an answer while it is on screen, but not later. Good for fast, simple questionnaires and easy to train interviewers in its use.

Screen Based. You can fill each screen with related questions, but in all other ways this format is like an item-based format. Branching is controlled by the programmer, not the interviewer, and a specified sequence of questions must be followed (of course, in any computer-based system, you can program in rotation to eliminate order bias). The screen orientation can be helpful when a questionnaire requires interviewer knowledge of previous answers, for example, in probing. Each screen can be made analogous to a page of a printed questionnaire, which helps avoid confusion with some of the more complex question structures. For example, it is very good with fill-in tables.

Form Based. Here the computer screen is analogous to a form, and the interviewer can fill in the form in any order. Cursor movement and editing is nonsequential in order to make this possible. (In fact, editing is often held until an entire screenful of form has been completed.) The added flexibility form-based CATI systems provide is really for the benefit of the respondent, not the interviewer. In some cases, information is available in different order from different respondents—for example, accounting information from a company will come in the order of the company's reports, not the interviewer's questions.

Newer systems often allow choice among these three modes. In other words, you can design a questionnaire that is item-based, but switches to a form-based section to collect background information such as company purchasing patterns. In some cases you can split the screen to show a form-based display of information already collected, which can be corrected or used for reference as the interviewer follows an item-based questionnaire on the other half of the screen.

CATI systems also allow greater flexibility in scripting. Scripts can be personalized to the respondent based on an existing database or based on their answers to previous questions. This and the other options discussed add up to greater flexibility in questionnaire design. A wide variety of unconventional and creative approaches are made possible, and it is useful to be aware of how CATI systems work in order to take full advantage of these new options in questionnaire format and design.

Here is a list of six capabilities offered by modern CATI systems, developed by William Nicholls of the U.S. Bureau of the Census.

Census Bureau Checklist of CATI Capabilities

1. *Sample management.* The entire process, from selecting the next prospect to updating the file with status information and maintaining links between input and output data, is performed by the computer system.

2. *Online call scheduling and case management.* The list can be managed by the system to reflect your preferences. Systems usually allow you to define priorities, sequences, and timing, which avoids accidental or purposeful biases introduced by interviewers as they select the next prospect in manual systems. It also makes complex priority and timing schemes feasible.

3. *Online interviewing.* Screen-based interviewer instructions, scripts, and so forth are all possible. Review the description of item-based, screen-based, and form-based CATI systems for details. Also note that skipping and branching structures are programmed into the system, allowing them to be based on any logical evaluation of the information collected. This means, for example, that mathematical computations may be used to drive branching and skipping patterns, since the interviewer does not have to understand or perform the computations.

4. *Online monitoring.* Auto monitoring is fairly common in manual systems, and a CATI system makes it possible for the supervisor to see a duplicate of the interviewer's screen display as well. This is like looking over the interviewer's shoulder without being seen. It is easy to detect misunderstandings leading to improper data entry and other errors that cannot be detected through audio monitoring alone.

5. *Automatic record keeping.* A CATI system can be programmed to track any useful information, from the length of each call to response rates.

6. *Preparation of data sets.* A CATI system spits out data files in whatever form is needed for processing and analysis.

References

William L. Nicholls, II, "Computer-Assisted Telephone Interviewing: A General Introduction," in *Telephone Survey Methodology*, eds. Robert Groves et al. (New York: John Wiley, 1988). Also see, in the same book, Michael F. Weeks (of the Research Triangle Institute) on the eight key components of a CATI Call Scheduling System, p. 405, in "Call Scheduling with CATI: Current Capabilities and Methods." And see Carol C. House and William Nicholls, "Questionnaire Design for CATI: Design Objectives and Methods." Their Checklist of Specification Topics on page 424 is useful.

Applications

- Comparing your company's competitor intelligence (CI) system with those of other companies.
- Identifying common problems and complaints with the CI function to design a better system.

Procedures:

Review the findings of the survey as background information. Also look at the description of four common forms of CI systems for ideas on how to design or improve a system.

Findings

Competitor intelligence was the hot new research technique of the 1980s. Where is it now? A recent Conference Board survey of 300 managers in marketing and sales reveals that competitor intelligence is now gathered at most companies, but that many systems are simplistic and misunderstandings about competitor intelligence persist. Here are the Conference Board's most interesting findings from the survey and a related study:

- Almost all marketing, sales, and planning managers consider it important to monitor competitors.
- Senior managers, however, consider it less important.
- The majority of competitor intelligence systems are not well developed.
- Many managers believe that it is very difficult to obtain competitor intelligence, when actually a good system will provide so much data that the main problem becomes identifying the most important information.
- Many managers continue to confuse competitor intelligence with general marketing research, not realizing that competitor intelligence can provide detailed insight into

competitor actions, plans, and motives. They may mistakenly "be inclined to think the company already has most of the information it needs to support strategic decisions."

- Information on competitor pricing, strategies, and sales are the most useful outputs from competitor intelligence systems for most managers.

- There are four common types of competitor intelligence systems:

    1. Competitor intelligence is gathered by the sales or marketing manager and staff. The emphasis is on collecting information and rumor from the sales force and distributors.

    2. A central office manages the collection, analysis, storage, and distribution of competitor information under the direction of a corporate or divisional competitor intelligence manager.

    3. Electronic network is used to communicate news about competitors among a network of managers.

    4. A team of managers from various departments is assembled on an ad hoc basis to analyze competitor information and provide interpretations and recommendations to upper management.

Sales Force Information

The Conference Board survey also revealed that the sales force is considered the most important source of information about competitors. Any company with an in-house sales force can take advantage of their regular contacts with customers and competitors' sales force to find out what the word is "on the street." A competitor intelligence system I developed for one large company is representative of the techniques used to gather and analyze sales force opinion and information. The company's large sales force called on industrial businesses, competing closely with a half-dozen national companies and many regionals. The local sales offices were linked to corporate headquarters via an electronic network, and each local sales office was required to provide a weekly report on competitor activities (the content of the report was not specified, however, and in practice most offices would not provide much information unless something unusual took place or something new was learned).

The raw data from these reports piled up rapidly, and nobody wanted to read them. So an analyst was given the job of sorting the reports by competitor, looking for patterns, and summarizing the raw data in a short weekly report to managers. The electronic transmission of the data from field offices made it possible to provide managers with day-old competitor intelligence, which was useful as an early warning system. For example, it frequently gave early warning of a new discounting or marketing program, allowing management to develop a counter strategy in time to respond effectively.

The weekly management reports were also utilized to prepare more long-term appraisals of competitor strategy during the preparation of marketing plans and strategic plans.

Another system developed for a large business-to-business company allowed management to gather detailed information about competitors' training programs and sales policies and procedures. A questionnaire was sent to all salespeople who had been working with the company for less than two years. It asked them to list previous employers and positions. Those who had worked in sales positions with major competitors were contacted and asked by a staff person (who should not be too closely associated with their supervisor) whether they would like to volunteer to answer some anonymous questions about their former employer. In practice, employees are generally quite willing to provide whatever information they can remember, and are often surprised to learn that management is interested in it.

References

"Keeping Up with Competitor Intelligence" *The Conference Board's Management Briefing: Marketing*, Vol 3, August/September 1988.

Howard Sutton, *Competitive Intelligence*, Conference Board Report (New York, 1988), p. 913.

ETHNOGRAPHIC RESEARCH METHODS

*If the goal of a study involves looking
at behavior in context, ethnography
should be used.*

—Hy Mariampolski

Applications

- Studying aspects of consumer attitude and behavior that are not reported accurately by respondents in surveys.
- Obtaining insights for new product development and marketing through "fly on the wall" observation.

Procedures

Review the background information on ethnographic research methods. Use QualiData Research's guidelines for designing a specific study (see the list of five guidelines following).

Background

Ethnographic techniques have recently been borrowed from social anthropologists to give marketers a new qualitative research tool when in-depth interviews or focus groups are inadequate. This is the case when it is important to "enter the subject's world" to see exactly how people interact socially, how they use a product, how slang is used in a particular context, or how a product fits into a ritualized pattern of behavior. In other cases it is necessary to enter the subject's world simply because it is difficult to get them to enter the researcher's world. The elderly, handicapped, busy executives, and other groups can be very difficult to recruit for a focus group or reach for a survey, so observational research is the only practical alternative.

Traditional ethnographic research involves a long-term effort to become accepted in a community, permitting both passive observation and in-depth one-on-one interviews once trust has been established. The length of an ethnographic study, combined with the fact that studies traditionally involve only a single observer, makes the method unsuitable for marketing. However, when a larger team is used, and observations are condensed into a short time period, the method becomes practical (at the possible expense of a deep understanding of the culture under study). Ethnographic market research makes use of videotape, tape recordings, and still photographs when possible to speed the collection of information and provide documentation for managers during the presentation of results.

Observers face the challenging task of noting behavior and its context—observers will definitely benefit from training in this method or at least will require experience in other forms of qualitative research.

QualiData's Ethnography Guidelines

Mr. Mariampolski, president of QualiData Research, Inc., suggests the following guidelines for ethnographic studies:

1. Close collaboration between researcher/research firm and decision makers is important in the development stage.
2. A long lead time is needed for ethnographic research projects.
3. Subjects need to be recruited as in any qualitative study, but in addition they should be selected for high motivation.
4. Subjects need to be given detailed information about the study and its objectives.
5. Plan photography or videotaping in advance, obtain permission from subjects, and have them sign releases if there is any chance you will want to use pictures of them later.

Examples

Young & Rubicam has used this method successfully for in-home studies of packaging and product use, where it gives researchers a rich source of information about how people use and store products and how different products interact within the home setting. This is a complex environment, and the close observation made possible by ethnographic studies helps identify product uses and problems and link them to specific behaviors and uses. Benefits: Ads are more consistent with reality; observations are a good source of new product ideas. Y&R's ethnographic research has included in-home studies of parent-child interactions and an investigation of the "new traditional woman" who has left the work force to raise children but plans to return. (See the Alsop article for details.)

QualiData Research has used the method to help a health management organization study the medical needs of the elderly, and has also studied the records management departments of banks, hospitals, and other organizations using the method. In the records management study, ethnographic techniques were helpful in discovering that many departments used multiple, incompatible computer systems, and were therefore especially receptive to any new products that either tied into existing systems or actually reduced their number and complexity.

Traditional Ethnographic Research

Because this method represents adaptation of traditional methods from social anthropology, it may be useful to present the standard method as conventionally practiced in this field. A researcher from Harvard University has used standard ethnographic techniques to study organizational culture. The procedure involved a several-week period in which the author acted as a nonparticipatory observer and waited until subjects grew accustomed to her presence. The data collected prior to this time are considered likely to be biased by the observer. According to the researcher, Alice Sapienza, "as it became clear to all that a "nonparticipant observer" was just that, the author found she was no longer even noticed for the remaining months." Clearly, the objectivity of the method depends on achieving this invisibility, and the truncated versions of ethnographic studies used in marketing are at risk for this reason.

The second feature of conventional ethnographic research is the use of unstructured interviews to explore topics of interest to the researcher. Interviews are conducted with certain subjects once trust has been established, and usually a series of interviews is conducted with the same individual in order to explore issues and questions arising from previous interviews or from observations. Here also the market researcher may compromise the method by shortening it, as multiple follow-up interviews are not practical in a short-term study.

References

Hy Mariampolski, "Ethnography Makes Comeback as Research Tool," *Marketing News*, January 4, 1988, pp. 32 and 44.

Alice M. Sapienza, "Imagery and Strategy," *Journal of Management*, Vol. 13, 1987: pp. 543–555; a description of the ethnographic method appears on pp. 545–549.

Ronald Alsop, "People Watchers Seek Clues to Consumers' True Behavior," *The Wall Street Journal*, September 4, 1986.

G.M. RESEARCH INFORMATION SYSTEM

Applications

- Improving utilization of information from market research.
- Planning and systematizing the application of research results.
- Auditing use of information to improve future research and reporting.

Procedures

Review the descriptions of information system functions and compare them with your organization's approach. If (as is likely to be the case) your organization does not systematize the evaluation, dissemination, and use of research as well as G.M. does, consider either "plugging the holes" by adopting formal mechanisms where the greatest gaps exist, or actually revamping the entire system to incorporate all the functions/methods described here.

Vincent Barabba, the executive director of market research and planning at General Motors Corporation, sees the research process as consisting of five steps:

1. Assessment of marketing information needs
2. Measurement of the marketplace (the actual research is performed here)
3. Storage, retrieval, and display of the data
4. Description and analysis of the information
5. Evaluation of the research and its utility

The interesting thing about his approach is that data collection is only one-fifth of the process. A great deal of attention is given to what happens after the data are gathered, and this attention benefits G.M. by ensuring that information reaches managers in usable form and that feedback from the managers reaches researchers so that future studies can be even more relevant.

The focus of this chapter is steps 4 and 5, in which the results of the research move from raw data in tabular form on to meaningful analysis, reports, and feedback. Many firms will benefit by giving a little extra attention to these steps, and G.M.'s approach will be instructive to those who do.

Description and Analysis of Market Information

This activity consists of a number of analytical functions, and each is described in the paragraphs that follow. Note the division of the analysis and report generation into four separate functions, to be performed sequentially. This approach ensures thorough analysis and summarizing of the data before any inferences are drawn, and requires thorough analysis, hypothesis testing, and generation of forecasts before the findings are used for decision making. Note also the involvement of decision makers at several of these stages. At G.M., decision makers presumably get the information they need because of this participation.

Descriptive Analysis. Basic statistical analyses are performed, as appropriate, and plots and graphs are prepared. Perform this work before data reduction and to aid in exploring the results. Output should be a summary of data.

Data Reduction. This activity uses techniques such as factor analysis, principal components analysis, and cluster analysis to generate product positioning maps. It may also be part of the exploration process, and should precede the inference stage. Recognize that it often takes longer than the descriptive analysis, and should involve collaboration between analysts and users of information. Output generally includes product positioning maps and other graphics, and an increased "knowledge of structure of underlying relationships in the data."

Inference. This activity uses techniques such as hypothesis testing and regression analysis to gain insight into the marketing environment of relevance to decision making. It is best undertaken in special studies directed at specific questions or hypotheses and requires good collaboration between research function and decision makers. Output may be specialized reports and insights that support prediction and decision making. Note that this stage is not initiated until descriptive analysis and data reduction have provided the information platform needed to do it well.

Prediction. This activity uses conjoint analysis, regression, smoothing techniques, and other methods to produce forecasts of relevance to decision makers (depending upon the nature of the data). Collaboration with users is of obvious importance. The output of descriptive analysis, data reduction, or inference may be used in forecasting.

Decision Making. While decisions are obviously made by the appropriate managers, the continued involvement of research personnel is less obvious. However, at G.M. the researchers need to understand the management decisions resulting from their studies in order to perform the functions described here.

Evaluation of the research and assessment of its usefulness consists of six functions that focus on the value and impact of the research for specific management decisions. Evaluation and assessment is concluded after the research, but it must be initiated at the beginning of a research project. The activities described next are carried on concurrent with research and analysis. Note that not all of them need to be used in any one study, and Barabba actually indicates that the use of some of them is fairly low. However, research and decision making both benefit from the inclusion of activities from this list, and this is probably a case of more is better.

Action Audits. Barabba's instructions are, "For each contemplated action, develop a set of research questions to determine its soundness." This requires a collaboration between managers and researchers before the project in order to identify specific actions or decisions that will be influenced by the research. In essence, G.M. engages in "backward market research" as described on page 242 of this book. The output should be an inventory of possible actions. This step requires a short meeting between researcher and manager. Problem: In some cases mangers are not willing to disclose possible actions.

Simulation of Final Results. The goal of this step is to rehearse the use of the research before the data are collected (simulated results are prepared by researchers). It is a way to hash out issues relating to the study and identify problems with the study design before the actual research is undertaken, and it fits in well with action audits. It is likely to lead to improvements in the selection of research instruments and also to give researchers better ideas about how to report the results.

Discrepancy Analysis. This method involves predicting the findings before performing the research, and then analyzing the discrepancies. Managers need to participate, but only briefly, in order to generate the predictions. Gather the predictions from managers after the research has been performed, but before it has been distributed (so that you know exactly what data they will be receiving and in what format). The output is a measure of the value of the information—if it was predicted accurately, it is of relatively low value, while a large discrepancy indicates that the information is of high value.

Assess Market Research Project. Barabba sums up the problems associated with research when he says that "Information is dysfunctional if it is technically flawed, misleading, irrelevant, poorly presented, incorrectly interpreted, or deliberately misconstrued." Yes, but, how do you make sure none of these problems arise, and how do you diagnose them when they do? The care taken in previous steps to ensure relevant and valuable information helps. However, it is also important to audit the research after the project is complete and find out whether any problems occurred. The method Barabba cites uses an auditor to quiz relevant managers (focus on all those who are the audience and/or use the information in decisions). Make sure all of the possible problems described in Barabba's quote are probed for. The output should include not only managers' gripes but a translation of these into guidelines for future projects. The auditor may find managers less than candid; a method ensuring anonymity may help with this problem.

Reference

Vincent P. Barabba, "The Market Research Encyclopedia," *Harvard Business Review*, January/February 1990: 105–116. Note: These methods will be covered in depth in a forthcoming book by Vincent P. Barabba and Gerald Zaltman, *Market Based Decision Making*, Harvard Business School Press, Boston.

THE PRIMARY RESEARCH TECHNIQUE SELECTOR

Applications

- Selecting the appropriate primary research technique.

- Considering the pros and cons of a technique and evaluating alternatives, that is, when reviewing a research proposal.

- Developing a detailed pro/con analysis as a preliminary to undertaking a particular project.

Procedures

Refer to the descriptions of specific techniques and their pros and cons in order to evaluate them. In the definition stage of a research project, review each of the techniques to find the one that is most appropriate to your situation and needs. When proposing or considering a specific technique, combine the pros and cons given here with cost/bid data and other situation-specific information to develop a formal pro/con analysis.

Researchers often have to balance the pros and cons of alternative research techniques in order to select the best one for a study. Here the pros and cons are described in detail to provide a generalizable strengths/weaknesses analysis for each technique. The analysis of each method is based on the author's experience and the advice of professional market researchers. If your company's experience with a certain technique suggests an additional strength or weakness, you might want to jot it down in the margin to make this list even more applicable to your specific situation.

Customizing Your Analysis

A strengths/weakness analysis is a good tool whenever research programs are designed or evaluated. There is a general tendency to use the same research firms and the same types of surveys for each project, but a careful strengths/weaknesses analysis before each could indicate that different techniques are advisable. Idea: Use these lists as the starting point for your own analysis. Work out cost estimates for different methods, and draw on your company's previous experiences and the knowledge of your research firms to determine what biases might apply for each method and how serious they are. Also assess your need for imagination-stimulating information versus cold hard numbers. Combine all this situation-specific analysis to develop a customized list of pros and cons for each method under consideration, using the following as your starting point.

Probabilistic Sample Survey Methods
(Produce Quantitative Output)

SELF-ADMINISTERED MAIL SURVEYS

Pro: Low cost (typically $5–10 per completed interview). Can cover wide area. Large sample size possible. Incentives can be effective at boosting response rates.

Con: Limited by quality of list. Low response rates (typically 5–25%) and potential for bias high as a result. Item non-response is common. Long field time. No probing possible.

TELEPHONE SURVEYS

Pro: Fast. Complex, flexible questionnaires are possible. Interviewer can be instructed to probe. Item nonresponse is uncommon. Respondents can be qualified accurately.

Con: Response rates vary widely, and can go as low as 20%. Difficult to exceed 15 minutes per survey. Cost per completed interview averages about $20, but can go as high as $100. Bias related to difficulty of reaching portions of the population by telephone is possible.

PERSONAL INTERVIEWS (IN-HOME OR AT RESEARCH CENTER)

Pro: High response rate—often 75% and up. Lengthy and complex interviews are possible. Probing and many open-ended questions are possible. Low item nonresponse rates. Minimizes misinterpretation of questions. Respondents can be shown a product, then questioned about it.

Con: Interview bias is likely. Requires large field staff and costs $100 to $500 per completed interview. Difficult to control interview quality.

Nonprobabilistic Studies
(Quantitative or Nonquantitative Output)

CONVENIENCE SAMPLES (PAPER-AND-PENCIL OR INTERCEPT INTERVIEW FORMAT CONDUCTED AT CONVENIENT HIGH-TRAFFIC LOCATION)

Pro: Inexpensive and fast. Does not require a priori knowledge of target or formal list development.

Con: Sample likely to be biased. Long and complex surveys are impossible. Often difficult to project results to a larger population.

FOCUS GROUP (STRUCTURED GROUP DISCUSSION USING A FACILITATOR AND SPECIALLY DESIGNED ROOM THAT ALLOWS UNDETECTED OBSERVATION AND VIDEOTAPING)

Pro: Possible to probe deeply and explore attitudes and beliefs. Good for evaluating new concepts. Group dynamics often of interest. Helps managers understand respondents' attitudes.

Con: Difficult to project results to a larger population. Facilitator bias is common. Uncooperative or overly outspoken participants can ruin a session (plan to do more than one). A bad moderator can ruin the entire project— management needs to participate in review and selection of moderator.

PRODUCT CLINIC (INTERVIEWING AT A CENTRAL LOCATION; MAY BE SELF-ADMINISTERED OR PERSONAL)

Pro: Puts the actual product in the consumer's hands prior to evaluation. Allows researchers to control conditions. Can be used to simulate usage or purchase conditions. Can provide unexpected insights into consumer attitude or behavior. A good intermediate step when new product design or packaging needs refinement prior to a test market. Can be designed to use a representative sample and produce generalizable results.

Con: Costly and often logistically complex. The clinic rarely simulates actual purchase and usage conditions accurately, and results are sometimes biased as a result.

Purchase-Oriented Studies
(Usually Nonprobabilistic, Qualitative and Quantitative Output)

SIMULATED TEST MARKET (CENTRAL LOCATION(S); USES MOCK-UP OF RETAIL ENVIRONMENT)

Pro: The closest thing to a real test market. A way to evaluate in-store purchase behavior without the cost of a full test market. Less likely to alert competitors to your intentions than a full-blown test market. Allows control over sample. Postshopping interviews and surveys can be conducted easily. Faster and less costly than test market.

Con: Does not give the feedback on promotional strategies that a real test market can. The simulated retail environment may introduce undetected biases. Does not allow assessment of competitor response. Sales projections based on simulated test markets may be inaccurate. Gives no information about trade response and difficulty of achieving desired shelving.

TEST MARKET

Pro: The best test of product performance in the marketplace. Results can give early warning of problems before rollout. Allows testing of packaging, advertising and promotional strategies, and other marketing variables. Can provide a solid basis for forecasting market performance. Allows comparison of performance versus key competitors.

Con: Costly and time consuming. Often stimulates competitor response, both in product development and marketing. Heavy promotions and dumping by competitors can make results hopelessly biased. "Leakage" of marketing outside of test market can confuse consumers. Can be difficult to find test markets that truly represent national markets.

Reference

See Vincent P. Barabba, "The Market Research Encyclopedia," *Harvard Business Review*, January/February 1990: 105–116, for another approach to identifying research needs.

PROJECTIVE TECHNIQUES

Applications

- Qualitatively exploring attitudes and feelings that are difficult to verbalize.
- Testing ad visuals.
- Exploring attitudes toward products when you suspect there is something more to the story than what was revealed by conventional product testing and surveys.

Procedures

Procedures vary and are described in the context of specific techniques. Readers should use this chapter as a guide to available techniques and thinking on the subject, and should pursue techniques that interest them by reading the referenced sources and seeking qualified research firms.

Projective research techniques present a subject with a vague stimulus and ask the subject to build some structure, image, or idea around this stimulus. In the process, the subject must project his or her personal attitudes and feelings onto the stimulus, since it is too vague and ambiguous to provide all the information needed. A good projective test will make it easy for the subject to do this—it will overcome emotional barriers to projecting personal attitudes and beliefs. Often projective research asks subjects to describe someone else in order to end-run the inhibitions against revealing one's own personality and beliefs.

In many cases marketers need to know not only what consumers think about a product, but also what consumers think about themselves. As Mason Haire, one of the originators of projective market research, puts it, "When we ask questions . . . about the product we are very often asking also about the respondent. Not only do we say "What is _____ product like?" but, indirectly "What are you like?" Our responses are often made up of both elements interwoven." The problem, of course, is that respondents are not very good about telling us what they are like. Projective techniques give researchers a way to explore this side of the equation in depth, and are likely to provide insights of use in advertising, packaging, product positioning, and product development as a result.

While the foregoing introduction to the method explains the concept adequately, it is unfortunately analogous to a projective test in that it leaves the reader to figure out most of the details of how actually to design and run a test. The area is broad, and the methods infrequently used, so there are no step-by-step instructions for researchers to follow. However, it may be useful to review some of the successful applications of the method to find an appropriate model or at least to provide a context for developing an original projective test that is better suited to your specific needs. Descriptions of a variety of tests follow.

Guide to Projective Techniques

Word Association Tests use a simple device to explore subjects' feelings about specific words and topics. These tests present a list of words, one at a time, asking respondents to say what word comes to mind immediately upon seeing each word on the list. According to Dillon et al., "The respondent's response and the time it takes to respond are recorded and analyzed according to the frequency with which a response is given, the amount of time elapsed, and the number of respondents unable to respond within the time allowed. Elapsed time is important because hesitation could indicate that the respondent was searching for a "socially acceptable" response.

The **Shopping List Test** is described by Haire in the referenced article. The design involves two groups of subjects, each exposed to a shopping list that is identical in every way except that one item differs. For example, Haire used the technique to study consumer attitudes toward instant coffee back when it was first introduced. Individuals in one group were asked to describe a woman based on a grocery list that included Nescafé instant coffee, and the other group did the same with a grocery list that had Maxwell House drip ground coffee on it instead of the instant coffee.

Earlier surveys had suggested that taste was the main reason for consumers' dislike of the instant coffee. However, the projective study revealed negative attitudes toward the woman who bought instant coffee—participants viewed her as "lazy, a spend-thrift, a poor wife, and as failing to plan well for her family." A careful follow-up proved that these negative attitudes were correlated with nonpurchase of instant coffee, and that those who did purchase instant coffee were likely to incorporate excuses for the purchase into their description of the "grocery-list woman" in the projective test. These excuses, for example, that she was a busy professional woman, provided a useful angle for advertisers to use in trying to overcome negative attitudes toward use of the product.

The Shopping List Test is sometimes classified as an example of **Third Person Tests** because an endless variety of tests can be devised in which respondents are asked to describe the feelings or beliefs of a third party, as in the Shopping List Test. Any written or visual description of a person and situation can be used to elicit projective feelings from subjects.

Thematic Aperception Tests are used by a variety of firms, often in the form of cartoons in which one of the speech bubbles has been left blank for the respondent to fill in. The cartoon is generally designed to be neutral—it does not make a positive or negative statement about the product, service, or behavior in question. The cartoon usually shows an action scene, requiring the respondent to complete the scenario or decide where the action is going. A similar test in concept is the **Unfinished Scenario Technique,** in which respondents are given a written description of a scenario with blanks to fill in.

Solutions Marketing Research (now part of Executive Solutions) is one of the new firms that makes extensive use of projective research, and its president, Sharon Livingston, described the techniques used by the firm in the referenced **Marketing News** article and speech. Techniques include:

The **Modified TAT** is a modification of the thematic aperception tests used in psychology (and sometimes in market research). It presents subjects with "an unbranded visual" that is under consideration for an advertisement. Subjects are asked to create a story based on the visual image, and the moderator guides them toward an exploration of the feelings and associations the image suggests through such questions as, "What are these people thinking about? How do they feel? What will they do next?" The test can be repeated after a brand name and copy have been added to explore the impact. The test can also be repeated to compare different versions of an ad and see which ones have the strongest and most positive associations. Interestingly, Sharon Livingston reports that "people from different segments of the population tell similar stories about the same photos or images."

In **"The Looking Glass"** (Solutions Marketing Research considers this name proprietary, but the technique can certainly be adapted and used by others provided the trademark is not used), the technique explores attitudes toward and positioning of brands. Participants are asked to imagine "the kind of door that would bear the imprint of a particular brand name. Subjects are then asked to walk through their imagined door and experience what's behind it," according to Livingston. How solid and attractive the door is, or how plain, shabby, and poorly maintained, will depend on how positive or negative the feelings about the brand are. This technique can be used in a focus group setting.

Group Storytelling is a guided effort by the group to fictionalize common experiences and attitudes. Livingston uses it in conjunction with The Looking Glass as follows:

> We often start with The Looking Glass, and lead respondents to a door labeled with the core concept. Respondents are invited to cross the threshold, guided through their experiences and then welcomed back into the room to jot down a summary of what happened on the other side of the door. They are then instructed to create a group story, including timing, setting, characters, plot and resolve with the same title as the core concept. The story must be based on the commonalities experienced by all or most, yet be garnished with flourishes of individual differences.

Laddering, or one-on-one interviews, is used to explore product benefits. The interviewer presents a basic statement of a practical benefit of the product ("This _____ brand of automobile provides transportation."). The respondent is then asked to list two additional benefits. For each of the benefits they identify, they are asked to come up with two more. This format is followed through as many as four rounds (giving a total of 16 benefits in the fourth round), or until the interviewer feels that the psychological and symbolic benefits of the brand have been fully explored. Respondents typically work from the more practical, tangible benefits to the more abstract and personal, with self-esteem–oriented benefits mentioned last. (This technique is sometimes called benefit chain analysis.)

Sentence Completion exercises can be used to explore attitudes and beliefs of relevance to an advertising or positioning strategy, either in a group setting or in one-on-one interviews. Livingston gives as an example the sentence, "Mother always said toothpaste . . . " and recommends having respondents complete the sentence several times.

Synesthesia asks participants to "fuse their senses and answer questions such as: What does a smooth shave sound, smell, look, and taste like?"

Scent-sations, another proprietary technique developed by Hollander, takes advantage of the fact that "scent can be used to trigger feelings about a particular aromatic product. . . . " For example, the feelings associated with coffee are best explored in the context of coffee's unique aroma. As Livingston explains,

> The respondents are asked to close their eyes and inhale the aroma of [an] unidentified product. This would be used as a catalyst to guide them to an early memory connected to their first use. They are then told the brand name of the product they sniffed to see how that alters their memories and feelings. The results can help marketers understand a product's emotional heritage, both positive and negative.

In **Brand and User Imagery,** participants develop quick descriptions of brand image and user image for comparison. In some cases, brand and user images are quit distinct. In others, the brand image is a role model for the user.

Category Sculpting extends brand imagery to an entire category of brands by having participants develop a family role and a set of character traits for each brand—with the category representing a family and each brand a member of it. The facilitator asks questions that are appropriate to describing a person and her relationship to the other family members. Example: One test labeled the cereal brand Lucky Charms as "The Family Pet," Shredded Wheat as "The Irresponsible Uncle," and Fruit Loops as "The Domineering Mother."

Focus Group Art, by Ziff Associates, Inc. of Winston-Salem, also uses projective techniques in market research, and Kathy Ziff has adapted a variety of art therapy techniques to the focus group setting. Her methodology generally involves "having participants draw pictures of situations involving product or service use" using plain sheets of copier paper and felt-tipped pens or fresh crayons. She recommends that participants be given "at least yellow, red, blue, green, orange, purple, brown, black, and pink" to work with and advises that "the typical drawing exercise last about 10 minutes, including time for drawing and brief descriptions by each participant." The moderator should look for meaning in the drawings through clues offered by use of color, anything odd or different in the way ordinary objects are drawn, the size and proportion of objects, what or who is missing, and what is in the middle of the picture. (She recommends Gregg Furth's *Secret World of Drawings* from Sigo Press for advice on interpreting the results.)

References

See William R. Dillon, Thomas J. Madden, and Neil H. Firtle, *Marketing Research in an Marketing Environment,* 2nd ed. (Homewood, IL: Richard D. Irwin, 1990), pp. 162–163. See also Maison Haire, "Projective Techniques in Marketing Research," *Journal of Marketing,* April

1950: 649–656; Sharon Livingston Hollander, "Projective Techniques Uncover *Real* Consumer Attitudes," *Marketing News,* January 4, 1988, and *Reflections Through the Looking Glass: 10/10 Vision* Speech, ARF, March 8, 1988 (available from Executive Solutions in Locust Valley, NY); and Kathy Ziff, "Focus Group 'Art" Reveals In-Depth Information," *Marketing News,* September 3, 1990: pp. 7 and 20.

SINKULA/HAMPTON STUDY OF MARKET RESEARCH DEPARTMENT STRUCTURE

Applications

- Reorganizing the research function to address problems or improve utilization of information.
- Controlling marketing research in a large organization, especially when research is decentralized.
- Designing or modifying organizational structure and responsibilities within the marketing department to tailor it to specific characteristics of the company and its environment.

Procedures:

1. Compare your organization's structure of the research function to industry norms based on survey results.
2. Identify alternative structures and decide how centralized or decentralized the function is at present.
3. Use the Organizational Problem Solver to find prescriptive advice specific to your organization's situation.

The decision to centralize or decentralize the market research function will have a profound effect on the way information is acquired and used in the firm.

—Sinkula and Hampton

In an interesting study of how the market research department is structured at 87 manufacturing and service companies in the United States, James Sinkula of the University of Vermont and Ronald Hampton of the University of Nebraska found the following:

- The market research function is centralized in the majority of companies, both large and small.

- Centralized research departments acquire more information from external vendors than do companies with decentralized research do. However,
- Companies with centralized research departments "make less use of externally supplied market research information." In other words, they waste more money on information they never apply.

The key organizational issues in market research are, first, whether to decentralize it to divisions and subsidiaries versus managing all research out of the corporate headquarters, and second, whether to subcontract to research firms for most of the information needed versus managing most studies in-house. Firms often adopt a centralized organization, combined with heavy use of subcontracting to the "pros," to improve the quality of research. However, the resulting studies are not necessarily of use to divisional managers, as Sinkula and Hampton's study found.

It is interesting to see that the key issues—extent of centralization and extent of in-house research—are closely related. Centralized market research departments generally use a lot more purchased information. When the function is decentralized, companies are less likely to hire a research firm. And it is striking to note that centralization, with its greater reliance on purchased information, generally produces a lot of unused reports. Perhaps this says something we do not want to hear about the quality of market research firms, but it is more likely to reflect the problems associated with centralized structure. The organization that centralizes its market research runs the risk that "not all decisions can be understood at one center, in one brain," so that the studies commissioned are not necessarily on target. Also, when a dynamic or volatile market requires innovative, rapidly performed research, a centralized department can be disappointingly inflexible and slow. Finally, the centralized department is not necessarily able to bring greater economy or quality to the research when the needs of individual divisions are unique.

These findings suggest many possible reasons for taking some of the research functions away from the corporate office. Sinkula and Hampton argue that managers should consider decentralization a viable option. But there are advantages to centralization as well. It increases the ability of a company to attract top employees to the research function, for example. It can provide economies. And centralization gives senior management greater access to research results.

With this combination of pros and cons, companies could, and do, debate the issue of how centralized to make market research *ad infinitum*. For this reason I have abstracted findings from the Sinkula/Hampton study and several related studies to compile a list of situation-specific prescriptions for organizational structure. When particular problems or complaints surface, use this list to find out what the research suggests is most likely to fix the problem in question.

Market Research Organizational Problem Solver

Dissatisfied with the performance of the market research function? Use this chart to help decide whether centralizing or decentralizing will fix the problem.

ORGANIZATIONAL FACTORS	PRESCRIPTION FOR RESEARCH FUNCTION
Rapid organizational growth	Centralize
Complex, varied research tasks	Decentralize
Dynamic environment	Decentralize
Authoritative decision making	Centralize
Participative decisionmaking	Decentralize
Underutilization of information	Decentralize
Inadequate research/information shortage	Centralize
Overreliance on external vendors	Decentralize
Overreliance on in-house researchers	Centralize
Emphasis on product development	Decentralize

ORGANIZATIONAL FACTORS	*PRESCRIPTION FOR RESEARCH FUNCTION*
Information is broadly applicable within company	Centralize
Information is specific in managers/departments	Decentralize
Costs of in-house research are out of control	Centralize
"Reinventing the wheel" by in-house researchers	Centralize
Low quality of research staff	Centralize

References

James M. Sinkula and Ronald D. Hampton, "Centralization and Information Acquisition by In-House Market Research Departments," *Journal of Business Research*, Vol. 16, 1988: 337–349. See also Rohit Deshpande, "The Organizational Context of Market Research Use," *Journal of Marketing*, Vol. 46, 1982: 91–101.

THOUGHTS ON APPLYING COMPETITOR INTELLIGENCE

Applications

- Making information and reports on competitors more action oriented.
- Increasing the utilization of competitor information by managers.
- Turning intelligence into decision support tools for managers.

Procedures

Review the collected ideas of competitor intelligence experts from various companies for ideas and techniques to apply in your company. Observations from competitor intelligence managers at American Telephone & Telegraph Co., Motorola, Inc., Pfizer, Inc., and Combustion Engineering, Inc., are quoted.

The material in this chapter comes from a conference on competitor intelligence, as reported in a Conference Board publication (see footnote). Many of the speakers addressed the question of how information is utilized, and most agreed that this is an increasingly critical issue. As companies develop databases and networks of sources, they become better at gathering and organizing large amounts of information about their competitors. But how does this information translate into better management and marketing decisions? This is the crucial issue of the 1990s in competitor intelligence, and it is really an internal marketing issue in that it comes down to communicating more effectively with the target audience and providing information services that better meet the audience's needs. The ideas and observations of companies that are wrestling with this issue may be of use in your organization as well. Here are salient quotes from experts who have made progress on the issue.

AT&T

OBSERVATIONS FROM:
BLAINE E. DAVIS, CORPORATE VICE PRESIDENT, STRATEGIC AND MARKET PLANNING

- The issue isn't acquiring enough information.

The issue is: How do you choose from all the information that you've got?

- We provide five-year forecasts, and all the data is sourced from the business units themselves, by the subject matter expert, with executive level sign-off. By that I mean that the responsible executives in the business units say, "This is the information we use to do our planning."

- We issue a competitive digest daily. . . . We select the top four to eight new items of the day, and we ask our experts what the competitive implications are for AT&T and for the industry.

OBSERVATIONS FROM:
MARTIN STARK, COMPETITIVE INFORMATION AND ANALYSIS MANAGER

- In effect, what we have is an electronic directory. . . . I'm not expected to have the answers, but I'm expected to know who in AT&T can supply them. There are very few questions I can't get answered. . . . We enlisted people in our database in a variety of ways. We published notices in company newsletters and electronic media. Probably the most effective way has been to go to a business unit and set up an AAA demonstration—"Access to AT&T Analysts"—in the lobby or just outside the cafeteria. It's a dial-in system, and if we can just sit them down at a PC or terminal and show how it works, we can prove we have information they need.

- We send participants their profile forms four times a year and ask them whether they're up to date . . . one of the entries on the user form is key words. You let us know what words are of interest to you, and we'll keep you up to date on changes in our database. We'll also let you know if other people search on your words of interest.

- The other thing we recently started is a broadcast message. Let's say you hear a rumor about a competitor, so you go into the system and type your message and say, "Send mail to. . . . " The message gets distributed to everyone who has previously expressed interest in that competitor.

- If I get an analysis of a competitor's announcement about a new product and it omits the implications for AT&T, I have to go after the analysts and say, "So what? Does that mean we should change our strategy? Does that mean we should pursue an additional alternative? Does this give us more of an opportunity? Should we proceed quicker?"

Motorola

OBSERVATIONS FROM:
JAN P. HERRING, DIRECTOR OF CORPORATE
ANALYTICAL RESEARCH

- When I met with a general manager, I would ask, "what are the five most important things you need to know about the external world?." . . . From those discussions, I drew up a list of about 35 key intelligence topics and assigned each a priority. That exercise produced the table of contents for our program. . . .

- Too many nice reports on competitors don't say what to do about them; there is no link to action. I'm not saying the analyst has to make the actionable recommendation, but there are ways of producing an analysis that highlights the alternatives, decisions, and actions that the reader should consider.

- Corporations have to go beyond competitor analysis. The most powerful tool I've run into is what I call competitive environmental analysis. You take apart a particular industry and see what's really driving the competition. Is it cost? Is it quality? Is it enabling technology? . . . When you look at the determinants of competition, it's more apparent why companies behave in the way they do. . . . if you're very sensitive to these competitive forces in the environment, you can really get out ahead.

Pfizer

OBSERVATIONS FROM:
WILLIAM L. SAMMON, MANAGER OF COMPETITIVE ANALYSIS, CORPORATE STRATEGIC PLANNING (NOW AT WOOD GUNDY, INC.)

- We try to feed competitive information in whenever we can. For example, we were evaluating a number of small Japanese and Northern European drug companies as potential acquisition candidates. It was decided that the report would include an addendum with an update on the top 40 global pharmaceutical companies that have a major research commitment.

- We've been fairly successful in making competitive analysis a part of the planning process. When managers come up for their annual strategic planning reviews, they know that senior management is going to press them on the competitive situation. They know that, if they try to blow smoke, they're going to be embarrassed. . . . If top management doesn't place that kind of emphasis on competitive intelligence, it is not possible to successfully set up a system.

- In the military, you have two types of briefings. One is an information briefing, and the other is a decision briefing. Both use intelligence. But in a corporation, an information briefing isn't deemed a valuable use of time.

Combustion Engineering

OBSERVATIONS FROM:
JOHN RHODE, VICE PRESIDENT OF MARKETING AND PLANNING, INDUSTRIAL GROUP

- We try to assemble both the business unit's top management team and those people who have competitor intelligence . . . I try to get as many of the management team members involved as possible, because they need to be committed to the strategies we invent. And these strategies have to flow from buying into the competitor analysis.

- When I first took over planning responsibility for the industrial group, one of the things that used to fry me was when a general manager would say, at the end of a planning period, "Boy, I'm glad that's over. Now I can get back to running my business." At first, I used to think, "What's the matter with those guys? . . . Then I realized they were saying that the planning we were doing and the way we were doing it was irrelevant to their decision framework. What was really important was having people in the planning department figure out how to give them decision-making tools.

- The competitive folder is one of the tools we developed. It helps general managers to decide how to react to pricing initiatives by a competitor and how to come up with tactical moves, as well as looking at the long-term strategic situation.

Reference

The Conference Board, *Competitor Intelligence* Conference Board Research Report #913 (New York, 1988) pp. 22–38.

WEYERHAEUSER DETERMINANT ATTRIBUTE ANALYSIS

Determinant attributes are those that are important yet also discriminate well among competing products or materials.

—Sinclair and Stalling

Applications

- Identifying the product (or service) attributes that customers use to differentiate among competing products or services.
- Refining the analysis of attributes to give strategists and marketers more meaningful information.
- Bringing attribute-based research and marketing to industrial markets.

Procedures

1. Develop a list of attributes.
2. Design a survey using the dual question method to capture the needed information concerning attribute importance and differentiation of competitors on each attribute.
3. Conduct the survey.
4. Calculate determinance by weighting attribute importance by perceived difference.
5. If desired, standardize each respondent's determinance scores using the T-score method (formula provided shortly) or a similar method.
6. Evaluate the results to identify the determinant attributes. Statistical significance can be assessed using Z-scores. If data have been cross-tabulated for multiple segments, use multiple discriminant analysis to assess differences between segments.

Marketers of major consumer brands are already expert in attribute analysis and may already have their own approaches to identifying which attributes determine consumer purchase behavior. But the vast majority of marketers are not. Many companies use survey research to identify the attributes consumers associate with a product and to ask consumers to rank these attributes in importance. Sometimes the survey will also ask consumers to rate competing products on these attributes. However, the list of attributes and their importance ratings may not necessarily translate into good marketing strategy. Interpreting the data can be frustrating.

For example, Consolidated Freightways conducted a series of surveys for its different subsidiaries several years ago. The importance ratings for one subsidiary, a less than truckload freight carrier, indicated that a number of service attributes (such as speed, loss and damage, and on-time delivery) were very important. Could the company differentiate itself on these attributes and gain share from its close competitors? Subsequent marketing communications stressed these attributes. But the strategy was limited by the fact that, in general, consumers saw little difference between service levels at Consolidated Freightways and its principal competitors. Probably for this reason, consumers continued to emphasize price in their purchase decisions, and paid less attention to service attributes than management hoped they would.

This problem is frequently encountered in commodity-oriented markets. Determinant attribute analysis helps by assessing the degree to which each attribute actually contributes to the decision. An attribute is only determinant if it differentiates competing products in a meaningful way from the consumer's perspective. It takes the idea of importance one step further, and in fact in some cases determinance and importance do not coincide.

Steven Sinclair of Virginia Polytechnic Institute and Edward C. Stalling of Weyerhaeuser Forest Products Company recently applied the concept of determinant attributes to the forest products industry to develop a better understanding of the markets for siding. Their methodology is broadly applicable and represents the state of the art. It forms the backbone for the following instructions, and their results provide illustrations as well.

1. Develop an attribute list through an exploratory study. An open-ended questionnaire, focus group, panel, or other exploratory research will help overcome any biases the researcher brings to the study. It may be helpful to generate a lengthy list of attributes through brainstorming, and then use exploratory research to bring the list down to a manageable number (the Weyerhaeuser study selected 23 attributes).

2. Design a survey that uses the dual question method to measure determinance. In this method, attributes are rated "in terms of: (1) how important each is thought to be in determining product choice, and (2) how much difference is perceived among the competing products in terms of each attribute," according to Sinclair and Stalling. In practice, this means having respondents rate each attribute's importance on a 5-place scale (ranges from "of no importance" to "critical"). Then they use a 4-point scale to indicate the extent to which competing products differ on each attribute (ranges from "very similar" to "very different").

3. Conduct a survey by mail or telephone. They mailed 3,271 questionnaires to a randomly selected list and received 412 usable returns. If you are concerned about timing or nonresponse errors, telephone interviews are preferable.

4. Calculate determinance by weighting the importance of an attribute by the perceived difference. Multiply the two ratings for each attribute (maximum score $= 4 \times 5 = 20$).

5. Optional. **Standardize each individual's determinance scores.** This creates scores that indicate how determinant each attribute is relative to other attributes for each respondent. This is an important refinement, as it compensates for the possibility that different respondents use the scales differently. It also makes possible the standardization of results so as to make them most easily intelligible by the managers who will base decisions on the information, and the analyst is certainly at liberty to adopt whatever method meets this goal best.

Any number of approaches might be used here, but Sinclair and Stalling use the T-score method, which gives each respondent's scores a mean of 50 and a standard deviation of 10. I will include the T-score formula because it does not appear in most standard references (in fact, it does not even appear in the source article due to a typographer's error—

thanks to Steven Sinclair for providing it!). The formula is as follows:

$$D_i = 10 \left[\frac{(P_i\, I_i - X)}{s} \right] + 50$$

where

D_i = determinance score for attribute i

P_i = perceived difference between competing products along attribute i

I_i = importance of attribute i

X = individual's grand determinance mean, or the mean of $(P)\,(I)$ for all 23 attributes

s = standard deviation of X

(10 and 50 are used to convert from Z-score into T-score.)

6. Evaluate the results. An eyeball approach can be based on the fact that scores deviate from the mean of 50 by standard deviations, making it quite easy to see when a score is fairly high or low (assuming you use the T-score method). A score of 60 is very high—one standard deviation above the mean. A score of 40 is one standard deviation below.

A statistical approach can also be used to identify those attributes with significantly high determinance scores. A recommended approach is to "use a one-tailed Z-test to identify those attributes which are significantly higher than the mean. In this method, the population and standard deviation are estimated with the grand mean from the sample." Z is the number of standard deviations away from the mean, formally defined as:

$$Z = \frac{\text{value} - \text{mean}}{\text{standard deviation}}$$

The probability of Z being greater than (or equal to) any particular value is ascertained by looking it up in a table giving probabilities in the right-hand tail of a standard normal distribution—any self-respecting statistics book contains this table.

If you have gathered survey data on more than one market segment, use multiple discriminant analysis (MDA) to test for differences across the segments (or just calculate separate determinance scores for each segment). MDA is commonly used in segmentation studies by consumer products companies, and discussed in depth in the referenced article by Perreault, Behrman, and Armstrong. It is probably best delegated to a research firm and will not be described in detail here.

7. Focus your strategic thinking. Focus on those attributes with determinance scores that are significantly greater than the grand mean—the ones that test as statistically significant at the 0.05 or 0.10 level using the Z-test. (Base interpretation on F-Test probabilities and the Newman-Keuls test of group differences if your perform MDA.)

In the Weyerhaeuser study of siding materials, 7 of the 23 attributes tested as significantly high. The results for one of the segments studied, single-family home owners, are as follows (other segments = multifamily, siding contractors, and repair and remodel contractors).

DETERMINANCE SCORES, SIDING MATERIAL ATTRIBUTES
SINGLE-FAMILY SEGMENT, WEYERHAEUSER STUDY

Attributes	Mean Determinance Scores
A. Determinant	
High-status/quality image	60.3
Competitive price	53.6
Resistance to impacts/dents	50.8
Beautiful appearance	58.3
Structural strength/rigidity	52.1
Low/easy maintenance	52.5
Weather resistant/long life	55.5
B. Nondeterminant	
Holds stains/paints	52.4
A "natural" material	48.9
Manufacturer service	44.3
Warranty/guarantee	48.4
Wholesaler/retailer service	46.4
Easy to repair	48.8
Variety in available sizes	44.5
Fade resistant	49.4
Thermal insulation	46.7
Wide color selection	46.4
Variety in textures/profiles	46.7
Fire resistance	46.7
Fast/easy application	48.7
Resists mold/mildew	49.1
Dimensional/shape stability	50.8
Availability	48.5

Determinance scores do not correlate closely with importance ratings in this study. For example, availability is not a determinant attribute, but it received one of the highest importance ratings (4 on a 1–5 scale). Retailer service also received a high importance rating but was not a determinant factor. The analysis of determinance is therefore likely to help management avoid the pitfall of focusing attention on retailer service or availability (unless, of course, management thinks it can redefine the market by differentiating on these factors and increasing their determinance scores—an ambitious and possibly foolhardy undertaking).

Some of the determinant attributes do not show up as being especially important, and so could have been overlooked entirely without the determinance analysis. High status/quality image and competitive price are both of only average importance (ratings are around 3.5 on the 1–5 scale), but are highly determinant factors. Why? Evidently consumers see real differences among products on both these dimensions, and are likely to base a purchase decision on these differences. This knowledge will be especially helpful in developing marketing strategy and marketing communications for Weyerhaeuser's siding products.

References

Steven A. Sinclair and Edward C. Stalling, "How to Identify Differences Between Market Segments with Attribute Analysis." *Industrial Marketing Management*, Vol. 19, February 1990: 31–40. See also Mark Alpert, "Identification of Determinant Attributes: A Comparison of Methods, *Journal of Marketing Research*, Vol. 8, May 1971: 184–191; Rowland T. Moriarty and David J. Reibstein, "Benefit Segmentation in Industrial Markets," *Journal of Business Research*, Vol. 14, December 1986: 463–486; and James H. Myers and Mark I. Alpert, "Determinant Buying Attitudes: Meaning and Measurement," *Journal of Marketing*, Vol. 32, October 1968: 18–20.

ZAP-PROOFING ADVERTISING

Applications

- Pretesting ads to eliminate those that are most likely to be zapped, skipped, or ignored (depending upon the medium).

Procedures

Much of the conventional wisdom concerning what works in advertising draws on advertising research in which subjects are not given the option of zapping their TV, turning the page, or tuning out the radio or billboard. Findings from forced-exposure tests of advertising often point to the effectiveness of fact-based ads and product comparisons. But when subjects are given the opportunity to ignore these ads, they usually do. Pretesting Co.'s president, Lee Weinblatt, argues that ads should be pretested under conditions that permit subjects to ignore them. How much attention an ad receives probably is the most important determinant of its effectiveness in today's cluttered, noisy message environment. Pretesting Co. has developed a methodology for evaluating how zapable TV commercials are and a related methodology for print advertisements (these are marketed under the names Simulated Network and PeopleMeter).

The basic concept behind them is that subjects are exposed to commercials in a way that gives them choice, and how they exercise this choice is observed and tracked. Test ads or commercials are inserted into a naturalistic situation in which regular programming (or articles) are combined with both test and control advertising. Subjects are then observed to measure how much time they choose to be exposed to the test ads, and they can also be questioned afterward to measure awareness, retention, and preference as in regular pretesting.

Study Design Note: A sample of more than 100 respondents was used in the referenced account of a TV pretesting study. Individual respondents were seated at a TV for an hour with a controller allowing them to switch among popular shows on the three networks. They were told they could switch back and forth and watch whatever they want. Three synchronized video recorders provided the signals, and each played commercials at the same time. (A pod was used consisting of three 30-second spots and two 15-second spots. Two of the 30-second and one of the 15-second commercials were different on each station, and the other two were the same (and appeared simultaneously.) These latter are the test commercials.

This type of pretesting gets at important observer behavior and gives agencies and advertisers insight into the attention their ads will—or won't—command. Pretesting Co. reports that many ads fail to measure up when pretested for zapping: "Our data clearly show that it is exceptionally difficult to force communication on an audience." Ads combining viewer interest with a strong, relevant and believable message are rare according to the firm. Further, 15-second spots are less likely to measure well than 30-second spots, even though one might expect it to be easier to hold the viewer's attention for 15 seconds than 30 seconds.

Ashok Pahwa of the Bloom Agency offers an interesting case to illustrate the impact of zapping—and the potential value of zap-proofed ads. In the 1988 Grammy Music Awards show, he reports that "the first ad in each of 11 sets of commercials was zapped by an average of 10% of the audience. But the Michael Jackson Pepsi ads were zapped by only 1%–2% of the viewers." This amounted to 2 million more viewers for the Pepsi commercial than for others. He argues that, given an average of 30 channels per household, advertisers must begin to provide "quality viewing" if they want their ads to be zap-proof. In his words, "The key may lie in creating commercials that more viewers would *want* to watch." Hopefully this philosophy, combined with pretesting that measures viewer interest and zap rates, will lead to commercials that are capable of holding viewer attention—without resorting to extreme and expensive tactics like roadblocking (simultaneous airings on multiple channels) and half-hour "infomercials."

References

Joe Agnew, "Researcher: Test Ads First to 'Zap Proof' Them," *Marketing News*, February 29, 1988, p. 18. Also see Ashok Pahwa, "Boom Generation More Receptive to Quality TV Ads," *Marketing News*, September, 17, 1990, pp. 8 and 17.

Chapter 8

Public Relations and Corporate Marketing

Bovee/Arens PR Checklist
Capsugel Crisis Management Checklist
Dowling's Corporate Image Measurement
Vielhaber's Crisis Communication Strategies
Word-of-Mouth Marketing Objectives

Also see:
Principles of Service Recovery

BOVEE/ARENS PR CHECKLIST

Applications

- Developing or evaluating a press release or news release.

Procedures

Review the checklist to identify problems with a specific press release or to develop a strategy and style for releases in general.

Cross-reference

See the Bovee-Arens Advertising Checklists in Chapter Two, Advertising and Promotion.

For a news release to be effective, it must be read and accepted by a busy editor who may have only a moment or two to glance at it. Here are some guidelines for producing successful press releases.

- ☐ Identify yourself. Include not only the name and address of the company (preferably on a letterhead) but also the name and number of whom to contact for further information.

- ☐ Provide a release date. Even if the item is marked "for immediate release," it is helpful to the editor to know when the item was sent.

- ☐ Use wide margins. Copy should be double-spaced for print and triple-spaced for broadcast media.

- ☐ Keep it short. One page is the preferred length. If the release needs to be longer, don't break in the middle of a paragraph.

- ☐ Proofread your copy. Typos and other mistakes will detract from your message.

- ☐ Update your mailing list. Editors change, offices move. Make sure you have the most recent information on the media you are informing.

- ☐ Don't call to see whether the editor has received your release. Editors don't like to be pressured into using PR materials; calling won't help your case.

- ☐ Don't ask for tear sheets. If the item gets published, don't expect the editor to take time out to send you a copy.
- ☐ Don't promise you'll advertise if the item is published. You will only offend the editor, who usually has nothing to do with the advertising department of the publication.
- ☐ Send a thank you. If an article is run, send the editor a note saying you appreciated the write-up.

Reference

Courtland L. Bovee and William F. Arens, *Contemporary Advertising*, 3rd ed. (Homewood, IL: Richard D. Irwin, 1989). Reproduced by permission of the publisher.

CAPSUGEL CRISIS MANAGEMENT CHECKLIST*

Applications

- Responding to a crises.
- Evaluating and improving current crisis management plans.

Procedures:

1. Develop a list of possible crises that could affect your business and industry.
2. Use the checklist to see whether your company is prepared for these possible crises. Develop a forecasting mechanism to make sure a crisis is recognized as early as possible.
3. Reduce the potential damage of future crises by making strategy conform to the approaches described in the checklist.
4. When a crisis occurs, consult the checklist to help develop contingency plans and guide reaction to the problem.

A 10-point checklist is used as a basis for creating crisis response plans and policies at Warner-Lambert's Capsugel Division. I have reproduced it as it appeared in *The Vest-Pocket CEO* because it still represents the "state of the art" in thinking about crisis management. Crisis planning was adopted at Capsugel after the Tylenol tampering cases devastated the market for capsules and created public suspicion of capsulized over-the-counter medications and their manufacturers. Management at Capsugel identified a number of policies and tactics that helped it and other companies in this market survive and maintain a positive public image. Their 10-point checklist and associated planning procedures may also help other companies survive crises. (See also "Vielhaber's Crisis Communication Strategies" in this chapter.)

Any organization can find itself in a crisis. Johnson & Johnson's Tylenol disaster, Union Carbide's Bhopal disaster, the Rushdie *Satanic Verses* inci-

*Alexander Hiam, *The Vest-Pocket CEO: Decision-Making Tools for Executives* (Englewood Cliffs, NJ: Prentice Hall 1990), by permission of the publisher.

dent, and NASA's disastrous 25th space shuttle mission are obvious examples. A recent survey of CEOs indicates that 70% of *Fortune* 500 companies and 20% of *Inc.* 500 companies have adopted crisis planning. These, and the many other organizations that have yet to address the issue, will find Capsugel's method to be of interest.

1. The first step in crisis planning is to anticipate possible crises. Try listing all the conceivable disasters that could befall your company and its industry. If the list is long, go back over it and rank them by how likely they are to occur. All may seem quite improbable, but some are bound to be more likely than others. Second, ask how significant the impact of each disaster might be. Try ranking them based on impact. Now take the most probable and the ones with the greatest potential impact and focus on them in your disaster forecasting and preparation.

Note: This step is the hardest for most CEOs, and the temptation is to delegate the task until it disappears. As Gerald Meyer, former chairman of American Motors, puts it: "Most executives don't like to think about crises. . . . They equate a crisis with bad management; things like that just don't happen on their watch."

2. Review the Capsugel checklist to see whether your company's policies, procedures, and philosophy violate any of the ten items. Make appropriate changes.

Focus especially on forecasting methods (see items 1 and 6 on checklist). Many companies do not systematically look for signs of crisis. Use the list developed in step 1, and think of events and information that could foretell each of the possible crises. Assign someone in publicity or strategic planning the job of monitoring the environment for early indicators of a crisis. Make sure the staff responsible for this function has direct communications with upper management and is not afraid to relay false alarms since no crisis forecasting system can be very accurate.

3. Integrate crisis preparation into strategic plans. Some of the items on the checklist are long-term in focus. They will do no good if not acted upon until after a crisis has been identified. But if implemented as part of the planning criteria, they will provide

protection against unforeseen events and make strategy more robust. Items 2, 7, 9, and 10 are especially relevant to strategic planning.

4. Crisis Response. If you are in the midst of a crisis, whether large, like Capsugel's, or of more modest proportions, the checklist may also be useful. Several of the items focus on how you respond during the crisis. Advice includes the following:

- Don't overreact.
- Stay close to the market.
- Watch your competition.
- Be prepared to give up some of your market.
- Don't assume a hostile environment.
- Develop a contingency plan.

See the checklist for specifics.

CRISIS MANAGEMENT CHECKLIST

1. *Look for signs that may foretell a crisis.* This task should be formalized and regularly reviewed by the chief executive. Ask yourself what events could have the worst impact on your organization.

2. *Have an alternative product or technology standing by.* Initiate product development now so that an almost-ready replacement will be in the pipeline.

3. *Speed is of the essence.* Your reactions in the first day or two of the crisis will establish consumer attitudes toward your company and product. Make sure your side of the story is included in the initial news coverage of the crisis.

4. *Don't overreact.* Make one person responsible for managing the crisis and have everyone else continue to take care of their work.

5. *Stay close to the market.* Market surveys and direct communications with customers are important. You need to track attitudes during the crises.

6. *Watch your competition.* Crises can create opportunities for you or your competitors.

7. *Be prepared to give up some of your market initially.* According to Charles Hoover, vice president of Capsugel, "It's ridiculous to think that you can manage a crisis with no damage. The idea is to minimize the damage, not eliminate the possibility of damage."

8. *Don't assume a hostile environment.* Many companies "clam up" in a crisis, which raises suspicions and leads to reduced confidence in your company and product. Do not act confrontational. (Include a PR person as well as a lawyer on your planning committee.)

    Example: Tenneco Oil's crisis policy statement includes the following: "When we must take a dose of bad publicity, it is better to release accurate information fast and as fully as possible."

9. *Build goodwill before the crisis.* A strong positive image will help you through crises.

10. *Develop a contingency or crisis plan in advance.* This will allow you to react effectively in the first hours of a crisis.

References

Management Briefing, Business Finance, The Conference Board, (New York: The Board, January 1987) (based on a presentation by Charles Hoover of Capsugel at a Conference Board marketing conference), and Paul Holmes, "Surviving crisis," in *Relate: Supplement to Adweek's Marketing Week*, March 27, 1989. (See page 10 for a description of the survey by The Goldman Group. Quotes from Gerald Meyer and Tenneco are also from this source.)

DOWLING'S CORPORATE IMAGE MEASUREMENT

Most companies do not measure and manage corporate image as well as they do brand image. Here are five ways to think and talk about corporate image and suggestions for how to research and manage image.

Applications

- Thinking about and managing corporate image.
- Developing specific image strategies and tactics for organizations.
- Measuring and tracking corporate image, including designing specific measures.
- Developing an image-based strategy and positioning the corporation's image relative to competitors'.

Procedures

Review the background on image and then try to apply the five models of corporate image listed here. One or more may be especially applicable to your organization. Use them to help verbalize and plan issues relating to corporate image. Refer to the technical note for specifics of how to measure corporate image.

A company's image among the general public, investors, government regulators, and other groups is of continuing interest to its mangers. However, most companies do not measure and track corporate image systematically. Grahame Dowling, a professor at the Australian Graduate School of Management (University of New South Wales), recently reviewed the options for measuring corporate image. Dowling finds there are a number of methods that can be used, and managers should find his list of options useful in developing a strategy for both measuring and managing corporate image. In addition, Dowling reviews the applicability of various research tools, providing pointers that will be of interest to market researchers. These findings are summarized in the technical notes at the end of this chapter, as others will have little interest in them.

Background

Images are formed by simple inference, as when "people feel that certain attributes of a company 'go together,' e.g., big is powerful." Images are also formed by the halo effect, as when "a person forms an overall image of a company (or object) by generalizing their impressions about attributes they are familiar with to those they know little or nothing about." For example, the insurance company that represents itself as an umbrella in its advertising encourages viewers to associate the protective power of the umbrella with the company.

Images give the mind organizing power, integrating a lot of information into a familiar and easily remembered 'big picture' or, in Dowling's words, a gestalt. Gestalt psychology "interprets phenomena as organized wholes rather than as aggregates of distinct parts and maintains that the whole is more than the sum of the parts" according to my handy desk encyclopedia. A corporation's image is truly more than the sum of the parts—one might associate lots of positive qualities with an insurance company because it is represented by an umbrella, even if one has virtually no specific information about the company. This example represents one of the ways images work: by activating a "knowledge structure." When companies can take advantage of people's existing knowledge structures they can create powerful, meaningful images quite easily. Another approach companies often take is to try to build up a knowledge structure through corporate and product advertising and publicity. McDonalds' Golden Arches had little meaning before the company created knowledge structures for people to associate with them. But enough of the background on why and how images work—here are Dowling's findings.

Approaches to Corporate Image Measurement and Management

Each of these five approaches suggests a basic framework and vocabulary for thinking about, measuring, and managing corporate image. In addition to these five approaches, managers should not overlook the obvious—the *strength* of a company's image as mea-

sured by percentage awareness or a comparative
strength measure might also be important!

1. Audience-specific image. Companies often
have multiple images, one for each of the segments
of its public. And image strategy can be tailored to
each group. For example, the image a company
ought to project to its shareholders and the financial
community is often different from the image it projects to its customers, and both will differ from the
image projected to employees. Image management
therefore requires the identification of distinct publics and the development and projection of appropriate images to them. Research into company image
needs to take into consideration the possibility that
different groups have different images, and it may be
necessary to customize the attributes used to measure image for each group.

2. Common image factors. Three factors have
been identified as important because many association structures can be derived from them—in other
words, they provide a framework or foundation for
many images. They are good–bad, strong–weak, and
active–passive. Therefore research can use these as
the basis for image measurement, and they can also
be used in the formulation of image strategy. One
approach is to think of these three factors as describing a three-dimensional mental space in which the
company can be, or is, positioned.

3. Hierarchy of images. In Dowling's words, "A
corporation's images may also be partially determined by a set of super and subordinate images." An
image associated with country of origin might be at
the top of the hierarchy, for example, with more
specific images beneath. Brand image is in most
cases at the bottom of the hierarchy. This suggests
the need to look for nested images and, when multiple images are discovered by researchers, to explore
the possibility of a hierarchical relationship. As far
as image management goes, it is important to note
that multiple images may be associated with a company and may be *interrelated* in a hierarchical structure. This suggests the need to consider the impact of
any planned shift in our creation of imagery in the
context of existing image structure.

4. Desired image. Many companies use a tag line
or a visual symbol to emphasize desired image attri-

butes. How well known and accepted are these desired attributes? Obviously one of the tasks of research is to answer this question.

Managers often define a desired image in a clumsy and heavy-handed manner. A tag line that proclaims the company is strong on service or the leader in its industry is not necessarily plausible to the public, and it does not take full advantage of the power of inference, halo effects, or existing cognitive structures, as discussed earlier under "Background." In developing and projecting a desired image, managers should find the other four items on this list a source of inspiration.

5. Image relative to other companies. Image can be a useful way to compare your company with competitors, and it can be a source of competitive advantage. Measuring image relative to competitors may require the development of different attributes than those used for measuring your company's image for other purposes. A separate effort is required by researchers.

Management may find it useful to know how the public, and especially customers, perceive the image of each major competitor. An image positioning strategy could be developed on the basis of this information.

Technical Notes

Unstructured interviews and *focus groups* can be used to measure company image. They are good for exploratory research, and it is not necessary to know the relevant attributes in advance. Their findings are qualitative.

Semantic differential scales are useful for descriptive studies in which attributes are known and qualitative or simple quantitative results are acceptable.

Simple space *multidimensional scaling* (MDS) does not require attributes to be predetermined, and Dowling finds it "the most appropriate nonattribute modeling procedure to represent a set of overall corporate images." In MDS, respondents rate the similarity of a set of companies, and one of the various statistical routines available is employed to map the companies using the minimum number of dimensions necessary to maintain the measured similarities among the companies. It produces both qualitative and quantitative results. Note: The dimensions are unnamed, leaving it up to the researcher's judgment whether and how to identify them. The number of dimensions is also somewhat arbitrary.

Dowling recommends using *joint-space MDS*, in which two images are mapped and scaled simultaneously, when management wants to compare perceived image with desired image, to compare image with a competitor's image, or to compare images of the company held by two distinct groups. Attribute-based methods include factor analysis and multiple discriminant analysis, and it is also possible to use similarity scaling methods combined with attribute-rating methods. Joint-space MDS methods require that attributes be known.

References

Grahame R. Dowling, "Measuring Corporate Images: A Review of Alternative Approaches," *Journal of Business Research*, Vol. 17, 1988: 27–34. Also see William H. Harris and Judith S. Levy, eds., *The New Columbia Encyclopedia* (New York: Columbia University Press, 1975).

VIELHABER'S CRISIS COMMUNICATION STRATEGIES

Applications

- Identifying and planning for communications problems that occur in crises.
- Incorporating crisis communication strategies into a crisis plan or strategic plan.

Procedures

1. Review your organization's plans and existing communication structures to see how communication will be handled in crises.
2. Adapt each of the strategies following to your organization, modifying your plans if necessary to do so. Make sure crisis plans include strategies to enhance the flow of communication, improve the accuracy of information, and ensure the timeliness of information.

Insight into the art and practice of crisis management is generally an unexpected positive outcome of major crises. Capsugel's experience as their primary product was decimated by the Tylenol poisonings resulted in the Capsugel Crisis Management Checklist (also in this Chapter) and the communication strategies following were developed by Mary Vielhaber of Eastern Michigan University after a careful study of communication during the Three Mile Island accident. If we could just have a few more major crises like these, we could get really good at crisis planning and management!

Vielhaber identified a series of communication problems that are likely to affect public safety and corporate image during other crises as well:

- The normal speed of communications with an organization is too slow during a crisis.
- The filtering of information that normally occurs as it flows through an organization is inappropriate during a crisis.
- The "natural tendency to suppress bad news," or at least to sit on it until the right time and way can be found to break the news to the boss, is counterproductive in a crisis.

- The informality of information gathering in most organizations makes it hard to coordinate and verify crisis information.

- Normally effective spokespeople are often less effective communicators when under the extreme stress a crisis creates.

- The division of authority based on function and expertise, while beneficial in ordinary circumstances, tends to lead to "too many cooks" and conflicting reports and releases during a crisis.

She recommends the following communication strategies be adopted to avoid these and associated problems. (The italicized strategies are quoted directly from the referenced source.)

STRATEGIES TO ENHANCE COMMUNICATION

1. *Know your purpose for communicating.* A misplaced sense of what is really important to the audience often characterizes public statements by companies during crises. If safety is an issue, then the public wants to know what the risks are and how to avoid getting hurt—they do not care to hear why the company thinks the accident happened or who they think is responsible. In disaster planning, it is helpful to write down the communication priority for each anticipated crisis or type of crisis.

2. *Limit the number of spokespersons who communicate with the public.* Preferably a single spokesperson should be chosen to represent the company and communicate all relevant information to interested parties. If multiple parties are involved, they should try to combine information and issue joint statements to the press and the public.

3. *Limit the number of filters a message must pass through before it reaches its intended audience.* It is best to have a direct link from the people who gather information to a central location where the information is analyzed and formed into corporate communications. The normal organization chart must

be bypassed. Using the CEO or a senior VP as the spokesperson helps to cut through organizational red tape.

STRATEGIES TO IMPROVE THE ACCURACY OF INFORMATION

1. *Communicate messages that are clear, direct, and audience centered.* While obvious, this is easier said than done. It might be a good idea for the spokesperson to have a staffer review each communication against these three criteria before release—an objective eye can pick up deviations more quickly than the author in the heat of crisis. Audience centered means the "force of the message" must clearly tell the audience what they need to know, especially if it concerns their safety. No double-talk, confusing technical details, or lengthy rationalizations can be permitted to confuse the message.

2. *Use a variety of channels of communication to reinforce the message.* According to Vielhaber, "in times of crisis, the emergency broadcast systems, newspapers, television, and radio can all be used to reach the public. When immediate danger has lessened, the variety of communication channels can be used to begin to restore the public's confidence."

3. *Monitor the feedback to the messages regarding the crisis.* Are you getting the message across? Is there confusion, misunderstanding? How is the company perceived? A "rumor control center" or 800 number for feedback helps, and telephone or intercept surveys may also be useful in some circumstances.

4. *Repeat messages.* Everyone knows this one— or do they? There is a tendency to assume that what you said in the release yesterday, and on TV this morning, is less important than the new information that just came in. But the core message to the public needs to be repeated regularly to make sure safety information gets through and to put new information into proper context.

1. Monitor the time it takes to communicate messages to the public. How long does it take to gather information, prepare a message, and communicate it to interested parties? If links in this chain of communication understand that they need to pass on information rapidly, and will be held responsible for any delays, the flow will be far quicker. Vielhaber recommends that "messages be sent on forms that have the time they were sent and the time they were received stamped on them as a reminder that timeliness is a key concern." Also consider scheduling regular press conferences to ensure continuous flow of information to the public.

References

Mary E. Vielhaber, "Crisis Communication: The Business Communicator's Strategies for Communicating Under Stress," *The Bulletin of the Association for Business Communication*, March 1990: 29–31. See also M. K. Pinsdorf, *Communicating When Your Company Is Under Siege*, (Lexington, MA: Lexington Books, 1987).

WORD-OF-MOUTH MARKETING
OBJECTIVES

Applications

- Setting objectives for word-of-mouth marketing and networking during marketing plan
  development.
- Increasing the benefits of word of mouth.

Procedures

Regis McKenna, the Silicon Valley PR whiz, says
that "word of mouth is so obvious a communications
medium that most people do not take the time to
analyze or understand its structure. . . . You never
see a Word-of-Mouth Communications Section in
marketing plans." If you did, what marketing objectives would it address? The main reason that word of
mouth is overlooked by marketers is probably that
we tend not to have a clear idea of what it can
accomplish. A plan needs to start with objectives.
Once you have clear and realistic objectives you can
start developing strategies. The following list of feasible objectives for word of mouth will help you
make your marketing strategy incorporate word of
mouth more effectively by pointing to specific objectives for it and helping you integrate those objectives
into the marketing plan as a whole.

The power of good word-of-mouth marketing is
legendary. McKenna writes (in his book *The Regis
Touch*) that "Word of mouth is probably the most
powerful form of communication in the business
world." McKenna has integrated word of mouth into
the publicity campaigns of Apple Computer and
many other computer-industry success stories. Harvey Mackay of Mackay Envelope relied heavily on
word-of-mouth in marketing his best-selling *Swim
with the Sharks Without Being Eaten Alive*. He says
that "If the house is on fire, forget the china, silver,
and wedding album—grab the Rolodex," and I am
sure he would. An *Inc.* magazine article about his
book explains that

> nowhere has Mackay's partnership with his
> Rolodex been more productive than in his

ability to convince about 45 famous people—
from show business, politics, the media, and
even academia—to endorse Swim with the
Sharks Without Being Eaten Alive, *giving the*
impression that Mackay was the jet set's own
treasured secret. In truth, Mackay knows few
of his flatterers.

The *Sharks* case illustrates one of the objectives of word of mouth: referrals. Most of us do not need referrals from 45 celebrities, but referrals from opinion leaders within your industry can be a very powerful marketing tool. There are five specific rules in soliciting and using referrals, as described here. Referrals are the most obvious objective of word-of-mouth marketing, but other objectives exist as well. This list comes from Frank Sonnenberg, director of marketing in the Management Consulting Group of Ernst & Young in New York:

Ernst & Young's Marketing Objectives for Word of Mouth

Knowledge. Word of mouth can be used to provide access to knowledge, especially specific information about business problems and projects. For example, if you are launching a product in a market that is unfamiliar to you, networking to obtain advice from managers with experience in this market would be a good objective.

Resources. Word of mouth not only lets people know you or your products are available, it also makes hard-to-find resources available to you. A network of contacts and "loose ties" can be used to put the word out when you need to hire someone with special skills or find special services or information. Even when you could find the resources on your own, it may make sense to use your network to locate them to keep the network of contacts active or expand it.

Positioning. Opinion leaders within target markets can be influenced or at least reached through networking, and these contacts provide access to useful opinions on how to position your product as well as a source of endorsements to help make your positioning credible in the marketplace. CEOs of leading companies, well-known editors and writers, stock analysts, professors, trade association heads, and consultants are often opinion leaders.

Opportunity. Word of mouth can provide access to opportunities. The more you talk with others in your industry, and the more visible you are within it, the more likely you are to hear about opportunities and to be approached by other companies with ideas for joint ventures. Speaking at conferences and participating in trade associations are both good ways to build a network and increase your exposure to opportunity.

Referrals. As discussed, referrals are one of the most powerful forms of word-of-mouth marketing. Some businesses find almost all their customers through referrals. In other cases, a referral or implied referral can be used to help close a sale or clinch a deal. (An implied referral is when you let it be known that a respected company is a customer.) Sonnenberg suggests five rules to follow:

1. Do not use anyone's name without permission.
2. If you are introduced to a contact, let the introducer know what happens.
3 When you use someone's name you have an obligation to provide "The same or better service to others" and to "make them look good," in Sonnenberg's words.
4. All referrals require thank yous.
5. If you ask someone to speak on your behalf, "make sure that you either know what they are going to say or see to it that you adequately prepare them with information to use."

Solidifying Existing Relationships. Word of mouth can provide details about customers' businesses and needs, making it possible to provide better and more personal service. Networking within customers is an important objective for business-to-business marketers.

Leads. In modern marketing leads are often generated through telemarketing, direct-response mailings, and other formal programs. However, word of mouth can be a useful source of leads, and the leads are usually of high quality. A sales force can be trained in networking and encouraged to develop word-of-mouth sources of leads.

References

Joshua Hyatt, "How to Write a Business Best-Seller," *Inc.*, March 1990, pp 64–75. Also, see Frank K. Sonnenberg, "How to Reap the Benefits of Networking," *The Journal of Business Strategy*, January/February 1990: 59–62.

Chapter 9

Pricing

Nagle's Pricing Income Statement
Oxenfeldt's Checklist of Pricing Objectives
Price Strategy Selector
The Pricing Advisor's Pricing Policy Audit
Ross's Proactive Pricing Test

Also see:
Performance Standards Checklist
Schultz's Four Challenges
Smith's Negotiating Tactics

NAGLE'S PRICING INCOME STATEMENT

The value of reorganization is that it first focuses attention on costs that are incremental and avoidable and only later looks at costs that are fixed and sunk for the pricing decision.

—Thomas Nagle

Applications

- Providing more accurate cost estimates to support pricing decisions.

- Evaluating a proposed short-term increase or decrease in price from the firm's cost perspective.

- Reorganizing the income statement to provide better information for pricing decisions.

Procedures

Thomas Nagle of Boston University recommends reorganizing the income statement before tackling pricing and related management decisions. The traditional income statement does not make it easy to separate sunk costs, and it also can "lead a manager to think about pricing sequentially, as a set of hurdles to be overcome in order." For example, gross profit—the first hurdle—focuses attention on maximizing sales revenue and minimizing cost of goods sold. But optimizing gross profit does not necessarily optimize net profit—the impact on other categories of expense must be taken into account. Sometimes decisions that produce less gross profit actually provide higher net profit.

A typical income statement follows the form:

```
        sales revenue
      − cost of goods sold
                  = gross profit
      − selling expenses
      − depreciation
      − administrative overhead
                  = operating profit
      − interest expense
                  = pretax profit
      − taxes
                  = net profit
```

Nagle's reorganized income statement follows a very different form:

    sales revenue
 − incremental, avoidable variable costs
                = total contribution margin (in
                   dollars)
 − incremental, avoidable fixed costs
                = profit contribution
 − other fixed or sunk costs
                = pretax profit
 − income taxes
                = net profit

Preparing it is a little more tricky than simply playing with costs from the last available income statement. The first and most important step is to identify the relevant costs for your specific pricing decision. These are the costs that are directly associated with the specific units the price change will apply to. According to Nagle (page 25), "The relevant cost to consider when evaluating a price reduction is the cost of the additional units that the firm expects to sell because of the price cut. The relevant cost to consider when evaluating a price increase is the avoided cost of units that the firm will not produce because sales will be reduced by the price rise."

Note also that the average of total variable costs is accurate from an historical perspective, but may not represent the variable cost per unit for the specific units under consideration. For example, a price increase that reduces demand might remove units that would have been produced on overtime labor rates, and thus a higher than average variable cost should apply.

Finally, note that Nagle's statement specifies avoidable variable costs. While managers generally equate the terms "avoidable" and "variable," they have different meanings. Variable costs are those that vary with the number of units produced. Avoidable costs are those that can be avoided, either because they have not yet been incurred or because they can be reversed. In practice, most variable costs can be avoided, but some cannot—be sure all the variable costs you use when calculating price are truly avoidable.

Also be sure to consider costs that are classified as fixed, but could be avoided anyway. Unless they have already been paid for, and cannot be returned/refunded, fixed costs are usually still avoidable. A custom bottling machine may be an unavoidable expense to the bottler that owns it, since there is probably not an established market for it. But a leased forklift in good working order might well be an avoidable expense. If a price increase reduced volume, the bottler could probably return the forklift or sell the lease. Thus the monthly payments on the forklift should be subtracted out as "incremental, avoidable fixed costs" just as the labor needed to run the bottling machine and forklift should be subtracted on the line above as "incremental, avoidable variable costs." An advantage of Nagle's reorganized income statement is that it encourages the decision maker to think more accurately and carefully about costs.

A careful look at costs also reveals that most depreciation figures are inappropriate for pricing decisions. Depreciation calculated for income taxes uses an accelerated schedule. Formulas used for financial statements generally estimate depreciation more accurately, but apply depreciation to historical costs. Nagle argues that, "For pricing and any other managerial decision making, however, depreciation expenses should be based on forecasts of the actual decline in the current market value of assets as a result of their use." The wisdom of this approach is obvious in the case of assets which have been fully depreciated on a company's financial statements. If these assets still have a market value, and that value is affected by a pricing decision, this effect ought to be part of the cost analysis. Ignoring it because they are listed as fully depreciated is unrealistic and distorts the analysis of costs.

Two additional warnings are important to the user of this method. First, it is easy to assume that each line item on the company's income statement is either relevant or irrelevant. But in many cases, a portion of it is relevant and the rest is not. If some of the applicable labor costs must be paid under the terms of a contract, whether or not the labor is performed, then this portion must be treated as sunk. Second, opportunity costs are easy to overlook when analyzing pricing decisions. Opportunity cost are any profits that are forgone due to the pricing decision in question. A lower price and corresponding higher volume may displace other products and therefore sacrifice some of their profits. The forgone profits are therefore relevant to the pricing decision.

With these cautions in mind, identify the relevant costs and organize them according to Nagle's format. The resulting statement (which may be used on a spreadsheet program for evaluating multiple scenarios) answers a number of important questions:

- What is the minimum price at which additional units can be sold profitably?
- Which costs are most easily controlled?
- What is the best estimate of total contribution margin?

Cautions: This pricing method's focus on cost analysis is valuable, but in general, pricing decisions must also reflect customer perceptions as well as company costs. Use an analysis of costs to better understand the constraints imposed on a decision by relevant costs. But do not base price decisions solely on cost analysis.

Reference

Thomas T. Nagle, *The Strategy and Tactics of Pricing: A Guide to Profitable Decision Making*, (Englewood Cliffs, NJ: Prentice Hall, 1987) pp. 23–28.

OXENFELDT'S CHECKLIST OF PRICING OBJECTIVES

Applications

- Identifying strategic objectives for pricing.
- Checking whether a particular marketing objective can be addressed through pricing.
- Thinking about pricing strategy in the context of planning, development, or new product positioning.

Procedures

Use the checklist as a source of potential pricing objectives or to see whether an objective of your organization is easily addressed through pricing.

CHECKLIST OF POTENTIAL PRICING OBJECTIVES

- ☐ Maximize long-run profits
- ☐ Maximize short-run profits
- ☐ Growth
- ☐ Stabilize market
- ☐ Desensitize customers to price
- ☐ Maintain price-leadership arrangement
- ☐ Discourage entrants
- ☐ Speed exit of marginal firms
- ☐ Avoid government investigation and control
- ☐ Maintain loyalty of middlemen and get their sales support
- ☐ Avoid demands for "more" from suppliers—labor in particular
- ☐ Enhance image of firm and its offerings
- ☐ Be regarded as "fair" by customers (ultimate)
- ☐ Create interest and excitement about the item
- ☐ Be considered trustworthy and reliable by rivals
- ☐ Help in the sale of weak items in the line
- ☐ Discourage others from cutting prices
- ☐ Make a product "visible"
- ☐ "Spoil market" to obtain high price for sale of business
- ☐ Build traffic

This list usually surprises marketers because of the wide variety of objectives that pricing can accomplish. Many marketing plans give little attention to the subject of pricing, assuming that prices will be set more or less as they were last year, or as competitors set them. In other cases, cost-based formulas are used that have nothing to do with specific marketing objectives. However, price can be a powerful variable for achieving marketing objectives on both the strategic and tactical levels. This checklist is very helpful in putting marketing objectives on the agenda whenever pricing is to be discussed, and vice versa.

Some readers may notice that, while the checklist identified many legitimate objectives for pricing, it fails to describe how to achieve any of them. Unfortunately, there are few simple formulas, and in many cases a great variety of approaches might be used depending upon the circumstances (especially those created by competitor pricing actions). Examples: In most cases a smaller margin will be prescribed whenever the objective is to discourage entrants. But growth may be achieved in a price-sensitive environment through low penetration pricing and in a status-oriented market by high psychological pricing.

In general, it is wise to start with the objective and then talk with representative customers and intermediaries to see how best to achieve it through pricing. This input, combined with information about industry and economic trends, competitor pricing actions or signals, and any other relevant intelligence ought to provide the platform for a customized pricing strategy that fits the circumstances. Next, a comparison of the pricing strategy with any other options (utilizing nonprice marketing variables) should be performed to see whether a price-based pursuit of the objective is the most cost-effective approach.

Reference

Alfred R. Oxenfeldt, "A Decision-Making Structure for Price Decisions," *Journal of Marketing*, Vol. 37, January 1973. The checklist is from Exhibit 1.

PRICE STRATEGY SELECTOR

Applications

- Finding the appropriate pricing strategy in any specific situation.
- Evaluating pricing options.
- Solving specific pricing problems or customer complaints (see the applications section of each strategy description for specifics).

Procedures

Use the descriptions of pricing strategies, their applications, and their tactics to evaluate the wisdom of existing price structures or to select an appropriate strategy upon which to base new prices.

Geographical Pricing Strategies

Applications. Achieving geographic marketing objectives, such as building share in distant markets. Protecting margins when shipping costs or other costs make some areas more expensive to serve than others. Resolving customer complaints concerning freight charges.

Tactics. Many pricing tactics focus on geographic objectives. *FOB origin pricing* requires customer to pay the freight charges, which will be higher for more distant customers. *Uniform delivered pricing* applies a standard shipping charge to all customers, regardless of distance from origin. *Zone pricing* sets standard prices within geographic zones to reflect differences in shipping to different zones—the customer pays the shipping in this case also. *Basing-point pricing* establishes a specific city as the basing point, charging all customers the freight from that city to their location—even if the shipment did not originate in that city. *Freight-absorption pricing* waves the freight charges to customers. Sometimes used to help develop a specific regional market.

Introduction Pricing Strategies

Applications. Introducing new products. Building image, market share, or market size. Protecting the market from later entries. Maximizing short-term profits to benefit from being first to market. Pricing an imitative new product so as to differentiate its position from established competitors.

Tactics. All introduction pricing strategies are short term. Most involve low prices and tight margins, and so run a slight risk that the market will not permit the prices to be raised later.

Penetration pricing involves low pricing and low margins, with consequently low short-term profits. Its goal is to maximize long-term market share and, usually, to give the product a dominant share of market in the long run. Presumably the short-term investment in market share will yield greater returns in the long run. Dow Chemical often uses penetration pricing for its many commodity-type products (see the *Business Week* article). Penetration pricing is sometimes broken out into four different strategies:

- *Restrained pricing* puts a lower limit on prices so as to protect margins, especially during periods of rapid inflation.

- *Promotional pricing* differentiates the penetration price from the regular price in the consumer's mind. Purchasers of shoes at factory outlet stores understand that the stores' promotional pricing gives them lower than usual prices.

- *Elimination pricing* is designed to push competitors with higher costs out of the market (and requires a clear understanding of the legal issues).

- *Keep-out pricing* attempts to prevent the entry of new competitors by setting price just low enough to make the market unattractive to them.

Warning: Penetration pricing will not work unless the target market is sufficiently price sensitive. In many cases prices have been lowered without market share increasing in return. Use customer surveys, focus groups, or test markets to evaluate the importance of price and to make sure the proposed change will be noticed by consumers and will motivate them.

Skimming is the opposite of a penetration strategy. Prices are set high initially to make the maximum profit from those customers who have the greatest interest in the new product—usually a minority of the potential market. It is usually accompanied by heavy spending on promotion. As the segments willing to pay a premium for the product are penetrated, and as competitors enter the market, the price is gradually lowered. Skimming is appropriate when a novel product is expected to diffuse slowly through the market, when the early adopters are not expected to be price sensitive, when heavy R&D expenditures need to be recovered, and when competitors are not expected to enter the market with a similar offering in the immediate future. Most patented pharmaceuticals are priced in this manner—penicillin was introduced at $20 in 1942, sold at $2 two years later, and cost only a few cents for the same quantity by 1949. (For a description of Du Pont's use of the skimming strategy, see the *Business Week* article in the footnote.)

Relative pricing is used to position a new product relative to other, similar products. A useful approach is to develop a value map for the competing products and to give the new product a unique and desirable combination of quality and price. Kotler uses a quality/value matrix with nine cells and suggests evaluating the competition and growth rate in each cell before selecting a specific positioning strategy:

	PRICE		
PRODUCT QUALITY	HIGH	MEDIUM	LOW
High	1. Premium strategy	2. Penetration strategy	3. Superb-value strategy
Medium	4. Overcharging strategy	5. Average strategy	6. Good-value strategy
Low	7. Rip-off strategy	8. Borax strategy	9. Cheap-value strategy

When you want to position a new or existing product to compete directly with an important competing product, use relative pricing to do so. Price it the same to support the perception of it as a direct substitute, a little higher to position it as better, or a little lower to position it as a better value than the competitor.

Product Mix Pricing Strategies

Applications. Pricing in the context of a portfolio of products in one or many product lines. Simplifying prices for the benefit of customers or intermediaries. Taking advantage of established price points or grades that are recognized by consumers. Maximizing profits on an item by associating it with other items or pricing it in logical relationship to other items. Maximizing profits on a razor blade–type product. Selling additional associated or optional products when a principal product is purchased.

Tactics. Look at price in the context of the total product line. Individual products may have to be priced at or even below cost because they are necessary to the line. Others may provide additional profits if their prices are raised to fill gaps in the line or to position them in a recognized category or price point. The driving logic of product mix pricing is that the profits of the entire product portfolio should be maximized through pricing, which is not necessarily the result when an effort is made to maximize the profits from each product individually.

There are various types of product mix strategies:

Product-line pricing arrays a number of product options along a value line, offering the consumer a logical set of options ranging from less expensive to more expensive with features added as the price increases. The size of the price step between each pair of items is important. Small steps may lure the consumer to higher-priced models, but too many options can be confusing. Too few can create opportunities for competitors.

Note: Cost differences do not have to drive price differences, and sometimes a group of products will be priced over a larger range than that spanned by their costs. The low-priced items in the group therefore have smaller margins and the high-priced items have larger margins. The goal with this type of pricing is to sell items in the middle and top of the price range.

Price increases need to be carried out across the product line, and any price points should be maintained. If consumers are accustomed to buying at a particular price point (i.e., top-of-the-line camera equipment), they will usually continue to purchase at this price point after a price increase.

Product line pricing is especially suited to consumer products where status or image is an important attribute, such as automobiles, clothing, or cosmetics. The price structure of the line and its relationship to competing lines is one of the most important signals of image.

Optional-product pricing addresses the pricing of ancillary (though not always truly optional) products and services such as the drinks and salads served with a restaurant meal or the spare tire offered as an option on your new car. The separate pricing of such products and services makes sense when they are not wanted by the majority of consumers. But when they are desired in most cases, making them optional is generally a way to reduce the sticker price of the item in a deceptive manner. The real cost of a meal includes something to drink, but the perceived cost may be based on the published prices of entrees on a menu rather than by the unpublished (or deemphasized) prices of the drinks. For this reason, optional product margins are often high relative to their primary products.

Optional-product pricing can be used to take advantage of the fact that consumers generally are more price-sensitive to some elements of a complex purchase than to others. The car buyer will be hounded by in-laws for all eternity if he or she brings home a car whose sticker price is obviously a rip-off. But the same buyer can happily purchase an overpriced car stereo because of its status benefit. By separating the car's price from the stereo's price, the manufacturer and dealer can take advantage of the relative lack of price sensitivity on the stereo while advertising a low price on the car.

Optional-product pricing can provide a basis for market segmentation. Within a group of consumers who are all willing to pay exactly $20.00 for a restaurant meal, there may be some who are more price sensitive when it comes to food and others who are more price sensitive when it comes to drinks. Two different restaurants could coexist to serve this group, one pricing its drinks high and the other pricing its food high.

Captive-product pricing concerns the pricing of a principal product and any products that must be used with it (cameras and film; film and processing; razors and blades; photocopiers and toner; computers, training, and service). It is common to keep the price of the principal product low and profit from the sale of the captive products. In many cases, some primary product competitors do not make the captive product, giving the companies that do the ability to price the primary product low relative to competitors (example: Kodak cameras). The company that first develops a primary product–captive product pair usually has the option of protecting the captive product or making it an open standard to invite competition. Competition is sometimes desirable, as it can build the market more quickly and help create an industry standard. However, it usually places downward pressure on the price of the captive product. Example: Gillette continues to innovate in razor blade technology in part because competitors eventually adopt each new blade design and start competing with Gillette on the basis of price.

Cost-Based Pricing Strategies

Applications. Ensuring profit margins in pricing. Obtaining a desired return on the capital required to produce and distribute a product. Creating simple formulas for pricing or bidding. Setting price to maximize profits based on assumptions concerning both break-even point and demand versus price.

Tactics. A great many formulas and methods have been developed based on analysis of costs. All have in common a focus on the company and not the customers or competitors, and so should be balanced by consideration of these perspectives as well (i.e., by using one of the other strategies described earlier). The danger of cost-based pricing is that prices will not appeal to customers. The danger of other pricing strategies is that they may not provide sufficient profits or returns.

Cost-plus pricing sets list price by adding a certain amount or proportion of profit to the cost per unit (use average total cost). Often used for products for which demand is well known, stable, and not very price-sensitive, such as milk, bread, and paper clips. Intermediaries such as wholesalers and retailers often use cost-plus pricing under the term *market pricing*, in which they add a profit margin to their delivered cost (the wholesale price or the wholesale price plus shipping).

Target return pricing is designed to obtain a specific return, expressed either as an absolute dollar amount or as a percentage of the capital dedicated to producing and distributing the product. It treats the return in the same way fixed costs are treated, summing the return and the fixed costs, then allocating these costs over the number of units produced. Per-unit variable costs are also allocated. When fixed costs and profits are added to variable costs for any projected production run or sales volume, the resulting total is the price at which the target return will be achieved.

Break-even pricing sets price so as to ensure, at the minimum, total revenues at or above total costs. It can also be used to pick the price that maximizes total revenues relative to total costs, given a set of assumptions about demand and price.

Start by estimating demand (in units sold) for the product at a variety of price points. Create a table, as in the exhibit, and multiply demand by price to estimate total revenues for each price point. Next calculate the break-even point (in units) using this formula:

$$\text{break-even (in units)} = \frac{\text{total fixed costs}}{\text{selling price} - \text{variable cost per unit}}$$

Compare estimated demand with the breakeven point. If demand is below breakeven for a specific price point, then that price point obviously will not allow the company to recoup its initial investment. To calculate total profits, calculate the total cost of the units sold, which equals fixed costs + (variable costs × number of units). Subtract this from total revenues. See the exhibit for an example.

BREAK-EVEN ANALYSIS

UNIT PRICE	MARKET DEMAND AT GIVEN PRICE	TOTAL REVENUE	BREAK-EVEN POINT (UNITS)	TOTAL COST OF UNITS SOLD	TOTAL PROFITS
23	7	161	16.7	190	− 29
29	6	174	5.6	170	4
32	5	160	4.2	150	10
42	2	84	2.3	90	− 6

Source: Schewe's *Marketing Principles and Strategies*, p. 330. Assumes fixed cost of $50 and variable cost of $20 per unit.

References

Subhash C. Jain, "Pricing Strategies," *Marketing Planning & Strategy*, 3rd ed. (Cincinnati: South-Western, 1990), pp. 471–510; "Pricing Strategy in an Inflation Economy," *Business Week*, April 6, 1974, p. 43; Philip Kotler, *Marketing Management: Analysis, Planning, and Control*, 5th ed. (Englewood Cliffs, NJ: Prentice Hall, 1984), pp. 505–537; and Charles D. Schewe, "The Nature of Pricing," in *Marketing Principles and Strategies*, (New York: Random House, 1987).

THE PRICING ADVISOR'S PRICING POLICY AUDIT

Applications

- Reviewing pricing policy to identify problems and improve practices.
- Setting and updating pricing policy.
- Evaluating or developing pricing strategy for marketing plans and product plans.

Procedures

1. Identifying marketing objectives and relate them to pricing policy.
2. Analyze buyer behavior and relate it to pricing policy.
3. Conduct a cost/profitability analysis and relate to pricing policy.
4. Review traditional practices and policies to make sure they still make sense.
5. Analyze perceived value of products or services and relate to list prices.
6. Track competitor prices and price changes and relate them to pricing policy.
7. Assess the overall impact of pricing pressures to predict whether prices in your market will move upward or downward.

The Pricing Advisor and its president, Eric Mitchell, have developed a series of simple analyses that can be used to conduct a thorough audit of price policy. It runs you through all the important considerations for setting or modifying prices, discounts, and other elements of pricing policy. Use it to review policy if you haven't looked closely at all aspects of pricing in the last year or two. Also use it—or relevant sections of it—as an aid to price analysis and development of pricing strategy when facing a pricing problem, preparing a marketing plan, or whenever a close look at pricing is needed.

THE PRICING POLICY AUDIT

To answer this question, define the marketing mission for the products (or services) and geographic area in question. How important is market share expansion, geographic expansion, and so on? Refer to the most recent marketing or strategic plan if available. Specific, detailed objectives are helpful. For example, if your plan calls for gaining share through increased business with existing customers and the creation of a national account system, your analysis of discount policies will indicate that quantity discounts are less appropriate than a dollar or volume discount structure.

Next, quantify the *gap between list prices and the actual transaction prices* after discounts, free goods, and so on. And answer these questions:

- ☐ How wide is the gap between list and transaction prices?
- ☐ Has it been holding steady or widening in the past few months or years?
- ☐ If widening, why?

Note: A widening spread between list and transaction prices may be due to growing competition, selling to the wrong class of customers, a depressed industry, or other factors. In some industries, especially those in which products or services are quoted at $X\%$ off list, wide gaps are normal. Example: The furniture industry seems to thrive despite gaps as large as 80%. Except for its value as a pivoting point, the list price in this industry is meaningless. However, in most industries widening gaps lead to pricing problems and throw margins and profits off target.

Now look at discount structure and make sure the right discounts are being used, in the right circumstances, given your marketing objectives. Identify which of these discount structures are in use:

- ☐ *Dollar or volume discount structures.* These serve the purpose of inducing customer repurchase because buyers want to qualify for the next discount level. Sometimes called *relationship pricing.* They are effective for broad product lines and for products that are purchased habitually and with relatively little price analysis by the customer. They are best used in situations where it is feasible to maintain a relatively small price spread, or band, between the highest and lowest price for a product (the typical price band ranges from 100% of list down to 95% or 90%). They are helpful in developing national account programs. They can also be used as replacement for prompt payment discounts. However, if they are not used in any of these contexts, or a large price spread is employed, flag these discounts in your audit as a source of trouble.

☐ *Quantity discounts.* Best for encouraging individual rather than repeat purchases. Preferably quantity discounts reflect your actual savings on fixed costs associated with increased quantity. If costs of raw materials, production, freight, selling, and so on are reduced on a per-unit basis when customers purchase in greater quantity, this cost reduction can be reflected in quantity discounts to customers and/or the channel. However, if they do not reflect underlying cost structure, they may not make sense from a marketing perspective. The price spread or price band on quantity discount schedules should be wider than the band on volume discount schedules, for example ranging from 100% of list at low quantities down to 60% of list at high quantities. *Note:* In some industrial markets it is common to use quantity discounts that exceed cost savings. This may be justified by a different competitive environment for large versus small customers.

Example: Newspapers offer maximum discounts of as much as 40% on display advertising—which is far in excess of their quantity savings. Low prices are used to lure large advertisers away from local TV, an indirect competitor that does not compete as effectively for small advertisers. However, unless there is a strong marketing rationale (and unless a volume discount cannot be employed for this purpose), the quantity discount schedule should be fairly close to the cost structure.

☐ *Bids/contracts*. More and more contracts are being converted from routine purchases to formal bidding processes. The conversion is almost always a symptom of heightened buyer price sensitivity. It should signal any incumbent supplier that historical price levels will no longer hold this customer. Many marketers fallaciously rationalize this year's low-price bid as an investment in next year's sales. In fact, the intrusion of bid requirements means all previous bets are off. Once the buyer has turned to bidding, the marketing process for that customer should be viewed as a *one-time effort* rather than a customer-retention or loyalty-based marketing effort. Sweetening your volume discount schedule, for example, is inappropriate. Contract/bid requests signal overly price-sensitive customers. So price low if you need the business and high if you don't. The only cost rationalization needed is variable cost. Note: Consistency between published and bid prices is unnecessary.

☐ *Are you using discounts properly?* They should reflect the marketing environment and your marketing objectives. Volume discounts make sense when repeat purchases are important and price is not the customer's sole issue. Quantity discount schedules are better tools for accommodating heterogeneous buyers (some bargain shoppers and some willing to buy at list price levels), but they are a passive means of communicating price and meeting competition. If matching competition or fending off increased competition is your main goal, there are not enough quality discount schedules in the world to get the job done. Bids are one-time efforts. Don't bid low today in hopes of gaining more profitable business next time around. Bid to suit your current objectives.

Identify which of the following types of buying behavior are found in your market and check that you
are using pricing structures that are consistent with
this buying behavior, as described here.

☐ Complex buying behavior, characterized by
   high involvement on the part of the buyer
   and high differentiation among product
   choices. Usually associated with a long buying cycle where the buyer's choices are perceived as significantly different. Infrequent
   and/or expensive purchases and any purchases that are perceived as high risk fall
   into this category. Pricing policy should establish price differences between your products and the competition. Bundle features to
   increase perceived value. Complexity is all
   right in price lists. Customers have to learn
   about the products to make the purchase,
   and there is nothing wrong with putting
   them through a learning process on prices
   also.

☐ Dissonance-reducing buying behavior, characterized by high involvement in the purchase
   decision but low differentiation between
   brands. Example: Wall-to-wall carpeting requires significant involvement because it is
   an infrequent and expensive purchase, but
   consumers probably consider most brands of
   carpet in a general price range to be basically
   the same. There is usually a short buying
   cycle, and since there is little customer
   learning required, the customer's precon-
   ceived notions about what price range or
   price slot they want to buy in will be the
   determinant. If your products or services fit
   into this category, matching your price to
   your brand image is of primary importance.
   Don't nickel-and-dime these buyers. Prices
   that include warranty and service are essential. Pricing structure should be simple. A

complex structure may create pre- or post-purchase doubts about the value of your offering vis-à-vis those of competitors.

☐ Variety-seeking buying behavior, characterized by high differentiation between brands but low involvement on the part of the buyer. The buyer is really seeking variety, and brand switching is a way of life. Cookies and potato chips are consumer examples; file cabinets and plant supplies, industrial ones. Even though buyers have some beliefs about the product, they will choose a brand without much evaluation. If they switch brands after repeat purchases, it is usually out of boredom, not dissatisfaction. If you are a market leader in this category, you'll do best by maintaining stable prices and fighting brand switching by dominating shelf space, frequent sales follow-up with purchasing agents, and consistent quality and delivery. Avoid stock-outs. If you are not the share leader, rely more on promotional pricing structures—free samples, free trial programs, coupon deals, and frequent price cuts.

☐ Habitual buying behavior, characterized by low differentiation among brands coupled with low buyer involvement in purchase decisions. The buying cycle is short and habit often governs choice. Examples include salt, milk, office paper, and raw materials. These buyers place their monthly orders dutifully or go to the store and simply reach for their favorite brand—in either case, avoiding the belief/attitude/behavior sequence. Any learning that occurs is passive learning. Stable prices are important. Roller-coaster pricing—like that found in the supermarket for soft drinks—does not work for undifferentiated products. But you can try to convert these buyers to higher involvement by linking the product to some issue like quality. Moves toward more product differentiation and customer involvement will help delay (and occasionally reverse) the inevitable drift toward commodity pricing status for these products.

STEP 3. ARE PRICES "EATING AWAY" AT PROFITS UNNECESSARILY?

Although pricing strategy needs to be driven by marketing considerations, it also needs to produce the maximum profits. Your audit should look at the cost side as well as the marketing side. In this audit method, emphasis is placed on price change analysis on the assumption that you already have fairly good gross margin figures on your products, but that companies are less likely to have gone beyond the traditional static accounting models to a dynamic examination of price change. When you run the numbers to see what sales volume change is needed in order to profit from a given increase or decrease in price, you may find a new price level is more likely to optimize profits than the current one. The calculation is fairly simple, and it makes sense to examine a number of alternative price scenarios whenever you perform a pricing policy audit.

☐ *Price increase analysis.* How much of a decline in sales volume could a product absorb and still yield higher profits if its price were raised? If the "indifference point" is well below the decline you might expect, consider raising the price.

Here is how you figure how much volume you could lose following a price increase while still maintaining your current revenues. Say your product carries a 20% gross margin. You plan to increase its price by 5%. The formula would be:

$$\frac{20\%}{20\% + 5\%} - 1 = \frac{20\%}{25\%} - 1 = -20\%$$

That tells you that the product can absorb up to a 20% decline in its sales volume and still yield as much as or more dollar revenue contribution than it does now. Here is a table showing some "breakeven" sales points for price increases.

PRICE INCREASE (%)	GROSS MARGIN (%)						
	20	30	45	50	60	70	80
	SALES CAN DECLINE BY AS MUCH AS x%:						
5	20	14	10	9	8	7	6
10	33	25	18	17	14	13	11
15	43	33	25	23	20	18	16
20	50	40	31	29	25	22	20

Note that products with smaller gross margins are better candidates for price increases than are those with huge margins.

☐ *Price cut analysis.* The same formula can be used to calculate the break-even volume given a proposed price cut. The price cut is plugged into the formula as a negative in the denominator. For example, a 5% price cut in the foregoing example would be calculated as 20%/(20% − 5%) − 1. Here are some break-even sales points for price cuts:

PRICE CUT (%)	GROSS MARGIN (%)						
	20	30	45	50	60	70	80
	SALES CAN DECLINE BY AT LEAST x%:						
5	33	20	13	11	9	8	7
10	100	50	29	25	20	17	14
15	300	100	50	43	33	27	23
20	NA	200	80	67	50	40	33

As might be expected, products with low gross margins are poor candidates for price cuts.

STEP 4. ARE TRADITIONAL PRACTICES AND POLICIES NO LONGER APPROPRIATE?

Long-established trade practices and pricing policies are often assumed to be sacrosanct. While they may provide enough incremental profit to justify their costs, they just as frequently create a serious and unnoticed drain on profit. Part of the audit process is the evaluation of these "sacrosanct" policies with care and judgment. Be especially aware of the potential for price and profit erosion that lurks within otherwise innocent-looking practices. In general, these practices were adopted years ago because they were consistent with a specific marketing objective. Is that objective still valid, and is the practice still a good way to pursue it (if it ever was)? Once these practices become institutionalized, they no longer function as elements of the marketing mix. Buyers take them for granted, and their impact is reduced, even if it is not negative. Identify any longstanding practices (from the following list) and discontinue their use unless they can be justified anew.

- [ ] *2%-10 days, net-30* seems harmless enough, even though most customers will claim the discount without earning it. But over a year's time, the discounts add up to a large cost for money 20 days early. Recommendation: Drop your 2%-10 day discount. Grandfather it only if key customers start to bellyache.

- [ ] *Collection procedures.* These can be a source of profit and price erosion as well as gain. If receivables average 60 to 90 days, that imposes a considerable penalty. Recommendation: If cutting average receivables time isn't feasible, consider building your historical receivables aging costs into your price levels.

- [ ] *Freight policy.* If freight is prepaid, that's money out of your pocket—a considerable burden should the customer be slow in paying. If freight is FOB origin, however, the problem is eliminated, because the burden shifts to the customer. Furthermore, with FOB origin freight terms, the buyer takes title to the merchandise when it is shipped, shifting insurance cost from you as well. Note: To add value to your offering you may choose to pick up the insurance cost on even FOB shipments.

- [ ] *Volume rebates and discounts.* These are a valuable sales aid *if* the discounts take the form of additional merchandise and not price concessions. For example, terms of "one case free with every ten" create a 10% discount for the buyer, but not for the seller. If manufacturing costs are 40% of the selling price, then buyers have their 10% discount at a cost to the seller of just 4%.

☐ *Extended terms and "dating."* These give buyers a certain amount of time to pay after they take receipt of the merchandise and are traditional in some lines of business and may be valuable sales aids. But they may also cause serious profit erosion. Their value in obtaining advanced bookings must be weighted against the cost of maintaining an expanded inventory. Do the math before continuing your present terms.

☐ *Exchange and return policies.* These require scrutiny, because if there's a loophole in the policy, customers will find it. Then, obsolete merchandise will turn up for credit against current sales.

☐ *Warranties.* The volume of claims ought to be compared with the cost of administering them. Often, it is cheaper and makes a better impression on the customer to replace a product without question than to maintain a complex system of paperwork and supervision.

☐ *Dealer and distributor discounts.* They may be deep enough to permit the reseller to undercut the factory on a large order. That kind of direct competition from a reseller plays havoc with established supply relationships.

The process of developing better operational policies begins with understanding how your current policies work in the market and what effect they have on your profits. Once you know, you must decide how and when to follow traditional or industry-standard pricing practices and, more important, how and when to deviate from them.

STEP 5. DO PRICES MATCH PERCEIVED VALUE?

How do customers perceive your products and services relative to the competition? Consumer companies typically invest in research to determine an offering's perceived value both prior to market launch and periodically thereafter. Business-to-business marketers usually do not do as extensive research, and sometimes lack an accurate reading on how the customer values a product. Trade-off analysis (in which customers compare competing products) may be necessary if perceived value is uncertain. If formal, quantitative research is out of the question, at least consider an informal poll of customers in which they are asked to value the product, both in absolute terms and relative to competitors. Once you have a realistic fix on what customers believe you have to offer vis-à-vis the competition, you can examine your price positioning to determine if it matches up logically with those perceived differences. The Pricing Advisor uses a *Relative Value Assessment Form* to help assess perceived value. Their method is summarized in the following steps—use it or something similar to summarize recent customer research or, if one has been conducted, to perform a quick-and-dirty survey of 10 or 20 customers:

☐ Determine the five or six key customer criteria that go into the buying decision for your product or service. (Do not include price.) Weight the importance of each criterion using percentages that add to 100%.

☐ Next, rate (or preferably have customers rate) your firm and two or more primary competitors on each criterion. Use a 10 = highest/best to 1 = lowest/worst scale.

☐ Calculate a weighted average score for you and for each competitor. (Multiply the percentage importance weighting for each criterion by the customer rating of each firm on that criterion. Then sum the weighted ratings for each firm and divide by the number of criteria.)

☐ Calculate the score differences. What percent higher or lower than your firm's average score is the score of each competitor?

☐ Identify the price for your product/service and each of the competitor's. Calculate the price differences in the same way, and compare the percentage difference in price with the percentage difference in customer rating score.

When the score differences are compared with price differences, you will note that the product differences are generally much greater than the price differences. Value differences should not be captured percentage point for percentage point with price differences. However, the stacked ratings for price and quality should be similar.

This analysis should be the fundamental starting point for business-to-business pricing. Industrial and commercial markets are less price elastic than their consumer counterparts. Fewer people buy. Therefore, being 10% cheaper than your competitor results in less increase in demand when Coke is priced 10% lower than Pepsi. Second, business-to-business companies cannot compensate for product deficiencies through advertising and company image reinforcement as much, or as frequently, as consumer companies can.

STEP 6. *WHERE ARE COMPETITOR PRICES GOING?*

Compiling and correctly interpreting your competitor's prices are also important in a pricing audit. Make sure you are getting regular and accurate information on competitor prices from your sales force, wholesalers, and distributors. If the information indicates that lower-priced competitors are a problem (or that a new "insurgent" is entering the market with lower prices), diagnose and respond to the problem by identifying which one of these four situations applies:

☐ Low-priced competitor targeting customers who are *price-sensitive and do not consider product quality/features to be very important.* Typically high-volume users but small accounts. Insurgent competitors generally cherry-pick among these customers first, offering them no-frills products at low prices. These customers are difficult—perhaps futile—for incumbents to defend.

☐ Competitor targeting customers who are *not very price-sensitive and who place high value on product quality and features.* Typically loyal accounts of small and medium size. Price is not a major issue for these customers, and the low price position of the competitor will not succeed unless the price/value mix is improved. No immediate price response is necessary. Reinforce loyalty by giving these customers more attention—letters, sales calls, and so on.

☐ Competitor targeting customers who are *very price sensitive, but also consider product quality and features to be important.* Typically infrequent users, "insatiable" customers. Defend your position with these customers by offering additional quality, service, and product guarantees. Do not reactively match the insurgent's low price, but do not merely repeat old pricing policy either. A small movement on pricing will help defend against the insurgent in both this situation and the one directly above.

☐ Competitor targeting customers with *low price sensitivity but high interest in product features/quality.* Typically national accounts, large users. The low-priced imitator typically tries to pick up a big early hit in this customer group. Many incumbents, panicked at the very possibility, offer price action even before the customer requests it. Too bad, because the national accounts are generally incumbent's safest ground. Usually insurgents and imitators are unprepared to play the national accounts game. Only poor marketing and sales moves—such as arrogance, refusal to be flexible in terms of price, or benign neglect—will turn a national account over quickly to an unknown, price-oriented insurgent. So reinforce your position through fair pricing and extra service, but do not overestimate the ability of insurgents to pick up national accounts.

If there is no significant low-cost competitor moving into your market, you still need to audit other possible sources of pricing pressure that can move competitor prices downward or upward. General market trends are important, and your audit should include a review of:

☐ *Economic demand trends.* These primary data signal whether customers are willing and able to buy your products. For example, the Conference Board issues monthly reports on consumer buying trends. Trade magazines such as *Quarterly Purchasing Manager* and *Purchasing World* provide data on business purchasing patterns, and your trade association is also a likely source of data.

☐ Trends involving substitute products. The growth of new technologies like electronic printing and the decline of older technologies like offset printing are closely watched by plain-paper copier companies like Xerox. When superior new technology cannot be matched, lowering prices is often the only choice.

☐ *Trends for parasitic or complementary products.* The supplies used in copier machines are generally leading indicators of sales and price trends for copiers.

☐ *Direct competitor trends.* Look at both small and large competitors for clues to the pending need to change prices. Smaller firms in any industry can least afford to ride out hard times, so they will often assume price leadership and cut prices based on what they perceive as a cut-or-perish situation. Note: A smaller firm's price cut does not mean you have to respond. Make sure the price is really a clue that overall industry prices are too high in relation to customer demand before you adjust your prices. And tailor your response depending on what types of customers the price cutter is targeting.

STEP 7. WHAT IS THE OVERALL IMPACT OF PRICING PRESSURES?

Eric Mitchell recently contributed to *Marketing News* an interesting article on how to anticipate upward or downward pressure on prices. Now that you have examined competitor pricing trends, looked at customer perception, and generally steeped yourself in the pricing environment, you should find it fairly

easy to use his model of pricing pressures to anticipate future change. Forecasting future price changes
is, as Mitchell writes, "one of the most difficult strategic tasks facing any marketing executive." But despite its difficulty, the effort is well worthwhile, and
a good way to end your pricing audit. Mitchell's
model identifies all likely sources of pricing pressure and divides them into upward and downward
pressures. Check all that apply in each category; then
make a judgmental assessment as to whether the
upward or downward pressures dominate—or
whether they are in balance and equilibrium will be
maintained.

UPWARD PRESSURES

☐ Price deflectors (structural changes)
☐ Inflation
☐ FUD (fear, uncertainty, and doubt about
   switching vendors)
☐ Product extensions
☐ Product enhancements

DOWNWARD PRESSURES

☐ Price-driven competition (or changes in com-
   petitive management)
☐ Customer experience
☐ Changes in technology
☐ Increase in the number of competitors
☐ Increased internal expectations/high sales fore-
   casts (and sales force reactions)

After evaluating these as external variables and
assessing their current impact on prices in the market, also consider how you might influence any of
them. For example, the FUD factor can be created or
strengthened through advertising and customer support and can be reinforced through strong guarantees
and warranties and excellent product performance.
Anything you can do to raise the perceived risks of
switching will elevate the FUD factor and increase
the balance of upward prices. If you think of the
equilibrium price as an outcome of a series of upward and downward pressures, you may think of

ways to counter a downward pressure by mitigating other downward pressures or strengthening upward pressures, even if you cannot alter the downward pressure.

References

Pricing Bonus Report, The Pricing Advisor, Inc., 1990. The pricing policy audit is adapted by permission of The Pricing Advisor Inc., Atlanta, Georgia. See also Eric Mitchell, "Balance Upward and Downward Pressures to Keep Your Equilibrium," *Marketing News,* November 20, 1989, p. 10.

ROSS'S PROACTIVE PRICING TEST

Applications

- Diagnosing problems in pricing.
- Evaluating an organization's pricing to see if it is proactive and contributing to marketing objectives.
- Determining whether an organization uses pricing strategically or not.

Procedures

Answer each of the 20 questions that follow. (Photocopy the pages if you want to use the chapter as a diagnostic form.) Read "Evaluating the Answers" for insights into current pricing policies and procedures and suggestions for improvement.

Idea: Hand out this diagnostic test to people at different levels and in different functions within sales and marketing to gain insight into where specific strengths or problems may be located within the organization. Use as a basis for a working meeting on improving pricing—the first meeting should include all the people who were given a copy of the diagnostic.

IS YOUR ORGANIZATION A PROACTIVE PRICER?
Answer the following diagnostic questions with a "yes" or "no."

---

yes	no	1.	Is your market share constant or declining while prices are falling in real terms?
yes	no	2.	Do you have a nagging suspicion—but no real evidence—that you are regularly bidding too high for contracts?
yes	no	3.	Do your salespeople keep complaining that your prices are several percentage points too high, although your share is holding steady?
yes	no	4.	Do your contribution margins for the same product vary widely from customer to customer?
yes	no	5.	Are you unsure who is the industry price leader?
yes	no	6.	Do your pricing approval levels seem to be functioning more as a volume discount device than as a control mechanism?
yes	no	7.	Would you have trouble describing your competitors' pricing strategies?

yes no 8. Do you find that too many pricing decisions seem aimed at gaining volume, despite an overall nonvolume strategy?

yes no 9. Are most of your prices set at minimum approval levels?

yes no 10. Do your competitors seem to anticipate your pricing actions with ease, while theirs often take you by surprise?

yes no 11. Do you have a planned method of communicating price changes to customers and distributors?

yes no 12. Do you know how long to wait before following a competitor's price change?

yes no 13. Are your prices set to reflect such customer-specific costs as transportation, setup charges, design costs, warranty, sales commissions, and inventory?

yes no 14. Do you know how long it takes each of your major competitors to follow one of your price moves?

yes no 15. Do you know the economic value of your product to your customers?

yes no 16. Do you use the industry's price/volume curve as an analytical aid to price setting?

yes no 17. Do you know whether you would be better off making a single large price change or several small price changes?

yes no 18. Do you know how to go about establishing price leadership in your industry?

yes no 19. Are your prices based strictly on your own costs?

yes no 20. Do you have a consistent and effective policy for intracompany pricing?

(From the *Harvard Business Review* article.)

Evaluating the Answers. Each question addresses a common practice in pricing. Those in the first half are generally considered poor practices and a "no" is the preferable answer to questions 1 through 10. Those in the second half are generally considered good practices, and a "yes" to questions 11 through 20 is good news.

What should you do about answers that do not fit this pattern? They indicate a deviation from what Elliot Ross, and many other experts on pricing, would consider to be good strategic pricing practice. This does not mean your organization must drop everything and do an about-face. It does mean, however, that a closer look at this element of your pricing policy is needed. The advantage to working through these questions in a group is that the implications of each question can be discussed and the merits of a change identified by all those with responsibility for pricing. In many cases, companies will find that they make a number of the mistakes diagnosed by questions 1 through 10 and that they do not utilize all the proactive pricing policies and strategies identified in questions 11 through 20. If many of the answers are incorrect, a serious look at pricing is needed. It should involve upper management as well as the marketing and salespeople who are involved in routine pricing decisions.

Reference

Elliot B. Ross, "Making Money with Proactive Pricing," *Harvard Business Review*, November/December 1984: 147.

Chapter 10

Marketing Management

FIREKING'S CHANNEL MANAGEMENT STRATEGY

Applications

- Implementing repositioning strategies where the distribution channel is dominant over manufacturers and pull strategies are impractical.

Procedures

This is not a prescriptive or systematic method. The key to implementing it is simply to develop dual marketing strategies—strategies that reposition a product in the minds of consumers *and* dealers at the same time. Consumer and dealer perceptions can be, and usually are, different, so it is necessary to develop different positioning strategies for each. The two strategies need to compliment each other, however, for the plan to work.

In 1974 FireKing was in sixth place with a 3% share of the fireproof file cabinet market in the United States. By the late 1980s share had grown to 40% and FireKing was the number 1 manufacturer. A series of repositioning moves and product developments differentiated FireKing's products on the basis of high quality, and clever management of the distribution channel allowed FireKing to build support at the dealer level for its products and new strategy. FireKing's relationship with dealers was critical to the success of its strategy.

In 1974 FireKing's products had the reputation among consumers as the best. So why was the firm doing poorly? Dealers were unenthusiastic about the cabinets. Fireproof files contain heavy insulation that makes them expensive to ship, and FireKing's were the heaviest. Management considered slimming down the product, but recognized that weight was important to the customer perception of quality. The first move management took was to promote FireKing's quality in a way that meant more to dealers. Some competitors used a quicker, cheaper production method that did not guarantee that the poured, plasterlike insulation would dry completely. This meant that rust was a problem. Fire-King launched a campaign to tell dealers that its products would not rust while in inventory—a quality benefit that dealers cared about more than customers since the dealers were usually stuck with rusted cabinets.

Next FireKing focused on the dealer's perceived problem with shipping costs. Research indicated that dealers were leery of being surprised by a high freight bill that would eat up most of their margin. FireKing switched to contract truckload carriers, allowing it to negotiate transportation prices in advance—and to communicate this fixed cost to dealers before they put a price on the cabinets. The strategy took the surprise out of the shipping costs and made dealers more receptive to FireKing.

The next major move involved an upgrade and simplification of the product line. Fireproof cabinets are rated C by Underwriters Laboratories if they are impact resistant, D if they are not. FireKing and other manufacturers produced a broad line of both C- and D-rated cabinets, but FireKing's D cabinets were pretty close to achieving a C rating because they were built more heavily. So the company upgraded all its products to the C category without altering prices significantly. This move pleased customers, of course, but it was also carefully designed to please dealers by simplifying their inventories and giving them a clear differentiation to make selling FireKing's cabinets simpler.

Two themes have run through FireKing's dealer strategy. First, the price structure has been designed to give dealers good margins. According to Van Carlisle, "From the end-user standpoint, we're the best. From the dealer standpoint, we're the most profitable." Second, FireKing has consistently made a greater effort than competitors to get close to dealers so that FireKing understands what motivates them and they understand and appreciate the products. Each positioning move was directed at both the consumer and the dealer, with specific benefits for each group. And strategies like giving all the dealers their own FireKing file cabinets ensure dealer knowledge and understanding of the product.

Reference

David E. Gumpert, "Which Customer Is Always Right?" *Inc.*, June 1987, pp. 145–147.

GARFIELD'S PRINCIPLES OF CUSTOMER TURNOVER REDUCTION

Applications

- Reducing customer turnover by providing better service.
- Investing marketing resources in existing customers to increase sales volume most efficiently.
- Managing the handling of customer complaints and problems.

Procedures

Measure customer turnover and begin setting specific goals for turnover as a way of increasing sales. Apply Garfield's four principles when developing a strategy for managing customer turnover.

Customer service is an important management issue, touching on the effectiveness of many marketing functions. The "Principles of Service Recovery" chapter addresses strategies for coping with specific "moments of truth" in the customer-company relationship. Maynard Garfield of Persuasive Communications agrees that the problems in service delivery have the greatest impact on the long-term relationship, and he focuses on managing these to maximize customer retention. The argument is simply that existing customers are less expensive to keep than new customers are to find, and therefore marketing ought to make reducing customer turnover a primary goal. As Garfield explains,

> Increased sales come from only three areas: acquiring new customers, upgrading existing customers, and reducing turnover of customers.

In fact, most companies do not even measure customer turnover, and those that do are unlikely to give it the prominence of market share and growth figures when it comes to planning and goal setting. But customer turnover is generally fairly easy to manage, and does not require the expensive marketing and promotion techniques used for new customer development since you are already communicating directly with existing customers.

Garfield identifies four principles that apply to reducing customer turnover:

1. You don't have a good customer until you have been through a crisis together. Of course, it is the crises that often lead to customer turnover as well. How you handle a crisis or customer complaint shapes and strengthens the customer's perception of your company, for better or for worse. Garfield tells a story to illustrate this principle:

> A friend's wife changed laundries, and he asked her whether the new laundry was superior to the old. "I don't know," she said. "I haven't had any trouble with them yet."

2. A complaint or grievance is a golden opportunity to solidify a business relationship. Sounds a lot like Jan Carlson (see "Principles of Service Recovery" later in this chapter). But at most companies complaints are considered unpleasant experiences and are avoided by everyone with sufficient authority to delegate. The person who does handle complaints usually lacks the authority, knowledge, concern and courtesy to turn the complaint into an opportunity for retaining a customer and building loyalty.

3. Physical restitution is merely incidental to handling customer complaints. Companies that replace defective merchandise often think they have solved the problem, and are surprised to find that this alone does not reduce customer turnover significantly. It should be considered an essential, but small, first step.

4. The real answer is "psychological" restitution. By this, Garfield means you have to deal with the customer's anger and disappointment, which is directed both at the company and at himself or herself. Garfield recommends the following sequence be applied consistently in handling customer complaints to make sure the psychological dimension is handled properly:

- ☐ Listen without taking offense.

- ☐ Show empathy—the customer needs to know you care.

- ☐ Repeat the complaint, stating it factually (rather than emotionally, as the customer did) and making sure you understand it.

☐ Don't tell how it happened. The customer doesn't want to hear about your firm's problems, and you don't want them to either. The exception to this is when it is really the customer's fault. Then a *very* tactful effort to educate them is needed so the problem will not be repeated.

☐ Reach mutual agreement on a solution. The customer should be more reasonable by this point. If not, start back at the beginning of this checklist and go through the process again.

☐ Follow up. Solve the problem as promised.

☐ Ask for another order. "This is a must. There is no better way to find out whether a customer is satisfied."

Reference

Maynard M. Garfield, "Reduce Customer Turnover for Long-Term Success," *Marketing News*, May 28, 1990, p. 20.

McCORMACK'S MEETING GUIDELINES

I would like to find the guy who first said, "There is no such thing as a stupid question," and force him to sit through the monthly meeting cycle of any major corporation.

—Mark McCormack

Applications

- Streamlining the decision-making process in meetings.
- Treating meetingitis—too many meetings with too many people in them in which nothing much is accomplished.

Procedures

Apply the rules aggressively. Question each scheduled meeting and see if there is a better way to run it—or whether it can be eliminated completely. Run a meeting by distributing in advance the time it will begin and end to each attendee by name. Distribute a topic agenda at the beginning of the meeting.

Every day, over a million meetings are held in the United States to discuss marketing issues. (Sometimes you just have to quote a statistic and hope no one calls you on it!) Marketing is meeting-prone, in part because most projects require coordination of multiple functions, and in part because marketers tend to be among the more sociable, and verbal, of managers. Meetings serve a valuable purpose—but not always. Sometimes they drag on without accomplishing anything. Most regularly scheduled meetings, such as staff meetings, degenerate into dull, time-consuming exercises unless strong actions are taken to keep them useful and defined.

Mark McCormack has developed some useful guidelines for managing meetings based on his philosophy that "Since they can't be eliminated, minimize their number, their frequency, and their length." Here they are abstracted and illustrated with quotes from his book.

1. A meeting's productivity is inversely proportionate to the number of people attending it. McCormack argues that "beyond four or five attendees, productivity decreases exponentially" and that "the longer a meeting has been in existence, the bigger it becomes." Some managers feel their importance is measured by the number attending their meetings. Others do not like to feel left out. It is essential that meetings not be allowed to become "part of the corporate merit system." Avoid giving them an official name or regular schedule, and invite only those who really need to be there (fewer than six).

2. Meetings—like corporate policies—should be reviewed regularly: for their frequency, their necessity, and their size. Meetings, even if informal and irregular to start with, tend to grow and become institutionalized. A regular review is needed to make sure meetings continue to operate effectively and efficiently, and to reduce the guest list and counteract the tendency toward formal scheduling. Many meetings can be eliminated, but are never reviewed critically and so continue to take valuable time away from other tasks. Some meetings, while necessary, are just as productive if held less frequently.

3. People who might otherwise wish to attend may be just as content to receive the minutes. Others might actually be pleased not to attend. Many meetings have unwilling participants. Since you are looking for ways to reduce the number of attendees anyway, figure out who does not want to be there and help them pack.

4. Both the frequency and purposes of most regularly scheduled meetings can be significantly altered without any loss of effectiveness. Really. McCormack argues that "meetings follow a reverse Parkinson's law: The number of subjects to be discussed contracts to accommodate the time available." You need not fear that cuts in meeting time will cripple your department. The shorter meetings, attended by fewer people, will do at least as much as long, overattended meetings used to.

5. Many meetings have parallel or overlapping functions which can easily be folded into one another or combined. This axiom follows from the reverse Parkinson's law of meetings. If you combine two separate meetings into one, and give it half the time the two meetings used to take, no loss of productivity or quality will result. If it does, you can increase the meeting time in small increments until you are satisfied that sufficient time has been made available. McCormack argues that setting a firm time limit on a meeting, or combining multiple meetings/ topics in a single meeting, will increase the productivity of the meeting rather than reduce the quality of discussions.

6. Scheduling a meeting is often the automatic response to dealing with those subjects which are slightly too complex to handle over the telephone. McCormack believes that "Meeting in hallways— that is, any short, informal gathering of three or four people to exchange information or to get quick consensus—is a better, more efficient alternative."

Reference

Mark H. McCormack, *What They Don't Teach You at Harvard Business School* (New York: Bantam Books, 1984), pp. 222–228.

McELNEA'S PROMOTION AGENCY SELECTION GUIDE

Knowing what you want is the easy part. Finding the agency that's right is another story.

—Jeffrey McElnea

Applications

- Planning the selection of a new promotion agency.
- Avoiding internal conflicts and conflicts with candidate agencies.
- Improving the quality of agency selection.

Procedures

Jeffrey McElnea, president of Einson Freeman, Inc., recommends a seven-step process for selecting a promotion agency. Why the big deal over agency selection? Sales promotion cuts across many functions within the firm, and there is sometimes disagreement among sales, marketing, advertising, brand management, and other functions concerning sales promotions. A process that involves all interested parties in agency selection lessens this problem. Another problem is that not all promotion agencies are equal, and it is entirely possible to select an agency that will not do a good job for your company and products. McElnea's selection process is designed to screen candidates carefully and give you maximum exposure to the agency's people and work before making your choice. The process is also intended to keep the agencies happy—even those you do not select—so that your reputation and future options remain intact. The recommended process follows these seven steps (adapted from *Marketing News*):

1. Form a selection committee.
2. Develop a candidate list.
3. Perform a brief initial screening.
4. Meet to brief each agency.
5. Request agency presentations and proposals in the format described presently.

6. Evaluate agency proposals.
7. Notify winners and losers.

The product manager or marketing manager is occasionally responsible for selecting new advertising and sales promotion agencies. Because this task is not routine, companies seldom give it the careful thought it deserves. It can be a difficult task, requiring considerable time and effort, and it does not always leave the client or the candidate agencies happy. Poor selection results in a poor relationship and, generally, in poor work as well. And if the selection process is not managed properly, all the candidate agencies can come away from it unhappy and less than enthusiastic about working with that client in the future.

Jeffrey McElnea's step-by-step guidelines focus on finding an agency to handle sales promotion, as this is his agency's specialty. However, the reader will find it easy to adapt this process to the selection of other agencies as well. His seven steps are described in his own words here—

Agency Selection

The following text is reproduced by permission of American Marketing Association. Thanks to the AMA also for providing additional and corrected material for this chapter.

Quality, innovation, expertise, compatibility, and efficiency are some of the most important attributes to evaluate when selecting a promotion agency.

Your new agency should provide maximum professionalism, be a source of creative innovation, and have knowledgeable insights about your brands, markets, distribution, and competition.

The agency must be equipped to deal effectively with the range of personalities, thinking patterns, and cultures that characterize your company. And it should be one with a sterling reputation for follow-through.

Knowing what you want is the easy part. Finding the agency that's right for you is another story.

The following seven-step selection method, which assumes that fairly specific promotional needs and an annual budget have already been established, brings some objectivity to this important decision.

1. The selection committee. Because the promotion agency generally works with several departments, a decision committee might include directors of marketing, sales, brand management, and advertising—in addition to the sales promotion director.

Depending on the size and structure of your company, the president or other top management might be included.

2. The candidate list. The sales promotion or marketing director is usually the point person for candidate selection.

The most logical sources for your initial list of candidates are promotion agencies that have solicited your business within the past several years, your ad agency account team, business associates, trade publications and industry directories, and the Council of Sales Promotion Agencies in Stamford, Connecticut.

3. Initial screening. Contact the agency presidents. This is not the time for an in-depth discussion of your needs. Instead, you should probe areas such as the agency's interest in building a partnership with your company, its related experience with parallel products and distribution channels, and its size as measured in revenues, staff, clients, and services offered.

Scrutinize the chemistry. Are you comfortable with the agency's top officer as well as the account manager who would be assigned to your business?

4. The briefing meetings. Brief the agencies with all members of the committee present. A complete agenda for their presentations should be discussed, including the unique requirements you will expect of the chosen agency.

Emphasize that you are not looking for specific "answers" during the presentation, but an in-depth demonstration of relevant credentials.

Give the agency principals your suggested format for a proposal, and agree on a response time (generally within three to four weeks).

5. Agency response and proposal. The agency presentation is your most critical tool in making a professional selection because it maximizes the objectivity of evaluation.

A good format enables each agency to demonstrate how well it absorbs marketing problems and responds with a clear "blueprint" of how strategy development and creative would be handled, as opposed to what would be produced.

My suggested format has three sections. The first provides a general overview of agency capabilities. The second details specific case histories from the past, providing insights into how the agency analyzes market situations, draws conclusions, develops strategic and tactical plans, and executes complete programs.

The third section might be called "interpretation," which essentially is a distillation of the information provided during the briefing. This section demonstrates how well the agency assimilates input that might have been communicated randomly, and how accurately it sets priorities for the essential tasks to be accomplished.

6. Proposal evaluation. Systematically evaluate the agencies' proposal letters. Dissect the evidence they have presented and analyze the depth and quality of their recommendations for past clients.

Use the agencies' reference list and talk to their clients directly. Consider circulating point-scale checklists to the committee covering each of the proposal format points to determine how well each agency addressed its capabilities in terms of analysis, planning, creative execution, and other key criteria.

The marketing director will want to review details of compensation with the finalist's top people, if any questions remain prior to selection. It's preferable to clarify potential misunderstandings at this stage. The "purest" form of compensation is the monthly retainer fee based on actual staff time and expenses.

7. Notifying winners and losers. Call the winner with congratulations and explain the next steps: orientation session, project briefings, media notification of the agency's appointment.

Equally important, tell the principals at the losing agencies why they *didn't* get your business this time around. This information will be helpful when they mount their next presentation.

The losers will appreciate your candor. Your company's reputation, as well as your personal reputation for fairness, will benefit.

Reference

Jeffrey McElnea, "7 Steps Guide Agency Selection." *Marketing News*, July 9, 1990, p.14 (Reprinted by permission of the American Marketing Association.)

THE MOTIVATION/LIFE-STYLE HELIX

The desires that flit through consciousness are most often desires for clothes, automobiles, friendliness, company, praise, prestige, and the like.

—Abraham H. Maslow

Applications

- Exploring new approaches to segmenting markets and understanding consumer behavior

Procedures

This is a new motivational model with intriguing implications but no quantitative support. Use it as a starting point for creative ideas about consumer segments and buyer behavior. Generate specific hypotheses for advertising communication strategies, product positioning, and customer segmentation; then by all means *test* these hypotheses before committing to them.

The Motivation/Life-style Helix is currently under development by Philip T. DiPeri of Stonehenge International and is included here because of its novel and thought-provoking nature. It may prove a good scaffolding for a VALS-type study and segmentation model and may also prove useful in advertising and other areas of marketing. In general, new models of consumer behavior translate into useful insights and novel strategies for marketers, and it will be interesting to see the uses this one is put to over the coming years.

Background

Abraham Maslow's theory of a need hierarchy, first postulated in 1943, has appeared in hundreds of marketing and management texts over the years. (You'll find it described on page 441 of this book.) But what use is it to the marketer? The texts never seem to get to the particulars. Here is a model that extends the Maslow schema to create something of potential value to advertisers and marketers, and also perhaps of use in sales force management and even strategic planning.

Maslow's model imagines five levels of needs and assumes that you have to satisfy lower-level needs before you turn your attention to higher-level needs. To put it most simply, hunger will motivate people to eat, and you can't sell a hungry person a status product until you have fed her. But once the stomach is full, motivation to buy a status product may increase.

In Maslow's model (illustrated in the One-Minute Guides to the Marketing Classics at the back of this book), a pyramid-shaped diagram divides the population into groups based on what their primary motivation is. At the bottom are those who are motivated by physiological needs—survival and reproduction—because this is assumed to be the largest group and because these are the most basic of needs. Next up comes a focus on safety, then social needs, then self-esteem, and, at the apex of the pyramid, self-actualization or self-fulfillment needs. This fifth and final category of needs cannot be pursued, so the theory goes, until the other four needs have been met. And most of society is not focused on self-actualization, so this is the smallest group at any one time.

Maslow's model has also been extended to describe the human life cycle, in which people start as babies with a strong focus on survival, then gradually work their way up the hierarchy of needs. Many satisfy physiological and safety needs, then go on to the pursuit of social and esteem needs. A minority then move beyond the pursuit of these needs to the pursuit of self-actualization. Note that the VALS typology is derivative of this model, with the Survivor and Sustainer segments focused on physiological and safety needs, for example (see the Values and Life-styles entry in Part 3, "One-Minute Guides").

Philip DiPeri started with the insight that people do shift their focus, but not over as long a time frame or as predictably as a life-cycle model implies. In fact, one can imagine working through the entire Maslow pyramid in one evening, starting with a quick dinner from the microwave (physiological), a cab to a friend's house to avoid walking through a bad neighborhood (safety), a cup of coffee with a group of friends (social), an outing with your friends to listen to jazz at a well-regarded nightclub (esteem), then, sated by these pleasant activities, a quiet cab ride home in which you contemplate your life, decide that your current job does not allow you to achieve your potential, and vow that you will prepare a resume tomorrow morning (self-actualization).

Of course, this scenario suggests that motivation is extremely unpredictable, and so it is of little use to marketers either. Whether the consumer had a good breakfast may well determine her predominant motivational focus throughout the day! But DiPeri sees a middle ground, in which people move through a slower cycle, over months and even years, one that provides a general undercurrent of focus to their motivations. In his model, people cycle gradually through the different motivational states in order, and when they reach the end, they start around again. However, their needs are *different* each time they move through the cycle—there is an underlying directional movement. DiPeri describes this movement as increasing one's distance from immediate threats to survival—he calls it survival distance. For example, John Doe may feel more secure once he joins the local country club and develops social ties with his town's elite—his perceived survival distance is greater because he now has farther to fall.

This suggests a *reason* for the cyclic movements through different motivational states. People generally try to move "upward" in society, or to "improve their lot," to increase their survival distance—to increase their *likelihood* of survival in the future. And the consumer society feeds this process by providing an endless sequence of ladders to climb, uptowns to move up to, groups to join, and status symbols to advertise the latest social position achieved. Static models of social class structure are inadequate to describe this complex and fluid process as it exists in modern society. They also fail to capture the *personal* nature of this quest—each individual draws his or her own map and plots his or her own course through society on a psychological/social terrain that is not clearly defined by externally imposed class lines.

At the base of DiPeri's upward spiral through repetitions of this motivational cycle are the basic physiological and safety needs that also characterize the base of Maslow's pyramid. The driving force in the model is the effort of people to distance themselves from the personal destruction that failing to meet these base survival needs implies. In a complex modern society, one can get pretty far from concerns about where the next meal will come from. But that does not mean survival needs are not revisited in future cycles—just that survival will be defined differently. Because a movement down implies a reduction in survival distance, and this is undesirable. People, it is postulated, will be highly motivated to maintain their current position—the most recently achieved social environment—and they will see this as a survival issue that is almost as pressing as physiological survival or base survival would be. John Doe's purchase of appropriate country club attire, and his efforts to earn a large commission to cover his country club dues, may in his perception be essential to survival in his new social environment—even though dress clothes are generally classified by marketers as status goods rather than survival goods.

This brief introduction is perhaps sufficient to clarify the basic concepts behind both Maslow's and DiPeri's models—concepts that can seem very simple when they are fresh in the mind, but somehow become quite muddled if encountered without sufficient preparation. Here is DiPeri's formal explanation of his model, based on working papers from Stonehenge International.

The MLH Model

Premise. The Motivation/Life-style Helix is based on the premise that a person's instinct for survival controls all decision making—even decisions seemingly removed from imminent physical danger.

Parameters and Mechanisms. The model proposes three stages of individual focus: environmental, associative, and renewal. It assumes that lifestyle and purchase decisions are made to increase the probability of survival (termed survivability). Survivability increases with increased survival distance. Two mechanisms influence survival distance: the development of survival efficiency and the generation and inventorying of a survival energy surplus.

How It Works. Each cycle starts with the environmental stage. It has two phases—the now phase, in which attention is focused on the operational environment on a moment-by-moment basis, and the future phase, in which attention is turned to increasing future survivability. A surplus of survival energy is needed to move from the now phase to the future phase, and also on to the second stage of the cycle.

The second stage is the associative stage, consisting first of the membership phase and then the contribution phase. The stage is characterized by a focus on achieving and sustaining group membership. Membership in groups increases survival energy. As membership is gained, the individual accepts more and more of the group's norms, and (assuming membership proves valuable) fear of losing the membership motivates the individual to more active participation and the creation of reciprocal obligations. In the contribution phase, membership is ensured through increased status in and value to the group.

The third stage is the renewal stage, in which the individual steps back from the tasks of maintaining position in the current environment (for stage 1) and gaining membership in a new group (stage 2) to assess his or her situation and redefine wants and needs. Specifically, this involves a redefinition of the possibility horizon to reflect any recent changes in the individual's social and physical environment and the options and potentials that now come into view. After the possibility horizon is adjusted (phase 1), the renewal stage shifts to personal growth planning (phase 2), in which the individual redefines his or her view of the world and defines a new operating environment which supports recently expanded expectations. To summarize, renewal starts with the realization that there are still more lands to conquer and shifts to the development of new goals and desires as a result. It then enters a third phase in which the individual seeks new challenges. This pushes the individual into a transition again and reduces survival energy surplus by spending it in pursuit of a more expensive environment. The individual must

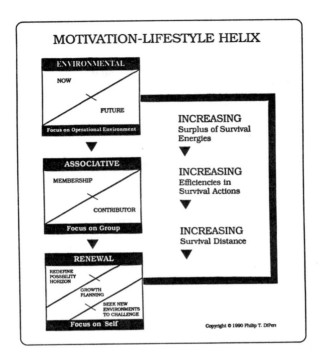

now focus on establishing a position in this newly defined environment and maintaining it—which brings the individual back to the beginning of the cycle.

Implications

One possible segmentation strategy might be based on the rate at which people move through this cycle. Some people presumably move more rapidly than others, and some may stabilize or even move backward. Their needs ought to differ. For example, more rapid cycles will be associated with more frequent change in possibility horizons and group affiliations, and therefore more rapid changes in consumption habits, a stronger interest in new products, rapidly shifting brand loyalties, and shifts in reference groups and decision influences.

Another implication is that luxury or status products do not always play the same functional role. An individual who is just moving into a group will consider this group's status symbols as necessary for growth (much as traditional views of status products suggest). But the individual who has come to consider that group a cornerstone of his or her environment will consider the same products as necessities of continued survival in the current environment—they will become staples rather than status symbols. This line of reasoning might support segmentation strategies and product differentiation strategies for premium and status products, and segments might vary according to how price-sensitive they are, how involved they are in the product decision, and how important the purchase decision seems to them.

Idea: Does the model also work for companies or strategic business units (SUBs)? Growth may go through similar cycles, and recognizing where the organization is in its cycle may be helpful in deciding where to focus efforts, that is,

> Stage 1: Maintain share, strengthen awareness with customers, distributors. (Environmental).
>
> Stage 2: Build market positions relative to leaders—associate products in desired reference groups. (Associative).
>
> Stage 3: Use strength of market position as a springboard to find and pursue new opportunities. (Renewal).

Reference

No published materials available. Contact Stonehenge International or my office for background information.

P&G'S BRAND MANAGEMENT TEAMS

We've made watershed changes at P&G, the most significant changes since the Second World War. They will bear fruit well into the next decade.

—John Smale, retiring CEO, P&G

Applications

- Bringing the perspectives of sales, R&D, and manufacturing into the brand management process.
- Speeding new product introductions.
- Reducing errors in product introductions.
- Turning around underperforming brands.

Procedures

Requires creation of a multidisciplinary working group to plan and manage the brand, replacing the individual brand manager. Can be implemented on a one-time basis, with team members reporting to the brand manager. Can also be implemented formally through changes in the organization chart and the use of elections for team leaders in order to reduce the autonomy of the brand manager.

Procter & Gamble invented product management. But that was 1931, and by the mid-1980s the system had developed some shortcomings. The dominance of the brand manager at P&G, whose role is often described as the hub of a wheel, meant that sometimes the research, sales, and manufacturing people out on the rim did not have sufficient input. The introduction of Pringles potato chips (the ones that are stacked in a tube) is a good example. Marketing championed the product on the basis of its innovative packaging and good test market results. Research and manufacturing was concerned about taste, consistency, and high production cost. But marketing prevailed due to the strength of the brand manager structure, and as it turned out the introduction was a disappointment and P&G had over invested in new Pringles plants.

There were other problems as well. Some analysts believe that P&G was slow at capitalizing on research breakthroughs that did not fit the strategic script of the brand-oriented marketing management dominant at the company. Olestra, a no-cholesterol, no-calorie fat substitute, wasted decades in R&D because it did not fit into the product-oriented organizational structure and culture according to Hercules Segalas, a Drexel Burnham Lambert analyst and former P&G researcher. Another problem arose from the isolation of brand managers—product introductions tended to be slow and gradual, allowing competitors to beat P&G to the punch on some introductions. Brand managers were limited in their ability to make any major changes by the need to seek permission through three or four layers of management, and with as many as 14 brand managers per division, it was difficult to get the attention of the division chief. And finally, in the traditional brand management structure, individual P&G brand managers and their brands competed against each other as well as against non-P&G brands. This competition was not always in the interests of the company, as it did not guarantee optimal investment in P&G's portfolio of products. A P&G brand manager is quoted by *Fortune* as saying, "The brand managers were butting heads. There was a lot of cannibalization. You'd issue coupons at the same time for P&G's liquid and powdered detergents."

To address these problems, P&G experimented with approaches that increased communication and broadened the strategic perspective of brand management. One successful approach, in use at many packaged goods companies now, is to create a new position, above traditional product managers, with responsibility for a product line (the title is generally "category manager"). A company like P&G with many brands in major product lines can benefit from the coordinated strategies and shared resources this approach makes possible. For example, P&G used category managers to increase standardization of packaging and production in its line of 13 laundry detergents, gaining significant cost savings in the process. And according to *Fortune,* the category managers "have the spending power and decision-making authority to respond to fast-changing markets."

Business Teams. P&G first used the team approach in 1980 to salvage Pringles. The team consisted of representatives from sales, research, production, and marketing, and all shared in the analysis and solution of the problem. New flavors and an ad emphasis on flavor rather than package came out of this group. The repositioning strategy revitalized Pringles and demonstrated the value of a team approach. Teams are now used on an ad hoc basis on top of the traditional product management structure when a problem must be solved or a novel approach is desired. Teams typically consist of 10 to 20 members, and can be led by the brand manager or can elect a leader. They generally make decisions by consensus, which means that decision making can be difficult and lengthy. However, decisions seem to be more careful and, by drawing on multiple perspectives, can be more creative as well. And implementation is faster if the team members include everyone needed to implement the chosen strategy.

Problem: This approach can lead to conflict between the brand manager and other team members because the brand manager is used to a high-paced, high-risk environment that differs from the slower pace of the research and production cultures at most companies. (Brand manager positions are usually of short duration, and brand managers are expected to show results rapidly in order to qualify for promotions.) It is therefore important to define the time frame and objectives of the team up front and make the required commitment clear to everyone. A strong problem-solving focus will help. Idea: Some P&G groups meet away from the company in order to help them develop their own culture and identity, distinct from the culture of any single department or function.

Sales Teams. Sales teams are also in use, and their structure and function is similar. Before 1987, P&G's 4,000 salespeople were divided among 11 national sales forces, which meant the retailer had to deal with many independent salespeople. Consolidation at the retail level has shifted power to the retailer—over the last 20 years the top 100 grocery accounts have grown from 15% of P&G's business to 80%, for example. Now P&G serves top accounts with multidisciplinary teams drawn from manufacturing, distribution, finance, and other functions. For example, a team of about a dozen people is dedicated to WalMart and has added value through projects like a just-in-time delivery system that reduces store-based inventories of bulky disposable diapers. (See Recompetitive strategy in Chapter Six for advice on how to set up and manage customer teams to solve problems such as this one.)

Category Profit Centers. The category management system was developed along with the team approach, and in response to the same problems. However, category profit centers provide a permanent structure in comparison with the more informal team structures. P&G's category management system stems from 1987, at which time approximately 100 brand managers were organized into 39 product categories. Each category is assigned to a category manager who has total profit-and-loss responsibility for a product line and up to $1 million in spending authority. According to John Smale, who created this system as P&G's CEO, "The creation of these category profit centers was really a continuation of the basic philosophy that small is good, that you bring focus to a specific business when you create a standalone operation."

Brand Teams. The category managers frequently use brand teams to launch new products or reposition existing ones. They are structured as described (see Business Teams) and often include the brand manager and finance, sales, and manufacturing people. When the team's mission is to introduce a new product, the category manager may assign leadership of the team to a "product supply manager" who takes primary responsibility for pushing development through the various departments, from engineering to production to distribution, shortening the development time as a result.

References

Julie Solomon and Carol Hymowitz, "P&G Makes Changes in the Way It Develops and Sells Its Products," *The Wall Street Journal*, August 11, 1987, pp. 1 and 12.

Brian Dumaine, "P&G Rewrites the Marketing Rules," *Fortune*, November 6, 1990, pp. 34–48.

PRINCIPLES OF SERVICE RECOVERY

Applications

- Improving customer service.
- Managing the inevitable service snafu so as to retain customers at a higher rate.
- Improving frontline employees' response to service problems.

Procedures

1. Measure the costs of recovering from different types of service problems.
2. Break customer silence to find out what customers really think about your service.
3. Anticipate needs for recovery and prepare for rapid response.
4. Act fast to keep the customer's costs from escalating.
5. Train employees to deal with service problems.
6. Empower the front line by giving them the authority, incentives, and responsibility for solving service problems.
7. Close the customer feedback loop by responding to complaints and suggestions thoughtfully, rapidly, and respectfully.

Optional: Use Carlzon's principles of good service as an aid to implementing service improvements. Use Sonesta's criteria for evaluating service response (in principle 5, following) for training employees or for assessing a company's responses to customer problems.

Service recovery is important because, as the authors of the following principles explain, ". . . in services, often performed in the customer's presence, errors are inevitable." The application of quality concepts from the world of manufacturing has improved and standardized customer service in many companies, but it cannot eliminate the possibility of error because, "Unlike manufacturers that can adjust the inputs and machinery until products are uniformly perfect, service companies cannot escape variation. Factors like weather and the customers themselves are beyond a company's control."

This means services never achieve zero defects—they will always be a source of problems for customers. Reducing the rate at which these problems occur is an important project, but it is perhaps even more important to manage the mess-ups so as to avoid angering the customer. A problem solved can be more impressive to the customer than problem-free service since it communicates the company's concern for that customer. But recovering from service snafus is not always easy, even at a company as service oriented as SAS. The following case illustrates the concept of service recovery clearly.

*A Service Recovery at SAS**

One day an SAS flight across Sweden had fallen far behind schedule because of snow. Taking responsibility for the situation, the purser decided on her own to compensate the customers for their inconvenience by offering free coffee and biscuits. She knew from experience that, because she was offering them at no charge, she would need about 40 additional servings. So she went to catering and ordered extra coffee and biscuits.

The SAS catering supervisor turned her down. It was against regulations to request more than the amount of food allotted to a particular flight, and the supervisor refused to budge. But the purser wasn't thwarted. She noticed a Finnair plane docked at the next gate. Finnair is an external customer of the SAS catering department, and as such is not subject to SAS internal regulations.

Thinking quickly, the purser turned to her colleague in the Finnair plane and asked him to order 40 cups of coffee and 40 biscuits. He placed the order which, according to regulations, the catering supervisor was obligated to fulfill. Then the SAS purser bought the snack from Finnair with SAS petty cash and served the grateful passengers.

In this case, the purser dared to meet the customers' needs. . . . At the same time, however, the catering supervisor couldn't understand why a lowly purser had the right to make decisions that had always been in his purview and so became confused and angry.

*From Jan Carlzon, *Moments of Truth: New Strategies for Today's Customer-Driven Economy*, p. 67-68. Copyright 1987 Ballinger Publishing Co.

What he hadn't realized—what we hadn't adequately explained—was that he never should have questioned her authority or in any way interfered with her attempt to satisfy customers. In that "moment of truth," the purser had to act quickly or forever lose an opportunity to satisfy those customers. . . .The catering supervisor could have questioned the purser's decision later, but no one has the authority to interfere during a moment of truth. Seizing these golden opportunities to serve the customer is the responsibility of the front line. Enabling them to do so is the responsibility of middle managers.

Jan Carlson of SAS sees snafus as "golden opportunities," but most customers of airlines, health plans, banks, and other service businesses see them as frustrating and occasionally horrible problems. Consumers interact with service businesses and the service facades of product businesses (retailers, repair services, etc.) every day. Most have an experience that makes their blood boil at least once a week, and no one who has a bad experience with a company ever forgets it. But whether they remember it as a reason never to do business with the company again, or as a reason never to do business with the competitors, depends on how well the company manages the fine art of service recovery.

There are many wonderful stories of service recoveries, some no doubt apocryphal. My favorite is told in the article by Hart, Heskett, and Sasser about a Domino's Pizza delivery-truck driver who spotted a family sitting on the front step of their just-burned house. He talked to his supervisor and, a half hour later, arrived with two free pizzas. Perhaps a poor consolation for losing your house, but the startled customer was later quoted as saying, "Do you think I'd ever buy pizza from anyone else?" These stories are inspiring, but most involve a heroic effort by a low-level employee who breaks the rules to keep customers happy. In these stories, someone like the SAS purser has to "dare to meet the customer's needs," as Carlzon puts it, in order for good service to be provided. Which is a fine way to manage service, if you can ensure that all your front-line people are heros. The problem is, you can't. Employees are conditioned not to break rules and deviate from the routine, and it is unlikely that all front-line employees would come up with good solutions in a hurry even if they were motivated to—anyway, it would be poor management to leave it entirely up to them. As Hart, Heskett, and Sasser bluntly put it, "Companies have made service delivery idiot-proof. But idiots can't solve problems."

Christopher Hart, president of the TOM Group, teamed with Earl Sasser and James Heskett of Harvard Business School to develop an approach that makes service recovery easier and more routine. The power of their concept is that it takes the heroics out of service recovery, or at least makes it legal to be a hero. Their principles provide a foundation for the management of service recovery. And since service providers cannot eliminate bad service entirely, it is essential that they begin to manage the bad service as well as the good. These principles will be useful to managers who want to examine and improve their company's management of bad service.

1. Measure the Costs of Recovery. The cost of unhappy customers is usually underestimated and rarely measured. When it is measured, it is most commonly defined as the short-term costs to the company, such as warranty work, refunds, replacements, and the operating expenses of the customer service department. These figures need to be collected and presented to management, but they are only part of the picture. Long-term opportunity costs may be very high if the dissatisfied customer goes forth and spreads the bad word. Every source of negative word of mouth reduces the number of future customers, or raises the cost of obtaining them. And every dissatisfied customer that leaves has to be replaced. This imposes a short-term burden on the company in the form of higher marketing costs, since it typically costs something like five times more to get a customer than it does to keep one. (This is the generally quoted figure, but there is no firm evidence to support it, and the real difference is likely to be much higher in most companies.)

However, even if the company's real costs are estimated accurately, there is some question as to whether these are the costs to consider. After all, the customer's view of the costs of poor service is very different. Hart, Heskett, and Sasser note that ". . . dissatisfied customers almost always get stuck with certain costs—the money they spend for phone calls, the time they spend making their cases, and the aggravation they must endure throughout. . . . Many service companies conveniently overlook these hidden costs, but the customer surely won't." It is important to identify all the expenses your customers commonly incur when your company's service fails them, and to consider reimbursement as one of your company's costs of dealing with a problem.

It is very important to try to nail down the actual cost of a lost customer. This is likely to be the biggest cost to the company, and if reimbursing the customer for all costs he or she incurs avoids the loss of that customer, the net result is usually in the black. For example, Club Med estimates that a lost customer costs, on average, $2,400 (based on an average of four returns at $1,000 a visit and a contribution margin of 60%). With this figure in hand, it is a lot easier to justify reimbursing a customer for a few phone calls or a taxi ride needed to overcome a travel problem, even if Club Med's management does not feel directly responsible for the problem.

Note: To refine the calculation, a present value of future business could be calculated. (For example, Club Med could discount the revenues from future visits based on how far in the future they expect each to be.) Also, the cost of losing the customer could be weighted by the probability of retaining the customer via reimbursement and resolution of the problem. This figure may range widely—in a recent survey for the U.S. Office of Consumer Affairs retention rates after problem resolution ranged from 54% for service problems that cost the customer more than $100 up to 70% retention for problems costing customers less than $5. Observation of your customer behavior is the best way to establish an appropriate weighting. (It is also likely that you can manage the retention rate and move it closer to 100% through the use of these principles.)

2. Break Customer Silence. Managers face a problem of their own when they decide to turn customer problems into "opportunity for the company to prove its commitment to service," as Hart, Heskett, and Sasser put it. The problem is how to find out about customer problems in the first place. Some customers are very vocal about their complaints, but most are not—at least, they do not talk to the service provider. They may talk to everyone else, of course.

Once a "silent majority" of dissatisfied customers is recognized, the company can search for ways to find them and identify their problems. Start by examining the complaint process. Is it easy and inexpensive for customers to complain? If not, add an "800" number and helpful, trained people to answer it, as American Express has. Or put in a round-the-clock hot line, as Marriott installed in its hotel rooms.

Next, go out and ask customers what they think of the service. Train employees to ask if anything is wrong, and make sure there is a mechanism for remembering and reacting to the answers. The traditional suggestion box can also be effective, as long as you make clear who will read the suggestions and how they will be used. And as long as you actually use them! British Airways has a new twist on this approach—it installed video booths at Heathrow where customers can tape messages to management about their trip. Rewards or compensation to customers who break the silence are sometimes helpful. Main Savings Bank encourages complaints by offering $1 for every suggestion letter a customer sends in.

All these techniques increase the number of customers who volunteer information about a problem. But even if you double the number of squeaky wheels, you can still count on a silent majority. One strategy for reaching these people and learning about their problems is to "look for trouble in the making." Front-line employees can be trained and encouraged to observe customers carefully and intervene when they see a potential problem. Another strategy is to talk with customers (or better yet, ex-customers) through a formal research program to find out what kinds of problems they encountered. An outreach effort costs more up front, but can identify the major sources of trouble in a less biased manner. The information from such a study can lead to strategies for reducing the worst problems and for identifying trouble as it happens so that intervention and recovery is possible, even with customers who do not break the silence.

3. Anticipate Needs for Recovery. Many problems are "waiting to happen," and anticipating them means effective recovery strategies can already be in place when they do happen. Study the organization to find likely sources of customer problems, for example where interdependent events must be properly scheduled to make service work right. Anywhere that a small error can cause a big problem, a service recovery mechanism needs to be put in place. When new services are introduced, resources need to be allocated to deal with any confusion resulting from unfamiliarity. Where new employees interact with customers, either because a service is new or just because turnover is high, service recovery strategies are needed.

Research plays an important role as well. It should be used to find out where errors occur and which ones recur most frequently. If this information is combined with information about customer perception of errors, management can focus on those errors which are most devastating or stressful to customers and which occur most frequently.

When recovery needs are anticipated, recovery can be planned. It is true that many problems are not predictable as individual events, but it is usually easy to predict the general rate and location of such errors, which means that policies, resources, and employee training can be focused where errors will occur. A hotel does not know which customers will lock keys in the trunk of their cars, and it cannot control the occurrence of these events. But it *does* know that this will happen occasionally, and that when it does the customer will be pleased if the hotel can solve the problem rapidly. Therefore it can have a local locksmith agree to provide rapid service under a long-term contract, posting the locksmith's number for employees and instructing them to call as soon as a problem occurs. And, like the Sheraton in Boca Raton, it can even purchase a heavy-duty rolling jack so that the car can be moved out of the driveway while waiting for the locksmith to arrive. The cost of these preparations is remarkably low, but the benefit to the customer—and to the hotel's image—is high.

4. Act Fast. According to Hart, Heskett, and Sasser, "Service problems quickly escalate, so the opportunity to prove one's commitment to the customer is fleeting, especially if the company is at fault."

The inconvenience, aggravation, and cost to the customer does escalate as a problem remains unsolved. A faulty product is a minor irritation if it can be rapidly and easily exchanged. But if the customer must wait in line to exchange it, or make a long-distance call, or package and mail it himself, or wait two weeks for a replacement to arrive, the faulty product has become the stuff of modern nightmares.

How rapidly does your company respond to customer problems? This is an interesting bit of research, and not as simple as it at first sounds. An average elapsed time, as reported by your customer service department, is of little value in answering the question. First, many problems are not handled centrally, and no record of these recoveries exists. It may be necessary to send researchers out to the front lines for a few days to identify and track a sample of service problems. Second, customer perception of the speed of response is what matters here. A survey of customers and employees would probably reveal that employees feel most problems are solved quickly, but that customers think most are not. Standards for response time need to originate with customers, not the company.

A fresh look at the question of response time is likely to precipitate changes in how you handle problems. Many companies handle complaints by letter, especially if they normally do business with customers via the mail, as mail-order businesses do. But the mail is usually too slow for effective service recovery. For example Smith and Hawken, the garden catalogue merchandisers, used to respond to complaints by form letter, but switched to telephone calls in order to speed recovery efforts. In general, the customer wants recovery to happen at a pace that is *faster* than the normal pace of service. If you normally perform a service overnight, recovery should be effected in a single day. If it usually takes a half-hour to purchase a product at your stores, then it should only take a minute to exchange it. If your auto repair shops usually schedule visits a week in advance, a second visit for the same problem should be scheduled the same day as the call.

5. Train Employees. The SAS purser who provided free coffee and biscuits on a late flight had an intimate knowledge of the workings of the organization, and was able to use it to circumvent policy roadblocks and solve the problem. Unfortunately, most front-line employees are so specialized that they develop "tunnel vision." An important goal for training is to broaden this vision. According to Hart, Heskett, and Sasser, "A worker who understands the entire service delivery process is more likely to understand the interconnectedness of the system and find a quick solution. The most direct way to develop this perspective is by rotating workers through different jobs and departments."

Training can also prepare front-line people for specific problems. Role-playing and discussion based on descriptions of problem situations is in use at some companies. Sonesta Hotels does role-playing exercises in the form of a game in which one employee team draws a card describing a problem, and a second team draws a card describing possible solutions. The second team gives points to the first "depending on how well the responses fit the general criteria of keen observation, responsiveness, care and concern, and compensation for true loss," as Hart, Heskett, and Sasser explain it. Note: Sonesta's criteria are applicable in most training situations and provide a set of general principles against which to measure the effectiveness of recovery efforts.

A related issue is whether some employees are simply not suitable for front-line contact with customers. It is certainly true that those employees who have not been made part of the solution through training and empowerment (see the next principle) are eventually going to become part of a customer's problem. But whether some employees are untrainable, or not worth the high costs of training, is a debatable point. Hart, Heskett, and Sasser do not suggest removing the worst employees, but Karl Albrecht and Ron Zemke do. They argue that

> It should go without saying that service people need to have a certain level of maturity and social skills to do an effective job. Yet it is remarkably common to find downright toxic people placed in frontline contact jobs, even crucially important jobs.

If a few "toxic" individuals are at the root of many complaints and problems, they need to be retrained or removed from direct customer contact. And personnel needs to screen people for the "level of maturity and social skills" requisite for customer interaction and problem response. Unfortunately, this is relatively new territory and there are few firm guidelines to follow. One approach is to screen candidates with the same role-playing exercises used in training. At least it would be easy to see how a candidate's responses compare to experienced employees and to established training goals and standards. The larger the gap, the more training a candidate needs. And if the candidate is not even in the ballpark, training is going to be more expensive than searching for a better candidate.

6. Empower the Front Line. "Organizations that empower workers make it clear that they are permitted to use their judgment to make phone calls, credit accounts, or send flowers." If you want employees to solve problems, you have to give them the authority to do so. Traditionally, front-line employees are too low on the totem pole to have any spending authority, yet most problems require some expense. McDonald's has as standard operating procedure that employees should offer a free replacement if the customer complains that her burger is cold. Otherwise, the employee would not be able to respond immediately to the problem without the possibility of getting in trouble for giving away free food—something that restaurants cannot in general condone. Other companies leave the specifics up to employees by giving them a certain amount of spending authority. At one Marriott installation, employees can spend up to $10 on customers without management approval, which is sufficient for the majority of recovery efforts.

In addition to the authority to solve problems, employees need to be motivated. Training is part of the motivation process, but it must be reinforced by reward systems, internal communications, and management example. The third element of empowerment is responsibility—solving problems needs to be written into the job description. If employees are told that they *must* solve customer's problems, they are more likely to use the training and authority they are given.

7. Close the Customer Feedback Loop. Research by Hart, Heskett, and Sasser reveals that "more than half of all responses to letters of criticism either reinforce or fail to counter the senders' original negative perceptions." Companies are not good at "closing the loop" by telling customers what they are doing in response to a complaint. Basically, companies have three options. They can ignore or deny the customer's allegations—the given statistic shows that this is the most common response. They can take corrective action and tell the customer about it—an effective way to close the loop. Or, third, they can explain clearly why they cannot take corrective action, which can also close the loop effectively.

The loop referred to here is simply the give and take of normal communication. In conversation a statement by one person must be responded to appropriately by the other for real communication to take place. But the standards we apply to conversations are seldom applied to customer-company communication. As a result, companies often respond inappropriately, giving the (usually valid) impression that they did not pay close attention to the customer's communication. To close the loop means to pay attention to what the customer says and to respond thoughtfully. It requires taking each problem seriously, and when companies take customer problems seriously they find it easy to close the loop. They ask for more information if needed, and they act to prevent future problems and to solve this problem. It is easy to communicate concern for the customer's problem if concern really exists.

The Need for Consistency

Even if you follow these principles, you will run into trouble unless your service goals are consistent with other goals affecting the employees. For example, GTE Corporation's GTE California unit recently provided service training for telephone operators in weekend seminars in which employees were taught that, "when you pick up the phone you own the problem." But when employees went back to work, they were still evaluated on the basis of how fast they handled calls. According to a recent *Wall Street Journal* article, "Nine-year customer service veteran Ramona Kies-Moore says she now tries to 'own the problem' when a customer complains. For instance, if an installer is late, instead of writing up the problem for her manager to solve—as she is supposed to—Ms. Kies-Moore says she will sometimes take a few extra minutes to track down the installer herself. Unfortunately, she says, 'that shows up bad on your talk time.' "

Eventually GTE's service training will be forgotten, employees will go back to productivity-based performance, and service quality will be unchanged. Unless GTE's management assesses the costs of poor service and decides that the bottom line is better served by improving service quality rather than maximizing the speed of service contacts. If this fundamental change in attitude takes place, then performance measures will change, the role of supervisors will shift from solving frontline problems to supporting frontline problem-solvers, and customers will begin to notice a real change in the character of the organization.

Carlzon's Principles of Good Service

Since this chapter was introduced by Jan Carlzon, it seems appropriate to let him close it. He focuses on four simple principles at SAS and argues that they are applicable wherever managers are trying to improve the quality of service. They provide a useful backdrop to the principles of service recovery, and if service recovery is managed in a service environment such as that developed at SAS, it is much more likely to take root. Here are Carlzon's principles as quoted in the front material of *Moments of Truth*:

- Everyone needs to know and feel that he is needed.*

- Everyone wants to be treated as an individual.

- Giving someone the freedom to take responsibility releases resources that would otherwise remain concealed.

- An individual without information cannot take responsibility; an individual who is given information cannot help but take responsibility.

---

*"Everyone" presumably includes the women in your organization, so you may want to change the "he" to "he or she" if you use these principles in training.

References

Christopher W. L. Hart, James L. Heskett, and W. Earl Sasser, Jr., "The Profitable Art of Service Recovery," *Harvard Business Review*, July/August 1990: 148–156. See also Jan Carlzon, *Moments of Truth: New Strategies for Today's Customer-Driven Economy*, (New York: Ballinger, 1987), which is the source of the SAS material, and Karl Albrecht and Ron Zemke, *Service America*, (New York: Warner Brooks 1990), p. 100.

Joan E. Rigdon, "More Firms Try to Reward Good Service," *Wall Street Journal*, December 5, 1990: B1 and B6.

RAPP & COLLINS' DOUBLE-DUTY ADVERTISING

Applications

- Maximizing returns from advertising by giving it a double focus.
- Reviewing ad campaigns and advertising plans to reduce costs and increase efficiency by exploiting synergies.

Procedures

Review current advertising by your company to identify the function each advertising campaign performs. Look for ways of combining functions in single ads or campaigns. Use the list of double-duty advertising techniques as a source of ideas.

"Single-duty advertising may be the most costly mistake you can make in advertising today," proclaim Stan Rapp and Tom Collins of Doyle Dane Bernbach. The concept of multifunction advertising is not widely accepted, but it makes good sense. In many cases, a creative approach can produce advertising that can be used for more than one purpose and that addresses more than one marketing objective. In fact, as the consumer's environment becomes more cluttered with advertising messages, this approach makes more sense. The cost of grabbing the audience's attention is high, and once attention is there it makes sense to do as much with it as possible.

The double-duty advertising strategy is something that marketing managers may have to talk their agencies into. After all, if one ad accomplishes two tasks, half as many ads will be needed!

Multiple-duty ads are beginning to appear for consumer products under the rubric "line campaigns." Examples include a television commercial from Colgate-Palmolive that,

> . . . starts with a tired little kid marching up to the sink for a morning brush with Colgate Junior toothpaste. Then the ad shifts to an older kid stuffing a tube of *regular* Colgate into a backpack. Cut to a shot of construction workers jackhammering the street—

and a pitch for Colgate anti-cavity mouth rinse. Then on to Colgate tartar control toothpaste and two types of Colgate toothbrushes. All in 60 seconds. (*The Wall Street Journal*, June 21, 1990, p. B1.)

Ralston Purina, Johnson & Johnson, and Guinness aired similar line campaigns in 1990. Some line campaigns have taken considerable flack. A split-screen TV commercial with two pitchmen simultaneously promoting Heineken and Amstel Light beers probably went too far, although Bob Fiore of Warwick Baker & Fiore, the developers of this ad, defends it on the ground that the audience for the two brands is almost identical. *The Wall Street Journal* qualifies this defense with the comment, "He adds, though, that cost was one strong factor in deciding on the double pitch." Of course, from a cost perspective the split-screen appeal has to be less than half as effective as a traditional single-brand ad to have failed, and this one probably wasn't.

Note: This approach is inappropriate in some contexts. Older consumers do not process complex messages very well, and a double message may not work with them. And some messages are too important to adulterate. Also, it is necessary that the multiple functions an ad addresses are compatible. You cannot advertise quality at a premium price to one group and super discounts to another in the same ad! And Beatrice Cos. unintentionally demonstrated several years ago that ads attempting to bring an unrelated group of product categories under a single corporate umbrella are not very effective.

1. Combine awareness and sales promotion. Especially applicable to print ads. Where possible, combine brand-building copy and artwork with a sales promotion such as a clip-out coupon. The communication of a sales promotion is commonly carried out separately from awareness-building and positioning ads, but in many cases they can be combined in a common message strategy. Combining them often reduces the visibility of the sales promotion (as less space or time is allocated than in a single-purpose ad), but the brand-building effect of the ad can make up for this.

Problem: In many cases, different managers and even different agencies are responsible for sales promotion and brand-building ad campaigns. The mar-

keting manager may need to intervene to force cooperation.

2. Promote two channels of distribution. This
flies in the face of the conventional wisdom that
your principal distribution channel will not tolerate
direct competition. However, in many cases companies do use multiple channels—in fact it is frequently a requirement for survival. Many companies
find that direct marketing is necessary to build demand and pull a product through retail distribution.
For example, Borland International introduced its
software products (such as Sidekick) through ads in
computer magazines in the early 1980s. The ads
included a coupon that invited direct orders. However, they also used the banner, "Available at better
dealers nationwide. Call 800-556-2283 for the dealer
nearest you." Initially direct sales dominated, but
eventually dealers saw the light and the products are
now sold heavily through computer retailers.

For more of Rapp and Collins' ideas on combining
direct and indirect marketing, see Either-or Selling
in "Rapp & Collins' Direct Strategies for Indirect
Marketers" (in the Direct Marketing chapter of this
book).

3. Do well by doing good. "You can tie your
corporate contributions to a cause through donation
based on the number of sales of your product, or you
can simply lend corporate support to the cause for
the public relations value." American Express used
this strategy to raise $1.7 million for the restoration
of the Statue of Liberty. A penny was contributed for
every charge card transaction and a dollar for every
new card. A Nabisco promotion sent free packages of
Almost Home cookies to members of the armed
forces when their families sent in three proof-of-
purchase seals. Promotions such as these cross the
boundary between advertising and sales promotion,
on the one hand, and corporate contributions and
PR, on the other. They make the donated dollars
work harder for the company and add PR value to
the advertising and sales promotion efforts.

4. Sell an event while selling a product. A tie-in
event is often a good way to attract attention in a new
market or for a new product. Companies can promote an event or create their own, and dual-purpose
advertising can be used to promote the event and
build awareness of the product.

5. Share the advertising (and its cost) with another advertiser. It is not uncommon to see two related products appear in the same sales promotion, especially if they are made by the same parent company. But there is no reason why unrelated advertisers cannot combine forces when their products make sense together and do not compete (coffee and sweetener, barbecue sauce and meat, etc.). The only risk is that the fates of the two brands become tied together to some extent, and if one turns out to be a dog the other will suffer as well.

American Express, Publishers Clearinghouse, and other companies that do mass mailings have begun to subsidize their mailing costs by including coupons from other companies or, in Amex's case, actually order taking for a variety of products much as a catalogue does. Catalogues are also exploring this strategy by accepting paid advertising from manufacturers with products targeted at their audiences. Automakers have run ads in catalogues such as Nieman-Marcus and The Sharper Image.

6. Support one medium while advertising in another. This generally means using an ad in one medium to alert the audience to look for marketing communications in another medium. A print or TV ad can include the information that a special promotional package is on its way by mail. Or print advertising can be used to notify prospects of a special event promoted by the company or an "infomercial" on cable TV. According to Rapp and Collins, ". . . if you are selling electric power tools, and you used just an inch or two of your advertising pages in *Popular Mechanics* and *Popular Science* to announce the networks and times for your home workshop program on cable, you could build up an audience for a 30-minute infomercial."

7. Promote your brand while promoting a separate profit center. "Jack Daniel Distillery operates the Lynchberg Hardware General Store and Catalogue as a separate profit center. The catalogue is filled with country-style items, all chosen for their value in enhancing the image of Jack Daniel's whisky." In addition to providing some $5 million in annual sales, the store and catalogue operation attracts 300,00 visitors and reaches 2.5 million households by mail every year. All of these exposures build awareness for and reinforce the positioning of the Jack Daniel brand. Diversification into retail and direct-mail sales makes sense in this case, since the new profit center's marketing activities and revenues help support the brand.

Other examples include Coca-Cola and Ronald McDonald clothing lines. Some are more successful than others, and the tightness of the link between the core brand or line and the new profit center may be a determining factor. While McDonald's may see children's clothing as an attractive new source of revenues and exposures to the brand name, children and their parents may not see any clear link between burgers and shirts—at least none that a little laundry detergent can't erase. The strategy requires customer perception of a unique, well-defined life-style represented by McDonald's (or Coke or Jack Daniel) that carries over to other consumer products. And this can be hard to establish. The alternative is to stick closer to home with diversification into products that are related in other, more obvious ways. The dual marketing of gourmet ice cream brands through retail shops and supermarket freezers is a good example.

8. Use your brand name to sell your premium and your premium to sell your brand name. Premiums tend to look like afterthoughts. They rarely tie in strongly with the advertising and sales promotion components of a marketing plan. (In fact, they are often purchased by different managers and from different agencies, so this lack of synergy is not surprising.) A strong premium program, however, can add strength to the brand and can be used to build awareness and stimulate trial. One acid test for any premium is whether it would stand on its own as a consumer product. If not, it is just piggybacking on the brand's identity, not adding anything unique of its own. But a strong, stand-alone product can make a wonderful premium item, as Glenmore Distilleries has found. Its immensely popular *Mr. Boston Official Bartender's Guide* (10 million copies sold) is an important brand in its own right, and tie-ins with Glenmore's liquor brands give them a boost most premiums cannot offer.

9. Advertise the brand while you advertise the distribution channel. Manufacturers already do this by offering co-op advertising funds to their distributors and retailers. But it can be taken farther and, in many cases, implemented more effectively. In many markets, retailers do not use all the available co-op funds because they find them too restricted, because the manufacturers do not pay quickly and fairly, and because tie-in materials are lacking. Poorly organized co-op programs, lacking in customer orientation, do not produce dramatic results. However, if programs are designed with the needs of the retailers in mind (and, perhaps, by a panel of retailers?), the effectiveness of this form of advertising could increase significantly.

References

Stan Rapp and Tom Collins, *MaxiMarketing: The New Direction in Promotion, Advertising & Marketing Strategy,* (New York: McGraw-Hill, 1987), pp. 171–181.

Thomas R. King, "Firms Squeeze More! Products into a Single Ad," *The Wall Street Journal,* June 21, 1990, pp. B1, B6.

PART II

ETHICAL ISSUES IN MARKETING AND MANAGEMENT

INTRODUCTION: ETHICS AND THE CUSTOMER RELATIONSHIP

We conduct our business with uncompromising integrity. We expect HP people to be open and honest in their dealings to earn the trust and loyalty of others. People at every level are expected to adhere to the highest standards of business ethics and must understand that anything less is totally unacceptable. As a practical matter, ethical conduct cannot be assured by written HP policies and codes; it must be an integral part of the organization, a deeply ingrained tradition that is passed from one generation of employees to another.

—from the Mission Statement of
Hewlett-Packard Co.

The man who will use his skill and constructive imagination to see how much he can give for a dollar, instead of how little he can give for a dollar, is bound to succeed.

—Henry Ford

Ethics most obviously concerns marketers because it can get them in trouble, trouble that will make them look bad in the public eye later or even lead to legal problems. But ethical issues can also be fundamental to the *quality of customer contacts*. A lack of strong, ethical values can infuse marketing communications, customer service, and other customer contacts with hidden negatives, as the following transcript of a recent telephone call I received on my last birthday illustrates:

Me: Hello?

Caller: This is James Mortimer from American Express. I'm calling to update our files. Do you still have a checking account at Barclays Bank?

Me: No. I don't think I ever did. And I'm about to sit down to dinner. Can't you call me during the day at my office to do this?

Caller: It will only take a minute, sir. I just need information about all your checking and savings accounts—where they are, the account numbers, and balances.

Me: Well, I don't have that information at hand. If you call me at my office I can give it to you.

Caller: We're just cleaning up our records. Oh, by the way, your card has been inactivated.

Me: What? You mean I can't use it? Why?

Caller: You have a past-due balance of $30 on your sign-and-travel account.

Me· But that's the interest on some airplane tickets that were supposed to be refunded.

Caller: My records show that the dispute was resolved a few days ago, and our policy is to inactivate cards when any amount is seriously past due.

Me: How was it resolved? Will I be charged for the tickets or not?

Caller: I don't know. that's another department. You'll have to call during office hours to find out.
Pause

Me: Well, I see in my checkbook that I sent you a payment for several hundred last week anyway. I'm sure that will cover the $30 you say is past due.

Caller: I don't show any record of receiving it. I'm going to give you the number you need to call to report all the bank information we need. It's (800) XXX-XXXX. You should call tomorrow. It's important that we have updated information so that we can check your balances whenever there is a problem.

Me: Are you saying that I can't use my card until you contact my banks?

Caller: Just call up tomorrow and give them the information. Thank you.

Happy birthday! This type of call is familiar to most consumers. We don't really expect courteous behavior out of behemoths like American Express, and their competitors are likely to be equally rude if given half a chance, so bad behavior does not necessarily have an obvious impact on their market share. But what is it about this call that is so irritating?

The real problem here is that the Amex representative appears to have a disguised intent. As the call opens, it is presented as a request for information. But as the call progresses, the information request is linked to continued use of the product. Is the use of the card contingent upon revealing personal information about bank accounts? The implication is certainly there. (Strangely, the threat was apparently a red herring. The card still works, the bill was in order—and Amex never followed up on the information request.)

Anyone receiving this type of call might conclude that the continued use of his or her card is being held hostage to the personal information Amex has demanded. And, whatever they conclude, they are going to be irritated and disinclined to use the card in the future.

In this case, and no doubt in millions of other cases where service contacts have multiple agendas, it is very easy for the company to cross the bounds of propriety. Perhaps Jim Robinson, chairman of Amex, would think this a clever new ploy for speeding collections. If so, he is a candidate for "inactivation" of membership in the American Marketing Association. It's code of ethics (reproduced elsewhere in this book) prohibits deceptive communications, insists upon "rejection of high pressure manipulations, or misleading sales tactics," and prohibits "selling or fund raising under the guise of conducting research," which we might reasonably extend to collections as well. It also calls on communicators to "Avoid manipulation to take advantage of situations." I'm sure he's all shook up at the prospect. But, more likely, the caller was acting on his own initiative or the advice of a supervisor, and senior management is unaware of the behavior.

The real issue for managers is how they can ensure that customer communications do not cross ethical bounds, and those arising from disguised intent are especially treacherous. The issue is tough because managers often disguise their intent, even to themselves. The entire corporate culture is usually at fault, not any single renegade manager or employee.

We can be reasonably sure that American Express would not intentionally bribe its customers for their banking records—yet they unintentionally do it nonetheless.

The disguised intent problem appears in other guises as well. Reformulations of product, for example, may be thought of by management as in the interests of their customers, but seen by customers as a rip-off. Consumers who recently repurchased an outlandishly expensive bottle or tube of liquid soap known as Bagno Crema al Miele, a brand belonging to the Italian firm Perlier S.p.A., may have been surprised to find that the strong, distinctive aroma of Acacia honey for which the product is loved by its users has been reformulated out of it. The scent has faded, but the label and packaging are identical. Only the price has gone up—to $40 for a 1,000 ml container, making this a rather expensive surprise to those consumers who buy the product for its scent!

I recently sat in on a management meeting at a manufacturer of hand tools for household use. The issue: Their primary competitors' costs were going down, and they felt obliged to follow suit. The competitors have been cutting costs by cutting out materials, an ounce here and a penny there, over the years. Today's tools weigh less and are of weaker materials than what the competitors sold under the same item number five years ago. The argument was put forward at the meeting that the products are *functionally* the same, and the "extra" material is wasted on the consumer. Perhaps, but is it ethical to reformulate the product without notifying customers, even when you can assume customers may not notice? Shouldn't consumers decide for example whether a heavy-handled screwdriver with a stronger shaft is no better than a lighter one with an untempered shaft? An alternative approach would be to "blow the whistle" and tell consumers that "Our competitors have been cheating you for years. Ours are the only screwdrivers still made with heavy materials and a tempered shaft."

Of course, the high road sounds easy from an armchair, but it often requires a new tack, and greater risk, for managers whose corporate culture or (in this case) industry culture dictate otherwise. The scrupulously   honest   screwdriver   manufacturer would have to overcome the fact that consumers probably do not pay any attention to the finer points of screwdriver quality at present, and the added problem that distributors and retailers discourage comparison shopping through tight limitations on display space for screwdrivers. The "right" approach—probably to develop a new line of low-priced products and reposition the old line as high-quality products—requires breaking through habitual buyer behavior and a distribution bottleneck in an industry that has never advertised direct to the consumer! Far easier to follow the leaders by convincing yourself and deceiving your customers with the argument that a little less material every year won't do anyone any harm.

At the core of many ethical transgressions and service problems alike is the essential conflict of interest between company and customer. The marketing concept holds that companies should take the customer's perspective and try to give customers what they want. But too often this becomes a trade-off of interests, and companies or their employees fail to see the possibility of a win-win relationship. The result, at best, is a company that does not show its customers it cares about them. At worst, it is a company that actively deceives the customer through disguised intent, misleading ads, undisclosed reformulations, and other acts that an informed consumer would clearly see as violations of ethics, if not laws—even if managers are inclined to overlook the ethical dimension.

The cost of this common type of ethical transgression is higher than the risk of occasional fines or suits suggests. As was argued at the expense of American Express, ethical issues are fundamental to the quality of customer relationships. This places marketing on the front lines of the growing struggle to come to terms with ethics in business, and it places ethics at the heart of service management, product development, marketing communications, and in fact, all the variables of the marketing mix. It makes ethics a potential source of competitive advantage and share gains, not just an occasional puzzle for the corporation's lawyers.

How do companies manage to deal with ethical problems arising out of the perceived conflict of interest between customer and company? As already discussed, a common solution is to disguise the company's intent—to itself. Self-deception or at least a studied lack of attention to the entire issue is commonplace. That it is necessary to even argue the point that ethical choices permeate the entire marketing function is evidence of this, for most of us compartmentalize ethics into a small, and generally insignificant, secondary issue. Something to put on the back of an application form, where the American Marketing Association's code appears. But not something to consider whenever marketing plans and marketing communications are developed.

All right, you get the picture. There is a strong argument to be made for front-and-center attention on ethics in marketing. The following methods and approaches to the subject are important for that reason. Each provides a slightly different perspective on ethics, since it continues to be a slippery subject. My personal favorite is the Moral Theory of Marketing model advanced by Williams and Murphy. What it lacks in specifics of application it more than makes up for by providing a strong, value-based concept of leadership that translates into ethical behavior throughout the corporation. I believe this conceptual approach is a better safeguard than lengthy regulations and guidelines for employees, which unfortunately are no more likely to be followed than the AMA's code of ethics is likely to influence Jim Robinson and his crew. However, be forewarned that this is an underdeveloped subject, and that the state of the art in ethical management leaves much to the invention and judgment of managers.

WILLIAMS AND MURPHY'S MORAL THEORY OF MARKETING

A theory of virtue enables business organizations to develop consciously their own ethical corporate culture.

—Oliver Williams and Patrick Murphy

Applications

- Creating an ethical corporate culture that guides the actions of employees and adds an ethical dimension to the company's values.

- Improving adherence to standards of ethical behavior.

- Understanding the implications of a company's principles and values on specific marketing decisions (as a guide for managers or to bring consideration of ethics to the market planning process).

Johnson & Johnson's one-page credo starts with the statement,

> We believe our first responsibility is to the doctors, nurses and patients, to the mothers and fathers and all others who use our products and services. In meeting their needs everything we do must be of high quality. We must constantly strive to reduce our costs in order to maintain reasonable prices. Customers' orders must be serviced promptly and accurately. Our suppliers and distributors must have an opportunity to make a fair profit.

And it ends with the statement that

> When we operate with these principles, the stockholders should realize a fair return.

When containers of Johnson & Johnson's Tylenol brand were poisoned in 1981 and 1984, Williams and Murphy argue that "The firm's recall of the Tylenol capsules was a result of the culture in place at Johnson & Johnson for a long time and was more that just clear reasoning about the company values." A senior executive once explained that "Our code of conduct was such a way of life in the firm that our employees, including me, would have been scandalized had we taken another course. We never seriously considered avoiding the costly recall." (See Laura Nash's referenced analysis.)

For many companies, the decision would have been far harder. Nestlé's managers persisted in selling infant formula to Third World countries for six years after the World Health Organization asked it to stop because these formulas were a major health risk. "Even after it became clear that consumers were using the product incorrectly, Nestlé still did not see the issue as its problem," explain Williams and Murphy. "The problem at Nestlé was not that decision makers were not thinking clearly, but rather that managers were adverting to the wrong features of their experience. This is a problem explicitly addressed by the formation of an ethical corporate culture, for the culture does, indeed, shape one's vision."

Nestlé's culture placed maximizing immediate profits over its responsibility to its customers—quite the opposite of Johnson & Johnson's value system as expressed in their credo and actions. Management's vision was focused on the wrong issues from an ethical standpoint, and it took Nestlé six years and a massive consumer boycott to change its focus. The ethical dimension of corporate culture is indeed a powerful force!

Had Johnson & Johnson faced the same decision as Nestlé, its managers would probably have come to the same conclusion in days rather than years. The trade-off between profits and ethical behavior assumed by Nestlé would not be apparent to Johnson & Johnson, where it is a matter of faith that principled actions will allow shareholders to realize a fair return. And in fact this faith in the long-term profitability of principled action has guided Johnson & Johnson to profitable growth, even through the traumatic Tylenol crisis.

A sense of virtue permeating management decisions brings a wonderful clarity to what otherwise would appear as difficult, ambiguous ethical decisions. In fact, it can go farther, by making the moral dimension of a decision apparent where it would not be otherwise. But this sense of virtue is lacking in many corporate cultures.

The case of R.J. Reynolds Tobacco Co.'s new Uptown brand of cigarettes is a good example. Targeted specifically at black males, the brand was conceived of as a classic application of marketing segmentation

strategy by Reynolds' managers. It was test marketed
in Philadelphia early in 1990 because of the high
(40%) proportion of blacks in this city, but was
hastily withdrawn in the face of massive, national
protests.

Reynolds does not see a compelling ethical case
against the brand, as Peter Hoult, executive vice
president of marketing, explains:

> We regret that a small coalition of antismoking zeal-
> ots apparently believes that black smokers are some-
> how different from others who choose to smoke and
> must not be allowed to exercise the same freedom of
> choice available to all other smokers.

This attitude is explained in part by Reynolds'
historical stand that cigarette smoking is a matter of
personal choice, that the medical evidence against
smoking is inconclusive, and that cigarette advertising does not influence people to smoke. Years ago,
when first faced with the health issue, the company
and industry chose to come down on what has
turned out to be the wrong side of an ethical decision
in favor of maximizing its profits, rather than protecting its customers. As the evidence against its position has strengthened, it has moved onto shakier and
shakier ground in defense of that position.

But with Uptown, Reynolds also made a new
ethical choice—probably without realizing it was
doing so. Opponents of the brand argued that the
targeted market segment was indeed different (and of
course black smokers are, or a segmentation strategy
would not have been pursued in the first place). The
mortality statistics alone support this contention.
While cigarettes cause one in every six deaths in the
United States on average, their impact is about twice
as negative among black men as among white men.
For example, blacks lose twice as many years of life
on average as do whites as a result of smoking. Other
arguments were also advanced to make this case. For
example, widespread poverty, lack of education, and
poor job prospects among inner-city youths are
thought by many to make them more vulnerable to
the "glamour, high fashion, and nightlife" emphasis
of the Uptown ads—just as they are more at risk from
illegal drugs' false promises of leisure and riches. To
those working against the oppressions of drugs and
poverty, the Uptown ad campaign's impact is a nega-

tive countervailing influence. Only the myopia brought on by a corporate culture without a strong sense of virtuous behavior would blind managers to these issues.

Burger King faced an interesting ethical decision when it elected to advertise on Channel One, the Whittle Communications in-school TV channel that has attracted controversy because of its plan to be advertiser supported. Should advertisers be allowed to target children at their desks in the forced-attention classroom context? Perhaps not, but so far they are, and advertisers have begun to use this new medium to air what *The New York Times* describes as "standard-product advertising." With one exception. Burger King and its agency, D'Arcy Masius Benton & Bowles, have run a series of lengthy commercials by noted documentary filmmakers on the "traumas faced by dropouts and of lives marred by prostitution, pregnancy, drugs, crime, homelessness and solitude. . . . All that identifies Burger King as the sponsor is fine print at the beginning, a small logo, and a slogan—"Sometimes breaking the rules means staying in school"—which echoes Burger King's regular slogan (New York Times)."

Burger King's management has seen the Channel One issue in ethical terms, and has hit upon an interesting, and more ethical, communications strategy than other advertisers as a result. Why? Again, the difference is something rooted in the value system of different corporate cultures. But how does a positive value system get there, and how can it be reinforced? Or, to put it in Williams and Murphy's words, how can you avoid the problem that, "A business organization can so shape persons that they do not "see" the ethical dimensions of the professional world?"

Step 1. Throw Out the Rule Book! Williams and Murphy argue that principles, such as those delineated in a corporate code of conduct, are useless without "a context, a vision of what constitutes the good life." Johnson & Johnson's vision, as expressed in its credo, fills this role. As the philosopher William Frankena has expressed it, "principles without traits are impotent." This means that the common theoretical approaches to business ethics (which are grounded either in classic teleological or deontological theory, and which it will not benefit the reader to elaborate upon here), are not very useful in bringing consistent, value-based ethical behavior to marketing. They lead to a "moral reasoning" approach, which tends to produce the end result the reasoner wants—note that both Nestlé and Reynolds justified their unethical behavior in the foregoing examples using freedom of choice—a *moral* argument.

Williams and Murphy's approach is grounded in a third, less popular ethical theory, Aristotle's theory of virtue. They put the meat of it in a nutshell when they explain,

> It takes virtuous people to make right decisions, and virtue is learned by doing.

Observing others, practicing, and imitating the behavior of role models is how virtuous behavior was learned in ancient Greece, and how it is learned in modern society. This implies that you cannot expect ethical decisions from managers and other employees unless they have learned the requisite virtues in the context of their work and corporate culture. Williams and Murphy explain that "Moral virtue is understood to be essential to making good assessments and judgments; that is, without having cultivated generosity, compassion, forgiveness, and so on, one will not 'see' all that is there."

Step 2. Cultivate moral virtue. Of course, this assumes senior management possesses moral virtue and can translate it into a practical vision of management. Johnson & Johnson's credo did not *create* any values; it simply put core values down on paper as the firm grew and the moral vision of the founders was at risk of dilution. Similarly, Hewlett-Packard's enlightened philosophy of personnel management was initially an expression of its founders' sense of what constituted virtue, and only came to be codified 20 years after founding in order to help preserve that vision. And when the Dana Corporation's one-page credo, "The Philosophy and Policies of Dana," states that "Laws and regulations have become increasing complex. The laws of propriety always govern," this charge of ethical responsibility is given weight by the fact that

> . . . company folklore remembers the 1969 incident when former President Ren McPherson publicly

dumped into the trash a sizable collection of detailed Dana policy manuals. (Rogers and Swales, p. 296)

Dana's corporate culture supports and values the judgment of its employees, and does not tie their hands with excessive or detailed policy manuals. Employees are given the freedom and support to make their own judgments, and this is what emboldens them to shoulder the burden of virtue. You can't throw out the policy manuals and allow the "laws of propriety" to govern unless you are confident your organization teaches and reinforces these laws of propriety.

In each of these examples, and probably in every example, virtuous behavior originated with a strong leader. *If* the CEO doesn't give a damn whether anyone dies after using the company's products, the rest of the company won't. *If* the director of marketing does not care to hear about possible negative influences of an advertising campaign, no one else is likely to worry either. But if these role models bring a consistent focus on the social impact of their decisions to work with them, the rest of the organization is likely to follow suit. Cultivating moral virtue seems to be the responsibility of whoever sits at the top of the organization chart. As Theodore Hesburg, former president of Notre Dame University, put it, "The very essence of leadership is [that] you have to have a vision. It's got to be a vision you articulate clearly and forcefully on every occasion. You can't blow an uncertain trumpet" (*Time*, May 1987).

Step 3. Reconcile values and goals. Ethical decisions can be ambiguous and unnerving because they can pit self-interest against propriety. What happens when you tell your product-development people to create new, profitable products, and also charge them not to do any harm to consumers? If you run a tobacco company, you are probably blowing an uncertain trumpet that leaves employees the unhappy task of deciding which tune is strongest. This is most likely to happen when you reexamine an organization's core values and try to inject them with a little more virtue than they currently have. If a tobacco company were to "get religion" at this late date, it would face the daunting task of developing harmless substitutes for its products and profits, starting basically at square one.

Given the possibility of short-term competition between performance goals and virtuous corporate behavior, management needs to identify the most difficult conflicts and articulate a specific strategy and philosophy for dealing with them. It needs to be consistent with the vision of "moral virtue" that management is trying to cultivate. But it also should recognize history and circumstance. For example, if a product line's impact is judged harmful, but the company is addicted to its profits and the customer is addicted to its active ingredients, a thoughtful, long-term withdrawal plan must be articulated by management in order to make virtuous behavior realistic.

Step 4. Identify a moral framework for marketing decisions. Williams and Murphy observe that "The theory of virtue has a bearing on the type of marketing mix decisions a company or manager makes." For example, "For product decisions, the theory of virtue would emphasize the product's effect on consumers' lives." For each important marketing decision, certain general questions can be asked that help place it in an ethical context. Marketers need to know what these questions are, and managers should consider requiring that they be answered in marketing plans. Williams and Murphy suggest the following candidates for this purpose.

Product. Does the product have the potential to harm consumers? (Look at both physical harm and less tangible harm such as "eroding the formation of virtue.")

Pricing. Are prices confusing to the target market? Are exceptions to the list price, such as discounts, clearly defined to the consumer? Is there a reasonable and apparent relationship between price and value?

Place. Are dealings with all channel members honest and cooperative in nature? Is unreasonable coercion being used?

Promotion. Are salespeople short-term oriented to the exclusion of honesty, integrity, and other desirable traits? Do salespeople treat customers as though they expect a long-term relationship? Does advertising have a negative influence on its recipients, either directly or by shaping them in inappropriate and potentially harmful directions?

By asking these questions, marketers bring the social implications of their actions into clear focus— hopefully during the planning stages and not after they have developed a vested interest in the outcome.

References

Oliver F. Williams and Patrick E. Murphy, "The Ethics of Virtue: A Moral Theory for Marketing," *Journal of Macromarketing,* Spring 1990: 19–29.

Laura L. Nash, "Johnson & Johnson's Credo," in *Corporate Ethics: A Prime Business Asset,* The Business Roundtable, February 1988: 77–104.

Associated Press, "RJR Cancels Test of 'Black' Cigarette," *Marketing News,* February 19, 1990, p. 10.

John Marcom Jr., "Feed the World," *Forbes,* October 1, 1990:110–118 (for the opposing view of Nestlé).

"Burger King Spots on Staying in School," *The New York Times,* May 29, 1990, p. D15.

Priscilla S. Rogers and John M. Swales, "We the People? An Analysis of the Dana Corporation Policies Document," *The Journal of Business Communication,* Vol. 27, Summer 1990: 293–313.

OVERCOMING MORAL MUTENESS

It is impossible to foster greater moral responsibility by business people and organizations without also facilitating more open and direct conversations about these issues by managers.

—Frederick Bird and James Waters

Applications

- Encouraging managers to see and articulate the moral dimensions of their behavior.
- Overcoming the serious obstacles to discussing ethics that exist in most business organizations.
- Paving the way for the creation of a stronger vision of ethics in the marketing function and the business in general.

Bird and Waters report that "Current research based on interviews with managers about how they experience ethical questions in their work reveals that managers seldom discuss with their colleagues the ethical problems they routinely encounter." This "moral muteness," as the researchers call it, leads managers to deny the ethical dimension of their decisions, even when the decisions are consistent with ethical norms of behavior. An alarming footnote to this finding is provided by a recent study that identifies a "generation gap in business ethics" and concludes that younger managers "appear less exacting in their moral judgments on a broad range of issues." This suggests a gradual slipping in the strength of managers' moral convictions over time. If firms allow managers to continue their moral muteness, and to continue to believe that most decisions are not ethical in nature, the result may be a deterioration in ethics rather than a continuation of the status quo.

In fact, ethical norms of behavior drive daily decisions concerning customer relations, pricing policy, dispute and conflict resolution, fair treatment of employees, and so on—they create standards for behavior that typically lead managers to fulfill obligations and behave in a trustworthy manner. But managers explain their behavior as designed to optimize revenues or profits, not as based on ethical standards or analysis of competing moral obligations.

Why don't managers like to admit the ethical basis of their actions? And, perhaps of more relevance to practitioners, how might this hinder efforts to build an ethical marketing program? Bird and Waters answer the second question when they report that, in the long term, moral muteness has the following organizational costs (as quoted from the footnoted article):

- Creation of moral amnesia.
- Inappropriate narrowness in conceptions of morality.
- Moral stress for individual managers.
- Neglect of moral abuses.
- Decreased authority of moral standards.

These are significant impacts, and it is clear that the problem of "moral muteness" must be overcome by any firm that is serious about implementing and living by a code of ethics or an ethical corporate culture.

To understand how to overcome the problem, it is helpful to see how it occurs. Bird and Waters found that managers do not like to articulate the ethical dimensions of their decisions for three reasons. First, moral loquaciousness is viewed as a threat to the organization's harmony. "Moral talk is intrusive and confrontational and invites cycles of mutual recrimination" is how they sum up managers' explanations.

Second, moral talk is often viewed as a threat to efficiency. They explain that managers generally believe that "Moral talk assumes distracting moralistic forms (praising, blaming, ideological) and is simplistic, inflexible, soft and inexact." They also find that "such moral talk frequently seems to be narrowly self-serving" or designed to protect the speaker's self-interests. A final efficiency concern is the fear that articulating specific promises, obligations and rights will limit the manager's flexibility in the future. Better to leave things vague and be able to "change the rules" should the need arise!

Third, moral talk is commonly viewed as a threat to managers' effort to "present themselves as powerful and effective." This is because moral talk is generally considered "too esoteric and idealistic, and lacks rigor and force." For example, "many managers experience futility after they attempt unsuccessfully to change corporate policies which they feel are morally questionable."

These findings provide clear signposts toward better articulated ethical decisions in marketing. Most simply, the threats or negative impacts of moral talk need to be reduced. Threats to harmony, efficiency, and the manager's image of power and effectiveness must be removed in order to take the risk out of openly considering moral and ethical issues.

Less obviously, the benefits of moral talk need to be increased. This is the other side of the equation, after all, and even if some risks remain, managers may be willing to break the silence if they perceive greater rewards. Each of these strategies is discussed in turn, although the reader should be cautioned that the research findings cited in this article have yet to be translated into firm, well-tested methods by managers. On the bright side, this means readers can probably think of creative approaches beyond those I have thought to list. On the negative side, it means readers must operate in uncharted waters. Hopefully the following ideas will help them chart a safe course.

1. Taking the risk out of discussing ethics

Clarify the responsibility of managers to their organizations. It is often seen as "a moral standard," according to Bird and Waters, and as such it conflicts with other ethical considerations (as when it will cost the company money to do something ethical). It helps to define the responsibility of managers to their organizations more clearly, for example, by putting it in the context of other social and moral obligations. Where does it fit in a hierarchy of values and obligations? If it should not be placed above public safety, for example, then make sure managers know this!

Do not punish managers for their moral views. This follows from the clarification of responsibility to the organization. Bird and Waters found that, "From the perspective of the managers we interviewed, their organizations seemed to expect from them unquestioning loyalty and deference." And as a result, they expected to be "personally blamed, criticized, ostracized, or punished" if they expressed moral views that ran counter to this unquestioning loyalty.

Increase the authority of moral standards. "Moral arguments possess compelling authority only if the discourse in which these arguments are stated is socially rooted," explain Bird and Waters. Programs designed to define and strengthen shared moral values within the organization can provide this social context (see the section on Moral Theory of Marketing). In addition, managers can make sure that employees are aware of the cases in which moral standards dictated company actions—they can tell relevant stories in staff meetings, or see that the stories are conveyed in an in-house publication. If the company draws attention to the impact of moral standards, their perceived authority should grow.

Encourage collaboration. Collaboration works because "shared values provide a common vocabulary for identifying and resolving problems." While charismatic leadership or dictatorial command can be used to increase teamwork in the short run, in general collaboration builds on (and will help build) a balance of obligations among collaborators— obligations that need to be defined according to a shared value system if the participants are to work together in harmony. This argument suggests that organizing for and requiring more collaborative work and less solo work will contribute to the creation of strong, shared values. And this shared value system could provide the social roots that give moral standards their strength and authority.

2. Increase the benefits of discussing ethics

Do not neglect abuses—or assertions—or moral conventions. Bird and Waters found that "organizational silence on moral issues makes it more difficult for members to raise questions and debate issues." Organizations are often silent, preferring to ignore or disguise improper behavior in order to avoid embarrassment, bad press, employee disputes and suits, or possible legal actions by regulators. But this organizational silence encourages individual silence by showing managers that unethical behavior is not punished and that ethical behavior is not rewarded.

Bird and Waters report that "Managers we interviewed readily cited moral lapses of colleagues and competitors." Without clear negative consequences for poor ethical choices, and clear rewards for good ethical choices, there are few personal benefits compelling managers to discuss and work out the ethical dimensions of their decisions.

Bring the relevant moral issues into the open. For example, you might circulate recent articles on companies that have been "forced to change . . . ads because of action by attorneys general, who have become increasingly aggressive in policing advertising" since "the Federal Trade Commission became less active in doing so," as a recent article on Miles, Inc., and its advertising for One-A-Day vitamins explains. Discussing the ethical and legal sides of product claims with your product managers and ad agency is one way to make sure they cannot "stonewall" moral questions by arguing that the issues involved are ones of "feasibility, practicality, and the impersonal balancing of costs and benefits," as do many managers according to Bird and Waters. By making sure these issues are understood, you demonstrate an interest in seeing managers resolve them ethically.

Help managers learn how to discuss and resolve moral issues in a constructive manner. If they find that talking through ethical problems helps them resolve these problems, they will see the benefits much more clearly. But the trouble is, managers have little training or experience in moral reasoning or moral discourse. How can you ask people to do something they are not trained to do? Fortunately, Bird and Waters find that, "Learning how to talk ethics is neither as simple nor as difficult as it seems to be to many managers." The two keys are to train managers how to recognize and use "several of the typical forms in which moral arguments are stated" and to train them to avoid abuses of moral expressions (when they are used to attack others or advance one's own position). A straightforward methodology in which moral talk is used "to identify problems, to consider issues, to advocate and criticize policies, and to justify and explain decisions" might best be taught through role-playing and case analysis exercises as part of ongoing management training.

Encourage open discussion of moral issues and their relevance to company policy. While it no doubt would be inefficient to have managers constantly raise questions about the ethicality of routine policies and decisions, they must be given a time and place to raise such issues. An analogy to marketing strategy is appropriate here. Strategy is not questioned and altered daily, but there is a formal, scheduled opportunity to reevaluate it in the planning process at most companies, and there are informal ways to redirect it in the interim in case something goes obviously wrong. The same should be true of ethics, and the annual planning process could provide a good forum for delving into tough ethical questions. Furthermore, some procedures must be in place so that managers can raise the unexpected ethical problems that they encounter between planning sessions. For example, you might establish the custom of writing a "moral issue memo" directly to the boss, in which the moral arguments and ambiguities of a tough decision are laid out so that constructive feedback can be provided.

References

Frederick B. Bird and James A. Waters, "The Moral Muteness of Managers," *California Management Review*, Fall 1988: 73–88.

Justin G. Longenecker, Joseph A. McKinney, and Carlos W. Moore, "The Generation Gap in Business Ethics," *Business Horizons*, September–October 1989: 9–14.

"Miles to End Health Claims on Vitamins," *The New York Times*, August 30, 1990, p. D17.

ETHICAL ISSUES IN MARKETING RESEARCH

Applications

- Identifying and discussing a number of sensitive issues to bring the ethical considerations behind them into the open within an organization.
- Teaching market researchers ethical behavior in on-the-job or orientation training.
- Testing the ethics of your research staff versus industry norms.

Kelley, Ferrell, and Skinner* recently studied the relationship of age, sex, and other demographic descriptors to the ethics of marketing researchers. They found, interestingly, that "female marketing researchers, older marketing researchers, and marketing researchers holding their present job for ten years or more generally rate their behavior as more ethical." Perhaps some marketers will begin to incorporate age and sex criteria into job descriptions—but I doubt it! In my opinion the most useful result of their findings for practitioners is the list of ethical issues they compiled in the process of doing their research.

Their list is derived from 70 candidate issues that came out of interviews with marketing researchers. From these, a panel of 11 marketing researchers selected only those items for which there was unanimous agreement that they possessed face validity, meaning that the list is a careful selection of problems commonly encountered by researchers, presented in a clear and valid manner.

Each of the items on this list provides an interesting test of personal ethics and a good case for discussion of and instruction in ethics as it relates to research. You could use them in staff training or as a basis for a short "retreat" in which ethical issues are discussed.

You might also find it interesting to test your own or your staff's self-assessment on these items, using the same "6-point Likert-type format with anchors of Definitely Agree and Definitely Disagree" that the

*Note: Kelley and Skinner are professors at the University of Kentucky. Ferrell is a professor at Memphis State University.

researchers used. (Anonymity is important!) If you do, you can compare your mean scores with the mean ratings for respondents under 31 (generally on the low side) and respondents over 50 (which represent the high end of the scale in most cases). Both are shown here. (These means are based on a response rate of 550 usable questionnaires from a mailing to 1,500 marketing researchers nationwide.)

If you run a research department or a market research firm, you should also consider what guidelines and policies your organization provides in each of these situations. If the areas are left ambiguous, employees are more likely to take an amoral stance. Consider developing specific suggestions and guidelines for each situation—and any others that your review of issues may bring to mind.

SENSITIVE ISSUES CONFRONTED BY MARKETING RESEARCHERS

ISSUES	MEAN SCORE, UNDER 31	MEAN SCORE, OVER 50
Sometimes I compromise the reliability of a study to complete the project.	5.1	5.7
I never divulge the identity of a respondent if I promised anonymity.	1.3	1.3
Sometimes I only report part of the data because I know my client may not like the results.	5.5	5.9
I sometimes have to cover up nonresponse and sampling error to please my clients.	5.3	5.8
I have continued a research project after knowing I made errors earlier.	4.8	5.3
I have altered the results of studies to gain conclusions sought by clients.	5.8	5.9
Sometimes I have to alter the sample design in order to obtain enough respondents.	4.2	4.9
Sometimes I claim to use the latest research techniques as a selling tool, even though I don't use the techniques.	5.6	5.8

SENSITIVE ISSUES CONFRONTED BY MARKETING
RESEARCHERS (*CONTINUED*)

ISSUES	MEAN SCORE, UNDER 31	MEAN SCORE, OVER 50
I have promised respondents a copy of results, and then failed to provide them with such a report.	5.5	5.8
Sometimes I use the name of a fake research firm to collect data.	5.4	5.4

An interesting, although unintended, use for
these data is to see what kinds of ethical transgressions are most common among market researchers.
Given nothing but the means, this question can only
be answered by eyeball. However, it appears that
alteration of sample design "to please the respondents" is the most common ethical error, followed
by continuing a project "after knowing I made errors." Both reflect a strong emphasis on getting the
job done, even if it isn't done perfectly.

Among older researchers, the next most "popular" ethical transgression is using "the name of a fake
research firm to collect data." Among younger researchers, the next most popular is compromising
the reliability of a study "to complete the project."

It is also notable that most of the means are quite
close to the limits of the scale—the research does not
indicate that any of these behaviors are the norm. In
general, researchers seem to agree that these behaviors are improper and they violate the norms only in
a minority of cases.

Reference

Scott W. Kelley, O. C. Ferrell, and Steven J. Skinner, "Ethical Behavior Among Marketing Researchers: An Assessment of Selected Demographic Characteristics, *Journal of
Business Ethics* 9, 1990: 681–688.

SOCIAL RESPONSIBILITY MATRIX

Applications

- Classifying companies by their attitude and behavior regarding social responsibilities.

- Choosing a managerial approach to specific social issues.

- Identifying and evaluating alternative responses to social issues.

Procedures

Use the matrix to analyze options in specific decisions to bring ethical issues into the open. In any specific situation, two choices (or a spectrum on a dimension of the matrix) are available.

Also use it as a tool for analyzing overall company position. Follow these procedures to analyze your company (or another you are considering doing business with):

1. Identify important stakeholders and assess the organization's degree of concern for each. (The source article rates concern either high or low, but as most firms fall in between, I prefer a 5-point scale.) Solicit the ratings of multiple managers and employees if you wish to verify your perception. Use the average score.

2. Review legal records, talk with managers and lawyers within the firm who are familiar with the issues, and assess compliance with regulations. (A 5-point scale ranging from low to high is preferred. You may also calculate an average score for this dimension.)

3. Prepare a matrix and plot your position.

4. Prepare additional matrices to reflect the perceived position of the firm from the perspective of key stakeholders, either by imagining what they think (based on previous conversations and secondary sources) or actually asking them to do the ratings in "1" and "2."

5. If the position(s) are undesirable, move the firm within the matrix. An undesirable position from management's perspective requires changes in policy. An undesirable po-

Social Responsibility Matrix

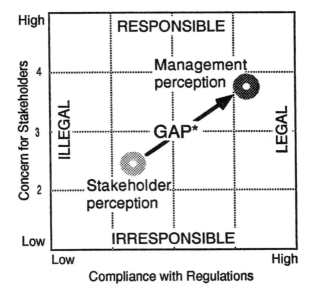

* Close gap through PR and policy changes.

Based on Dalton and Cosier (1982).

---

sition from a stakeholder's perspective, if inconsistent with management's perceptions, requires either a PR effort or a change in management's perception combined with policy changes.

This matrix describes social responsibility according to two dimensions: concern for stakeholders and compliance with regulations. It captures the sometimes conflicting relationship between ethics and the law. Stakeholders are defined as people with a vested interest in the company, such as employees, stockholders, customers, competitors, unions, governments, civil rights activists, and environmentalists. Regulations include all the legislation designed to protect various stakeholders' interests. But note that regulations do not guarantee complete protection of stakeholders, and do not necessarily represent their interests well in any given situation—hence the need to look at their interests on a separate dimension.

The matrix represents four decision states:

High Concern, Low Compliance. This is the "Illegal Responsible" position, in which the company has considered and acted on stakeholders' interests, but is not in compliance with specific regulations. Sometimes this reflects ambiguity or inconsistency in regulations. Sometimes it is the result of overemphasis of certain stakeholders' interests without proper consideration for others (as when stockholders' profits are maximized by avoiding costly environmental compliance).

Example: A good example of the problems associated with this position is encountered when companies go overseas to produce products and have to decide whether to pay bribes. If the bribes are small and customary, they may be in the interest of customers, vendors, owners, and other stakeholders (because they make possible better products, lower prices, and higher profits). But they are prohibited by the Foreign Corrupt Practices Act. The alternative in this case is "Legal Irresponsible" position, in which concern for stakeholders is traded for compliance with regulations.

Low Concern, High Compliance. The "Legal, Irresponsible" position is the alternative to the "Legal Responsible" position, illustrating the fact that this matrix provides two diagonal decision dimensions. Many decisions fall onto one of the diagonals. Low concern for stakeholders is possible even when compliance with regulations is high, and in fact there is sometimes a (diagonal) trade-off, as the example illustrates.

High Concern, High Compliance. In other cases, managers may have to choose between a "Legal, Irresponsible" position and a "Legal, Responsible" position (in which case the dimension is vertical, not diagonal—see the matrix). Simple compliance with regulations will often lead to a legal, but irresponsible, position, since regulations do not protect and represent all the interests of stakeholders. To be both legal and responsible, it is necessary to analyze stakeholders' interests in detail, understand how the firm's actions advance or harm those interests, then act out of concern for those interests—along with the effort to be in compliance with applicable laws. This position is probably rare in companies, and can be difficult to achieve. Sometimes stakeholders have conflicting interests, and some stakeholders seem more important than others (the environmental lobby may not seem as important as the votes of stockholders, for example). Further, even when firms act out of concern for stakeholders, the stakeholders are not necessarily happy. The position does not guarantee harmony. But it does minimize problems in the long run, and it certainly is an appropriate goal for all managers.

Low Concern, Low Compliance. This position will get you in trouble in a hurry. Illegal activities combined with a low concern for stakeholders (or some of them) sounds so dumb that it ought to be rare. But it isn't. Many firms are out of compliance with regulations, especially those relevant to employees (withholdings, minimum wages, equal rights), customers and distributors (pricing, disclosure, false claims), and the environment. Add to this a general lack of concern for, or interest in, stakeholders, and the firm is in an "Illegal, Irresponsible" position by default. Unless careful analysis of stakeholders' interests is conducted on occasion, combined with a rigorous look at compliance issues, the firm is likely to be at risk on both dimensions of the matrix.

References

Dan R. Dalton and Richard A. Cosier, "The Four Faces of Social Responsibility," *Business Horizons*, May–June 1982: 19–27.

R. Edward Freeman, *Strategic Management: A Stakeholder Approach* (New York: Ballinger, 1984).

ALTERNATIVE DISPUTE RESOLUTION

Lawyers shoulder much of the blame for the expense of litigation. Their economic self-interest may prolong some cases that might otherwise have been settled. What's more, few chief executives actively manage their legal disputes.

—Stephen Solomon

Applications

- Managing conflicts and disputes to minimize the cost of resolution.
- Preparing contracts that make it easier to manage disputes.
- Laying the ground rules for use of alternative dispute resolution.

Procedures

Follow the guidelines from attorney John Wilkinson to incorporate alternative dispute resolution (ADR) into all contracts. Use ADR techniques to manage legal costs more effectively and minimize negative PR.

Disputes are increasingly common, and many of them result in multiyear legal battles, cost hundreds of thousands of dollars, and wreak havoc on employee morale, customer perception, and management time. Alternative dispute resolution is a valuable alternative, often providing negotiated solutions at lower cost, in a shorter period of time, and with far less negative publicity. And ADR is more likely to be helpful when it has been planned in advance, when contracts and agreements are first designed.

Example: The Pulse network of automatic teller machines is a nonprofit activity operated for the benefit of financial institutions in Texas and adjoining states. In 1987 Pulse lowered fees paid to banks for cash withdrawals from their ATMs by other banks' customers. This benefited the hundreds of smaller member banks (whose customers often have to use other banks' ATMs) but cut an important source of revenues for the large First Texas Savings

Association, also a Pulse member. First Texas prepared for a suit against Pulse, but the high costs of an antitrust suit and the likelihood of a dreadful business relationship afterward convinced both parties that arbitration made more sense. Both parties signed an arbitration agreement in March 1988, and the dispute was resolved in June in favor of First Texas—the arbitrator ruled that their actions violated antitrust laws, and recommended that they use a flexible fee system instead.

The CEO of Pulse, Stan Paur, figures that arbitration saved 80% of the legal fees of litigation and condensed the preparation time from several years to several months. (Note: First Texas was later taken over by the FSLIC and is now reorganized under new ownership and named First Gibraltar Bank FSB.) (The source of this material is "The Case of the Price-Fixing Cartel," *Inc.*, October 1989, p. 112.)

This example illustrates the use of an arbitrator. Both parties agreed on the selection of the arbitrator, and also agreed on a schedule and a cap on the award. Arbitration works best when the parties agree that it will be binding.

The minitrial is another useful technique under the ADR banner. It creates a sort of moot court in which executives and their lawyers argue the case in a single day and then try to negotiate an out-of-court solution. The process of arguing your case, and hearing the opposition's, brings considerable objectivity to the dispute and helps both parties find room for movement (a mediator may also be used).

The strongest argument for using alternatives to court is that most disputes are settled out of court anyway—but not until too much money and time has been wasted on them. According to Solomon, "About 95% of all suits settle before trial, often on the courthouse steps. The ADR movement attempts to accelerate the settlement process so that companies can get back to work."

An accelerated process is often beneficial from a marketing perspective. As soon as a suit is filed, it is available to the public and the press. Disputes make good reading, and trade magazines report many that do not make it into the newspapers. Customers, suppliers, distributors, shareholders, lenders, and other important parties usually take a dim view of legal disputes, while competitors see opportunity in them. The liability they represent is difficult to quantify, and they often present the risk of a large negative settlement. Legal disputes are therefore likely to harm a company's reputation and scare away customers, distributors, and others the company wishes to do business with. The negative perceptions created by visible legal disputes are difficult and costly to counter through marketing, often requiring special efforts and expenditures in sales, advertising, and public relations. ADR can minimize the negative impact of disputes on the marketing function.

Further, marketing is a common source of disputes in many companies. As the given example illustrates, pricing is a frequent subject of disputes. Agreements with sales representatives, joint marketing agreements, ad agency contracts, and many other agreements with third parties are signed by people in the marketing department. The incorporation of ADR principles in these contracts is advisable.

How do you build alternative dispute resolution into contracts? John Wilkinson of Donovan Leisure Newton & Irvine suggests that ADR provisions incorporate these principles (adapted from *Inc.*, October 1989, p. 107):

1. Specify pre-ADR negotiation. Define the time period and parties.

2. If negotiation does not resolve the dispute, a neutral third party must be appointed to arbitrate during the ADR planning. The arbitrator is to be agreed upon by both parties, or, if agreement is not reached, appointed by an independent party such as the American Arbitration Association (New York).

3. Both parties to the dispute must agree on the form of ADR (including rules and format of the proceeding and extent and type of pre-proceeding fact finding). The arbitrator will resolve any differences concerning the form of ADR.

4. The confidentiality of proceedings must be agreed to by both parties to the contract. The proceedings, and the information provided

   during them, can be used for no other purpose but dispute resolution.

5. A lawsuit can be filed by either party in the
   event that settlement has not been reached
   within an agreed-upon period of time following the initiation of ADR.

Include clauses that establish these guidelines for
dispute resolution in contracts so that an agreed-
upon framework exists for dispute resolution in case
anything goes wrong. Then manage the process aggressively, maintaining control rather than handing
the whole mess to the lawyers. In most cases it will
be possible to resolve disputes without ever filing
suits or going to court.

Reference

Stephen D. Solomon, "Contempt of Court," *Inc.*, October
   1989, pp. 106–114.

AMERICAN MARKETING ASSOCIATION CODE OF ETHICS

Can't remember where you put your copy of the AMA's code? That is because it was on the back of the application form you sent in when you first joined—and you probably have not seen it since. However, it is a thorough and thoughtful treatment of the entire subject of marketing ethics, and well worth reviewing or calling upon in moments of doubt. Here it is reproduced in full:

Members of the American Marketing Association (AMA) are committed to ethical professional conduct. They have joined together in subscribing to this Code of Ethics embracing the following topics:

Responsibilities of the Marketer

Marketers must accept responsibility for the consequences of their activities and make every effort to ensure that their decisions, recommendations, and actions function to identify, serve, and satisfy all relevant publics: customers, organizations, and society.

Marketers' professional conduct must be guided by:

1. The basic rule of professional ethics: not knowingly to do harm;
2. The adherence to all applicable laws and regulations;
3. The accurate representation of their education, training and experience; and
4. The active support, practice, and promotion of this Code of Ethics.

HONESTY AND FAIRNESS

Marketers shall uphold and advance the integrity, honor, and dignity of the marketing profession by:

1. Being honest in serving customers, clients, employees, suppliers, distributors and the public;
2. Not knowingly participating in conflict of interest without prior notice to all parties involved; and

3. Establishing equitable fee schedules including the payment or receipt of usual, customary, and/or legal compensation for marketing exchanges.

Rights and Duties of Parties in the Marketing Exchange Process

Participants in the marketing exchange process should be able to expect that

1. Products and services offered are safe and fit for their intended uses;
2. Communications about offered products and services are not deceptive;
3. All parties intend to discharge their obligations, financial and otherwise, in good faith; and
4. Appropriate internal methods exist for equitable adjustment and/or redress of grievances concerning purchases.

IN THE AREA OF PRODUCT DEVELOPMENT AND MANAGEMENT,

- disclosure of all substantial risks associated with product or service usage;
- identification of any product component substitution that might materially change the product or impact the buyer's purchase decision;
- identification of extra-cost added features.

IN THE AREA OF PROMOTIONS,

- avoidance of false and misleading advertising;
- rejection of high pressure manipulations, or misleading sales tactics;
- avoidance of sales promotions that use deception or manipulation.

IN THE AREA OF DISTRIBUTION,

- not manipulating the availability of a product for purpose of exploitation;
- not using coercion in the marketing channel;

- not exerting undue influence over the re-sellers' choice to handle a product.

IN THE AREA OF PRICING,

- not engaging in price fixing;
- not practicing predatory pricing;
- disclosing the full price associated with any purchase.

IN THE AREA OF MARKETING RESEARCH,

- prohibiting selling or fund raising under the guise of conducting research;
- maintaining research integrity by avoiding misrepresentation and omission of pertinent research data;
- treating outside clients and suppliers fairly.

Organizational Relationships

Marketers should be aware of how their behavior may influence or impact on the behavior of others in organizational relationships. They should not de-mand, encourage or apply coercion to obtain unethical behavior in their relationships with others, such as employees, suppliers, or customers.

1. Apply confidentiality and anonymity in pro-fessional relationships with regard to privileged information;
2. Meet their obligations and responsibilities in contracts and mutual agreements in a timely manner;
3. Avoid taking the work of others, in whole, or in part, and represent this work as their own or directly benefit from it without compen-sation or consent of the originator or owner;
4. Avoid manipulation to take advantage of situations to maximize personal welfare in a way that unfairly deprives or damages the organization or others.

Any AMA member found to be in violation of any provision of this Code of Ethics may have his or her Association membership suspended or revoked.

PART III

ONE-MINUTE GUIDES TO THE MARKETING CLASSICS

ASSAEL'S BUYER BEHAVIOR GRID*

Useful source of insight into how people purchase specific products and how to communicate with them concerning the product and their experience with it. Postulates four different types of behavior depending upon whether the available brands are similar or differentiated, and whether the consumer is involved in the purchase or just treats it as routine. Applications: Advertisers sometimes try to shift behavior in order to get customers to notice the benefits they are offering. Where dissonance is an expected result, marketers use advertising to help consumers reduce it.

	High Involvement	Low Involvement
Brands Different	Complex buying behavior	Variety-seeking buying behavior
Brands Similar	Dissonance-reducing buying behavior	Habitual buying behavior

Involvement is high with expensive purchases, and with products that are purchased infrequently and are highly expressive or risky. Differentiation of brands should be measured in terms of customer perception—technical difference may be insignificant to the market.

Complex buying often involves learning, is slow, and is carefully considered. Details are welcomed, and advertising needs to help the customer evaluate and compare.

Dissonance-reducing buying is often price based, rapid, and influenced by convenience since the customer does not see sufficient differences in brands to justify a more formal approach. But since the purchase is important and involving, the consumer does not want to be confused or to make a wrong choice. The marketer needs to use price and location to make the sale, then communicate favorable informa-

*Henry Assael, Consumer Behavior and Marketing Action: (Kent, 1981), p. 80.

tion afterward to make sure the customer feels good about the purchase.

Variety-seeking buying occurs where customers are not very involved, but marketers give lots of options. Brand loyalty is hard to maintain, and boredom may cause a change in brands.

Habitual buying is common for low-profile products like salt. Marketers need to increase involvement, either by increasing the importance of the purchase or by increasing the differences among brands. The new "lite salt" brands do both by bringing the risk of heart problems into the purchase decision and offering a reduced-sodium benefit other brands do not have.

DEFINING THE MARKET

Planners and forecasters need a model for defining the market that tells them not only how big it is, but how much of it is accessible at the moment. The *potential market versus the total population* is one way to look at this problem—in general, only a small percentage of the population are potential buyers for a product.

Potential market can be further broken down as in the following:

CATEGORY	%
Potential market	100
Available market	30
Qualified available market	15
Served market	10
Penetrated market	3

The **penetrated market** is the percentage of the potential market that currently buy the product. The **served market** is the percentage that the marketers choose to target (in the example, they have landed only 30% of their targeted market to date). The **qualified available market** is comprised of consumers who have an interest in buying (available) and the means to (are qualified).

DISTRIBUTION/LOGISTICS

Costs. The costs of physical distribution vary significantly from one product to another, ranging from a third of the price tag for many foods to a sixth or less for most textiles. Because physical distribution accounts for a significant percentage of total costs, efficiencies in distribution can have a significant impact on costs and margins. On average, distribution makes up about 14% of manufacturers' costs and about 25% of resellers' costs.

Transportation is the largest component of physical distribution costs, averaging about 46%. Warehousing averages 26%, followed by inventory carrying at 10%, receiving and shipping at 6%, packaging at 5%, administration at 4%, and order processing at 3%.

Just-in-time inventory management, a Japanese import, is used by some manufacturers to minimize their raw materials and parts inventories. They require suppliers to make very frequent deliveries of just the parts or materials needed immediately. If a just-in-time system of supply operates efficiently, the manufacturer not only reduces inventory costs but also eliminates shortages. However, it usually takes a powerful manufacturer and dedicated local or regional suppliers to make it work.

Transportation. The *reliability* or predictability of delivery by freight carriers is an emerging issue, as it can have a significant impact on perceived service and also is essential to any just-in-time system. Measure using the variance of deliveries around scheduled arrival date or plot a histogram.

EOQ MODEL

Inventory management with EOQ. The economic order quantity (EOQ) model is sometimes used to determine the quantity of a reorder when supply must be maintained but costs need to be minimized (by minimizing carrying costs and by taking advantage of quantity discounts or economies of scale). To find the economic order quantity, Q,

1. Calculate D, the annual demand for the product from your inventory.
2. Calculate I, inventory carrying costs as a percentage of the inventory value (these are variable costs).
3. Determine Co, the unit cost of ordering the inventory item.
4. Determine Ch, the unit cost of carrying the item in inventory, or the holding cost (base this on inventory carrying costs as a percentage of inventory value, for example).

Now use your figures in the EOQ formula:

$$Q = \sqrt{\frac{2D \cdot Co}{Ch}}$$

The quantity suggested by this formula balances inventory carrying and ordering costs and, with accurate figures and fairly constant demand, will help minimize inventory costs.

Optimal Order Frequency. You can also compute the *cycle time,* or the optimal frequency for placing orders, using these figures. The formula for cycle time, T, is $365Q/D$.

FAMILY LIFE CYCLE

Family life cycle models are used to understand and predict consumer buying behavior. Preferences and purchase processes vary depending upon the consumer's family status. The basic model identifies nine possible stages (various researchers and marketers modify it for their purposes):

1. *Bachelor stage.* Young, single. Opinion-leaders in fashion goods. Buy basic household furnishings, vacations, products for "mating game."

2. *Newlyweds.* Young, no children. Spending more money now. High purchase rates. Buy many durables, from cars to refrigerators.

3. *Full nest 1.* Youngest child under six. Buy homes. Short of cash. Buy children's products, household equipment, new products. Influenced by advertising.

4. *Full nest 2.* Youngest child six or over. Financially stronger. Both parents may work. Buy large-sized packages, equipment, and toys for older children. Less influenced by advertising.

5. *Full nest 3.* Older married couples, dependent children. Financially even better. Both parents often work, and some kids do. Even less influenced by advertising. High purchases of durables. Replace household furnishings and luxury goods.

6. *Empty nest 1.* Older married couples, no kids at home, still working. Strong financial position, saving, compared to other stages. Own homes. Purchase travel, recreation, luxuries. Contribute to nonprofits. Little interest in novel products.

7. *Empty nest 2.* Older, married, no children at home, retired. Income down. Still own home. Increased purchases of medical/pharmaceutical products.

8. *Solitary survivor, working.* May sell home. Has fairly strong income and purchasing power.

9. *Solitary survivor, retired.* Living on fixed income. Increased need for attention, affection, security.

MARKETING CHANNELS

Form. Channels take on a *vertical, horizontal,* or *multichannel form.* Vertical channels are those in which each member plays a unique role, taking the product a step farther on its path from production to consumption. Horizontal form is when different kinds of companies cooperate to perform the functions of a single tier of the channel. Multichannel systems are those in which more than one vertical channel system is used by a producer, either to reach a single market or to reach different markets.

Length. The *number of levels* in a vertical channel varies widely. A channel in which consumers buy direct from the producer is called a zero-level channel. A *producer–retailer–consumer* channel is single level. Two-level channels (where a wholesaler is added) and even three-level channels are fairly common. Here is a four-level channel: *Producer–national distributor–independent rep–wholesaler–jobber–consumer.*

Who Performs What Functions. The members of a distribution channel add value through one or more of the following functions:

- Finding and contacting prospective buyers
- Advertising and promotion
- Market research
- Tailoring the offer to the buyer's needs
- Negotiating price and other terms
- Distributing and storing goods
- Financing the functions performed by the channel
- Sharing the risk with producers and retailers

How these functions are shared within the channel, and the skill with which they are performed, are a frequent source of conflict. For example, manufacturers often complain that their reps do not provide adequate market intelligence. Each function is a cost, of course, and the more powerful members of a channel will try to shift costs to the less powerful, or else will try to shift profits from the less powerful members.

Power is often balanced among members of a channel. With a fragmented structure and many alternate players at each level of the distribution channel, members can bargain at arm's length on fairly even terms, and are able to behave relatively autonomously. But if these conditions are not met, the power may no longer be balanced. Where a product is only available from a single supplier or is scarce, the supplier will have considerable power over intermediaries and retailers. When alternative sources of supply become available, intermediaries gain power over the traditional manufacturers (as is the case when imports become popular in a market). And when there are only a few intermediaries or retailers and many suppliers, the suppliers have very little power.

Shifts in channel structure occur fairly frequently, but nonetheless channel members are usually surprised by them. Innovations in distribution may precipitate change, as when a producer vertically integrates to distribute direct to retailers or end consumers and bypasses the traditional distribution channel. The recent emergence of high-volume discount retailers (such as Staples in office supplies, the Waldenbooks chain of book stores, and the various consumer price clubs) has shifted the balance of power toward the retailer in many industries. And it is forcing producers to sell direct to large retailers where they traditionally used intermediaries. Conflict with the traditional intermediaries may result as they attempt to prevent the new discounters from purchasing direct, obtaining superior service and deeper discounts, and gaining market share.

MARKET COVERAGE STRATEGIES

Which segments, and how many, should be covered? Options are:

- *Undifferentiated marketing* (address entire market with one offer)
- *Differentiated marketing* (target several segments, each with a special offer)
- *Concentrated marketing* (maximize share by concentrating on one or a few segments)

See the One-Minute Guide to Market Segmentation.

MARKET SEGMENTATION

Market segmentation consists of identifying the bases for segmenting a market and then developing profiles of resulting segments. It is generally followed by market targeting (in which the target segments are selected) and product positioning (in which products are positioned and a marketing mix developed for each segment). To segment a market, select one or more descriptors of the market, favoring those in which considerable variation occurs. Divide the market into two or more groups based on these descriptors. See if the groups are discrete and have unique needs that will support a targeted product offering and promotion strategy. Here are some of the descriptors that others have found useful in segmenting markets.

SEGMENTATION VARIABLES

GEOGRAPHIC

County
Zip code area
Size of city or metropolitan area
Climate

DEMOGRAPHIC

Sex
Age
Education level
Stage in family life cycle
Income
Religion
Race
Types of pets owned
Family size

BEHAVIORAL

Occasion of use
Benefits sought
New versus experienced user
Rate of use
Attitude toward product or use

PSYCHOGRAPHIC

Life-style
Social class
Personality
Values

MARKET SHARE

Any measure of performance relative to competitors. **Market share** is generally defined in one of these ways:

- Sales as percentage of total industry sales
- Sales as percentage of served (or targeted) market

Market share is also expressed as share relative to leading competitor(s)—termed **relative share**. It is generally calculated one of these ways:

- Share of industry sales divided by the sum of top three competitors' share of industry sales
- Share of industry sales divided by largest competitor's share of industry sales

Overall market share, the percentage figure resulting when your sales are divided by total industry sales, is the most commonly used. Total industry sales are generally available from a trade association or government reports. Most companies track overall market share and use it as a barometer of how they stand in their market(s). Market share measures are very important in planning, product management, media mix decisions, and almost every other marketing decision, since most product environments are dominated by intraproduct competition (exception: early stage of product life cycle).

Warning: Because market share figures generally use available industry and competitor data, and because it is useful to have a time series for comparison, there is a tendency for share calculation methods to become institutionalized. This creates opportunities for competitors who define the market differently (i.e., as larger or smaller) and develop novel strategies as a result. This makes market share measurements a potential source of "marketing myopia" as well as a source of insight. It is a good idea to calculate share multiple ways and to look continually for new and emerging ways to redefine your markets. It is also important to check your perception of market boundaries against customer perception from time to time.

MASLOW'S HIERARCHY

Abraham Maslow's classic model of human motivation is widely cited by marketing experts, and may even be of occasional use in understanding the whys and whens of **buyer behavior**. But nobody can get the drawing quite right when they try to sketch it on a napkin, so here it is.

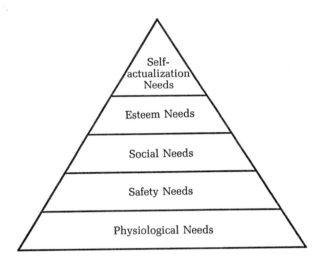

Hierarchy of Needs. The lowest needs are most important. When the lowest is satisfied, the next one up can be pursued, and so on all the way to the top. You can't sell someone a status symbol when they are starving. The model also helps understand some less obvious buying behavior—in many cases it is not immediately obvious what need a product addresses, and in fact the same product may be purchased by different people to satisfy different needs. Segmentation and promotional strategies can be based on insights into need-based buying behavior.

PERCEPTUAL MAPS

Provide a visual display of how competing products are positioned on two (sometimes three) decision variables according to **customer perception**. Usually generated by market research firms after surveying customer attitudes. Typical map consists of two axes, each representing the weightings of a decision variable. The axes usually are crossed in the middle of the page, as in the following example:

PERCEPTUAL MAP
FOOD ESTABLISHMENTS, TIMBUKTU

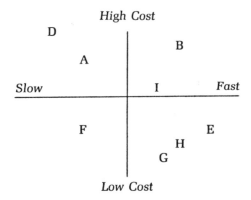

Where would you rather eat? The slow, expensive place or the cheap, fast one? Actually, it's rather hard to say, since an important dimension seems to be missing: how good the food tastes! In this respect, the example is not unlike many of the maps produced by market research firms, and managers must always be cautious in interpreting them.

Ps AND Cs

Marketing Mix. The marketing mix is the combination of product characteristics, price, promotion, and place or location that combine to make up a specific offering. Application: Planners, product developers, and product managers use the concept to make sure they have defined an intended offering clearly and to analyze success factors or compare competing products. Also used in allocating marketing dollars.

The **Four Ps** of the marketing mix are defined by the marketer using the following variables:

Product	Quality
	Features
	Options
	Name
	Packaging
	Service
	Warranties
Price	List
	Discounts
	Allowances
	Payment and credit terms
Place	Distribution channels
	Coverage
	Locations
	Logistics
Promotion	Advertising
	Personal selling
	Sales promotion
	Other communications

Three Cs. Describes the three important players in the company's environment. They are the company, customers, and competitors. Applications: In planning, used to identify the populations whose reaction to a strategy must be anticipated before it is chosen. Sometimes the list of major actors is broadened to include suppliers, marketing intermediaries, and publics in addition, and a good *situation analysis* will look at these along with the Three Cs. Too bad they don't start with "C" too. The "Three Cs, the S, I, and P" just doesn't stick in one's memory.

PLANNING AND STRATEGY MODELS

McKinsey 7S Framework. A model of the factors driving business success. Formed the jumping-off point for Peters and Waterman's *In Search of Excellence*. It is usually drawn as a chart with six circles encircling a central circle, with lines interconnecting them all. The central circle is labeled Shared Values, and the others are labeled (starting at 12 o'clock and going clockwise): Structure, Systems, Style, Staff, Skills, Strategy. Application: Focuses attention of planners on the many issues, both internal and external, that will effect the success of the plan.

Threat Matrix. Used to illustrate the potential impact of future threats in order to put them in context for planning purposes. Application: Planning for competitor moves and other threats to strategy. Drawn as follows (rate threats on both dimensions qualitatively, then plot on this chart):

	Probability of Occurence	
Seriousness	High	Low
High		
Low		

Opportunity Matrix. Often used with the threat matrix in planning. Identify opportunities, then rate them qualitatively in terms of probability of success (plot on horizontal axis) and attractiveness (plot on vertical).

Strategic Planning Gap. A graphical representation of the gap between desired sales and projected sales. Both are drawn as curves on a graph with sales (in units or dollars) on the vertical axis and time on the horizontal. The gap between projections of the normal growth expected for current business and the desired growth needs to be filled through **intensive growth** (market penetration, market development, or product development), **integrative growth** (forward or backward integration, horizontal integration), or **diversification**.

Ansoff's Product/Market Expansion Grid. Used to identify possible growth strategies and as an aid to brainstorming new product and new business concepts during planning. Drawn as follows (usually planners try to think of several ideas for each cell):

	Current Products	New Products
Current Markets	1. Market penetration strategy	3. Product development strategy
New Markets	2. Market development strategy	4. Diversification strategy

PRODUCT LIFE CYCLE

The product life cycle assumes that a product, when new, gradually picks up steam as it is adopted by more consumers. At first it has no competition, but its success attracts emulators. The competitors gradually draw closer to the original leader. Growth slows as the possible market is penetrated and competition becomes more intense. Competitors attempt to differentiate their offerings and extend their product lines in a fight for share. If the product is displaced by another innovation, usage gradually declines and the number of competitors and offerings falls. Eventually the product may become so antiquated that no one buys it or bothers to make it anymore—it dies.

Applications: If you can peg a product to one of the four stages of the product life-cycle model you can make certain predictions about market characteristics and can select marketing objectives and strategies that make the most sense for this stage:

1. Introduction stage. Sales are low and costs high. No profits. Only innovators buy, and there are few competitors.

Marketers try to build awareness and trial. Pricing is cost-plus, and distribution is built selectively. Promotion may be used extensively to stimulate trial. Advertising is relatively low and directed only at early adopters and the distribution channel.

2. Growth stage. Sales start to increase at an accelerating rate, and costs on a per-customer basis are moderate, allowing profits to grow. Early adopters purchase the product and new competitors enter the market.

Marketers try to maximize market share through penetration pricing, product line extensions, service and warranty offerings, and intensive distribution. Advertising targets the mass market to build awareness and interest, but promotion is reduced.

3. Maturity stage. Sales reach their peak and flatten or begin to fall. Costs are low and profits high (at least for those with strong market share). The middle majority of customers now purchases the product (innovators have already moved onto something new). Competition stabilizes.

Marketers try to "milk" their brands for maximum profit through the minimum marketing needed to maintain share. New brands and models are introduced. Pricing is competitor oriented as customers do more comparison shopping. The coverage provided by distribution is important. Promotion is increased to encourage brand switching, and advertising focuses on differentiating brands.

4. Decline stage. Profits decline, despite continued low cost per customer, as sales volume falls. A shakeout reduces the number of competitors, and marketers find that the primary customers are the late adopters or laggards. Most of the market has moved on to another product.

Marketers attempt to reduce exposure and continue to milk their brands by cutting weak items, dropping prices, and switching to selective distribution. Advertising and sales promotion are greatly reduced and targeted at maintaining the loyalty of old customers.

Graphing the Product Life Cycle

The PLC is generally depicted as a regular sigmoid curve rising to a peak, then gradually falling. However, actual products may be less regular and sometimes cycle in and out of maturity as innovations revive their growth temporarily.

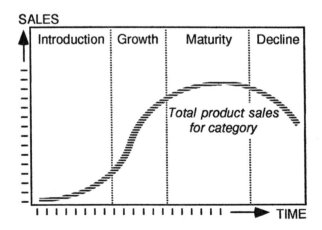

STAGES OF THE BUYING PROCESS

AIDA MODEL

Attention
↓
Interest
↓
Desire
↓
Action

ADOPTION MODEL

Awareness
↓
Interest
↓
Evaluation
↓
Trial
↓
Adoption

INDUSTRIAL BUYING PROCESS, FIRST-TIME PURCHASE

Problem recognition
↓
General need description
↓
Product specification
↓
Supplier search
↓
Proposal solicitation
↓
Supplier selection
↓
Order-routine specification
↓
Performance review

INDUSTRIAL BUYING PROCESS, REBUY

Product specification
↓
(Proposal solicitation)
↓
(Supplier selection)
↓
Performance review

STRATEGIC BUSINESS UNITS

SBUs. General Electric originated the term to describe the stand-alone businesses from a marketing perspective that they broke their larger divisions into for planning purposes. Defined according to the following criteria:

> Single business or collection of closely related businesses with:
>
> Distinct mission
>
> Unique competitors
>
> A responsible manager
>
> That will benefit from being planned independently of other businesses.

Application: Usually the unit of choice for planning and business portfolio management. Used in Boston Consulting Group Growth/Share Matrix and GE Matrix (see *Vest-Pocket CEO*).

VALUES AND LIFE-STYLES

Psychographics has been applied to life-style–based segmentation, and the VALS framework (Values and Life-styles) from SRI is the standard for this work. Survey research provides the basis.

Research uses the **AIO Framework** to measure *attitudes, interests,* and *opinions.* Ad agencies may use this framework to develop custom psychographic segmentation schemes for consumer product positioning. Marketers also use published classifications such as the VALS framework.

VALS GROUPS

Survivors. Very poor, despairing. 4% of population.

Sustainers. Poor but trying with some hope to improve their situation. 7%.

Belongers. Conservative, conventional, try to fit in. 33%.

Emulators. Upwardly mobile, status-conscious, ambitious. 10%.

Achievers. Leaders who work within the system and live well. 23%.

I-am-mes. Young, internally focused, impulsive. 5%.

Experientials. Hedonists and those who are eager for new experiences. Inner directed. 7%.

Societally conscious. Socially responsible, working against injustice and other social problems. 9%.

Integrateds. Mature, combine inner-directed and outer-directed traits. Balanced psychologically. 2%.

The VALS concept includes a life-cycle model in which people move from a need-driven stage (survivors or sustainers) into either a series of outer-directed stages (belongers, emulators, achievers) or an inner-directed series (I-am-mes, experientials, societally conscious). Some few move from one of these two series of stages on to the integrateds stage. VALS data are available by subscription and are updated regularly.

Glossary of Marketing and Advertising Terms

Administered vertical marketing system: A vertical marketing system in which one member is informally designated as captain.

Advertising: Any impersonal form of communication about ideas, goods, or services that is paid for by an identified sponsor.

Advertising campaign: A set of messages with a single theme that is repeatedly conveyed to the target audience over an extended period.

Advertising platform: The issues and product benefits that a marketer wishes to convey in an advertising message.

Advertising target market: The specific audience toward which an advertising message is aimed.

Advertising theme: The parts of an advertising message that are repeated throughout the campaign.

Affective component (of an attitude): The emotional feeling of favorableness or unfavorableness that results from a person's evaluation of an object.

Agent: A wholesaling intermediary that does not take title to merchandise but serves primarily to bring buyers and sellers together and facilitate exchanges.

Annual plan: A plan in which the organization's managers set goals for a single year.

Area sample: A probability sample in which respondents are chosen at random from a complete list of the population in a specific geographic area.

Attitudes: Feelings that express whether a person likes or dislikes objects in his or her environment.

Auction company: A wholesaling intermediary that sells merchandise on an agency basis by means of auctions.

Augmented product: An expected product that has been enhanced by a set of benefits that consumers do not expect or that exceed their expectations.

Backtranslation: A process in which a questionnaire is translated into a second language and then translated back into the original language to see if it makes sense.

Contributed by Charles Schewe, Professor of Marketing, University of Massachusetts at Amherst. Reproduced by permission.

Bait-and-switch pricing: A pricing strategy in which a product is given a low price in order to lure customers into a store, where an attempt is made to persuade them to buy a more expensive model or product.

Barometric techniques: Forecasting techniques that use analyses of past trends to predict the future.

Barter: The exchange of one good for another without using money as a means of valuation.

Basing-point pricing: A geographic pricing policy in which the seller designates one or more geographic locations from which the rate that a buyer will be charged is calculated.

Brainstorming: A method of generating new product ideas that consists of holding group discussions in which a specific problem or goal is set and no suggested solution is criticized.

Brand: A name, term, symbol, design, or combination of these elements that is intended to identify the goods or services of one seller or group of sellers and differentiate them from those of competitors.

Brand competitor: An organization that competes with others to satisfy consumers' demand for a specific product.

Brand extension: A new product category that is given the brand name of an existing category.

Brand mark: The portion of a brand that consists of a symbol, design, or distinctive coloring or lettering.

Brand name: The portion of a brand that consists of words, letters, or numbers that can be vocalized.

Breakdown method: An approach to sales force design in which the size of the sales force is determined by dividing the forecasted annual sales volume by the expected sales volume per salesperson.

Break-even pricing: An approach to pricing in which the price of a unit of the product is set high enough to cover the variable costs of producing that unit as well as the fixed costs of producing the product.

Broker: A wholesaling intermediary whose primary function is to supply market information and establish contacts in order to facilitate sales for clients.

Business definition: The way an organization answers the questions, "What business are we in?" and "What business *should* we be in?"

Buyer: In the exchange process, the purchaser of a product.

Buyer center: All the individuals and groups participating in the buying process that have interdependent goals and share common risks.

Cash-and-carry wholesaler: A limited-service wholesaler that sells on a cash-only basis and does not provide delivery.

Cash cow: An SBU that has a higher market share than its competitors and is in a low-growth market.

Cash discount: A discount that is offered to buyers who pay their bills within a stated period.

Cash flow: The flow of cash into a company; maintaining a steady cash flow is sometimes used as a pricing objective.

Catalogue showroom: A discount store at which customers review catalogues and then place orders and wait for delivery.

Causal studies: Research in which the cause-and-effect relationships between various phenomena are explored.

Chain store: A retail organization that consists of two or more units under a single ownership.

Channel captain: A channel member that is able to influence the behavior of the other members of the channel.

Channel management: The activities involved in anticipating and understanding the sources of channel conflict and trying to eliminate or minimize them.

Channel of distribution: The route taken by a product and its title as it moves from the resource procurer through the producer to the ultimate consumer.

Cognitive component (of an attitude): A person's evaluation of the characteristics of an object.

Cognitive dissonance: The state of anxiety or uneasiness that follows a purchase decision and creates a need for reassurance that the decision was the best one.

Combination store: A type of superstore that places emphasis on nonfood items and on services.

Commission merchant: An agent that performs selling functions for manufacturers, normally on a one-time basis.

Common carrier: A transportation company that transports products on a specified schedule and according to regulations and standards established by government regulatory agencies.

Common costs: Costs that must be allocated among two or more functional areas.

Communication: The process of exchanging meaning.

Comparative advantage: A theory that states that if a country has a relative cost advantage in a particular product, specializes in the production of that product, and trades it for products in which other countries have a relative cost advantage, more products will be available at lower prices than would be the case without specialization and trade.

Conative component (of an attitude): The intention or tendency to act that results from a person's evaluation of an object.

Concentrated strategy: A media scheduling strategy in which the marketer limits its advertising to specified periods.

Concentration strategy: A marketing strategy that aims at a single market segment.

Conclusive stage: The stage of the research process in which the researchers develop a plan for collecting data, implement the plan, and provide the resulting information to decision makers.

Consolidated Metropolitan Statistical Area (CMSA): A population unit that contains a major metropolitan area and has a total population of more than 1 million.

Consumer: In the exchange process, the person who uses a product.

Consumer market: A market in which goods and services are actually used up.

Consumer panel: A variation of the mail survey in which respondents are given some form of remuneration for participating in an ongoing study by filling out a series of questionnaires or keeping detailed records of their behavior.

Containerization: The use of large, standardized, easy-to-handle containers in which smaller packages can be loaded for shipping.

Contest: A sales promotion technique in which consumers are offered prizes for performing a task such as making up a slogan.

Continuity strategy: A media scheduling strategy in which advertisements are spread out over the entire period of the campaign.

Contract carrier: A transportation company that agrees to transport a specified number of shipments to specific destinations for an estimated price.

Contractual vertical marketing system: A vertical marketing system in which channel members draw up a legal agreement that specifies the rights and responsibilities of each party.

Contribution margin technique: An approach to cost analysis that ignores nontraceable common costs.

Control: The process of monitoring action programs, analyzing performance results, and, if necessary, taking corrective action.

Convenience products: Inexpensive, frequently purchased goods and services that consumers want to buy with the least possible effort.

Convenience sample: A nonprobability sample in which respondents are selected to suit the convenience of the researchers.

Convenience store: A store that is located near the residences or workplaces of its target customers and carries a wide assortment of products.

Cooperative organization: A retail organization that consists of a set of independent retailers that combine their resources to maintain their own wholesaling operation.

Corporate culture: A set of values that create a distinct pattern that is reflected in all of an organization's activities.

Corporate mission: A statement of an organization's overall goals, usually broadly defined and difficult to measure objectively.

Corporate vertical marketing system: A vertical marketing system in which one member gains control through ownership of both production and distribution systems.

Cost-per-thousand: The dollar cost of an advertisement per 1,000 readers or viewers.

Cost-plus pricing: An approach to pricing in which the list price is determined by adding a reasonable profit to the cost per unit.

Coupon: A certificate that entitles a consumer to a price reduction or a cash refund.

Cross elasticity of demand: A situation in which a change in the price of a product affects sales of another product.

Cue: An environmental stimulus that is perceived as a signal for action.

Culture: A set of values, ideas, attitudes, and other meaningful symbols created by human beings to shape human behavior and the artifacts of that behavior as they are transmitted from one generation to the next.

Cumulative quantity discount: A quantity discount that is applied to a buyer's total purchases over a set period.

Customary pricing: A pricing strategy in which the marketer maintains a traditional price level.

Custom research firm: A research firm that assists a marketer in designing a study, collecting information, and preparing a report.

Data bank: The component of an MIS that stores raw data that come in from both the external environment and internal records.

Dealer brand: A brand that is created and owned by an intermediary.

Decider: In the exchange process, the person who chooses an alternative that will satisfy a want or need.

Decoding: The process whereby a receiver extracts meaning from a transmitted message.

Delegation: Assigning specific responsibilities to specific people.

Delphi technique: A forecasting technique in which a panel of experts is asked to assign rankings and probabilities to various factors that may influence future events.

Demand: The composite desire for particular products as measured by how consumers choose to allocate their resources among different products in a given market.

Demarketing: A marketing tool whose objective is to persuade consumers to use less of a product while maintaining the same level of satisfaction.

Demographics: Statistics about a population, such as sex, age, marital status, birthrate, mortality rate, education, income, and occupation.

Department store: A store that offers a wide variety of product lines and is divided into departments to facilitate marketing and merchandise management.

Derived demand: Demand that is dependent on the demand for another product.

Descriptive label: A label that explains the important characteristics or benefits of a product.

Descriptive studies: Research that focuses on demographic information about markets and their composition.

Determining (behavioral) variables: A set of variables that determine whether or not a consumer is a member of a particular market segment.

Difference threshold: The smallest change in the intensity of a stimulus that can be noticed.

Differentiated marketing: A marketing strategy that aims at several market segments, varying the marketing mix for each segment.

Direct costs: Costs that can be assigned to a specific functional area.

Direct marketing: An approach to marketing that uses one or more advertising media to effect a measurable response.

Discount: A deduction from the list price in the form of cash or something else of value.

Discount store: A self-service general-merchandise store that combines low price with high volume.

Discretionary income: The amount of disposable income that is left over after spending on essentials such as food, shelter, and clothing.

Display unit: The component of an MIS that permits the user to communicate with the system.

Disposable income: The amount of income available for spending after taxes have been deducted.

Distinctive competencies: Activities that a firm can perform better than other firms.

Distribution: The process of making sure that a product is available when and where it is desired.

Distribution center: A storage facility that takes orders and delivers products.

Dog: An SBU that has a low relative market share and is in a low-growth market.

Drive: A strong motivating tendency that arouses an organism toward a particular type of behavior; see also *motive*.

Drop shipper: A limited-service wholesaler that sells goods but does not stock, handle, or deliver them.

Dumping: A situation in which a product is sold at a lower price in a foreign market than in a domestic one, or at a price below the cost of production.

Early adopters: Consumers who buy a product early in its life cycle and influence other people to buy it.

Early majority: Consumers who wait and watch others before adopting a new product.

Economic order quantity: The optimum quantity of a product to order at a given time.

Economic system: The way in which society organizes its resources to produce goods and services that will satisfy its members' wants and needs.

Economies of scale: The savings that result when fixed costs are spread over more units of a product.

Effective demand: The combination of desire to buy and ability to buy.

80-20 rule: A term used to refer to the fact that a large percentage of a company's sales and profits may come from a relatively small percentage of its customers or products.

Elastic demand: A situation in which a percentage change in price brings about a greater percentage change in quantity sold.

Emergency products: Goods or services that are needed to solve an immediate crisis.

Encoding: The process whereby a source translates a message into words and signs that can be transmitted, received, and understood by the receiver.

Engel's laws: A set of statements concerning the proportional changes in expenditures that accompany increases in family income.

Environment: A set of forces external to the organization that the marketer may be able to influence but cannot control.

Environmental scanning: A set of procedures for monitoring the organization's external environment.

Evaluator: In the exchange process, an individual who provides feedback on a chosen product's ability to satisfy.

Even pricing: A form of psychological pricing in which the price is an even number.

Evoked set: The set of alternatives that come immediately to mind when a consumer seeks a solution to a problem.

Exchange: An exchange occurs when two or more individuals, groups, or organizations give to each other something of value in order to receive something else of value. Each party to the exchange must want to exchange, must believe that what is received is more valuable than what is given up, and must be able to communicate with the other parties.

Exclusive dealing: A method of control over distribution in which the manufacturer forbids dealers to carry competitors' products.

Exclusive distribution: An approach to distribution in which the number of intermediaries is limited to one for each geographic territory.

Exempt carrier: A company that is exempt from state and federal transportation regulations.

Expected product: A generic product plus a set of features that meet additional expectations of consumers.

Experience curve: A graphic representation of the effect of experience on the per-unit cost of producing a product.

Experiment: A research method in which the effect of a particular variable is measured by making changes in the conditions experienced by a test group with respect to the variable and comparing the results with those of a control group that did not experience the change.

Exploratory stage: The stage of the research process in which the problem is defined, objectives are set, and possible solutions are explored.

Express warranty: A statement that specifies the exact conditions under which a manufacturer is responsible for a product's performance.

Expropriation: A situation in which a host country

denies a foreign corporation the right to engage in business there and seizes its assets.

Extended family: A nuclear family plus aunts, uncles, grandparents, and in-laws.

Extensive distribution: An approach to distribution that seeks the widest possible geographic coverage.

Factory outlet mall: A shopping center that focuses on quality, name brand items offered at lower than usual prices.

Family of orientation: The family into which a person is born.

Family of procreation: The family that a person establishes through having children.

Feedback: Information that tells an organization's managers about the performance of each marketing program.

Fixed-cost contribution: The portion of a selling price that is left over after variable costs have been accounted for.

Flexible-price policy: A pricing policy in which the marketer offers the same products and quantities to different customers at different prices, depending on their bargaining power and other factors.

Flighting strategy: A media scheduling strategy in which there is heavy advertising during some parts of the campaign and no advertising in between.

F.O.B. pricing: A geographic pricing policy in which buyers pay transportation costs from the point at which they take title to the product.

Focus group: A form of personal interview in which a group of 8 to 12 people are brought together to offer their views on an issue, idea, or product.

Form competitor: An organization that competes with others to satisfy consumers' wants or needs within a specific class of products or services.

Form utility: The satisfaction that buyers receive from the physical characteristics of a product (e.g., its shape, function, or style).

Franchise: A legal contractual relationship between a supplier and one or more independent retailers. The franchisee gains an established brand name and operating assistance, while the franchisor gains financial remuneration as well as some control over how the business is run.

Freight absorption: A geographic pricing policy in which the seller charges the same freight rate as the competitor located nearest to the buyer.

Freight forwarder· A transportation company that pools many small shipments to take advantage of lower rates, passing some of the savings on to the shippers.

Frequency: The average number of times that the average prospect will be exposed to a specific advertisement in a specified period.

Full-cost approach: An approach to cost analysis that takes both direct and common costs into consideration.

Full-service wholesaler: A merchant wholesaler that performs a full range of services for its customers.

Functional account: An accounting category that reflects the purpose for which money is spent.

Functional satisfaction: The satisfaction received from the tangible or functional features of a product.

General-merchandise retailer: A retailer that carries a wide range of products.

General-merchandise wholesaler: A full-service wholesaler that carries a wide variety of product lines.

Generic competitor: An organization that competes with others to satisfy consumers' wants or needs within a general category of products or services.

Generic name: A brand name that has become associated with a product category rather than with a particular brand.

Generic product: A set of tangible or intangible attributes that are assembled into an identifiable form.

Governmental market: A set of federal, state, county, or local agencies that buy goods and services for use in meeting social needs.

Grade label: A label that identifies the quality of a product by a letter, number, or word.

Gross rating points: The reach of an advertisement multiplied by its frequency.

Horizontal conflict: Conflict that occurs between channel members at the same level of the distribution channel.

Horizontal cooperative advertising: Advertising in which marketers at the same level in the distribution system advertise jointly.

Horizontal market: A market that is made up of a broad spectrum of industries.

Horizontal price fixing: A form of price fixing in which marketers at the same level of the distribution system get together and decide the price at which all of them will sell the product.

Hypermarche: A combination department store and supermarket.

Hypothesis: A statement about possible relationships between objects or events.

Ideal self-image: Our mental picture of ourselves as we would like to be.

Implementation: The actual execution of a strategic plan.

Implied warranty: A legal promise that a product will serve the purpose for which it is intended, whether stated by the manufacturer or not.

Impressions: The total number of exposures to a specific advertisement in a specified period.

Impulse items: Convenience products that are purchased not because of planning but because of a strongly felt need.

Independent retailer: A retailer that owns a single outlet that is not affiliated with any other retail outlet.

Industrial distributor: An independently owned operation that buys, stocks, and sells industrial products.

Industrial market: A producer market that consists of firms that engage in the manufacture of goods.

Industrial marketing: The process of anticipating, discovering, and designing product and service specifications that will satisfy the requirements of industrial customers.

Industrial marketing research: The systematic gathering, recording, and analyzing of data for use in solving problems related to the marketing of industrial goods and services.

Inelastic demand: A situation in which a percentage change in price brings about a smaller percentage change in quantity sold.

Influencer: In the exchange process, an individual who provides information about how a want or need may be satisfied.

Informative label: A label that advises consumers about the care, use, or preparation of a product.

Initiator: In the exchange process, the person who first recognizes an unsatisfied want or need.

Innovators: Consumers who are ready and willing to adopt a new idea.

Institutional advertising: Advertising that develops and maintains a favorable image for a particular industry or company.

Institutional market: A set of not-for-profit organizations that buy goods and services for use in achieving a particular goal or mission.

Intensive distribution: An approach to distribution that seeks the largest possible number of outlets in a given territory.

Interactive MIS: A computer-based marketing information system that allows managers to communicate directly with the system.

Intermediary: An independent or corporate-owned business that helps move products from the producer to the ultimate consumer.

Intermediate market: A set of wholesalers and retailers that buy goods from others and resell them.

Intrapreneurship: An approach to new product development in which a small team of employees is set apart from the rest of the organization and freed from ordinary bureaucratic requirements long enough to develop a particular product.

Joint demand: Demand for two products that are complementary.

Judgment sampling: Nonprobability sampling in which respondents are selected on the basis of criteria that the researchers believe will result in a group that is representative of the population being surveyed.

Jury of executive opinion: A forecasting technique in which executives from various departments of the company are asked to estimate market potential and sales and then try to reach a consensus.

Just-in-time purchasing: An approach to inventory management in which products are bought in small quantities to reduce inventory carrying costs and obtain delivery just in time for use.

Label: A tag or part of a package that supplies information about a product or its seller.

Laggards: Consumers who are strongly oriented toward the past and very suspicious of new concepts; they are the last to adopt a new product.

Late majority: Consumers who are committed to familiar ways of doing things and skeptical of new ideas.

Lead: The name of any individual or organization that may be a potential customer.

Learning: The process by which people's experiences produce changes in their behavior.

Leveling: A cognitive process in which the information retained becomes shorter and more concise.

Limited-line retailer: A retailer that offers only one or a few lines of related merchandise.

Limited-service wholesaler: A merchant wholesaler that performs a limited number of services for its customers.

Line extension: A new variety of a basic product.

List price: The initial price of a product; also termed the *base price*.

Long-range plan: A plan in which the organization's managers set goals for a period of more than one year.

Loss leader: A product that is given a lower than normal price in order to attract customers to a store.

Macromarketing: Bringing about exchanges between individuals and/or groups so as to provide satisfaction of a society's wants and needs.

Macrosegmentation: A process in which an industrial market is divided into segments based on types of buying organizations.

Mail interview: A survey technique in which questionnaires are mailed to potential respondents.

Mail-order wholesaler: A limited-service wholesaler that sells to industrial, institutional, and retail customers by means of catalogues.

Major innovation: An item that has never been sold by any other organization.

Manufacturer's agent: An independent sales representative who works for several manufacturers of related but noncompeting product lines.

Manufacturer's brand: A brand that is owned and marketed by the manufacturer that produces it.

Manufacturer's sales branch: A wholesaling establishment that is owned and operated by a manufacturer separately from its factories.

Manufacturer's sales office: A wholesaling establishment that is similar to a manufacturer's sales branch except that it does not carry inventory.

Marginal cost: The cost of producing one more unit than the most recent unit produced.

Market: A group of people with unsatisfied wants and needs who are willing to exchange and have the ability to buy.

Market aggregation: A marketing strategy that uses a single marketing program to offer the same product to all consumers.

Market atomization: A marketing strategy that treats each individual consumer as a unique market segment.

Market breakdown technique: A forecasting technique in which the sales forecast for a large unit is broken down into forecasts for smaller units.

Market buildup technique: A forecasting technique in which information on a few specific market segments is aggregated to arrive at a total sales forecast.

Market-driven economy: An economic system in which supply, demand, and price determine what products will be produced and who will receive those products.

Marketing audit: A comprehensive, systematic, independent, and periodic examination of an organization's marketing environment, objectives, strategies, and activities.

Marketing concept: The management philosophy that recognizes that the consumer should be the focal point of all activity within an organization.

Marketing control chart: A chart that combines trend analysis with the performance standards set by the organization.

Marketing decision support system: A coordinated collection of data, models, analytic tools, and computing power by which an organization gathers information from the environment and turns it into a basis for action.

Marketing information system (MIS): A set of procedures and methods for regular, planned collection, analysis, and presentation of marketing information.

Marketing intelligence system: Within a marketing information system, the set of activities whose purpose is to monitor the external environment for emerging trends or events.

Marketing mix: The combination of activities involving product, price, place, and promotion that a firm undertakes in order to provide satisfaction to consumers in a given market.

Marketing research: A systematic, objective approach to the development and provision of information for decision making regarding a specific marketing problem.

Market segment: A group of buyers within a market who have relatively similar wants and needs.

Market segmentation: A marketing strategy in which a large, heterogeneous market is broken down into small, more homogeneous segments and a separate marketing program is developed for each segment.

Market share: The total number of units of a product (or their dollar value) expressed as a percentage of the total number of units sold by all competitors in a given market.

Market share analysis: A forecasting technique in which it is assumed that the firm's market share will remain constant and sales forecasts for the firm are based on forecasts for the industry.

Matrix organization: An organizational structure in which projects are assigned to task forces made up of people drawn from various functional departments.

Mean: The sum of all the numbers in a set of scores divided by the number of scores.

Median: In a list of numbers, the number above which half of the numbers in the list fall and below which the other half fall.

Merchant middleman: An intermediary that takes title to the products it distributes.

Merchant wholesaler: A wholesaling intermediary that is an independently owned business and takes title to the goods it sells.

Message: An idea that is to be conveyed from a source to a receiver.

Message channel: A vehicle for delivering a message.

Micromarketing: Strategically managing human and organizational exchange relationships so as to provide socially responsible want and need satisfaction throughout the world while achieving the marketer's objectives.

Microsegmentation: A process in which industrial market segments are subdivided on the basis of characteristics of the buying center and individual participants.

Mill supply house: A general-merchandise wholesaler that operates in an industrial setting.

Miniwarehouse mall: A type of shopping center in which a large warehouse offers space to a variety of sellers, including both retailers and wholesalers.

Minor innovation: A product that was not previously sold by the company but has been marketed by some other company.

Mode: In a set of data, the number that occurs most frequently.

Model bank: The component of an MIS that contains mathematical marketing models that show relationships among various marketing activities, environmental forces, and desired outcomes.

Modification: Any adjustment of an existing product's style, color, or model; any product improvement; or a brand change.

Modified rebuy: A purchasing situation in which the organization has bought the good or service before, but some aspect of the situation has changed.

Monopolistic competition: A competitive situation in which there are many buyers and sellers, imperfect market information, some barriers to entry, and differentiated products.

Monopoly: A competitive situation in which there is only one seller of a product and entry to the market is restricted.

Motive: A need or want that is activated by a particular stimulus and initiates behavior toward some goal.

Multinational corporation (MNC): A corporation that operates in more than one country and makes all of its decisions within a global framework.

Nationalization: A situation in which a national government becomes involved in the ownership or management of a business organization.

Natural account: An accounting category that reflects how money is actually spent.

Need: Something that is lacking that is necessary for a person's physical or psychological well-being.

New task purchase: A purchasing situation in which the organization is making the purchase for the first time.

Noise: Any distraction that interferes with the effectiveness of a communication.

Noncumulative quantity discount: A quantity discount that is offered on each sale made to a particular buyer.

Nonprobability sampling: A sampling technique in which respondents are selected partly on the basis of researchers' judgment.

Nontraceable costs: Common costs that are assigned to functional areas on an arbitrary basis.

Norms: Rules that tell the members of a particular cultural group what behavior is correct in certain situations.

Nuclear family: A husband and wife and their children.

Nutritional labeling: A form of labeling in which consumers are informed of the amounts of protein, fat, carbohydrates, and calories in a processed food product.

Observational approach: A research method in which researchers observe people's behavior and record what they see but avoid direct interaction.

Odd pricing: A form of psychological pricing in which the price is an odd number or a number just below a round number.

Off-price store: A discount store that buys manufacturers' overruns, and end-of-season goods at below-wholesale prices and resells them at prices significantly lower than the regular department store price.

Oligopoly: A competitive situation in which a few firms account for a large percentage of the industry's sales and in which there are substantial barriers to entry.

One-price policy: A pricing policy in which the marketer assigns a price to the product and sells it at that price to all customers who purchase the same quantity of the product under the same conditions.

Open dating: A form of labeling in which consumers are informed of the expected shelf life of a product.

Opportunity: An unsatisfied want or need that arises from a change in the organization's environment.

Organization: All the activities involved in getting ready to carry out a strategic plan.

Organizational structure: A set of relationships among individuals with different responsibilities.

Original equipment manufacturer (OEM): An organization that purchases industrial goods to incorporate into other products.

Others self-image: Our mental picture of ourselves as we believe others see us.

Packaging: All activities that are related to designing and producing the container or wrapper for a product.

Penetration: A pricing strategy in which the initial price is set at a low level in order to generate the greatest possible demand for the product.

Perception: The process by which a person attaches meaning to the various stimuli he or she senses.

Perfect competition: A competitive situation in which there are many buyers and sellers, perfect market information, few or no barriers to entry, and homogeneous products.

Personal interview: A survey technique in which respondents are questioned in a face-to-face setting.

Personal selling: Person-to-person communication in which the receiver provides immediate feedback to the source's message.

Phantom freight: A term used to refer to the difference between the true freight cost and the cost charged to the buyer in situations in which the buyers is charged an amount greater than the actual cost.

Physical distribution: All the activities that provide for the efficient flow of raw materials, in-process inventory, and finished goods from the point of procurement to the ultimate consumer.

Physical obsolescence: Obsolescence that results when products are built to last only a limited time.

Piggyback service: A transportation service in which loaded trucks are taken directly onto railroad flatcars.

Place utility: The satisfaction that buyers receive from having a product available at the appropriate place.

Plan: A written document that specifies resource requirements, costs, expected benefits, and activities necessary to achieve a goal.

Planned obsolescence: A product management strategy in which a marketer forces a product in its line to become outdated, thereby increasing replacement sales.

Planning: The process of predicting future events and using those predictions to set courses of action that will achieve the organization's goals.

Point-of-purchase promotion: A sales promotion technique that consists of locating an attention-getting device at the place of actual purchase.

Positioning: A process in which a marketer communicates with consumers to establish a distinct place for its product or brand in their minds.

Possession utility: The satisfaction that buyers receive from having the right to use or own a product.

Postponed obsolescence: Obsolescence that occurs when technological improvements are available but are not introduced until the demand for existing products declines.

Premium: A product that is offered free or at less than the regular price in order to induce the consumer to buy another product.

Price: That which the buyer gives up in exchange for something that provides satisfaction.

Price lining: A pricing strategy in which prices are used to sort products into "lines" based on an attribute such as quality, prestige, or style.

Price-off: A price reduction that is used to induce trial or increase usage of a product.

Primary data: Data that are collected specifically for use in a particular research project.

Primary demand: Market demand for a product class rather than a particular brand.

Primary demand advertising: Advertising in which the marketer attempts to create awareness of and provide information about a type of product.

Primary group: A group that is small and intimate enough so that all of its members can communicate with one another face to face.

Private carrier: A company that owns the goods it transports.

Private warehouse: A warehouse that is owned and controlled by its users.

Probability sampling: A sampling technique in which all members of the population being surveyed have a known chance of being included in the sample.

Producer cooperative: A member-owned whole-sale operation that assembles farm products to sell in local markets.

Producer market: A set of buyers that purchase goods and services and use them to make other products.

Product: A combination of functional and psychological features that provides form utility; the entire set of benefits that are offered in an exchange, including goods, services, ideas, people, places, and organizations.

Product differentiation: A marketing strategy that uses promotion and other marketing activities to get consumers to perceive a product as different from and better than those of competitors.

Product life cycle: A sequence of stages in the marketing of a product that begins with commercialization and ends with removal from the market.

Product line: Within a company's product mix, a broad group of products that are similar in terms of use or characteristics.

Product mix: The various products that a company offers to consumers.

Product portfolio: A company's product mix viewed from a strategic perspective; a set of products or brands that are at different stages in the product life cycle.

Product relaunch: A product management strategy that focuses on finding new markets and untapped market segments, new product uses, and ways to stimulate increased use of a product by existing customers.

Professional advertising: Advertising that focuses on the benefits offered by professional services.

Program evaluation and review technique (PERT): An implementation technique that uses detailed flowcharts showing which tasks can be carried out only after certain other tasks have been completed and which tasks can be done simultaneously.

Promotion: Any technique that persuasively communicates favorable information about a seller's product to potential buyers; includes advertising, personal selling, sales promotion, and public relations.

Promotional discount: A discount that is offered to intermediaries as compensation for carrying out promotional activities.

Prospecting: The process of locating and classifying potential buyers of a product.

Protectionism: The erection of barriers to trade in an attempt to protect domestic industries from foreign competition.

Psychological pricing: A pricing strategy in which the product is given a price that is psychologically appealing to consumers.

Psychological satisfaction: The satisfaction received from the intangible benefits of a product, such as a feeling of self-worth.

Publicity: Any message about an organization that is communicated through the mass media but is not paid for by the organization.

Public relations: A promotional activity that aims to communicate a favorable image of a product or its marketer and to promote goodwill.

Public warehouse: A warehouse that is owned by an independent contractor, which rents space to users.

Pull strategy: A promotional strategy in which each channel member attempts to persuade the next member in the system to handle and promote the product.

Pulsing strategy: A media scheduling strategy in which a continuous campaign is combined with short bursts of heavier advertising.

Push strategy: A promotional strategy in which the producer uses mass promotion to stimulate demand in the consumer market, thereby causing intermediaries to want to carry the product.

Qualifying (descriptive) variables: A set of variables that allow or qualify an individual to be a member of a particular market segment.

Quantity discount: A discount offered to buyers that purchase larger than normal quantities of the product.

Question mark: An SBU that has a low relative market share and is in a high-growth market.

Quota: A specific limit on the number of items of a particular kind that may be imported.

Quota sampling: A form of judgment sampling in which the population is divided into subgroups on the basis of one or more characteristics and a specified proportion of respondents are chosen from each subgroup.

Rack jobber: A limited-service wholesaler that supplies nonfood products to supermarkets, grocery stores, and drug retailers.

Reach: The percentage of total prospects that are exposed to a specific advertisement in a specified period.

Real income: Income that has been adjusted for the effects of inflation.

Real self-image: Our mental picture of ourselves as we think we really are.

Receiver: The audience that is the target of a message.

Recruiting: The activity of locating skilled salespeople and inducing them to apply for employment.

Reference group: Any set of people that influences an individual's attitudes or behavior.

Reinforcement: The extent to which satisfaction is derived from a response to an aroused need.

Relative market share: An organization or SBU's market share divided by that of its largest competitor.

Repatriation: The transfer of profits to a parent firm from an affiliate in a foreign country.

Research design: An overall plan for conducting a research project, including the choice of the method that will be used to achieve the goals of the research.

Response: Whatever occurs as a reaction to an aroused need.

Retailer: An intermediary that sells products primarily to ultimate consumers.

Retailing: All activities undertaken by intermediaries whose primary function is to sell goods and services to ultimate consumers.

Retention: The extent to which one remembers what one has learned.

Reverse elasticity: A situation in which anticipation of a steady increase (decrease) in price causes buyers to make more (fewer) purchases of a product.

Role expectations: The rights, privileges, duties, and responsibilities that are associated with a particular role.

Role theory: An approach to the study of group influence that recognizes that people conduct their lives by playing many roles, each of which is accompanied by a certain range of acceptable behaviors.

Rollout: An approach to new product introduction in which the product is launched in a series of geographic areas over an extended period.

Sales manager: The person who designs and manages the activities of an organization's sales force.

Sales potential forecast: A forecast of total potential sales for the firm for a specific time period.

Sales promotion: The array of techniques that marketers use to stimulate immediate purchase.

Sales variance analysis: A method of data analysis in which data on actual sales are compared with quantitative sales objectives.

Sample: A group of respondents who are representative of the population being surveyed.

Sampling: Giving free samples of a product to consumers or offering a trial size at a very low cost.

Scenario analysis: A forecasting technique in which researchers develop a subjective picture of several possible futures by identifying cause-and-effect relationships and following them to their logical conclusions.

Scientific method: A research process that involves the development of a hypothesis that can be confirmed, modified, or rejected on the basis of information gathered by objective means.

Scrambled merchandising: The practice of carrying any product line, however dissimilar from other lines carried, as long as it yields a profit.

Seasonal discount: A discount that is offered to customers who purchase a product during a season when demand for that product is low.

Secondary group: A large group whose members have a shared goal but do not engage in face-to-face communication.

Secondary source: Data that have been collected for a purpose other than the research project in question.

Selective demand: Demand for a particular brand.

Selective demand advertising: Advertising in which the marketer attempts to create awareness of and provide information about a specific brand.

Selective distribution: An approach to distribution that involves the use of a limited set of outlets in a given territory.

Self-liquidating premium: A premium for which the buyer pays all or part of the cost.

Selling: The process of assisting and/or persuading a prospective customer to buy a good or service or to act favorably on an idea.

Selling agent: An agent that handles the entire marketing function for a manufacturer.

Sensory thresholds: The upper and lower limits on the ability of human sensory processes to perceive increases or decreases in the intensity of a stimulus.

Service: A deed, act, or performance.

Sharpening: A cognitive process in which the information retained becomes more vivid and important than the event itself.

Shippers' cooperative: A group of shippers that pool shipments of similar items in order to benefit from lower freight rates.

Shopping center: A group of retail stores at a single

location that is planned, developed, and controlled by one organization.

Shopping mall intercept: A form of personal interview in which respondents are approached or intercepted as they pass a particular spot in a shopping mall.

Shopping products: Goods and services about which consumers will seek information before making a purchase.

Shopping store: A retail outlet that is favored by consumers who are shopping for a certain type of product.

Simple random sampling: Probability sampling in which respondents are chosen at random from a complete list of the members of the population.

Simple trend analysis: A forecasting technique in which managers review historical data and use the rates of change to project future trends.

Single-line wholesaler: A full-service wholesaler that carries only one or two product lines but offers considerable depth in each.

Skimming: A pricing strategy in which the initial price is set at a high level with the goal of selling the product to people who want it and are willing to pay a high price for it.

Slice-of-life advertising: Advertising that portrays consumers in realistic situations that are consistent with consumers' perceptions of their own life-styles.

Social class: A relatively permanent and homogeneous category of people within a society. The members of a class have similar values, life-styles, interests, and behavior.

Socialization: The process by which we learn the values and norms of our culture.

Sorting: A process in which products are brought together at one location and then divided up and moved in smaller quantities to locations closer to the ultimate buyers.

Source: The originator of a message.

Specialty-line retailer: A limited-line retailer that carries only one or two product lines, but offers substantial depth and expertise in those lines.

Specialty-line supplier: A research firm that specializes in one aspect of the marketing research process.

Specialty-line wholesaler: A full-service wholesaler that carries a limited number of products for customers with specialized needs.

Specialty products: Goods and services for which there are no acceptable substitutes in the consumer's mind.

Specialty store: A retail outlet for which customers develop a strong preference based on the assortment of products offered, the service, or the store's reputation.

Spokesperson: The person who delivers the message in a testimonial.

Standard Metropolitan Statistical Area (SMSA):   The Census Bureau's standard urban population unit. An area is classified as an SMSA if it contains a city with a population of at least 50,000 or an urbanized area of 50,000 with a total metropolitan population of at least 100,000.

Staple items: Convenience products that consumers plan to buy.

Star: An SBU that has a high growth rate and a high relative market share.

Statistical bank: The component of an MIS that offers statistical techniques to be used in analyzing data.

Straight rebuy: A purchasing situation in which the organization has bought the good or service before and is likely to reorder from the same vendor.

Strategic business unit (SBU):   One or more products, brands, divisions, or market segments that have something in common, such as the same distribution system. Each SBU has its own mission, its own set of competitors, and its own strategic plan.

Strategic information scanning system: A formal structure of people, equipment, and procedures to obtain and manage information to support strategic decision making.

Strategic market planning: The managerial process of developing and implementing a match between market opportunities and the resources of the firm.

Strategic plan: A long-term plan covering a period of three, five, or sometimes ten years.

Strategic planning: The process of developing a long-range plan that is designed to match the organization's strengths and weaknesses with the threats and opportunities in its environment.

Stratified random sampling: Probability sampling in which the total population is divided into subgroups, or *strata*, and a random sample is chosen from each subgroup.

Structured question: A question that limits respondents to a specific set of replies.

Style obsolescence: Obsolescence that occurs when the physical appearance of a product is changed to make existing versions seem out of date.

Subculture: A smaller cultural group within a society that reflects geographic, religious, or ethnic differences.

Supermarket: A large self-service store that carries a full line of food products and, often, a number of nonfood products.

Superstore: A combination of a general-merchandise discount operation and a supermarket.

Survey approach: A research method in which researchers use personal interviews, telephone interviews, or mailed questionnaires to question a group of people directly.

Sweepstakes: A sales promotion technique in which prizes are tied to chance and consumers are encouraged to buy a product as part of the entry procedure.

Syndicated service: A research firm that periodically compiles specific types of data for sale to marketers.

Tactical plan: A short-term plan that specifies the activities necessary to carry out a strategic plan.

Target marketing: A process in which the marketer evaluates a number of market segments, decides which one or ones to serve, and develops and implements a unique marketing mix for the targeted segment(s).

Target return on investment: An amount of income equivalent to a certain percentage of the firm's investment; this amount is set as a goal to be achieved through pricing.

Target return pricing: An approach to pricing in which the marketer seeks to obtain a predetermined percentage return on the capital used to produce and distribute the product.

Tariff: A tax on imported goods.

Technological obsolescence: Obsolescence that results when technological improvements are made in a product.

Telemarketing: The sale of goods and services by telephone.

Telephone interview: A survey technique in which respondents are questioned by telephone.

Testimonial: An advertising message that is presented by someone who is viewed as an expert on the subject.

Test marketing: The controlled introduction of a new product to carefully selected markets for the purpose of testing market acceptance and predicting future sales of the product in that region.

Threat: An unfavorable trend or situation that could prevent the organization from satisfying a want or need.

Time utility: The satisfaction that buyers receive from having a product available at the appropriate time.

Total fixed costs: Costs that ordinarily do not change over time, no matter what quantity of output is produced.

Total variable costs: Costs that fluctuate, depending on the quantity of output produced.

Traceable costs: Common costs that can be assigned to two or more specific functional areas.

Trade deficit: The amount by which a nation's total imports exceed its total exports.

Trade discount: A discount that is offered to intermediaries as compensation for carrying out various marketing activities.

Trademark: A brand that is given legal protection because it has been appropriated exclusively by one marketer.

Trading down: A product management strategy in which a marketer that is known for selling high-priced products offers lower-priced products.

Trading stamps: A sales promotion technique in which customers receive stamps in quantities depending on how much they purchase, and can redeem the stamps for merchandise.

Trading up: A product management strategy in which a marketer that is known for selling low-priced products offers higher-priced products.

Transaction: An exchange between two or more parties.

Transfer pricing: Raising the price of a product shipped to a foreign affiliate in order to increase the amount of profit transferred from the affiliate to the parent firm.

Trial: The consumer's initial purchase and use of a product or brand.

Truck wholesaler: A limited-service wholesaler that specializes in selling and delivery services.

True prospect: A lead that can benefit from the use of the product, can afford to buy it, and has the authority to do so.

Tying agreement: A method of control over distribution in which the producer forces the dealer to buy additional products in order to secure one highly desired product.

Uniform delivered pricing: A geographic pricing policy in which the seller offers the same delivered price to all buyers, regardless of their location and the actual freight expense.

Unitary demand: A situation in which a percentage change in price brings about an equal percentage change in quantity sold.

Unit pricing: A form of pricing in which the price of the package is accompanied by the price of the product in terms of some standard measure of quantity.

Unsought products: Goods and services for which consumers have no felt need.

Unstructured question: A question that allows respondents to answer as they wish and does not limit the length of responses.

Value-added tax: A tax that is levied every time a product is sold to another member of the distribution channel.

Values: The deeply held beliefs and attitudes of the members of a particular society.

Variety store: A retailer that offers a wide assortment of low-priced items.

Vertical conflict: Conflict that occurs between channel members at different levels of the distribution system.

Vertical cooperative advertising: Advertising in which marketers at different levels in the distribution system advertise jointly.

Vertical market: A market that consists of a single industry.

Vertical marketing system: A distribution channel whose members are integrated into a single organization.

Vertical price fixing: A form of price fixing in which marketers at different levels of the distribution system get together to set retail prices.

Voluntary chain: A retail organization that consists of a set of independent retailers that agree to buy most of their merchandise through a single wholesaler.

Want: Something that is lacking that is desirable or useful, it is formed by a person's experiences, culture, and personality.

Warehouse club: A no-frills, cash-and-carry discount store that operates in a poor location; to shop there, the customer must become a member and pay dues.

Warehouse showroom: A discount store that follows a strategy based on low overhead and high turnover; customers pay cash and must transport the merchandise themselves.

Warehouse store: A no-frills supermarket that stocks a wide variety of food and nonfood items and sells them at lower prices than the typical supermarket price.

Warranty: A manufacturer's promise that a product will serve the purpose for which it is intended.

Wearout: The tendency of consumer response to a sales promotion to diminish over time.

Wholesaler: An intermediary that distributes products primarily to commercial or professional users.

Wholesaling: All of the activities provided by wholesaling intermediaries involved in selling merchandise to retailers; to industrial, institutional, farm, and professional businesses; or to other types of wholesaling intermediaries.

Wholesaling intermediary: Any firm that engages primarily in wholesaling activities.

Work load approach: An approach to sales force design in which the size of the sales force is determined by dividing the total work load in hours by the number of selling hours available from each salesperson.

Zero-based budgeting: An approach to budgeting in which each part of the organization must justify each item in its budget before it will be granted the funds it needs.

Zone pricing: A geographic pricing policy in which the seller divides a geographic area into zones and charges each buyer in a given zone the base price plus the standard freight rate for that zone.

Index